THE SPIRIT OF THE ENGLISH LANGUAGE

"John Wulsin's collection will inspire high school English teachers, new or seasoned, and will charm poetry lovers of any age. Starting with his subtle, engaging introduction to the sounds of poetry, readers will find abundant riches here. Biographical sketches show how poets help to create the culture and consciousness of their particular historical times. A mix of approaches to the poems themselves shows how the 'spirit of language' dwells in the 'lyrical activity' of various groups of poets—the Rosicrucian and Neo-Platonic 'metaphysical' poets, the British Romantics with their supernatural capacities for perceiving nature, and finally the American Romantics with their insistence on newness and singularity. To open Wulsin's book is to open the door of a lively classroom."

—Gertrude Reif Hughes, Professor Emerita, Wesleyan University, author of *Emerson's Demanding Optimism*

I0809418

Other books by John H. Wulsin Jr.

The Laws of the Living Language

Proverbs of Purgatory

The Riddle of America (editor)

Books for the Journey (coeditor)

THE SPIRIT OF THE *English Language*

A Practical Guide

for Poets, Teachers & Students

How Sound Works in English & American Poetry

JOHN H. WULSIN JR.

LINDISFARNE BOOKS
2008

Lindisfarne Books
An imprint of SteinerBooks / Anthroposophic Press, Inc.
610 Main St., Great Barrington, MA 01230
www.steinerbooks.org

COVER AND BOOK DESIGN: WILLIAM JENS JENSEN
FRONT COVER IMAGE © BY ANNA DICKIE

Library of Congress Cataloging-in-Publication Data

Wulsin, John H.
The spirit of the English language : a practical guide for poets, teachers & students / John H. Wulsin, Jr.
p. cm.
Includes bibliographical references.
ISBN 978-1-58420-063-5
1. English language—History. 2. Poetics—History. 3. English literature—History and criticism. 4. Poets—Biography. I. Title.
PE1075.W75 2008
420.9—dc22

2008028408

ISBN-13: 978-1-58420-063-5
ISBN-10: 1-58420-063-4

Contents

Acknowledgements:

To the students of both the Eurythmy School of Spring Valley, New York, and the Green Meadow Waldorf School, Chestnut Ridge, New York, whose ears led me in many of these explorations. To my long–time colleague David Sloan, who initially urged me to write this book. To Eastern Frontiers for a writers' retreat, allowing significant momentum. To Green Meadow Waldorf School, fertile field, for support during a sabbatical year. To Eugene Schwartz, who initially passed the torch to me for teaching the Poetics courses at the Eurythmy School, and for proofreading the text early on. To Thendara Foundation and Dr. John Wulsin for funding help to make the publication possible. To Lindisfarne Books, for its commitment to the book and the process. For Nicky Heron's demanding, persistent, extremely helpful copyediting, definitely bettering the book. For Julie Goldberg's super-sleuthing of a few elusive sources. For William Jensen's final editorial efforts. For the interest of my children, Lara and Seth, Gillian and Shannon. And for the ever-patient support of my wife Jane over the book's long years.

To Rosamond Foster Reed Wulsin
for her gift of the mother tongue

Introduction

Most of us remember the thrill of pretending to write, probably at home while playing school. We pretended that our scribbles and signs meant something, had meaning, and were important. The next stage of our relationship to the mysterious activity of writing is savored in Waldorf, Steiner education in the first grades, as children experience revelations through attention to each letter of the alphabet, to its shape, its story, its character and its flavor. It may be that mountains become an M, a fish becomes F, a king K, a bear B, as a story engenders large gestures in a drawing that later distills into the actual shapes of letters. Children experience consonants as distillations of the outer world, while the teacher helps them experience the vowels as reflections not of the outer world, but as mirrors of moods, or attitudes of soul. Thus, a story that evokes protectiveness may lead to the letter O. A story of openhearted wonder may foster the "ah" sound of the letter A, as boys and girls open their arms wide in awe at the rising Sun. For children at this stage, the whole alphabet resonates with multidimensional connotations that echo forms of the outer world and feelings of the inner world.

However, as we learn to read more fluently, we also begin to read through the signs, or letters, to the content suggested by the letter group, or words. Increasingly, we read through the words on the page to the meaning, and we hear through the sounds in our ears to the meaning. The more we become conscious of the content of stories, the more we become unconscious of the language itself, the medium in which the stories live. Although literature expands our awareness of the human condition, we can dreamily lose ourselves in literature, the stories of others. By contrast, certain self-awareness is quickened through attention to language itself. We awake by pulling back some of our focus on the message and by looking to the language of the story.

Thoreau remarked that, to know something in nature—a woodchuck, for example—one must look out of the side of one's eye. This book is an attempt to understand the spirit of the English language. We will look at stages in the story of English and American poetry, from the ninth century's Old Anglo-Saxon in *Beowulf* through the nineteenth century's "primal/modern" language of Gerard Manley Hopkins. Along the way, we will take a slanted glance at, or a slanted listen to, language itself, as the evolving nature of the language suggests the evolving consciousness of the English-speaking peoples.

As a longtime teacher of teenagers, I have included reflections on the relationship between the evolving stages of the English language and the developmental stages of adolescents. How might our understanding of evolving English become a key to helping adolescents in their development? Or, how can the spirit of the English language best help adolescents in their development? My focus, based largely on my experience as a Waldorf teacher, is from the context of a Waldorf curriculum. Waldorf education, initiated in 1919 by the Austrian philosopher Rudolf Steiner in Stuttgart, Germany, is an independent form of education devoted to teaching children in ways consistent with their stage of development. There are currently more than a thousand Waldorf schools worldwide. These reflections on adolescents should be of value to any teacher of adolescents. The reflections on the language of adolescents should be of interest to the general reader, as well, since in certain ways adolescents are most sensitive to new activities of language and, hence, to new activities of the spirit of the language.

The Story behind the Work of the Spirit of the English Language

As an experienced teacher of poetics to adults in a four-year training in the art of movement called eurythmy (in which the artists strive to embody objectively the sounds of speech and music through gesture), I have lived with this question: How can we tell the story of the work of the spirit of the English language? At its best, education strives to serve the mysterious evolution of each student's individuality, ideally in ways appropriate to each stage of development. Each class and each school has a particular character. Each ethnic group has a particular character. The same is true of each language. Linguists pay attention to the structure and behavior of the body of the language. Through attention to the sounds of the language, we can become more aware of the activity of the individuality, of the evolving "spirit," of the English language.

The impetus of this book is an exploration to better understand the activity of the spirit of the English language. Other books have laid the groundwork, including McNeill and Lehrer's *Story of the English Language,* which articulates part of the gesture, helping us understand in lay terms the major developments of accents, phrasing, patterns, and meanings have in evolving English language. Linguists have noticed, with brilliant accuracy, certain changes in sounds and syntax over time, generally not presuming to articulate implications of such changes. Owen Barfield's *History in English Words* explores the evolving English language through the way words change meanings over centuries and reflect changing consciousness in the peoples using them. Faulkner-Jones' *The English Spirit* comes closest to being a trailblazer for the present book, which tracks the activity of the spirit of the language through the activity of the sounds in poetry, in and through sequential stages of the evolving language. How can we, in our rational, skeptical age, even imagine gleaning the work of the spirit of a language?

The ancient Greeks spoke of muses, the guiding spirits of the various arts, especially the literary arts. The epic poets start, "Sing in me, O Muse." Behind Delphi's temple stands Mt. Parnassus, where Apollo presided over the nine muses, including Calliope, muse of epic poetry; Erato, muse of love poetry; Euterpe, muse of lyric poetry; Melpomene, muse of tragedy; and Thalia, muse of comedy. The human writer experienced being a vessel through which the gods, spiritual beings, could find expression.

In a parallel stream, Dionysius the Areopagite, the Greek early Christian, elaborated ancient Hebrew traditions by articulating nine spiritual hierarchies with differentiated tasks: seraphim, cherubim, thrones, kyriotetes, dynamis, exusiai, archai, archangels, and angels. Contemporary esoteric streams of various traditions continue to recognize the validity in such characterizations. Rudolf Steiner (1865–1925), scientist, philosopher, educator, and scientist of the spirit, discerned that, whereas an angel attends to an individual, archangels work in groups of people, especially in the activity of human language.

Most people today do not speak (and hence do not think) in such terms; we nevertheless use the term "spirit of the times," or "the spirit of the age." There is also the term "folk spirit," or spirit of a people. Imagine, as the ancient peoples experienced clearly, that a spiritual being presides over, orchestrates, and informs the various activities, the shifting and evolving, of a language. For the purpose of this book, we will imagine a spirit of the English language, at least as a way to focus on ways that the evolving language works.

The German, Dutch, Danish, Norwegian, Swedish, French, Spanish, Italian, English, and English-speaking "American" peoples all have distinct characteristics. Their languages, even when related to one another, nevertheless have distinct characteristics. Even though the Teutonic languages tend to be more rooted in sensory experience, the German language has become more capable of philosophical conception than the Scandinavian languages. Moreover, although the "Romance" languages, with their Greco-Roman base, may naturally support more abstract explorations than do the Teutonic languages, French is notably more intellectual and Italian more sentient. It is fascinating to discern differences in the ways more than twenty nations use Spanish as their common language in Latin America. Argentinean Spanish is more lilting, rising at the end of a line, whereas Mexican Spanish almost sings in a more regular, steady, rhythmic cadence. Chinese, Japanese, and Korean languages share some origins, yet they have evolved quite distinctly.

Consider the evolution of language as Europeans began to colonize different parts of the world. How have English, French, and Portuguese altered in various African countries, while serving as the "common" languages for many different local languages? How is the French spoken in Niger of the Sahel desert distinct from that spoken in coastal, central Cameroon? How does the Portuguese of Angola differ from that of Brazil? How does the spirit of the English language work differently, with different folk, in different lands, in Australia, South Africa, Canada, the United States, and in different parts of the United States? This book will focus specifically on the activity of the spirit of the English language in England and in the early United States of America.

As language evolves over time and in relation to place, consciousness evolves; as consciousness evolves, language evolves. In the effort to recognize the implications of evolving language in relation to evolving consciousness, I will at times use several ensuing terms coined by Rudolf Steiner.

The first is "sentient soul" consciousness. This can be characterized by the traditional stage in early adulthood when a young person leaves home and village to go off and know the world, perhaps as a soldier or sailor. This stage is symbolized by the warrior, the lover, passion, impulsiveness, and living strongly in one's feelings and in the elements, the winds, the sun, the storms. Think of the Vikings as a culture that embodied this stage; they followed the winds and their swords in almost all directions, to explore, pillage, and settle. While this characteristic role has not been so true for women until recently, moving as a young spouse to a new family, often a new locale, and quickly being immersed in the primal experiences of motherhood perhaps has parallels to the wandering warrior in the world. We can characterize such a relationship to life and the world as sentient soul consciousness. One lives vigorously in the senses, strongly experiencing one's likes and dislikes. One finds one's way in the world through wishes, desires, and will. When one's youthful forces are most developed and when the adult consciousness is just emerging, one lives in sentient soul consciousness.

Rational soul consciousness is the second stage. In the late twenties and early thirties, one's youthful forces start to recede. No longer do we ride the teeming tides of life, acting, reacting, responding, loving, and hating. Whereas we formerly relied on vitality, to some degree we are forced to become more conscious, to consider, take a step back and reflect, discern laws and principles, and make sense of the seeming chaos of life. Greater responsibilities weigh upon our shoulders. Examples of the rational soul include pre-Socratic Greek philosophers such as Heraclitus, Thales, Plato, and Aristotle, as well as the vast perspective of Homer's epics. Other examples are Roman law and the rational order of Roman armies as they built roads through wilderness, extending their web of organized culture. Consider the medieval Christian philosophers Albertus Magnus, Thomas Aquinas, and Duns Scotus, and efforts by the Nominalists and the Realists to rationally articulate the nature of reality. The pursuit of the rational soul in "right thinking" could also lead martyrs to die for their beliefs. By contrast, the shadow side of identifying with one's thinking could lead to being willing to kill another for "wrong thinking," as in the Inquisition. All of these examples of the actively reasoning consciousness can be referred to as the rational soul.

The rational soul is less motivated by what one likes or dislikes, and more motivated by ascertaining what is good or evil, right or wrong, true or false, just or unjust, and essential or nonessential. During the late twenties and early thirties, a person becomes more involved in abstracting the underlying principles from the teeming life surrounding the laws that apply on various levels of life. We exercise reason and practice judgment and discernment in the rational soul stage of consciousness.

It is more difficult to describe the third stage, the spiritual soul, experienced in the next stage of life, the late thirties and early forties. Often following or including a mid-life crisis, this stage involves inwardly stepping back further from life. One may separate from family, change work, or move to a new location. Whether primarily outer or inner, one often discovers a new quality of detachment, enabling one to see things more in their own right. For example, in a person's evolution as a teacher, one may go through a primary stage in which the main challenge is to make things happen and vitalize one's students. This is the sentient soul stage. The focus shifts and one becomes preoccupied with mastering the subject. Finally, as master of the classroom dynamic and the material, the teacher becomes newly free to focus more wakefully on what is happening with each student and the essence of the educational task. The ability to see the other's individuality objectively goes hand-in-hand with one's ability to see the natural world as it is, independent of one's feelings or preconceptions. This is the spiritual soul stage. Faulkner-Jones, in *The English Spirit*, has written that "the spiritual soul springs from union of sense observation and creative imagination" (23).

The thirteenth- and fourteenth-century artists Dante, Giotto, and Chaucer mark the threshold of a newly emerging consciousness. Dante the poet tells the story of Dante the pilgrim in the folk language of his Tuscany. His autobiographical, individual focus is new, as is the elevation of folk language. Giotto's capacity to render perspective in painting is new. Chaucer's threefold blend of Anglo-Saxon, Latin, and French words is new; rhyming couplets in iambic pentameter is new in English, as is his attention to physical particularities reflecting soul traits. The historical periods of the Renaissance and the Reformation saw the birth of artistic perspective; understanding of the heliocentric universe; Shakespeare's plays and poems; geographic exploration of the New World; and the birth of natural science based on weight, measure, number, all of which show great shifts in Western culture. In general, this new consciousness suggests increasing ability to objectify reality by separating from one's likes and dislikes, judgments, and even beliefs. Considering the long scope historically of the development of the rational soul faculties, c.800 B.C.E to c.1400 C.E., humanity is still in the early stages of unfolding the many dimensions of this spiritual soul or consciousness soul.

To Read with an Ear

My intention with this book is essentially to offer focused attention to the ear; it is thereby an effort to glean the work of the spirit of the language. Biographical sketches for students, practitioners, and teachers of poetry accompany perspectives on the evolution of consciousness through the examples of poetry. Even with all my brilliant schoolteachers and world-renowned professors, I was not aware of much emphasis on the ear and the ways that sounds work. In my experience of poetry and in my teaching of poetry, I have struggled to become more conscious of the experience of the ear, outer and inner. I have become increasingly convinced that such close reading for sound-awakened listening is a crucial antidote in this era of constant, numbing cacophony.

The contemporary poet Carolyn Forche once told high school students at the Green Meadow Waldorf School that, in the poetry classes at her university, she could detect which students had watched television the night before. The rhythms in their writing were neither those of the experience they were trying to evoke nor those of their individual voice. The absolutely recognizable rhythms dominating the young writers' work were those conceived and produced by mass-media moguls in Manhattan and Hollywood, imprinting the minds of millions, stereotypically, like so many fast-food plastic cartons. Carolyn Forche was able to work only with those who could listen freshly and, hence, possibly uniquely.

George Orwell warned about the dangers of state powers controlling consciousness by contracting people's vocabulary. How comparable, and perhaps even more deeply insidious, are the dangers when corporations dictate and contract the rhythms through which we experience life as we subject ourselves to excessive media influence. These rhythms affect how we breathe, how our hearts beat, and how we can feel. Modern women have declared, "Take back the night." Modern ecologists, echoing the Romantic poets, have declared, "Take back the wilderness." Let us declare, "Take back the silence for the sake of the word, so we can listen."

I offer an introductory listen rather than a "look" into exemplary, symptomatic pieces of poets' works, hoping to glean and hear from the poets who are able to work with language, the spirit of the language, as it evolves. None of these readings presumes to be an exclusive way to read or hear a poem.

I approach these "close listenings" 1) as an exercise to heighten my awareness; 2) as, I hope, a catalyst to help others read poetry with a more attentive ear; 3) as, especially, a catalyst for teachers of young people, since becoming more conscious of the musical work of each syllable can be crucial to self-development and to listening to the music of others' language; and, 4) ultimately perhaps, as ways to sit at the feet of the spirit of the English language, in intimate tutelage, allowing it to better inform and eventually inspire us.

Biographies

The biographical sketches have been gathered and composed with a two questions in mind: 1) What is the relationship between the emerging individuality and the development of the poet? Hence, each biographical sketch begins with a glimpse of the person's life around the age of twenty-one, the time traditionally when one's individuality begins to take responsibility in life. 2) How might the poet's life reflect and contribute to the activity of the spirit of the English language?

It is possible to read this book like a telescope, with an interest in the large picture of the activities of the spirit of the English language. It is also possible to read this book with a microscope, intently focusing on the way particular sounds work in each line of poetry. One can also find interest in the activity of the spirit of the language in the lives of the poets, in gleaning a generally evolving story of English poetry, and in reacquainting oneself with a taste of the poetry. I hope that, over time, readers will come to read this book in all these ways, engendering macro-, mid-, and micro-listening.

On the Sonnet

If by dull rhymes our English must be chained,
And like Andromeda, the Sonnet sweet
Fettered, in spite of pained loveliness,
Let us find out, if we must be constrained,
Sandals more interwoven and complete
To fit the naked foot of Poesy:
Let us inspect the Lyre, and weigh the stress
Of every chord, and see what may be gained
By ear industrious, and attention meet;
Misers of sound and syllable, no less
Than Midas of his coinage, let us be
Jealous of dead leaves in the bay wreath crown;
So, if we may not let the Muse be free,
She will be bound with garlands of her own.

Keats, April 1819

PART I

Chapter 1

A Language Is Born

As we look at the origins of English language and literature, consider Ralph Waldo Emerson's statement: "The English language is the sea which receives tributaries from every region under heaven." We begin by recalling one of the primary sources of many such tributaries of the English language: Sanskrit. The Sanskrit word *pitar* is a source of the Latin *pater*, the German *vater*, and hence the English *father*. The Sanskrit *bhratar* is the source of the Greek *phrater*, the Latin *frater*, the Dutch *braeder*, the German *bruder*, the Russian *brat*, the Irish *brathair*, and our English *brother*. Linguists generally agree that the Indo-European languages migrated west over the ages from the region of present India.

For our purposes, we will begin by looking at the particular language that permeated the British Isles most during the centuries B.C.E: the Celtic tongue, or Gaelic. Subsequently, through waves of successive Roman, Angle, Jute, and Saxon invaders, the Celtic peoples were driven south to Cornwall and Brittany, West to Wales, and north to Scotland, while Ireland remained intact. With the retreat of the Celtic peoples, their language virtually evaporated from the new languages of the land, unlike its cloudy mists, which did not. Several of the twelve remaining Celtic words in Old English are *crag* and *tor* (high rock), *combe* (deep valley, as in *Wycombe*) and *puca* (evil spirit, as in *puck*). Nevertheless, the Celtic spirit has continued to infuse English language and literature through major writers in English who were of Celtic (Irish, Scottish, and Welsh) backgrounds. These include Jonathon Swift, Robert Burns, Sir Edmund Burke, Sir Walter Scott, Robert Louis Stevenson, Oscar Wilde, William Butler Yeats, James Joyce, Dylan Thomas, Samuel Beckett, George Bernard Shaw, and Seamus Heaney.

The Celtic language was still very much alive when Julius Caesar arrived on the shores of Britain in 55 B.C.E. He was so unfamiliar with the tides of the English Channel (much higher than the comparative bathtub of the Mediterranean) that his troops pulled their boats up high on shore and proceeded to forage inland. When they returned, a high tide had taken his fleet out to sea. Fortunately for Caesar, the Celts were unaware and did not attack. Reinforcements in Normandy soon restored his force, and the Latin-speaking Romans were able to advance, building roads and *castra* (camps) in such places as Chester, Manchester, Winchester, and Cirencester. After centuries, the collapsing Roman Empire withdrew from England around 410 C.E., leaving Latin influences in local languages.

As the Roman tide receded, a new tide arrived. The Angles from the German-Danish peninsula settled in the east; the Saxons from the North Sea Coast settled in the south and west; the Jutes from Denmark settled in the southeast in what is now Kent. In spite of the leadership of the historic King Arthur, the Celtic Britons were driven north into Scotland, west into Wales, and south into Cornwall and Brittany. "The English language arrived on point of sword" (McCrum, Cran, Macneil 60). The mighty new inhabitants began to call themselves Angelcynn (Angle-kin). They began to call their land Englaland (land of the Angles), and their coalescing language they called Englisc.

Toward the end of the sixth century, Christianity met Anglo-Saxon on the waves of Latin. In 597, Pope Gregory the Great sent the Roman Prior Augustine and fifty monks to England. King Athelbert, who eventually converted to Christianity along with many of his subjects, gave them a place in Canterbury, which has remained the center of English Christendom ever since. While the Anglo-Saxon warriors had words such as *God, Heaven,* and *Hell* from their Norse religions, new concepts for the Christian religion needed new words: Greek, Latin, and even Hebrew words such as *angel, devil, priest,* and *apostle*. In 635, the Irish Bishop Aidan resigned to go to Scotland as a monk and, at the invitation of King Oswald of North Umbria, begin to convert northern England to Christianity. By the end of the eighth century, England was permeated by the Christian, Anglo-Saxon culture, yet remained mostly illiterate.

In contrast to the sunlit world of the Greco-Roman culture of epic, dramatic, and lyric poetry, of philosophical treatises, of historical works, even of law, the people of the misty world still lived in a world of song, story, and action, but not yet in a world of written literature. The bards sang of the movements of the heavens and of human deeds. Druid priests read the shadows of the standing stones to divine times for agriculture and animal breeding or to augur other events, but on the whole, the people of the Northern Isles refrained from externalizing a reflective consciousness through written language far longer than did the more southern, Greco-Roman peoples.

In the Norse-Teutonic streams, there was certainly a tradition of reading signs. Although these people remained essentially an oral culture until about 800, a central imagination for these Norse peoples consisted of the God Odin reading the runes.

The Speech of the High One

I know I hung on that windswept tree,
Swung there for nine long nights,
Wounded by my own blade
Bloodied for Odin,
Myself an offering to myself:
Bound to the tree
That no man knows
Whither the roots of it run.

None gave me bread,
None gave me drink.
Down to the deepest depths I peered
Until I spied the Runes.
With a roaring cry I seized them up,
Then dizzy and fainting, I fell.

Well-being I won
And wisdom too.
I grew and took joy in my growth:
From a word to a word
I was led to a word,
From a deed to another deed.

The Poetic Edda C.1200 C.E.

As early as 98 C.E., the Roman historian Tacitus described the Germanic tribes thus:

> To divination and casting of lots they pay attention beyond any other people. Their method of casting lots is a simple one: they cut a branch from a fruit-bearing tree and divide it into small pieces which they mark with certain distinctive signs [*notae*] and scatter at random onto a white cloth. Then, the priest of the community, if the lots are consulted publicly, of the gatherer of the family, if it is done privately, after invoking the gods and with eyes raised to heaven, picks up three pieces, one at a time, and interprets them according to the signs previously marked upon them. (*Germania*, ch. 10)

So, a rune, carved on an individual stone or piece of wood and picked up with two other runes could be interpreted, like the *I Ching*, as a fluid, mobile, kinetic reflection of the will of the gods, the will of the worlds.

Three Viking ships have been found in a mound in the village of Tonsberg on the southeast coast of Norway, each remarkably light like the wind. Apparently, in such locations, the earliest carvings of the angular runes were for the dead, made on a stone lowered into the burial mound. Later, upright stones bore runes for the living. In Tonsberg, the earliest standing stone with runes, dated around the third century, use the traditional twenty-four *runastafr.* The staves of the runes were also known as the *futhark,* for the first six staves, or stones: *fu the ark.* As early as around 450 C.E., "*I*" appears carved in stone: "I by the name of Vive made the rune after Rovary the giver of Bread." The word *rune,* from gothic *runa,* means "a secret thing, or mystery" (Bo). Not only the ships but also the runes themselves accompanied the departed Viking king on his journey into the afterlife. It would be centuries before the Norse peoples, even those Anglecynn living in Englaland, could coalesce their consciousness into written versions of their stories for the living.

Chapter 2

Old Anglo-Saxon

In this misty, cold seventh-century world, warmed by action, song, and boast, we may imagine men gathered around a fire on a Northumbrian hillside, taking turns offering stories or songs. One modest soul, dreading his turn, slips away into the dark and falls asleep in the crofter's hay. In his sleep he is visited by a being who asks him to sing. He protests, however, having no clue of what to sing. The visiting presence urges him to sing then about the creation of the world.

The next day the young man, Caedmon, goes to the Abbess of Busby and tells her his story. When she asks him to sing, he sings of the world's creation. He becomes one of the noted singers of the time and area, though only about sacred subjects. Fortunately, someone wrote down, on paper, the following fragment, the oldest Anglo-Saxon literature on record.

Caedmon's Hymn

Nu sculon herigean heofonrices weard,
Metodes meahte and his modgethanc,
Weorc wuldorfaeder, swa he wundra gehwaes,
Ece drihten, or onstealde.
He aerest sceop eorthan bearnum
Heofon to hrofe, halig scyppend;
Tha middangeard moncynnes weard,
Ece drihten, aefter teode
Firum foldan, frea aelmightig.

Now must we praise of heaven's kingdom the Keeper
Of the Lord the power and his Wisdom
The work of the Glory-Father, as he of marvels each,
The eternal Lord, the beginning established.
He first created of earth for the sons,
Heaven as a roof, the holy Creator.
Then the middle-enclosure of mankind the Protector
The eternal Lord, thereafter made
For men, earth the Lord almighty.

By the ninth century, King Alfred the Great had so united the Anglo-Saxon kingdom that, when a new wave of Danish Norse Vikings invaded, he was able to defeat them in 878 at the battle of Ethandune, commemorated by a white horse carved in the hillside. After King Alfred reclaimed London in 886, the Norse stayed in the "Danelow," the northeastern third of England. Their language, however, strayed southwest of the border, permeating the Anglo-Saxon with more than nine hundred words of Norse origin, including *get, hit, leg, low, root, same, want, wrong,* and many words beginning with *sk*, such as *sky, skein, skin, scope,* and *scoop.*

King Alfred, through his individual will, used English instead of Latin to unite the various peoples as he rebuilt monasteries and schools. The language blends created dialects that varied according to both the different invaders over the centuries and the different geographical influences. Alfred translated Bede's *History of the English Church* into English, establishing a common written language for the folk. Alfred the Great's central southern blend of Anglo-Saxon became the enduring standard of what we now call Old Anglo-Saxon. The institutor of the Anglo-Saxon chronicle of English history can justly be considered the "savior of the English language" and "the founder of English prose."

In the context of Alfred's relatively secure England, with the living language of the people of the land becoming the written language of the land, emerges the first epic of the English language, composed by an unknown storyteller, told by many and written down by an unknown scribe. *Beowulf* is the story of a hero who rescues a besieged land. Hygelac, the king of the Danes, suffers because each night a monster named Grendel plucks a sleeping warrior from Hrothgar, Hygelac's great mead hall. Beowulf, prime vassal of the king of the Geats (southern Sweden), receives permission to sail with twelve companions to help the Danes.

After Beowulf is welcomed with a festive night of meat, drinking, and boasting tales, the monster Grendel visits the sleeping warriors and begins his feast, until Beowulf grips the arm of this beast, impervious to sword, axe, or arrow. The pure strength of Beowulf prevails as he rips the arm from its socket and hangs it high in the hall.

Grendel's dam, however, avenges the fatal blow to her son, and Beowulf chases her across the fens and moors, down to her lair beneath the sea. Beowulf dives below the depths of the sea and is nearly overcome by her, when he eyes and then grasps a sword in her treasure hoard. His long-resigned soldiers on the shore are distressed when they see the waters turn red, then surprised to see Beowulf surface in the blood-red sea, holding the head of Grendel's dam in his hand.

Not long after Beowulf returns to the land of the Geats, he becomes their king. Toward the end of his life, he has a third, mighty, and final encounter, this time with a dragon. Abandoned by all except one young warrior, Beowulf is wounded mortally, yet allows the young warrior to deal the deathblow to the dragon.

> Da co*m* of *m*ore under *m*ist-hleothum
> Grendel gongan, Godes yrre baer:
> *m*ynte se *m*an-scatha *m*anna cynnes
> sumne besyrwan in sels tham hean.
>
> From the stretching moors, from the misty hollows,
> Grendel came creeping, accursed of God,
> A murderous ravager minded to snare
> Spoil of heroes in high-built hall.
>
> *Beowulf* (tr. Kennedy), II. 710–714

Listening to lines of *Beowulf*, one first hears the four strong beats per line. Next, one realizes that in almost all lines of this old Anglo-Saxon verse, the first three strong beats coincide with the same consonant sound, *m,* in the first line, *g* in the second, *m* in the third, *s* in the fourth. The fourth beat in each line sounds openly, flexibly on any other consonant.

The four-beat alliterative line can sound outwardly almost as though the singer-speaker is banging a sword on a shield with each strong beat. Inwardly, it sounds like the heartbeat and pulsing of the blood. The number of weakly stressed syllables before and after the strong beats is flexible, variable and irregular. In relation to four-beat alliterative verse:

> Dr. Steiner portrays for us how, in alliteration, a longing lives for the innocent primeval condition of the human soul, a longing for the time when the language itself had not yet suffered the fall into the intellect, the time when one still spoke for the sake of the wisdom that lived in the sounds themselves, and not for the sake of the content; so that we may say that all that was spoken was in fact poetry at the time when Odin still lived in the speech. (Knottenbelt)

In the Old Anglo-Saxon of eighth century *Beowulf,* we have access to some of the earliest written language reflecting consciousness hardly affected by Greek literature, philosophy, and Roman literature of the previous 1600 years.

Before we turn our attention from the old English of the Anglo-Saxon mind of the ninth and tenth centuries, we must focus on a characteristic trait, which is less oriented to music or sound and more toward image, a characteristic of the Anglo-Saxon imagination.

A distinguishing trait of the early Greek imagination in the Homeric epics is the simile, in which we understand one thing or event better by comparing it consciously, through the words *like, as,* or *just so,* with another thing or event. Homer describes how Odysseus put out the eye of the Cyclops with a burning pole.

> In a smithy
> one sees a white-hot axehead of an adze
> plunged and wrung in a cold tub, screeching steam—

> the way they make soft iron hale and hard—:
> just so that eyeball hissed around the spike.
> The Kyklops bellowed and the rock roared around him,
> And we fell back in fear.
>
> *The Odyssey*, book IX, ll.424–430

This conscious linguistic form of comparison, occurring in Greece at the beginning of the human rational soul stage of development, had not yet become a capacity of the Anglo-Saxon mind even 1600 years later, during the early stages of its literature. However, there is an Anglo-Saxon activity of yoking together two normally dissimilar images. Both the mode and the purpose differ from the Greek simile. The Anglo-Saxon manner is not rational or reflective, but active, a deed in itself. The Anglo-Saxon purpose is not for better understanding, but actually to name. The form of this Anglo-Saxon activity of imagination was called kenning. In the kenning, two images are joined to create a new word-name. Examples of kennings include:

Whale-path
Bone-house
Mirth-wood
World-Candle
Hawks-land
Hawks-land-flame

Whale-path was the name for the sea. *Bone-house* was a name for a person's chest. *Mirth-wood* was a harp. *World-candle* was the Sun. *Hawks-land* is sky. *Hawks-land-flame* is lightning.

Through these kennings, the Anglo-Saxon mind intuits connections among things of the sensory world, creating a new language of interconnectedness. Through the kennings, the speaker recognizes and wills reunion, reintegrating the creation. Whereas the ancient Greek, especially through Homer's similes, quickened and engendered a capacity to make rational connections in the world, the Old Anglo-Saxon language, through both its four-beat alliterative verse and its metaphor-like activity of the kennings, embodied the northern peoples' more will-oriented, sentient-soul approach to life in the ninth century C.E. As we shall see, English poetry's particular capacity for metaphor, epitomized in both Shakespeare and Keats, has its seed origins in Old Anglo-Saxon kennings.

Chapter 3

Evolving English and Evolving Adolescents

Introduction

How do developments in the language of English literature reflect developments in adolescence? How, if we understand appropriately, can developments in the language of English literature affect, quicken, or at least enhance, or reinforce, adolescent developmental stages? There is no simple, categorical answer. But looking at the four years of high school as qualitatively as possible may yield helpful clues.

Reading literature can offer windows into many realms of human experience, beyond our daily sensory experience. However, understanding literature, as rich as it can be, is a window at best. Working directly with the language of literature itself, particularly poetry, can open the door, ushering one directly into the medium itself, the living "soul-flesh," of that recreated experience. Or, to take the metaphor further, direct work with the language of poetry can work as a key that unlocks otherwise dormant, unconscious layers of soul-experience in adolescents. The language of humanity's particular age stage can quicken the consciousness of the individual's corresponding age stage. Decades of work with adolescents serve as a context for the following characterizations of adolescent development in relation to the development of the English language. The accompanying exercises work to help both adolescents and adults of any age to live more immediately and consciously into qualities of the language of English poetry at dramatic stages of development in the language.

Ninth Grade (ages 14–15)

Since the Waldorf curriculum in ninth grade focuses primarily on modern history (from the American Revolution through the twentieth century), on the one hand, and on observation of the physical world on the other, it may be fair to say that the effect of language on consciousness is less conscious in ninth grade than in the other three years of high school. The main emphasis is to use language clearly, reflecting accurately the actual appearances of the physical world, using language as correctly as possible, and using language as playfully and enjoyably as possible. Students are affected by living in the English of Shakespeare (*A Midsummer Night's Dream*), Melville (*Moby-Dick*), Twain (his short pieces), Paton (*Cry, the Beloved Country*), Lee (*To Kill a Mockingbird*), Carter (*The Education of Little Tree*), Hansberry (*A Raisin in the Sun*), and other "outside" books.

Tenth Grade (ages 15–16)

In the context of the Waldorf Curriculum, tenth grade is the year when language needs to really get to work, quickening the student, vitally, artfully, and consciously or in Rudolf Steiner's terms—etheric, astral and spirit/ego. Historically, the tenth grade curriculum reaches back, to the origins of ancient cultures such as India, Persia, Babylon and Sumeria, and Egypt, and all the way forward to Ancient Greece, while looking at the question: How do cultures and civilizations form and evolve? Scientifically, students look at physiology, the activities of the nervous, circulatory, and metabolic systems. How do the processes of the body work? How do the processes of the whole Earth work? Whereas ninth graders need to be able to look at the world to see what it is, tenth graders need to look behind the world to understand how it works.

If one looks at the third seven-year period as the time when a young person's astral body (soul body) develops, it is possible, and wise, to consider the ninth grade year as a recapitulation of the student's physical development during the first seven years, so that the newly emerging soul body can orient well in the physical world. Similarly, as an educator helping students develop in the healthiest ways, one can work with the developing soul, or astral body, in the tenth grade, in a way that recapitulates and reinforces some of the characteristics of the child's life body as it developed in the second seven-year period, roughly between the change of teeth and puberty. With the activity of the formative forces in mind, how can we work with language in a way that quickens, activates, generates, and articulates the emerging astral body in an artful, lively, and healthy manner that helps it interweave with the more mature forces of the developed life body?

How can the newly "flowering" consciousness of the teenager best integrate with the healthy "leaves" of the prepubescent life forces? The primary way is through two courses that Rudolf Steiner recommended for the curriculum in the tenth grade. One he called "the evolution of the language" (the mother tongue); the other can be called "the elements of poetry," or "the art of poetry." In recent years, a number of schools have combined these two subjects to help students become aware of certain elements of poetry, in the medium of the evolving poetry, hence the evolving language and consciousness. One can introduce elements of poetry as the poetry of the language evolves historically.

The ultimate way for tenth grade students to begin thinking about their own language or language in general is through the creation myth, particularly the Judeo-Christian story of the world's origin, occurring through the saying activity of the Creator. The first human being, made in the image of the Creator, was given the task and opportunity of naming the other creatures. Hence, humankind, made in the image of the Creator, imitated the Creator's creative power by naming the creatures. The Tower of Babel is, of course, a picture of the differentiation of one original language into many, as a consequence of humanity's luciferic attempt to build the tower to God and to be too much like the Creator. Both naming others and speaking the words "I AM" remain important deeds throughout the stories of the Bible, as the tenth graders discover in later studies of the Bible as source of literature.

Students can learn some of the language and rhythms of the earliest Western written verse, the ancient Greeks of the early epics, lyrics, and dramas. In doing so, they can experience not only how the content of the epic (Homer's *Iliad* and *Odyssey*) guides a whole culture into being, but also how the rhythms—formed through the pace of the breathing lungs in relation to the beating heart—in fact helped the people listening to the stories to be able to breathe the long tales into their own being. "*Andra moi ennepe musa*, \ *polutropon hos mala pola*" (Sing in me, O Muse, of the man of many turns), the opening lines of Homer's *Odyssey*. On such a basis, students can easily imagine that early Greek rhythms even helped form the breathing and circulatory systems of the people themselves within a lifetime and of the folk as a whole over generations.

Not only does "The Art of Poetry" need to help students imagine back to the origin of our world and to the origins of Western literature, but it also needs to take them back to the origins of their own language as well. Tenth graders become aware of the ebbs and flows and gradual interweaving of Celtic, Roman Latin, Angle, Saxon, Jute, Norse, and Church Latin by the time that Alfraed (*raed* = "counseled by the *Alf*" = elfs) consolidated not only a kingdom, but also a language, by translating Bede's history of the Church into English and by instituting a *Chronicle of English History*.

Beowulf

Da co***m*** of ***m***ore under ***m***ist-hleothum
Grendel **g**ongan, **G**odes yrre baer:
mynte se ***m***an-scatha ***m***anna cynnes
*s*umne be*s*yrwan in *s*els tham hean.

From the stretching moors, from the misty hollows,
Grendel came creeping, accursed of God,
A murderous ravager minded to snare
Spoil of heroes in high-built hall.

Beowulf (tr. Kennedy), II. 710–714

As tenth grade students read ninth-century *Beowulf* and learn some of the lines by heart, speaking them day after day, and writing in imitation of the four-beat alliterative verse, they begin to experience:

1. The living sounds of our great-grandfather tongue, of our earliest English.
2. Sounds that are more immediately, primally, and freshly rooted in the elements (water, earth, air, and fire) than is the case in any more recent forms of English language. In particular, the thick texture of emphasis on consonants helps students incarnate into the physical world, helps developing astral bodies to be well grounded in relation to the physical world.
3. Rhythms (four-beat alliteration) that not only echo but also reinforce, generate, and strengthen the heartbeat and hence the health of the circulatory system at a time when the student's etheric heart is forming independently.
4. Sounds and rhythm, as well as imagery, that appeal to the will, that emanate from the will, that quicken the will, and that strengthen the will. In our contemporary era of information overload and weakening will, a hunger for action and power is reflected frequently in adolescent and street lingo filled with Anglo-Saxon four-letter words. Teenagers find an unparalleled fresh power in the fountain-force of the old Anglo-Saxon language.
5. Through kennings (explained in chapter 2), the activity of first seeing the connection between two different images—whale and path, for example—as in a simile forming a marriage between two normally separate parts of creation. At the same time the kenning crafter creates a new word, "whale-path," for the word *sea,* thereby generating language and fresh vitality.
6. Through riddles that quicken the tenth graders' souls to ponder, with practical wisdom, mysteries of life on Earth. Such a consideration generates imagination, the activity of gleaning an activity's essence.

7. Unconscious recapitulation of what Rudolf Steiner calls sentient soul experience. In one's life, the astral body (developed especially between puberty and becoming an adult, around age twenty-one) is then transformed by the individual's "I" into the sentient soul during the twenties.

Historically, humanity evolved through a sentient soul stage of development roughly during the two millennia between 3000 B.C.E and 1000 B.C.E., when Egyptian culture was ripest. Humanity's next stage of development, the intellectual soul stage, began around the time of the origins of Western literature in ancient Greece, c.800 B.C.E. Nevertheless, not all cultures developed simultaneously. The Norse peoples of the north remained illiterate longer as an oral culture and thus sustained a sentient soul relationship to life until much later.

As their own individual astral bodies are emerging, tenth graders have the opportunity, through the old Anglo-Saxon language, to experience a vital, potent, homeopathic dose of sentient soul life, which nourishes them with a certain raw distillation of a vast, rich cultural sustenance. They love the mysterious, atmospheric power of the sounds; they feel empowered, charged, reconnected with the elemental forces of the world; they feel made mighty, artfully.

> Well-being I won
> And wisdom too.
> I grew and took joy in my growth:
> From a word to a word
> I was led to a word,
> From a deed to another deed.
>
> Odin (from the Old Norse)
> *The Poetic Edda* (c.1200 C.E.)

Also in the "Art of Poetry," the tenth graders should learn of the linguistic developments after the Norman invasion, leading up to the time of Chaucer, some of whose iambic pentameter rhyming couplets the students should experience. They should learn something of the vowel changes in the fifteenth and early sixteenth centuries. They should work with a Shakespearean sonnet and try to write one. Through the works of Shakespeare or Milton, they should experience blank verse. They can also experience later Romantic poetry and the free verse of Walt Whitman.

For several reasons, it is helpful for tenth graders to have a main lesson on the Bible as source of literature. The mytho-historic development described in the Old Testament complements the history curriculum of ancient cultures. The Old and New Testaments together are a primary source of imagery and patterns for the whole Western imagination, and hence for Western culture. The King James translation, generated also in the time of Shakespeare, is the other wonder of the spirit of the English language (chapter 8), fashioning phrasings that still shape the minds of English-speakers.

To complement the Judeo-Christian stream, Homer's *Odyssey* offers the other major source of the Western imagination. In addition to the shape of the narrative and the wealth of the imagery, the Homeric similes specifically educate the tenth graders' minds in imaginative activity with rational discipline. Elaborating the details of a comparison stimulates and strengthens imaginative capacity. Both the language (like, as) and the lawful accuracy require logical clarity.

Study of the short story in tenth grade provides an excellent opportunity for students to become more aware of the narrative craft, especially plot, symbol, theme, and character. Although the modernity of this form makes it an exception to the general ancient Greek context of tenth grade, its accessibility makes it prime material for tenth graders to further develop their thinking by applying consciousness to form.

The Old Anglo-Saxon of Beowulf: A Possible Sequence of Exercises

The following series of exercises assumes that a large space is available, allowing substantial movement. If space does not allow a group to move so fully, it is possible to have a micro-version of the experiences, using fingers on desktops, instead of legs on floors.

1. Read aloud four to six lines of the original *Beowulf*. Have everyone speak together two to four lines of the old Anglo-Saxon. Then, speaking the lines again, have the students take a step, on each of the (four) strong beats in a line. What do they experience?
2. The teacher speaks the lines, tapping with a ruler or pencil, the weak, unstressed syllables, as the students step the strong beats. What do they experience? The students start to become aware of the regularity of the strong beats, and the varying, flexible irregularity of the weak beats. Then they can try stepping the weak beats lightly, and the strong beats heavily.
3. As the teacher speaks the line, the students step and call out the repeated consonant sound on three of the four strong beats. Then the students can do the same, this time banging their "sword hand" over onto their "shield hand" on each of the three repeated consonants. What is their experience?
4. No longer speaking the old Anglo-Saxon, have the students walk a straight line in any direction, stepping four strong beats, varying weak beats however they choose. However, each student calls out some consonant, repeating it on three of the four strong beats, then changes direction, and does the same, walking a four beat line, varying weak beats, repeating a new consonant sound for three of the four strong beats—and again, and again. What is their experience?
5. Have the students sit down and write an alliterative, four-beat line, repeating the same consonant three of the four strong beats, varying weak beats however they choose. The subject matter might be a battle or a journey, emphasizing the elements (earth, water, air, and fire) and physical phenomena as vividly as possibly. Writing four-to-six lines in class, they might take it further at night, to ten to fifteen lines, or more.
6. What was it like writing in that form? What was the experience, what were the effects?

Chapter 4

The Norman Conquest

Roughly two centuries after Alfred the Great had consolidated Anglo-Saxon culture, England's last Saxon king, Harald, was well aware in the spring of 1066 that William of Normandy was gathering forces on the shores of Northern France for an invasion of southern England. The previous Anglo-Saxon king, Edward the Confessor, had at one point promised the crown to his distant cousin, William of Normandy. However, in his dying days, he declared his successor to be Harald, the able son of the second most powerful man in England, Edward's father-in-law Godwin. Nine months into his reign, Harald mustered men all along the coast, from Dover to Cornwall, to stand watch for any signs of invasion, and to be ready as a standing militia to resist the outsiders. Across the English Channel, William gathered hundreds of ships, along with infantry and horsemen. However, because their ships used square sails, the wind had to be just right to take them downwind, on a south/southwesterly breeze, to England's shores. The winds were not just right in May.

After six weeks of militia duty, Harald's men returned to their neglected farms to bring in the first hay crop. Harald called them out again in July, then again in August. Still the wind was not right for William's fleet and still there was no sight of the supposed invaders. Morale yielded to skepticism among the defenders. By September most of the English felt that the danger of invasion had pretty well passed during that summer.

On the nineteenth day of September, King Harald received word from an exhausted messenger, who had ridden down the whole length of the country, that on the northeastern shores of England, outside York, a large Viking fleet had arrived, led by the notorious Norse king, Harald Hardrada. England's Harald called together his army immediately and led a forced march from London to York in four days and nights, where they did battle with the Vikings and overcame them. A week after Harald conducted the formal ceremony of the Viking surrender, a messenger all the way from London arrived in York to say that William of Normandy had landed with his fleet on the southern shores.

So Harald led his army, victorious but bloody and weakened, on another forced four-day march back to London. Meanwhile, William, unobstructed, had ample time to unload his ships and deploy his troops, including his fresh cavalry. On October 14, 1066, Harald's army met William's at Hastings in Sussex near London. The battle was fierce, and Harald was felled when an arrow pierced his eye. Owing to months of unusual winds and the extraordinary timing of the Viking invasion just days before that of the Normans, the tide of destiny was turned irrevocably, in spite of the almost superhuman efforts of the army led by Harald, the Saxon king.

During the next several centuries, the three different levels of people in England lived in three different languages. The Anglo-Saxons who worked the land continued to speak Anglo-Saxon. Scholars, practitioners of law (clerks), and the clergy worked and communicated in Latin. The Norman nobility, both at home and in court, continued to speak French. An extraordinary historical irony is that those Normans who sustained French among the Anglo-Saxons were in fact descendants of Norse Vikings who had invaded northern France a mere hundred and fifty years earlier. The Norman invaders had absorbed the French language and culture, making it their own to then export in 1066 to the Anglo-Saxons of Britain. Imagine the parallel coexistence and activity of the spirits of these three languages: Anglo-Saxon English, Latin, and French. Imagine the Anglo-Saxon servants in Norman courts; the Anglo-Saxon peasants and the Norman nobility in courts of law, where Latin was used; the use of English, Latin, and French in churches for marriages and funerals; and all three overlapping and rubbing shoulders in the marketplaces. Yet, essentially, the three languages remained distinct.

During what historians call the Hundred Years' War, between England and France, roughly from 1337 to 1454, the impetus grew for everyone in England to speak English, not French. From a certain perspective, these struggles can be seen as a mutual effort by the two folk souls to extricate themselves from their long intertwined connection to each other, for the French to become essentially French (culminating in Joan of Arc's actions and death), and for the English to become essentially English. In 1340, considered coincidentally to be the year of Chaucer's birth, the English House of Commons passed a new law, the Abolition of Englishry, which abolished any distinction between Norman English and Saxon English; all English men were Englishmen. The parliamentary House of Commons had become an organ through which the common people had acquired the power to act on their dissatisfaction at being treated differently from the "Normans" of the land. On a practical level, King Edward III was forced to acquiesce to the new law in order to muster common support among the common people for his imminent war with France to assert his claim as the rightful heir to the French throne.

Hence, a progressive banishment of the French language ensued: in 1349, from the schools; in 1356, from the courts of law; and in 1362, from parliamentary debates. In spite of the blending of Latin, French, and Anglo-Saxon, the resulting English language was itself four strands of vigorous regional dialects with differing sources, each virtually unintelligible to the others.

In the north, the Angles' English of Northumbria and Mercia, colored by Norse, was the medium for the Chester, York, and Townley Miracle Plays.

> Sir Knightis, saie, howe wirke we nowe?
> Zis, certis, I hope I holde this hande.
> And to the boore I have it brought,
> Full boxumly with-outen bande.
> Strike on than harde, for him to the boght.
>
> "Crucifixio Cristi," *York Miracle Play*, II. 97–101

In the west, the Saxons' English was tinted faintly with Celtic and generated *Sir Gawain and the Green Knight, The Pearl, Wynnere, Wastour*, and *Piers Plowman:*

> In a somer sesun, whon softe was the sonne,
> I schop me into a shroud, as I a scheep were;
> In habite as an hermite unholy of werkes
> Wente I wyde in this world wondres to here;
> Bote in a Mayes morwnynge on Malverne hulles
> Me bifel a ferly, of fairie, me-thoughte.
>
> WILLIAM LANGLAND, *Piers Plowman*

The Jutes' English permeated southeastern Kent, whereas London and the East-Midlands absorbed more Danish and Norman French than the other regions. As we shall see in the next chapter, Chaucer was able to give birth to a national language and literature though his London–East Midlands English.

> Whan that aprill with his shoures soughte
> The droghte of March hath perced to the rote
> And bathed every veyne in swich licour
> Of which vertu engendered is the fleur
>
> *Canterbury Tales* (opening lines, prologue)

In 1399, Henry Bolingbroke, grandson of King Edward III, successfully seized the power from his uncle, Richard II. At the coronation of Henry IV, an English king spoke, claiming his crown in the "Englische Tunge" for the first time in history. Chaucer died one year later. By 1417, Henry V became the first king to use English in documents. While he fought the French in France, he dictated letters in English. Although he was declared regent of France and married Catherine of Valois, the French king's daughter, Henry V performed his deeds as King of England in the English language. By 1422, the London brewers resolved to write in English. The spirit of the English language had almost fully permeated the people of the land.

How can we imagine the activity, influence, and even "interfluence" of the spirits of the Anglo-Saxon, Latin, and French languages, in the process of evolving English? One way may be through the people's relationship to their various patron saints. Initially, the Saxons, chafing under Norman rule, hearkened back to their last holy king, Edward the Confessor. They would utter his name when they needed strength, outer or inner, as though the individual spirit of King Edward I could inspire the folk soul of the Anglo-Saxon people. The Normans themselves had brought with them the guidance of the Archangel St. Michael from the island of Mont St. Michel on the northern coast of France. Thirty-three years later, in 1099, those first European (mostly French and Italian) crusaders who reclaimed Jerusalem for Christianity became increasingly more aware of the legends of St. George, associated especially with the region of Anatolia in present Turkey. Almost a century later, in 1194, England's King Richard I, the Lion-Heart, wholeheartedly brought veneration of St. George back to England upon his return from the Third Crusade in the Mideast. St. George, the earthly counterpart of St. Michael, appealed to the Norman-English soldiery.

Almost two centuries later, a moment of this spiritual fusion occurred. In 1349, Edward III, while besieging Calais, "drew his sword, and cried with ardour, 'Ha, St. Edward! Ha, St. George!' and fell with vigour on the French, and so defeated them" (Wyatt 195). Nine years after both the Abolition of Englishry and the birth of Geoffrey Chaucer, it is as though the Anglo-Saxon patron Saint Edward passed the sword of the Word to St. George, who was emerging as the Patron Saint of an England that thought, felt, and acted, even fought in one language.

Although Rudolf Steiner described how a particular archangelic being presides over each language, the general populace has had little clear awareness of such spiritual activity. Nevertheless, whole populations have been able to rally around and be inspired by a patron saint, a particularly spiritual person who has embodied the aspirations of a particular folk. Some cultures have even chosen an archangel such as St. Michael as their patron saint.

As we shall see, by the time of Chaucer's death in 1400, the three strands of Anglo-Saxon, Latin, and French have coalesced and been internalized into a new, unified, multidimensional, threefold braid of English, as though the guiding spirits of those three languages prepared, contributed, and then surrendered a significant element in their own languages, handing over tutelage to a new guide of a new, hybrid language. This fusion occurs right at the culmination of the intellectual soul stage of humanity's development, right at the dawning in the early 1400s, according to Rudolf Steiner, of the consciousness-soul stage of development. It is as if Edward, the patron of the earth-working Anglo-Saxons, and St. Michael, the heavenly patron of the ruling Normans gave way to St. George, patron of the people of England and their language, English, which would best enable new attention to the Earth through a new consciousness. What qualities of the new language would enable what kinds of new consciousness?

Chapter 5

Chaucer's Middle English

The Life of Geoffrey Chaucer (1340–1400)

IN THE LATE 1350s, the young Geoffrey Chaucer had already lived through an extraordinary spectrum of experiences, sandwiched among his studies of the Seven Liberal Arts. Having studied the trivium, grammar, rhetoric, and logic, in secondary school, he joined the court of Prince Lionel, son of King Edward III, who, inspired by Arthur, had a round table. By the age of nineteen, young Geoffrey had fought as a knight in France, been captured, and been ransomed by the King. Returning to England, he was able to immerse himself in studies of the quadrivium: mathematics, geometry, music, and astronomy. He then turned to law at the Inner Temple in London. Little could anyone imagine these experiences as preparation for Geoffrey Chaucer's most enduring contributions: the range of perennial character types embodied in his Canterbury pilgrims and, even more important, his literary language, the direct source of which has become our English language today, almost seven hundred years later.

Although his palette had been broadly prepared by his education and worldly exposure, this twenty-one-year-old nevertheless showed no outer signs of his future work with the spirit of the English language, becoming what linguists call the grandfather of contemporary English.

Into what world had Geoffrey Chaucer been born? Medieval England in the 1300s included numerous contrasts. On the one hand misogyny abounded. Woman, like Eve, might be seen as a source of evil, and husbands were permitted to beat their wives so long as it wasn't fatal. On the other hand, the atmosphere was still permeated with vestiges of the courtly love of Eleanor of Aquitaine, the earlier medieval virtues of chivalry by which a knight reverently aspired to serve an inspiring woman of great virtue. People ate with their fingers. Sauces, which both preserved and disguised foods, were messy. Without handkerchiefs, people wiped their mouths and hands with their sleeves. There were no glass windows; wooden shutters closed out the night. There were no chairs, only benches. There was little loneliness, boredom, alienation, or privacy, since most people slept several to a bed. Straw covered the floors. When dogs contributed, straw was added, not changed. London's streets were certainly darker than those of New York today, both for want of light and for the events that happened in them. Few went out after curfew. Murders and beatings with wooden staffs were common.

The typical English person of the time was quite different from the image of our overly polite, super-civilized contemporaries. "They were passionate,... quick to change moods." Chaucer's medieval contemporaries might greet one another with a hug and a kiss, then, "when insulted or injured, they snatched at their daggers without thinking" (John Gardner 62). This sentient soul behavior lingered, as though the English folk as a whole were essentially still young, almost adolescent, with their adult consciousness just beginning to emerge. The Anglo-Saxon language had surrendered its sentient soul alliteration in its literary forms to Latin and French influences, but its youthful vitality was still reflected in the British folk.

What many medieval English people called "The Ringing Isle" sounded with bells everywhere, at all times of day and night. Measured Time reached England only in the early fourteenth century. The streets resounded "with the clangs of iron on horses, hooves, the clatter of wooden cartwheels, dogs yapping, vendors calling out, 'Hot peascods, ripe strawberries, Paris thread, Sir, finest in the land, Mackeral, green thrushes, hot sheep's feet, pewter pots!'" (Gardner 61).

The "holy blissful martyr" St. Thomas Becket, who had been assassinated on the altar of Canterbury Cathedral by knights of Henry II, inspired Christian pilgrimages. The Church was omnipresent throughout the land. Nevertheless, especially from the North, the land of Macbeth, stories of witches, goblins and changelings abounded. Magic and witchcraft were everywhere; spells and superstitions were interwoven with prayers and ecclesiastical rites.

In 1340, the year that the English Parliament passed The Abolition of Englishry, Geoffrey Chaucer was born in London. His father John was a vintner, helping to supply wines for the chief butler serving King Edward III. Probably not weaned until age five, as was customary, young Geoffrey fortunately moved at the age of seven with his family to Southampton, where he began his studies of Latin, in French of course. The next year, 1348, the Black Death arrived in London from Genoa and Constantinople. The Church reinforced the growing sense in the nation that God was inflicting punishment for sin. Geoffrey turned nine when King Edward III rode into battle against the French, calling, "St. Edward! St. George!" uniting the spirit of the language. Also that year, England banished French from the schools and the Chaucers returned to London.

Geoffrey resumed his schooling there, now in English, pursuing the trivium of the classic medieval liberal arts education, grammar, logic, and rhetoric. At sixteen, Geoffrey joined the household of Prince Lionel, third son of Edward III, who ruled Ireland. Edward, inspired by King Arthur, had established both a round table and the Order of the Garter. After nineteen-year-old Geoffrey Chaucer served in the King's army in France, was captured, and was ransomed by the king, he returned to study the quadrivium at Oxford University. Philosophical studies included the medieval debates between Nominalism and Realism. He also translated texts from ancient Greek into Latin. His studies focused on common law at the Inner Temple in London.

At twenty-six, Chaucer was joined in marriage with Philippa Rouet, an acquaintance from his adolescence whose sister was the mistress of John of Gaunt, another son of King Edward. They shared three children, Thomas, Elizabeth, and Lewis. Over a period of seven years Chaucer translated the ideal and sensuous *Roman of the Rose*, written by Lorris and de Meun, from French into English. Valued for his diplomatic and linguistic skills, he was sent to Navarre in northern Spain for delicate negotiations in service of the king. John of Gaunt, his patron, also sent him to France. Later, at thirty-two and thirty-three, Chaucer was sent to Italy, where he feasted on music and architecture, met Petrarch, the father of humanism, and possibly Boccacio, whose tales in the *Decameron* powerfully inspired Chaucer with plots and human experience. In 1374, in appreciation of his diplomatic efforts over the years, King Edward III awarded Chaucer a gallon of wine per day for the rest of his life.

Then, when he was thirty-six and thirty-seven, Chaucer was sent on three mysterious missions to France to negotiate a potential marriage between the new King Richard II and a French princess, hoping to secure peace and end the Hundred Years War. However, no wedding occurred. Finally, in 1381, at the age of forty-one, Geoffrey Chaucer began to write the *Canterbury Tales*, on which he worked for the rest of his life. His services to the state were rewarded with several official posts during his later years, including Sub-Forester, Customs, and finally Clerk of the King's Works, making him responsible for the King's architecture. The security that came with such employment allowed him to write. When Henry IV overthrew Richard in 1399 and assumed the throne of England, Chaucer disappeared from public life. His tombstone, carved a hundred years later, states his death to have occurred on October 25, 1400 at the age of sixty. There are some scholars who wonder if King Richard's enemies may have murdered him. Nevertheless, as befitting a man of such public service to the monarchy, Geoffrey Chaucer was buried in Westminster Abbey. In 1556, his remains were moved to a more elaborate tomb, where Chaucer, the grandfather of English literature and language, became the first English poet buried in what is now known as Poets' Corner.

Chaucer: the Middle-English Language

Listening to lines of the Old Anglo-Saxon of ninth-century *Beowulf:*

> Tha com of more, unter mist hleothum
> Grendel gongan, Godes yrre baer,

and lines of Chaucer's *Canterbury Tales* about five hundred years later:

> Whan that Aprill, with his shoures soote
> The droghte of March hath perced to the roote
> And bathed every veyne in swich licour
> Of which vertu engendred is the flour,

one can hear a number of differences. First, the rhythm and length of the lines differ. *Beowulf*'s four-beat line has expanded to Chaucer's five-beat pentameter. Instead of the weakly emphasized syllable falling in any (varying) number among the strong beats, as in the northern, Anglo-Saxon verse, Chaucer's line includes a regular alternation between short and long syllables, more duration than stress, and rhythmical, regular, iambic (short-long) pentameter. "The ***droghte*** of ***March*** hath ***per***ced ***to*** the ***roo***te." The opening line could be read as trochaic pentameter, with the long syllable before the short. "***Whan*** that ***A***prill, ***with*** his ***shou***res ***soo***te." Yet the regular pattern of lines is iambic pentameter, as anyone conscious can hear. However, anyone familiar with the old English at the time of *Beowulf* can read Chaucer's *Canterbury Tales* with a second ear.

> ***Whan*** that ***A***prill ***with*** his ***shou***res ***soo***te
> The ***droghte*** of ***March*** hath ***per***ced ***to*** the ***roo***te

Not far below the even-tempered five-beat line brought up through the southern, Greco-Roman-French stream, especially through the gradual emergence of Norman influence, not far below still pulses the Northern, Anglo-Saxon counter-rhythm of the blood-pulsing four-beat line.

> ***Whan*** that ***A***pril with his ***shou***res ***soo***te
> The ***droghte*** of ***March*** hath ***per***ced to the ***roo***te

Not only the rhythms but also the sounds themselves yield different experiences in the Old Anglo-Saxon and the Middle

English. In the Old Anglo-Saxon, the consonantal sounds of the three beats of alliteration dominate the experience of the line,

> Tha co***m*** of ***m***ore ***unter m***ist hleothum
> Grendel gongan Godes irre baer.

In a culture only on the verge of literacy, the soul experience was primarily external, out in the elements of wind, water, rock, and terrain, out in the actions of battle. Hence, the sound experience of the language predominantly reflects, through the emphasized consonant sounds, the forms of the external, physical world, the *more*, moor, the *mist,* mist, and the *hleothum*, hollow.

We modern souls, moving from Old Anglo-Saxon to Chaucer's Middle English, can experience quite a relief, as the alliterative consonants surrender their domination of the line, receding into more proportional, balanced relationship with the vowel sounds. It is almost as though a storm abates, the battle is over, and the new language allows for more light, for the quieter interplay of more varying soul experience, more interplay between outer and inner, between consonant and vowel. A new consciousness is emerging, in a language that allows more time to breathe, time to reflect.

However, as the language in one earlier stage of humanity's soul development surrenders a certain formal security, what remains? Consider, in the old English, the certainty of soul is reinforced in every line, as the first strong beat sounds a certain consonant, and the speaker and the listeners (readers) know that the next two strong beats will reaffirm that same sound, no matter what. Rudolf Steiner spoke of the northern, alliterative verse as a sentient soul recollection, even hearkening back to humankind's original state of being. The fourth strong beat was open, variable, in terms of which consonant was stressed, allowing an element of unpredictable sound. Remember, too, that the pattern of unstressed syllables could vary completely.

> Da co***m*** of ***m***ore under ***m***ist-hleothum
> Grendel gongan, Godes yrre baer:

On the one hand, in the language of Chaucer, the interior of the line opens up, almost as though three standing stones (the required consonantal alliteration) had been removed from the stream. However, Chaucer's line is certainly not completely variable. We have seen that it sustains a musical rhythm of iambic pentameter: "And ***bath***ed ***e***very ***veyne*** in ***swich*** li***cour***...." And now, whereas the final beat of the Old English was open, the final beat of the Middle English assumes a new importance.

As the first line completes its statement, with the word-sounds "soote," the listening reader discovers that the next line concludes with a similar sound set: "roote." Although the third line ends in "licour," we are not surprised to hear the fourth line end in something like "flour." And, in fact, as we proceed through the ensuing pairs of lines, throughout the whole *Canterbury Tales*, we proceed with an absolute confidence that the end sound of one line will also include the end of the next line, in rhyming couplets. One experiences a combination of surprise, reassurance, and enhancing certainty. There is a delighted, knowing confidence in the mind of the writer and reader to find the rhyme come to closure.

The Old Anglo-Saxon had marched with a security of consonantal reverberation at each of the first three stresses of a line, with the final, fourth step being open. It is as though the sentient-soul warrior knew he was marching, but not knowing or perhaps even caring where. Think of the Vikings, who regularly fanned out in any direction each spring, south, west, north—out and out. By contrast, the soul in Middle English, riding the more regular, trotting rhythm of the iambic pentameter, is freed to experience much more variety of sound during the course of the line, being far freer in the interior of the line. Yet the certainty comes with knowing where one will end up at the end of each couplet.

In the beginning of Western literature around 600 B.C.E., in Greek epics, Greek dramas, and Greek lyrics, there was no end rhyme. The old English also has no end rhyme. Latin and Italian poets had been playing with kinds of rhyme, as Chaucer the translator well knew. The rhyming couplet, per se, emerges essentially at the culmination of what Rudolf Steiner calls the intellectual-soul stage of human development from approximately 700 B.C.E. to 1400 C.E. In fact, Steiner says of the end-rhyme experience:

> The final rhyme is closely connected with the remarkable soul condition that, after humanity has entered the present evolution, is expressed through the culture of the intellectual, or mind, soul. Fundamentally, the time in which the intellectual soul arose in human beings, during the fourth post-Atlantean period of civilization (essentially, the Greco-Roman and Medieval era) is also the time when, in poetry, memory dawned of the experiences of the ancient time that extended into the ancient *Imaginative* world. This memory is expressed in the end rhyme." (Faulkner-Jones 65)

One way to understand this concept is to consider the Greek philosophers (Socrates, Plato, and Aristotle especially) and the medieval philosophers (Albertus Magnus, Duns Scotus, and Thomas Aquinas), trying to reconcile Greek understanding with Christian faith.

In form, Chaucer's language carries barely heard echoes of the Anglo-Saxon alliterative, four-beat line, the suitable vessel for the action-experience of the sentient soul. At the crest of the wave of the mind soul's development, Chaucer's rhyming couplets have a vital, sustaining, intellectual beauty, allowing both refinement of feeling and more orderly mental reflection. Stretching the English consciousness beyond the Anglo-Saxon four-beat line, Chaucer virtually created the iambic pentameter in English. This iambic pentameter line becomes the medium in the English language for the imminent articulation of, and development of, what Steiner calls the consciousness soul, for at least the next six hundred years.

During the Prologue to *The Canterbury Tales*, Chaucer introduces each of the twenty-nine pilgrims who will travel together to Canterbury. The description of the Miller proceeds predictably, according to type.

The Millere was a stout carl for the nones.
Full byg he was of brawn, and eek of bones...
He was short-shouldred, brood, a thikke knarre.
There was no dore that he nolde heve of harre.

So far, so good; we are on the familiar terrain of a type of character, although the next line might catch us slightly by surprise, "Or breke it at a rennyng with his heed." This miller is starting to distinguish himself a bit from any other millers we have met, at least in literature, and at least in terms of his behavior. "His berd as any sowe or fox was reed." Okay, like any other choleric, door-bashing, fire-bearded miller, "And therto brood, as though it were a spade." This is a fresh simile—a beard is like a spade. But now, watch out:

Upon the cop right of his nose he hade
A werte, and theron stood a toft of herys,
Reed as the brustles of a sowes erys.
His nosethirles blake were and wyde.
II. 545–557

Some scholars of Old Anglo-Saxon might hear, as we noticed before, subtle undertone echoes of the sentient soul, four-beat line pulsing under Chaucer's iambic pentameter. Moreover, Chaucer's rhyming couplets freshly sustain a rational soul sound framework that most of us, in our third-millennium English, would find confining, even deadening. But these several lines of the word portrait of the miller serve as an early signal of a consciousness-soul capacity of the English language. I am not aware of a medieval description in literature, certainly in English literature, as dependent on sense-perceived particular features as Chaucer's miller, with the red, pig-like bristles growing out of the mole on his nose, right by his black, wide nostrils.

Wolfram von Eschenbach's Cundrie la sorcière in *Parzival* has a shocking composite of animal features, emphasized once, with almost allegorical, fairy-tale effect, and then not reinforced later, as Parzival changes inwardly. They are more a feature of imagination than of observation, more reflection of soul than features of an actual physical body. Most of Chaucer's description of the miller is inherited out of type, the categories of the medieval mind. But that "werte," and that "toft of herys, / Reed as the brustles of a sowes erys" were perceived by a consciousness capable of emancipating itself from feeling or preconception, free to perceive physical particulars in their own right, revealing, therefore, signs of a more individualized miller than ever rendered before. Such a sketch, probably written in the late 1300s, anticipates the emergence of the consciousness soul, a long development lasting more than two millennia, not really beginning generally until the early 1400s. The consciousness soul, as embodied in its early stages by the imminent emergence of natural science, will include humanity's new capacity for maintaining an objective relationship with the physical world.

Not only did Chaucer fashion iambic pentameter, the sound vessel for our first consciousness-soul explorations in English poetry, but he also drew brush strokes of content, leading the emerging attention to the physical world, the miller's wart, for example, characteristic of the consciousness soul.

Chaucer's Middle English: Possible Exercises

1. As a reminder, have everyone speak two-to-four lines of *Beowulf.*
2. The teacher speaks four to six lines of Chaucer's *Canterbury Tales.* Have the students speak two and then at least four lines. What do they notice, as qualities, in relation to the old Anglo-Saxon?
3. Speak the lines, asking the students to step the strong beats. Speak the lines, asking them to step the strong beats and clap the weak beats. What is the difference in quality between a four-beat and a five-beat line? What is the effect of the regular, short-long, (iambic) foot, in which the "weak" sound is generally as regular as the strong sound? What is it like not to have the threefold alliteration of each line? What is the effect of having the end sound of line two rhyme with the end sound

of line one? What does it mean, what is it like, to know, with certainty, that the next line will rhyme with the previous?

4. Have students cluster in the center of the room, each facing out toward the perimeter. As the teacher calls out, perhaps "short-long, short-long...," each student walks a straight line, in any direction, stepping five iambs, short-long; on the fifth iamb, each person calls out a sound, of his or her choice. Then each person turns in any direction, stepping the iambic pentameter, then curving back to the exact same end spot on the fifth foot (iamb), calling out the same sound on that last foot. Then walk an iambic pentameter line in a new direction, calling out a new end-sound, curving out a next line, ending at the same new end spot, calling out that same "new" end sound. Perhaps do this for ten lines, five rhyming couplets. What is the effect? How do students experience such lines?
5. Now have the students write lines in iambic pentameter, with rhyming couplets. The subject could vary; recommendations include a character sketch, a love passage/poem, or the beginning of a tale. Students could continue at home, writing at least twelve lines, reworking and improving them.
6. What was it like to write in that form? What was the experience, the effect?

Chapter 6

The Language Wakes up, Renewed

One of the greatest and quickest changes in the history of languages occurred during the 1400s and 1500s in England. Essentially, "English" in its various waves of influence, from the Celts, Romans, Angles, Saxons, and Jutes, down through the Normans to Chaucer, shared with common continental languages certain vowel sounds. Mysteriously, new sounds enter the English language during the 1400s and 1500s. The first major development consisted of changes in four long vowels. The "ah" of Chaucer's name became the "a" of our *name.* The "uh" of Chaucer's *ston* became the "oo" of our *stone.* The "ue" (as in our *hoof*) of Chaucer's *roote* became the "u" of our *root.* In a slightly slower process, the "ae" of Chaucer's *clene* became by Shakespeare's time *clean,* as in our *lane,* before it becomes the "ee" sound of our *clean.*

Middle English		Modern English
Name (ah) [na:mea]	becomes	name (a){[ne:m]
Ston (uh)[st:n]	becomes	stone (o)[sto:n]
Roote (ue)(our hoof)[ro:t]	becomes	root (u)[ru:t]
Clene (ae)[kle:n]	becomes	clen (our lane), then clean (I)[lkli:n]

(Baugh 288)

The short vowels (*a e i o u*) remained essentially the same, although *catte* ("ah") shifted slightly to *cat* ("ae"), while *bedd* remained *bed; scip* remained *ship; folc* remained *folk;* and *full* remained *full.*

Notice that, whereas the short vowels remain essentially the same, the shift in the long vowel sounds occur primarily as a shift from sounding back, deep in the mouth and throat, to sounding farther forward, more through the mouth, closer to the tongue and lips, the threshold to the outer world. In the second major shift, something unusual occurs with two of Chaucer's classic, continental vowel sounds "i" and "u," as in *five* [*fi:f*] and *down* [*du:n*]. These two vowels sound far forward into the mouth, toward the teeth and lips. The other vowel sounds moved forward and out during this great vowel shift. However, "those that could not move forward without becoming consonantal (*i, u*) became diphthongs" (Baugh 288). A diphthong is a sound created through the combination of two or more vowel sounds. The *u* of Chaucer's *doon* (*down*)[*du:n*] reaches back, gathers the *ah*, and becomes our word *down* [*daun*]. The "u" becomes "au," or, listening with enough sensitively, we can even hear *ah, o, u,* a threefold diphthong.

It is almost as though the sound experience had to reach back through, to regather its vowel character, fashioning the new hybrid vowel experience, *ai.* Thus, by Shakespeare's time, *feeve* (*five*) [*fi:f*] becomes *five* [*faiv*], as we say it today, with the diphthong, *ai.* Speaking the *i* slowly enough to bend it, as a prism bends light revealing color, we can hear "ah," "ee." Listening carefully, one may even hear a threefold blend, "ah, a, ee" = *i.* Of course, "I" becomes the quintessential experience for the new expression of one's individuality, the name no one else can speak for us, unencumbered even by the consonantal *ch* of the German *ich.* What new soul experience might the new diphthong reflect or affect? These two new sound experiences reflect neither a contraction nor, perhaps, even a further incarnation of the original vowel sounds. The diphthongs *ow* ("ah+o+uu") and *i* ("ah+a+ee"), reflect rather a freshly combined expansion of soul experience; new soul sounds had been created, each with three sounds in one, each ending with sound thrust forward in the mouth, again out toward the world.

Three minor shifts accompany these major vowel shifts. One is that the *e* at the end of a word becomes silent, surrendering its syllabicity (*nam-e* to *name*). A second minor change is that certain consonants become silent; *knight* [*knicht*] becomes *knight* [*nite*]; *through* becomes *through* [*thru*]; *droughte* [*drawchte*] becomes *drought* [*draut*]. The third minor change is that the vowel sound in unaccented syllables tends to become virtually indistinguishable, as in *ago, upon, opinion, drama, kingdom,* etc.

How should we understand these extraordinary metamorphoses of the language during a literary silent night? It is as though the language goes to sleep as Chaucer and wakes up, like Bottom in *A Midsummer Night's Dream*, translated into a language usable by Shakespeare and others. How should we understand the changes in consciousness enabled, or implied, by these new sounds? The most striking general observation is that a number of vowel experiences (*a*, *o*, *u*), which formerly sounded deep in the throat, move forward and outward, toward the outer world. The teeth and lips form, after all, the vocal doorway, the threshold between the inner and the outer world. Two vowel sounds that had already sounded relatively far forward (*u*, *i*) combine with other vowel sounds, creating a newly expansive, reaching sound/soul experience, as in *five* and *down*.

On the one hand, vowels reach out toward the world in a new way, while some sounds sacrifice themselves and go silent. One might think of the *e* on the end of a word, as in *name,* becoming silent, giving up its sound and its right to be a syllable in its own right, to intensify the main vowel sound of the word, in this case, "a" in *name.* Vowels reach out to the world in a new way, just as the great maritime explorers were on the verge of doing, including John Cabot, and later Sir Francis Drake, Sir Walter Raleigh, and Henry Hudson. On the other hand, some consonant sounds sacrifice themselves and go silent, as in *knight.* Since consonant sounds represent direct experience of phenomena, elements of the physical world, one might consider the silencing of certain consonants to be a reflection of being weaned somewhat from immediate, sentient experience of the physical world, making inner consciousness more available to reflect on the physical world. Such separation and reflection will be necessary for the consciousness soul to develop.

For the newly evolving English language to be inhabited by silent *e*, *k*, *g*, and *h* seems analogous to the Anglo-Saxon-Norman English still imbued with the spirit of the Celtic language of the original inhabitants of "Great Britain," even though few Celtic words actually survive in the English language. Consider words like "*drought, plough, thoroughfare,* and *pneumonia.*" Our "dead" silent letters give living words extra dimension, though we are usually unaware of them.

The question is, of course: Where did these new sounds come from? These are not the words that arrived in different waves from various lands during the earlier growth of the English language. Major external influences had already occurred. The greatest change in the history of language was not external but internal. In a sense, English literature went to sleep in the 1400s and early 1500s. Chaucer had finished *The Canterbury Tales.* Although Malory wrote *Le Morte d'Arthur* in the tower of London, his prose version is no great work of art, dear though it is to many hearts. In terms of English literature, that time was definitely an ebb, a *pralaya*, or interlude of silence.

Mysteriously, however, the genius, or spirit, of the English language was profoundly at work. Let us recall that this profound transformation of the English language occurred right at the threshold between the intellectual- and consciousness-soul stages of development, between the English of medieval Chaucer and the English of Renaissance Shakespeare. Rudolf Steiner also speaks of the English people, and hence the English language, as exceptionally capable of bearing the new capacity and orientation of the consciousness soul, particularly with its capacity for objectively viewing the physical world. In such a context, we can at least consider that the spirit of the English language remained at work during those "sleeping" centuries, fashioning new vowel sounds and new diphthongs and making the English language a suitable vessel through which a new consciousness could be able to explore and express in the new world.

For years, I wondered why Rudolf Steiner associated the diphthong *au* (as in *house*) with the Sun, whereas he associated the diphthong *ai* (as in *fire*) with the Moon. Recent reflections on the mystery of the "I" have led me for the first time to some understanding. What was my problem in thinking about sounds for the "I"? While the sounds of the *au* diphthong have had a certain sun-like quality for me (think of *round, found, sound,* a kind of arching reach), I have thought that, on some level, the diphthong *ai* really ought to be associated with the Sun as well. Consider our English pronoun *I* in relation to the "I AM," to Christ, to the Son of God, to the Sun of our universe. However, what is the inexplicable nature of the "I," one of the most mysterious riddles of our time? The Western world tends to think of the "I" as the self, who we are in this world, how people know us. When we are young and insecure, we want to fill our hollow space with achievements, roles, honors, and even stereotypes, forming a collage to create an identity. The Eastern world tends to think of this sense of self as *maya*, or illusion, to be transcended or released. Some Westerners may distinguish between one's persona, or personality (one's mask to the world), and one's true individuality. Others may speak of "higher self" and "lower self." How do we realize our true individuality, the part of each of us that is eternal, universal, and yet particular to each of us? What is the nature of the "I AM"? My "I" is not how people know me; no one else calls me "I." My "I" is not just what distinguishes me from others.

Steiner speaks of the essential nature of the "I" as having an experience of hollowness, or emptiness. One cannot strengthen the "I" directly or fill the "I" as an object in a reflexive manner. In fact, the mystery is that one's "I" grows only through knowing the "I" of another. In a certain way, we might say that the mystery of the "I" is less like the Sun, shining its light on everything and less like the full Moon glowing, and more like the new moon, especially the Grail moon, the slenderest sliver of "I," yet mostly evoking the glow, not of itself but of the other, the Sun.

When I am least filled with myself, I am most able to recognize the other fully. In this context, I finally experience the appropriateness of Rudolf Steiner associating the diphthong *ai* (I) with the Moon's influence.

"I and thou..." How mysteriously fitting that the "sun" sound informs *thou,* and that the "moon" sound informs *I* in the title of Martin Buber's important twentieth-century book of philosophy, *I and Thou.* The word *thou,* in its perhaps quaint, archaic form, still embodies a kind of sacred intimacy of the "I" Sun in the other person, a recognition of the other's higher self, in a way that is different from merely *you.* Like the Moon, "I" reflects the light of the other, essentially the only way that the sense of "I" is active, according to Steiner.

With an understanding of the great changes in the sounds of the English language during the "night" of the 1400s and early 1500s, when little literature was written, we can now better understand and appreciate the great awakening, the "Renaissance," of Elizabethan Literature during the late 1500s and early 1600s. Rarely in the history of languages and literatures has the spirit of a language fostered such a fertile birth.

Chapter 7

Elizabethan English and Shakespeare

The Life of Shakespeare

IN 1585, A country fellow named William Shakespeare left Stratford-on-Avon to find his way in London. He left behind his twenty-nine-year-old wife and their three children. Having seen dozens of performances by wandering thespians while growing up, this twenty-one-year-old headed for the theater to begin an unpredictable, uncharted career in a recently coalescing profession. Who could have imagined that this innocuous transplant would eventually become responsible for, in the words of critic Harold Bloom, "the invention of the human, the inauguration of personality as we have come to recognize it?" Even less than Chaucer two hundred years earlier, this young man did not seem to reveal any clues that he would eventually foster the most fertile relationship with the spirit of his language of any human being in history.

"So far from Shakespeare's being the least known, he is the one person, in all modern history, known to us" (Emerson 119). Emerson's point is that we all know Shakespeare through his plays, while far less is known about him with biographical certainty than perhaps any other great individual. Mystery even surrounds his identity, embodied perhaps even in the numerous ways his name has been spelled: Shaxpere, Shagspeare, and so on. Many people have deep convictions that Francis Bacon (clue, "Hamlet"), Christopher Marlowe, the Earl of Oxford, or perhaps even a woman actually wrote the more than thirty famous plays.

However, the common picture is that on April 23, 1564, William Shakespeare was born in Stratford-upon-Avon, in central western England to the glove maker, John Shakespeare, and his gentry wife Mary Arden. John, a Catholic, was hardworking and at times successful—a Stratford council member, High Bailiff, and even mayor at one time. William, the first son and third of eight children, would have enjoyed the Avon River, the fields, and the forests. The future playwright had clearly absorbed into his being the creatures of nature, for his plays include names of 150 plants and 100 birds.

In an era before there were any permanent theaters in England, young William, between his fifth and twenty-first years, might have seen as many as twenty-four traveling troupes of actors performing both medieval mystery cycles and secular dramas. Whereas a Puritan bailiff might have refused the actors permission, William's Catholic father would have welcomed them when he was High Bailiff, while William's youngest brother Edmund would later become an actor of note. The Shakespeare boys would have had free roam of the nearby Kenilworth Castle, where mother Mary's kinsman, Edward Arden, was the trusted right-hand man of the Earl of Leicester. At age eleven, young William would have witnessed the coronation procession of Queen Elizabeth I, with pageantry, pomp, and even a water show. Until at least age thirteen, William went to the local grammar school, endowed by the guild of the Holy Cross, where he learned Latin and probably read Cicero, Terence, Seneca, and Ovid, absorbing plots, language, and myth.

At age eighteen William Shakespeare became engaged to eighteen-year-old Anne Whately. The next day, however, a marriage bond was posted announcing his imminent marriage to a twenty-six-year-old Puritan, Anne Hathaway. Six months later she gave birth to Susanna, and two years later to twins, Judith and Hamnet. Within a year, William left his family in Stratford to seek his fortune in London.

In an era of wandering thespians, England's first permanent theater, "The Theatre," was built by James Burbage in 1576. Gradually, others followed. William Shakespeare began a seven-stage sequence of growing into his craft and calling. First he became a "hostler," holding the horses of wealthy theatergoers. Then he became a servitor, what we would call a "gofer," taking care of any needs of any of the company of actors. That led to becoming the prompter's attendant. Eventually, having proven himself, he became an actor in The Lord Chamberlain's Men, led by James Burbage, whose son Richard was the outstanding actor in London at the time. William was taught much of the actor's craft by the other great Elizabethan star Tarleton, also in the company, who, having been one of Elizabeth's jesters, became the model later for Shakespeare's wise fools. William then became a script-furbisher, making sure the actors' working scripts were all in order. That craft led, lo and behold, to writing plays. Finally, through a gift from the Earl of Southampton, Shakespeare became a share-holding actor, one of seven "housekeepers," each earning ten percent of the company's proceeds.

At that time in Elizabethan England, many fertile minds gathered at London's Mermaid Tavern, conversing, competing, and catalyzing what became perhaps the richest several decades in all literary history. Shakespeare's contemporaries at the Mermaid included the high and the low, from Sir Philip Sydney, author of the pastoral romance *Arcadia* and the sonnet cycle *Astrophil and Stella;* Sir Edmund Spencer, author of the chivalric romance *The Fairie Queen;* Sir Walter Raleigh, founder of the first English colony in the New World, Roanoke Island, Virginia; and many playwrights, including Ben Jonson (*Volpone, the Fox)*, the satirist Thomas Nashe, Beaumont and Fletcher, coauthors of tragicomedies such as *A King and No King* and *Love's Pilgrimage;* Christopher Marlowe (*Dr. Faustus*), who was later murdered in a tavern; Thomas Kyd, author of *The Spanish Tragedy;* and Richard Greene, who lived among thieves and whores and whose mistress's brother, the gangster Cutting Ball, served as his bodyguard. Fastidious Ben Jonson, who labored painstakingly at his plays, saw Shakespeare write a play at one sitting, with hardly a mistake.

During his play-writing years, Shakespeare seems to have gone through recognizable stages, throughout which he sustained annual visits back to Stratford-on-Avon to visit his family. During his twenties (the sentient-soul stage), young William must have been preoccupied with making his way and absorbing as much of life in the world as possible. In 1593, when Shakespeare was twenty-nine, the Puritan Aldermen of London sent a preacher to convert the dangerous "atheists" gathering at the Mermaid Tavern. After the poor preacher was returned tarred and waxed, Kyd and Marlowe were arrested. Kyd was strangled in prison, and days after his release Marlowe was stabbed to death in a tavern. The circumstances of both are mysterious and suggested causes range from petty quarrels to insidious efforts to repress new consciousness.

The Plague swept devastatingly through London, and the three major theaters at the time were forced to close, forcing the actors to go on tour for a year in the countryside, until the Plague subsided and the theaters reopened. Between twenty-eight and thirty-five (the intellectual-soul stage), one typically applies reason and wit to understand life. During these years, Shakespeare began to write plays, predominantly comedies and histories.

In 1597, when Shakespeare was thirty-three years old, James Burbage's lease for The Theatre expired, shortly after he did. The owner, Richard Alleyn, refused to renew the lease. On December 28, while Alleyn was out of town for Christmas vacation, the remaining Burbages, Mrs. and sons Richard and Cuthbert, along with Shakespeare and other company members, came with swords and carpenters' tools and pulled down the theater piece by piece, hauling all the wood in wagons across to the south side of the Thames. Meanwhile, William had purchased and was rebuilding the second largest house in Stratford for his family. He was granted a coat-of-arms, and was able to sign himself as a "gentleman." Also that year, Shakespeare suffered the death of his eleven-year-old son Hamnet. By 1599, the open-air Globe Theatre opened amid the surrounding bustle of streets, houses of ill repute, bear baiting, bull baiting, acrobats, and executions.

By the age of thirty-five, Shakespeare was acknowledged as the greatest Elizabethan dramatist. "As Plautus and Seneca are accounted the best for Comedy and Tragedy among the Latins, so Shakespeare among the English is the most excellent in both kinds for the stage" (Meres, contemporary). At thirty-seven, Shakespeare experienced the death of his father. In 1603, when Shakespeare was thirty-nine, the new king, James I, renamed the Lord Chamberlain's Men "the King's Men."

Between thirty-five and forty-two (the consciousness-soul stage), Shakespeare wrote, among others, the four great tragedies: *Hamlet, Othello, Macbeth,* and *King Lear.* His consciousness-soul stage allowed him the detachment and perspective needed to explore, in a multi-dimensional way, some of the greatest mysteries of human experience: vengeance, fate, free will, jealousy, ambition, guilt, trust, and love. As mentioned, a gift and necessity of early stages of consciousness-soul development is the capacity to detach oneself from the physical world sufficiently to behold it in the most objective way, in its own right, as natural science has endeavored to do. A further stage in consciousness-soul development would be the ability to behold one's soul as objectively as possible, as the more recent science of psychology endeavors to do, led four hundred years ago by William Shakespeare. Although we each go individually though our own stage of consciousness-soul experience between thirty-five and forty-two, all of humanity is still collectively in the early stages of consciousness-soul development, a process that will continue to ripen for almost two millennia.

In 1609, when Shakespeare was forty-five, his sonnets were published without permission. His mother's death a year earlier coincided with the first emergence of those mysterious plays that no one has been able to classify properly: *Pericles*, *Cymbeline*, *A Winter's Tale*, and *The Tempest*. They include depths of tragedy yet go beyond death, through the healing reconciliations of comedy, into a fairy-tale quality, resonant of a mystery drama. These plays are often called "Romances." Shakespeare was able to craft them with a wiser spiritual perspective following the strife of his own soul stages.

In 1613, after a performance of *Henry VIII*, the Globe Theatre burned down, leaving Shakespeare, after twenty-eight years in London, without a theater home. One actor had retrieved original drafts of Shakespeare's plays. William Shakespeare retired, age forty-nine, and returned to Stratford on Avon. He died of fever on April 23, 1616, allegedly the day of his birth, the day associated with St. George, by then long established as England's patron saint. It is fitting that Shakespeare, the epitome of English culture, shares the day of England's patron saint. Just as George, the knight of legend, saved a woman from the dragon, Shakespeare the dramatist wrested the modern personality from the imminent clutches of reductionistic materialism in the coming centuries.

General Language in Elizabethan England: New Sounds

In William Shakespeare's comedy *A Midsummer Night's Dream* (3.2.l.101–114), only Oberon sees sleeping Demetrius and proceeds to set straight Puck's mistake, since Puck put the love potion in Lysander's eyes, not Demetrius'.

> ***Oberon.***
> Flower of this purple dye,
> Hit with Cupid's Archery,
> Sink in apple of his eye.
> When his love he doth espy,
> Let her shine as gloriously
> As the Venus of the sky.
> When thou wakest, if she be by,
> Beg of her for remedy.
> [Reenter Puck.]
> ***Puck***
> Captain of our fairy band,
> And the youth, mistook by me,
> Helena is here at hand;
> Pleading for a lover's fee.
> Shall we their fond pageant see?
> Lord, what fools these mortals be!

Notice that Oberon's rhyme scheme undulates between two sounds, *i* of *dye,* and *ee* of *archery.* Young servant Puck's entrance speech begins with a couplet, hands and band, followed by a four-line sequence, ending in *me, fee, see,* and *be.*

When Lysander appears in hot pursuit of scornful Helena, each of these mortals speaks in regularly alternating rhyme, followed by a couplet.

Lysander
Why should you think that I should woo in scorn?
Scorn and derision never come in tears:
Look, when I vow, I weep; and vows so born,
In their nativity all truth appears.
How can these things in me seem scorn to you?
Bearing the badge of faith to prove them true?

Helena
You do advance your cunning more and more.
When truth kills truth, O devilish-holy fray!
Those vows are Hermia's: will you give her o'er?
Weigh oath with oath, and you will nothing weigh:
Your vows, to her and me, put in two scales,
Will even weigh, and both as light as tales.

The alternating rhyme in each speech suggests tension in each speaker: Lysander trying to convince Helena of his passion for her, and Helena weighing his words and finding them lacking. The third rhyme sound, in the closing couplet of each speech (*you, true, scales, tales*), suggests the conclusion to which each has come, on the one hand; on the other, the third rhyme sound also suggests, in contrast to the two-rhyme-sound speeches of the fairy folk, Oberon and Puck, an extra dimension of soul experience in these struggling, foolish mortals, these denizens of three-dimensional space.

Demetrius then awakes, struck by love potion, first beholding Helena, the previous object of his disdain.

[Awaking]
Demetrius
O Helen! Goddess, nymph, perfect, divine!

To what, my love, shall I compare thine eyne!
Crystal is muddy. O! how ripe in show
Thy lips, those kissing cherries, tempting grow;
That pure congealed white, high Taurus' snow,
Fann'd with the eastern wind, turns to a crow
When thou hold'st up thy hand. O! let me kiss
This princess of pure white, this seal of bliss.

Demetrius's speech begins with a naming conclusion, in the form of a rhyming couplet (*divine, eyne*). Demetrius then proceeds in a four-line rhyme (*show, grow, snow, crow*) to expound his passionate adoration, culminating with a couplet of will, or wish (kiss, bliss).

The final sentence of Demetrius' speech is a good example of new vowel sounds in the English language, an evolution from the classic sounds of Chaucer's fourteenth-century Middle English. "O! Let me kiss / This princess of pure white, this seal of bliss." The content of this line, culminating Demetrius' new potion-powered passion, funnels narrowly into the object of his desire, with the familiar short *i* reflecting the obsessive focus of his wish, in the sequence, "kiss... this,... princess, this,... bliss." The center of the line, in the word white, is the new vowel sound "i," the almost painfully expansive diphthong, and the ultimate quality of this "other" for whom he now yearns and for whom she has always been striving.

Having lived in the soundscape of Chaucer's Middle English, imagine that you have gone to sleep and you wake up in Shakespeare's Elizabethan English. Forgetting all that your twenty-first-century ears have heard, try to imagine the effect on your soul of hearing the many "dawn-fresh" sounds in just this simple eight-line speech by Demetrius:

Demetrius

O Helen! Goddess, nymph, perfect, div***i***ne!
T***o*** what, m***y*** love, shall ***I*** compare th***i***ne ***ey***ne!
Crystal is muddy. ***O***! h***ow*** r***i***pe in sh***ow***
Th***y*** lips, th***o***se kissing cherries, tempting gr***ow***;
That p***u***re cong***ea***led wh***i***te, h***igh*** Taurus' sn***ow***,

Fann'd with the ***ea***stern wind, turns t***o*** a cr***ow***
When th***ou*** h***o***ld'st up th***y*** hand. ***O***! let m***e*** kiss
This princess of pure wh***i***te, this s***ea***l of bliss.

All these sounds are essentially new experiences for the English-speaking soul. Of course, the vowel change did not happen overnight. The people of Shakespeare's time grew up hearing these sounds, which had evolved into the language during the preceding 150 years. Nevertheless, stepping back for a larger perspective on the evolving English folk soul over a thousand years, one can imagine that, in terms of dramatic literature's capacity to generate consciousness, audiences hearing these sounds at work in the Elizabethan theater may have in fact been inwardly experiencing the aural equivalent of fireworks, as they heard these "new" sound sequences.

Shakespeare: Rhyme and Rhythm

Helena, suddenly hearing love from the object of her own love, who has always spurned her, does not believe her ears, quickly concluding that both Lysander and Demetrius mock her.

Helena
O spite! O hell! I see you all are bent
To set against me for your merriment:
If you were civil and knew courtesy,
You would not do me thus much injury.
Can you not hate me, as I know you do,
But you must join in souls to mock me too?
If you were men, as men you are in show,
You would not use a gentle lady so;
To vow, and swear, and superpraise my parts
When I am sure you hate me with your hearts.

In contrast to the preceding speeches of Oberon and Puck, but also of amicable Lysander, of judgmental Helena herself, and of passionate Demetrius, Helena emphatically asserts here her conclusion in rhyming couplets. What is the effect of hearing lines of verse in rhyming couplets? We hear the end sound of the first line, "bent." During the second line we anticipate the culmination in a similar sound, "merriment." An aesthetic excitement, eagerness is present, even curiosity as to what form it may take. And yet, as couplet after couplet rhymes, "courtesy-injury, do-too, show-so," the curiosity about what word will rhyme is yoked with a knowing certainty of what sound will conclude the two-line thought. Helena hammers home the decisiveness of the conclusion about the two mocking lovers, in reinforcing rhyming couplets. In fact, some of Shakespeare's early comedies, like *Love's Labours Lost*, tingling with the witty exploration of resolving love problems with the eventual conclusion of marriage, usually flow in rhyming couplets. One can almost experience Shakespeare the playwright mastering his wit, like a fencer in a fencing school mastering his strokes.

By the end of *A Midsummer Night's Dream*, after Oberon and Puck have helped the lovers fall into right relationship, have restored Bottom to himself, and have even healed the rift between Oberon and Titania, the kingdom is ready for its ruler Theseus to unite in marriage with Hippolyta, queen of the Amazons. In act V, scene 1, Theseus speaks:

Theseus
More strange than true: I never may believe
Thee antick fables, not these fairy toys,
Lovers and madmen have such seething brains,
Such shaping fantasies, that apprehend
More than cool reason ever comprehends.
The lunatic, the lover, and the poet,
Are of imagination all compact:
One sees more devils than vast hell can hold,
That is the madman; the lover, all as frantic,
Sees Helen's beauty in a brow of Egypt:
The poet's eye, in a fine frenzy rolling,
Doth glance from heaven to earth, from earth to heaven;
And, as imagination bodies forth
The forms of things unknown, the poet's pen

> Turns them to shapes, and gives to airy nothing
> A local habitation and a name.

The ruler, the determiner of order in civilized society, has changed his former decree, acquiescing to the resolved unions of Hermia and Lysander, of Helena and Demetrius, acknowledging a human rightness made possible not in his lawful city but in the wild woods "that apprehend more than cool reason e'er apprehends," where more mysterious forces are at play in human destiny. Theseus's speech about imagination does not rhyme. It is not prose. The lines are usually iambic pentameter, five "feet" with a short-long, *u* -, rhythm. What is the effect of this non-rhyming, iambic pentameter of what is called "blank verse"?

When we listen to rhyming couplets, as in Helena's earlier speech, after Demetrius awoke, we establish the final sound of the first line ("bent") at the end of the five feet. Then we successfully anticipated the recurrence of the same essential sound ("merriment") at the end of the next five feet, the next line closure. The thoughts expressed in the couplet tend to conclude with the second rhyme sound. Therefore the form of the thinking remains limited. Since sense is reflected by sound, and the rhyme dictates the sound, the rhyme in a certain sense "dictates," or at least strongly requires, the sense. Certainly, the weaker the writer, the more the rhyme seems to determine, to affect, rather than to reflect, the content, even the direction of the poem.

Such crisp, lucid, artfully wrought statements in rhyming couplets are, in a way, the culmination and celebration of, what Rudolf Steiner calls the intellectual-soul stage of development in humanity. The capacity for thinking—generated by the Greek philosophers, externalized in Roman law, and Christianized by the Medieval Scholastics—took great joy eventually in the succinct, diamond-like articulations of the rhyming couplets. Steiner spoke of the end rhyme of the rhyming couplets as evoking in the rational, or intellectual, soul a memory of the human imagination before the Fall. How can we understand such a statement? The rhyming couplets provide the equivalent of the gates of the Garden of Eden, a security, as though within their confines the poet could tend the garden of human experience without undue fear of temptation by the serpent, of consequences of the Fall owing to the knowledge of good and evil.

Helena
If you were men, as men you are in show,
You would not use a gentle lady so;
To vow, and swear, and superpraise my parts
When I am sure you hate me with your hearts.

Helena wraps things up, firm in her conclusions, reinforced by the rhyming couplets. Chaucer, living at the culmination of humanity's intellectual soul stage of development (c.750 B.C.E. to 1400 C.E.), writes his *Canterbury Tales* in rhyming couplets. Later, after the Renaissance of Elizabethan literature, after Shakespeare's and Milton's mighty explorations through the medium of the non-rhyming iambic pentameter of blank verse, the English folk (or the spirit of the English language) almost slumps back in its chair. In the neo-classical, "Augustan" Age of Reason during the late 1600s to 1700s, Alexander Pope and John Dryden turn back to rhyming couplets, with dazzling technical virtuosity, in a kind of ebb tide, a return to an intellectual soul orientation.

Shakespeare: Blank Verse

However, William Shakespeare, already at the end of *A Midsummer Night's Dream*, finds himself reaching beyond the confines of rhyme, to express Theseus' reflection on the nature of imagination. If his thoughts are to range "from heaven to earth, from earth to heaven," Theseus's speech must stretch beyond the confines of the sensory sound of rhyme. Indeed, by the time Shakespeare is exploring the larger dimensions of riddles, as in the tragedies *Hamlet*, *Othello*, *Macbeth*, and *King Lear,* he virtually leaves behind the rhyming couplets of the earlier comedies. However, he resumes the rhythm and meter of his earlier iambic pentameter lines, finding the non-rhyming, yet rhythmic blank verse to be the suitable vessel for explorations of such scope as his contemporary Christopher Marlowe did in *Tamurlane* and *Dr. Faustus*.

To be or not to be,—that is the question:—
Whether 'tis nobler in the mind to suffer
The slings and arrows of outrageous fortune,
Or to take arms against a sea of troubles,
And by opposing end them?—To die,—to sleep,—
No more; and by a sleep to say we end
The heart-ache, and the thousand natural shocks
That flesh is heir to, 'tis a consummation
Devoutly to be wisht. To die,—to sleep;—
To sleep! Perchance to dream: ay, there's the rub;
For in that sleep of death what dreams may come,
When we have shuffled off this mortal coil,
Must give us pause:...

(*Hamlet*, 3. 1. 56–67)

Read or listen to Hamlet's, indeed Shakespeare's, best-known speech with the question: What is the effect of not hearing the end rhyme? In the silence at the end of the line, all sounds are possible, and hence all thought words are possible in terms of where the next line will go. Listening, wondering, and anticipating, we are more actively open to the scope of possibilities than if we know the culminating end sound and, hence, the sound contour or limit of the thought. Since our thought is freed from anticipating the regulated sound contour of the thought content as shaped by end rhyme, the thought terrain becomes unpredictably limitless in scope, as in Hamlet's groping struggle to put both the time and his kingdom back in joint. The English language in blank verse becomes freer than any language before, able to explore "more things in heaven and earth, Horatio, / than are dreamt of in your philosophy," as Hamlet says to his friend (I, v, 175–176), to explore things undreamt of in rhyming verse. Blank verse gives its writer a literary license and capacity comparable to the possibilities of the explorers of the New World.

As Faulkner Jones articulates in *The English Spirit*, the spirit of the English language sacrifices some of its musicality, to allow greater independence of thinking. Figuratively, English sacrifices some of its color, to allow greater translucency.

Thus the English language surrenders some of its substance, to allow the writer and, hence, the reader the freedom to generate the equivalent through the activity of their own thinking. Such withdrawal of the spirit from the "music body" of the language is just what allows a consciousness-soul experience of the world. Rather than imposing our own preconceived rhyme patterns on the world, we need our language to become transparent, or actually trans-listening, or per-listening, or per-phonic, enough, to allow the world thoughts to speak, (no longer sing, but speak-think) through it.

> To sleep! Perchance to dream: ay, there's the rub;
> For in that sleep of death what dreams may come,
> When we have shuffled off this mortal coil,
> Must give us pause:...
>
> (*Hamlet*, 3. 1. 66–69)

Having considered how the English language sacrificed musicality, particularly through blank verse, we should now ask: If Shakespeare, English master of dramatic verse, went so far, after *A Midsummer Night's Dream*, as essentially to abandon rhyming verse, and in fact dramatic verse altogether in favor of prose in *Much Ado About Nothing*, then why does he nevertheless reassume the rhythm and meter of blank verse for the explorations of the great tragedies and the later plays? Or, simply, what is the difference between blank verse and prose?

SHAKESPEARE: PROSE

Prose, one might say, surrenders itself to the world. The sounds come out as the thought allows, spilling over even to the edge, the limit, of the physical page on which they are written, contained simply by those limits. The words fit the page. By contrast, in poetry, or verse, the words fit, not the page, the outer world, but rather the breath and the pulse of the poet himself, of the speaker, the singer. The two-breath line of Homer's dactylic hexameter, the one-breath Northern alliterative tetrameter, the four-beat/

three-beat alternation of the ballad, with the singer breathing in at the end of the three-beat line, all are related, variously to the rhythms of heart and lung. What begins to emerge, in the 1300s with Dante, Petrarch, and Chaucer is a five-beat line.

> To every loving heart and captive soul
> Into whose sight these present words may come,...
>
> (Dante, *La Vita Nuova)*

> O You who hears in scattered verse the sound,
> Of all those sighs with which my heart I feel...
>
> (Petrarch, *Vanity of His Passion*)

It is as though the Greek, Southern hexameter ("*Andra moi enepe musa / polutropon hos malapola*") and the Norse, Northern tetrameter ("*tha com of more unter mist-hleothum*") somehow meet and merge in the middle in the English of Chaucer, with a new five-beat line, a pentameter, ("the droughte of March hath perced to the rote") emerging as the breath-pace bearing a new consciousness. And it is as though the ancient Greek consciousness of the Epic contracts from the hexameter to the pentameter, with the help of Dante and Petrarch. As epic poet, Dante, writing fifty years before Chaucer, fashioned his *Divine Comedy* in iambic pentameter. As lyric poets, both Dante and Petrarch, whom Chaucer visited, wrote their sonnets in iambic pentameter. Chaucer was profoundly influenced by contemporary Italian literature. However, the iambic trimeter of the ancient Greek tragedy expands into the pentameter of Chaucerian and Elizabethan English. Iambic pentameter sustains both Shakespeare's dramas and Milton's epics. The Old Anglo-Saxon tetrameter of the Norse also expands into Chaucer's pentameter.

The early epics of Homer (*Iliad* and *Odyssey)* and Virgil *(Aeneid*), guiding souls into life in the extent of the known world, were sung or written in an incarnating rhythm, especially the *__uu* of the dactyl, or the *__u* of the trochee. The dactyl (Greek for finger) is composed of one long measure (syllable) followed by two short measures. The Trochee is one long measure followed by one short, as in Longfellow's *Hiawatha:* "By the shores of

Guitchee-Goomie." The early dramas by Aeschylus, Sophocles, Euripides, and Aristophanes, guiding souls into the mysteries of soul and spirit, were sung usually in an excarnating rhythm, the *u_* of iambic. We have seen how Shakespeare wrote his early dramas in iambic pentameter, in varieties of rhyme.

Along the way, about midway between *Midsummer Night's Dream* and *Hamlet*, Shakespeare experimented, abandoning rhyme and indeed almost abandoning meter, the pace and form of dramatic verse, altogether. *Much Ado About Nothing* is written and spoken mostly in prose by most characters, whatever their levels of society, in most situations. Indeed, the main character, Benedick, is finally free enough inwardly to express his love for Beatrice, trying verse and then delivering what one could call Shakespeare's epitaph to "rime":

> Marry I cannot show it in rime. I have tried: I can find out no rime to "lady" but "baby," an innocent rime; for "scorn," "horn," a hard rime; for "school," "fool," a babbling rime; very ominous endings: no, I was not born under a riming planet, nor I cannot woo in festival terms.

Of course, what the audience hears as Benedick's confession, of his own limitations as a rhyming poet, we scholars of Shakespeare can hear as representative of the limitations of rhyming verse itself. Shakespeare, 'rime master,' has exhausted the form and abandoned it almost completely for the less confining medium of prose.

However, by the time he is exploring the tragic dimensions of the measureless mysteries of the modern soul, Shakespeare, having abandoned the confines of rhyme, abandons the boundlessness of prose, resuming the open, excarnating rhythm, the iambic pentameter of blank verse, as the breath of, the suitable medium for, his explorations, his articulations of the human being's spiritual soul in its development, as we saw in *Hamlet*. Although the blank verse lacks the constraints of rhyming couplets, its very rhythm makes it somehow more suitable than prose for exploring the deepest mysteries of the human soul. The artist needs the living rhythms of heart and lungs for the ultimate human explorations. Indeed, at his ripest, Shakespeare even chooses, needs, the medium of blank verse to accomplish the ultimate renunciation, the ultimate sacrifice, as Prospero articulates in his final speech in the final play, *The Tempest.*

Prospero
Ye elves of hills, brooks, standing lakes, and groves,
And ye that on the sands with printless foot
Do chase the ebbing Neptune, and do fly him
When he comes back; you demi-puppets that
By moonshine do the green sour ringlets make.
Whereof the ewe not bites; and you whose pastime
Is to make midnight mushrumps, that rejoice
To hear the solemn curfew; by whose aid
(weak masters though ye be) I have bedimmed
The noontide sun, called forth the mutinous winds,
And 'twixt the green seas and the azured vault
Set roaring war; to the dread rattling thunder
Have I given fire and rifted Jove's stout oak
With his own bolt; the strong-based promontory
Have I made shake and by the spurs plucked up
The pine and cedar; graves at my command
Have waked their sleepers, oped, and let 'em forth
By my so potent art. But this rough magic
I here abjure; and when I have required
Some heavenly music (which even now I do)
To work mine end upon their senses that
This airy charm is for, I'll break my staff,
Bury it certain fathoms in the earth,
And deeper than did ever plummet sound
I'll drown my book.

In the final statement of Prospero-Shakespeare, the final word-deed works, of course, in multiple manner. First, one hears in the final sentence *plummet* as noun and *sound* as verb, for a plummet is dropped to sound the fathoms of the bottom of a channel. But the clause works far more deeply on another level as *plummet* becomes verb, and *sound* becomes noun. The greatest artist of the English language, perhaps of any language, chooses to use not prose but words in blank verse, the instrument of his art, to reach beyond sound itself, for his ultimate book of meaning.

SHAKESPEARE: THE SONNET

During the thirteenth century, Pier delle Vigne, Chancellor of the Holy Roman Emperor Frederic II, fashioned the form of the sonnet. Dante and Petrarch during the late 1200s to 1300s in Italy each wrote a series of sonnets, inspired by their platonic love of a lady. Petrarch wrote 365 sonnets in honor of Laura, a married woman to whom he may never have spoken. Dante wrote his sonnets in particular in the autobiographical *La Vita Nuova*, reflecting on his experiences of love in relation to Beatrice, first seeing her at age nine, second, being spoken to by her at age eighteen, suffering both her rejection of him and her marriage to another, culminating in her death at the age of twenty-five. Beatrice most greatly inspired, of course, Dante's epic, *The Divine Comedy.*

However, Petrarch's form of sonnet remains the primary form, structure, even today. For example, in the early 1800s John Keats wrote:

ON FIRST LOOKING INTO CHAPMAN'S HOMER

Much have I traveled in realms of gold,
And many goodly states and kingdoms seen;
Round many islands have I been
Which bards in fealty to Apollo hold.
Oft of one wide expanse have I been told
That deep-brow'd Homer ruled as his demesene;
Yet did I never breathe its pure serene
Till I heard Chapman speak out loud and bold:
Then felt I like some watcher of the skies
When a new planet swims into his ken;
Or like stout Cortez when with eagle eyes
He star'd at the Pacific—and all his men
Look'd at each other with a wild surmise—
Silent, upon a peak in Darien.

While most sonnets share the common structure of fourteen lines of iambic pentameter, the Petrarchan sonnet has a particular dynamic within the fourteen lines. The first eight lines usually have a rhyme scheme of a-b-b-a, a-b-b-a. Two quatrains with the same rhyme pattern articulate a certain "terrain" of content. In fact, the opening eight lines of a Petrarchan sonnet typically pose a problem or question. For example, in Keats's sonnet, the "problem" of the first octave might be articulated as, "With all my readings in the worlds of imagination, I have never been able to experience directly Homer's worlds" (in part, because he did not read ancient Greek).

The final six lines of a Petrarchan sonnet usually have one of three variations of rhyme scheme: c-d-c-d-c-d, c-d-e-c-d-e, or perhaps c-d-c-e-d-e. Somehow, in terms of content, the final six lines, or the second half of the sonnet, offers a solution to the problem, an answer to the question. In this case the "solution" is Keats's experience reading aloud Chapman's English translations of Homer's epics that night with a friend.

The Petrarchan sonnet is clearly essentially twofold, in form and in content. Generated in the 1300s, in the final, twilight culmination of the intellectual soul era, the form of the Petrarchan sonnet reflects thinking oriented toward problem and solution, toward question and answer, cause and effect, characteristic of the rational soul frame of mind.

In the late sixteenth and early seventeenth centuries, dramatist William Shakespeare, usually inspired, one might say, by the muses *Melpomene* (tragedy), *Thalia* (comedy), and even *Clio* (history), also found himself frequently moved and inspired by *Euterpe,* the muse of lyric poetry. The ancient Greeks experienced Apollo as presiding over the nine muses up on Mt. Parnassus, behind the Temple of Delphi. The sun god Apollo, guiding the gradual emergence of the human individuality, guided these muses to inspire human beings in their nine forms of artistic expression, all as ways for the human individuality to eventually emerge.

The 154 sonnets that Shakespeare wrote, however, took a form different from Petrarch's classical form. For example, the much loved number 116:

Let me not to the marriage of true minds
Admit impediments. Love is not love
Which alters when it alteration finds
Or bends with the remover to remove:
O, no! it is an ever-fixed mark,
That looks on tempests and is never shaken;
It is the star to every wandering bark,
Whose worth's unknown, although his height be taken.
Love's not Time's fool, though rosy lips and cheeks
Within his bending sickle's compass come;
Love alters not with his brief hours and weeks,
But bears it out even to the edge of doom.
If this be error and upon me proved,
I never writ, nor no man ever loved.

Notice that the fourteen lines are not arranged in a twofold structure: a-b-a-b, c-d-c-d, e-f-e-f, g-g. There are three different quatrains of alternating, evolving lines, rather than the enclosing a-b-b-a. Not only do the lines evolve, a-b-a-b, but also each quatrain evolves into new sounds, c-d-c-d and e-f-e-f. Rather than a twofold dialectic, as in the Petrarchan sonnet, the Shakespearean sonnet is essentially threefold, engendering a dynamic evolution rather than a problem and its solution. Spenser, in his sonnets, and some other Elizabethan poets enjoyed a similar structure in their sonnets, but without the three quatrains remaining as distinct from each other: a-b-a-b, b-c-b-c, c-d-c-d, e-e.

This essentially threefold structure culminates in a fourth element, a final, concluding couplet. Typically, less substantial and less dynamic than the other three parts of the sonnet, the closing couplet nevertheless brings closure to the exploration. Keeping in mind that the critic Harold Bloom speaks of Shakespeare as the creator of the modern personality, and that Rudolf Steiner speaks of Shakespeare as, more than any other writer, the generator of consciousness soul, one can recognize that this threefold-fourfold structure of Shakespeare's sonnets in fact reflects, on some level, humanity's three soul faculties (thinking, feeling, and willing), while the concluding couplet acts as an equivalent of the human being's spirit, "I" activity, integrating the three soul activities.

Shakespeare's Blank Verse: Possible Exercises

1. Give the historical background of the great vowel shift of fifteenth- and sixteenth-century English.
2. Let students again hear and then speak some lines of *Beowulf*, the old Anglo-Saxon. Then let them again hear and speak some lines of Chaucer's Middle English.
3. Let students hear and then speak some of Shakespeare's rhyming couplets, from a play (perhaps Demetrius' speech in *A Midsummer Night's Dream*, III ii). Can the students hear the new sounds? Speak a Chaucerian couplet, then a Shakespearean couplet. Identify the new sounds.
4. Imagine never having heard or voiced these sounds before. What can one feel, experience, even articulate through sounding *a*, *o*, *u*, *ee*? What about the diphthongs *ow* and *ai*? Through sounding them, what can the soul experience that the English-speaking soul had never been able to experience before? Can the students hear any other differences between Chaucer's couplets and Shakespeare's couplets, in terms of sound?
5. Speak to the students a good number (10–15) of lines of Shakespearean blank verse. (Hamlet's famous soliloquy "To be or not be" would be good.) Any impressions? Have the students speak the first two lines of it, then the first four lines of it. What do they notice in terms of the activity of their ear, or related to sound possibilities? In addition to whatever qualitative observations they have, they should certainly become conscious of the fact that, on the one hand, the metrical line continues to be iambic pentameter, while on the other hand, the end rhyme of couplets has evaporated, disappeared.
6. Have the students cluster in the center of the room, facing out to the perimeter. As the teacher calls out the rhythm of the iambic pentameter, " short-long, short-long. . . . " the students step it, with a pause at the end of the line. Then each student may change to any direction to walk the next line of iambic pentameter, then choose a new direction, and so on,

at least five or six lines. What is the experience? How does the lack of rhyme affect the students? What is lost? What is gained? What are the effects of the sustained rhythm of the iambic pentameter within the lack of rhyme?

7. Ask students to write in blank verse, eventually at least ten lines. The recommended subject could vary. It might be autobiographical, philosophical, or epic, evoking some great journey or struggle. The next day, ask what it was like to write in blank verse. Hear the pieces. Share impressions of them. As a teacher, have in mind the question: What consciousness, or frame of mind, does the blank verse make possible or even engender?

It is the process that is important, not the results of this research.

In describing these exercises, I use the word *students* for anyone who may be engaging in this research of trying to waken to how the language we utter affects our consciousness. The degree to which we would ask the accompanying questions would vary according to the age of the teenage students, or according to the nature of the particular adult group.

Chapter 8

Expansion and Contraction

Shakespeare and the "King James" Translation of the Bible

"But for the uttering sweetly and properly the conceite of the minde... which is the ende of thought.... English hath it equally with any other tongue in the world."

—Sir Philip Sidney

Most people know that, if one cannot identify a quotation in the English language, the odds are that it comes from either Shakespeare or the Bible. What the Italian Renaissance offered the world in art and architecture, Elizabethan England offered in literature, especially in lyric and dramatic poetry. Milton's epics were soon to follow. After the outwardly unproductive, though linguistically transformative, literary slumber of the 1400s and early 1500s, a great awakening occurred, equivalent in literary richness perhaps only to the birth of Greek epic, lyric, and dramatic literature in the seventh (Homer's epics), sixth (Sappho's lyrics), and fifth centuries B.C.E. (Aeschylus' and Sophocles' dramas). Yet the renaissance of English literature occurred not over several centuries but several decades.

As discussed in the previous chapter, during the Elizabethan era, the spirit of the English language inspired Sir Philip Sidney, Sir Edmund Spenser, Richard Greene, Thomas Kyd, Christopher Marlowe, Ben Jonson, (Francis) Beaumont and (John) Fletcher, Shakespeare, and many others to write. The Mermaid Tavern in London became a meeting ground where many authors shared ideas and stimulated one another's work. Drama in particular exercised its perennially democratic tradition of speaking, even to those still illiterate, in language that stimulated and enhanced their consciousness. The ancient Greek dramas, once liberated from the elite mystery centers out into the open-sky amphitheaters, were performed for all levels of society to experience. For a while all members of the *polis* were even required to attend the drama performances, for the well being of the whole community. In a similar fashion, all members of English society attended the Elizabethan dramas. The spirit of the English language was so active in Elizabethan England that some people believe that, had Shakespeare rather than Marlowe been stabbed in the tavern at age twenty-nine, those thirty-seven plays would have been written anyway, by someone else.

The late sixteenth and early seventeenth centuries included great English explorations of new worlds, especially by Sir Walter Raleigh, who sponsored the Roanoke Island settlements in present Virginia, and Sir Francis Drake, the first English explorer to circumnavigate the globe. The discovery of the Bermoothe reefs (contemporary Bermuda) inspired the setting for Shakespeare's *Tempest.* Through such explorations, the English language began to receive words from languages quite beyond the confines of the British Isles, adding to its original strands of Anglo-Saxon, Latin, and French: *cupola* and *stucco* (Italian); *desperado* and *embargo* (Spanish); *smuggle* and *reef* (Norse and German); as well as English variations of the Low Dutch words *fokkinge* and *kunte.* During the Renaissance, the English language grew dramatically, acquiring ten to twelve thousand new words, including: *atmosphere, gravity, skeleton, encyclopedia, paradox, external,* and *chronology.* Certainly, new interest in the world, not only geographically but also scientifically, engendered many new words, as well as the eventual new Royal Academy of Science, which laid foundations for much of modern natural science. By the time of King James I, five to seven million people spoke English.

Today, in the early third millennium, the average, educated English speaker, reader, and writer (among seven hundred and fifty million speakers) uses a vocabulary of about fifteen thousand words. From what we can tell, the writer of Shakespeare's plays both used and generated a working vocabulary of about 30,000 words. To explore and articulate through his poetry the many "new" worlds of human experience, he created many new words himself, such as *accommodation, assassination, dexterously, dislocate, indistinguishable, obscene, pedant, premeditated, reliance,* and *submerged.* Among the words he used that had not appeared in English before his time are *allurement, emulate, emphasis, demonstrate, antipathy, critical, dire, horrid, modest, prodigious, vast, meditate,* and *initiate.* The spirit of the English language had both its most willing father/conceiver and its most able midwife in William Shakespeare, who, more than any other poet in any language, fashioned "fire-new" words. As Chaucer is considered the grandfather of our contemporary English, Shakespeare is rightly considered the father of our language today. When this generator of new consciousness needed to articulate a certain nuance of concept or feeling for which no word existed, he fashioned a new word suitable to incarnate and bear the concept or feeling, allowing anyone to become conscious of that experience. Rarely, if ever, has a language embodied such an expansion of consciousness through the growth of vocabulary in such a short time. It's as though the transformation of essential sounds in the 1400s spiraled out in an almost geometric progression of sound combinations, or words, in the 1500s and 1600s.

In an atmosphere of almost unparalleled fertility of growing consciousness through the expansion of language, there occurs a paradoxical mystery. Most people know that a camel is a "horse designed by a committee." Many people have suffered the frustration of trying to draft documents, to "wordsmith," in groups or committees. Muses traditionally visit individuals in solitude at home or out in nature. We imagine people eating, drinking, talking together at the Mermaid Tavern, but then retreating to solitude to write. There are rare exceptions: Beaumont and Fletcher, the Elizabethan playwrights, apparently worked pretty well together. Two centuries later, the English lyric poets Wordsworth and Coleridge enjoyed a rare collaboration on their long walks, for several years often fructifying and even offering lines to each other's poetry. The German poets and playwrights Schiller and Goethe inspired each other complementarily, often at a distance through letters. Thoreau fixed Emerson's grape arbors, but they certainly didn't write together. Melville visited Hawthorne at times over eighteen months, with no evidence that ever considered writing together. In our era, the prime collaborations have been between composers and lyricists such as Rogers and Hammerstein, Lerner and Lowe in the world of musical plays, and Lennon and McCartney in popular music.

The contrasting mystery to the picture of the cohorts of the Mermaid Tavern, separating to write their great works in solitude, is the picture of forty-eight English scholars working together to fashion one of the enduring masterpieces of world literature: the King James translation of the Bible. The other aspect of the mystery is that, in contrast to the expansive nature of the spirit of the English language at the time, the translation of one of the world's largest, most varied works of literature included a vocabulary of only about 8,000 words, an extraordinary contraction and distillation, comparable to the process of extracting a gallon of spirits from bushels of grain.

In 1604, the new King James I presided over a conference of Anglican and Puritan divines, all hoping to reconcile differences. They conceived a plan for a new English translation of the Bible. For six years, six teams of eight scholars each in Oxford, Cambridge, and Westminster worked from original Hebrew and Greek texts and from the five English translations already in existence: Tyndale's, Henry VIII's Great Bible; the Calvinist Geneva Bible; the Bishops' Bible; and the Rheims Bible. Their mission was to cull the best that the English language could offer and harmonize differing theological perspectives. The six leaders of the teams then worked together an additional year to fuse the language of the teams as seamlessly as possible into one style that would be, in the Protestant spirit of those times, accessible to everyone. People would no longer have to depend on priests and scholars to experience the Word of God.

By now, however, the King James Version of the Bible in the twenty-first century is just one of many English versions. Modern translations have greater scholarly resources to draw from, so they are more accurate and true to original sources. Furthermore, there are those today who cannot understand the King James

English; it does not speak their language. Nevertheless, the fact remains: the King James Version of the Bible is the most fertile piece of literature in the English language. It has inspired more minds and more great works than any other work of English literature. As George Steiner wrote in "The Good Books,"

> The King James Bible and the Luther Bible provided much of our civilization with its alphabet of referential immediacy, not only in the spheres of personal and public piety but in those of politics, social institutions, and the life of the literary and aesthetic imagination. That alphabet knits the poetry of Milton to the prose of Abraham Lincoln; it makes the messianic tracts of Trotsky kindred to the politics of spirit in Carlyle and in Ruskin, to the grammar of prophecy in Emerson.... We would not have the prose cadences of Hemingway without Ecclesiastes, or the dynastic sorrows of Faulkner without Chronicles and the Books of Kings.... Samuel Beckett's "Endgame" is an exact meditation on the instruments and the finality of the Passion.
>
> The shorthand of somber historicism and of hope in the speeches of F. D. R. and of Churchill was no less informed by the pulse of the Authorized Version than was that in the prose of Gladstone or the framers of the Constitution." (*The New Yorker*, January 11, 1988)

In 1989, Prince Charles was invited to speak at the celebration of the five hundredth anniversary of the birth of Archbishop Thomas Cranmer (translator of Henry VIII's Great Bible). Charles said, "I would have liked to begin with a ringing phrase from the King James Version of the Bible: 'Harken to my words.' But the New English Bible translates the phrase in less commanding terms, 'Give me a hearing.'" When Charles spoke of the importance of our words for our thoughts, he referred to the phrase from the King James Version of the Bible: "Why take ye thought for raiment?" He then offered the equivalent in the Revised Standard Version: "And why are you anxious about clothing?" One can experience the contraction of consciousness in the poverty of the more recent language.

The point of this chapter is neither to engage in theological arguments, nor to indulge in nostalgia for the King James Version of the Bible. The point is rather to recognize the timeless, inspiring power with which the spirit of the English language was able to work through those forty-eight translators during their seven years of labor. And, more particularly, in the context of this book, to acknowledge the phenomenon to which George Steiner alluded through two words, *cadence* and *pulse.*

The rhythms of the King James Version of the Bible, published in 1611, have continued to inspire our greatest leaders through our greatest crises: Lincoln in the Civil War of the nineteenth century; both Churchill and Roosevelt in World War II; Martin Luther King Jr. in the Civil Rights movement of the 1950s and 1960s; the great founding poets of the New World, Whitman and Dickinson; the first great American novelists, Hawthorne and Melville; our great writers in the twentieth century, Hemingway, Faulkner, and Beckett; and today, notably Bob Dylan (the most popular poet in the English language since Shakespeare) and the playwright August Wilson. Our most powerful "speakers" have been informed by the rhythms of the King James Version of the Bible.

In contrast to the rest of this book, I will give only selective insight into characteristic rhythms of the King James Version of the Bible, partially because most of it is in prose and it has such a large number of varying forms of literature within it. Nevertheless, rather than ignore this primary work in the canon of English literature, I think it apt to simply behold or listen to it again in the open-minded spirit of Adam sounding the names of the creatures, or Walt Whitman "listing" (listening to) the great sounds of the cities or the wilderness. Listen again, with an ear for the musical "pulse," the "cadences."

THE KING JAMES VERSION

GENESIS 1: 1. In the beginning God created the heaven and
the earth. 2. And the earth was without form and void;
and darkness was upon the face of the deep. And the
spirit of God moved upon the face of the waters.

The Good News Bible (1986)

Genesis 1: [1.]In the beginning when God created the universe, [2.] the earth was formless and desolate. The raging ocean that covered everything was engulfed in total darkness, and the Spirit of God was moving over the water.

The King James Version

Job 38:1: Then the Lord answered Job out of the whirlwind, and said, [2.]Who is this that darkeneth counsel by words without knowledge? [3.]Gird up now thy loins like a man, for I will demand of thee, and answer thou me. [4.]Where wast thou when I laid the foundations of the earth?... [6.]Or who laid the cornerstone thereof; [7.]when the morning stars sang together, and all the sons of God shouted for joy? [8.]Or who shut up the sea with doors when it brake forth, as if it had issued out of the womb?...

41: [1.]Canst thou draw out Leviathon with a hook? or his tongue with a cord which thou lettest down?...

[18.]By his sneezings a light doth shine and his eyes are like the eyelids of the morning. [19.]Out of his nostrils go burning lamps, and sparks of fire leap out.... [24.]His heart is as firm as a stone, yea, as firm as a piece of the nether mill stone. [25.]When he rouseth up himself, the mighty are afraid; by reason of breakings they purify themselves. [26.]The sword of him that layeth at him cannot hold: the spear, the dart, nor the habergeon...; [31.]He maketh the deep to boil like a pot, he maketh the sea like a pot of ointment. [32.]He maketh a path to shine after him; one would think the deep to be hoary. [33.]Upon earth there is not his like, who is made without fear. [34.]He beholdeth all high things; he is a king over all the children of pride.

The New International Bible (1973)

Job 38:33: Nothing on earth is his equal—a creature without fear.

34. He looks down on all that are haughty; he is king over all that are proud.

THE KING JAMES VERSION

PSALM 19:1: The heavens declare the Glory of God
And the firmament showeth his handiwork.
2. Day unto day uttereth speech,
and night unto night showeth knowledge.
3. There is no speech nor language,
Where their voice is not heard.
4. Their line is gone out through all the earth, and their words to the end of the world.

THE KING JAMES VERSION

ECCLESIASTES 3: 1.To every thing there is a season, and a
time to every purpose unto heaven: 2.a time to be born,
and a time to die; a time to plant, and a time to pluck
up that which is planted; 3.a time to kill, and a time to
heal; a time to break down, and time to build up; 4.a
time to weep, and a time to laugh; a time to mourn, and
a time to dance; 5.a time to cast away stones, and a time
to gather stones together; a time to embrace, and a time
to refrain from embracing; 6.a time to get, and a time to
lose; a time to keep, and a time to cast away; 7. a time
to rend, and a time to sew; a time to keep silence, and
a time to speak; 8. a time to love, and a time to hate, a
time of war, and a time of peace.

THE GOOD NEWS BIBLE (1966)

ECCLESIASTES 3: 1.Everything that happens in this world
happens at the time god chooses. 2.He sets the time for
birth and the time for death.

THE KING JAMES VERSION

SONG OF SOLOMON 4:12: A garden inclosed is my sister,
my spouse; a spring shut up, a fountain sealed. 13.Thy
plants are an orchard of pomegranates, with pleas-
ant fruits; camphire, with spikenard, 14.spikenard

with saffron; calamus and cinnamon, with all trees of frankincense; myrrh and aloes, with all the chief spices; [15.] a fountain of gardens, a well of living waters, and streams from Lebanon. [16.] Awake, O north wind; and come, thou south; blow upon my garden, that the spices thereof may flow out. Let my beloved come into his garden, and eat his pleasant fruits.

ISAIAH 2:4: ...and they shall beat their swords into plowshares, and their spears into pruning hooks: nation shall not lift up sword against nation, neither shall they learn war any more.

THE GOOD NEWS BIBLE

2:4: They will hammer their swords into ploughs and their spears into pruning-knives. Nations will never go again to war, never prepare for battle again.

THE KING JAMES VERSION

ISAIAH 51:3: For the Lord shall comfort Zion: he will comfort all her waste places; and he will make her wilderness like Eden, and her desert like the garden of the Lord.

THE GOOD NEWS BIBLE

ISAIAH 51:3: I will show compassion to Jerusalem, to all who live in her ruins. Though her land is a desert, I will make it a garden, like the garden I planted in Eden.

THE KING JAMES VERSION

ISAIAH 51: [9.] Awake, awake, put on strength, O arm of the Lord; awake, as in the ancient days, in the generations of old. Art thou not it that hath cut Rahab, and wounded the dragon? [10.] Art thou not it which hath dried the sea, the waters of the great deep; that hath made the depths of the sea a way for the ransomed to pass over?

54:1. Sing, O barren, thou that didst not bear; break forth into singing, and cry aloud, thou that didst not travail with child: for more are the children of the desolate than the children of the married wife, saith the Lord.

55:12. For ye shall go out with joy, and be led forth with peace: the mountains and the hills shall break forth before you into singing, and all the trees of the field shall clap their hands.

THE KING JAMES VERSION

JOHN 1: [1]In the beginning was the Word, and the Word was with God, and the Word was God. [2]The same was in the beginning with God. [3]All things were made by him: and without him was not any thing made that was made. [4]In him was life; and the life was the light of men. [5]And the light shineth in the darkness; and the darkness comprehended it not.

THE GOOD NEWS BIBLE

JOHN 1: [1]Before the world was created, the Word already existed; he was with God, and he was the same as God.

THE KING JAMES VERSION

1 CORINTHIANS 13: [1]Though I speak with the tongues of men and of angels, and have not charity, I am become as sounding brass, or a tinkling cymbal. [2]And though I have the gift of prophecy, and understand all mysteries, and all knowledge; and though I have all faith, so that I could remove mountains, and have not charity, I am nothing. [3]And though I bestow all my goods to feed the poor, and though I give my body to be burned, and have no charity, it profiteth me nothing.... [8]Charity never faileth: but whether there be prophecies, they shall fail; whether there be tongues, they shall cease; whether there be knowledge, it shall vanish away. [9]For we know in part, and we prophesy in part. [10]But when that which is perfect is come, then that which is in part shall be done away. [11]When I was a child, I spake as a child, I understood as a child, I thought as a child: but

when I became a man, I put away childish things. [12]For now we see through a glass, darkly, but then face to face: now I know in part; but then shall I know even as also I am known. [13]And now abideth faith, hope, charity, these three; but the greatest of these is charity.

The Good News Bible

1 Corinthians 13: [1]I may be able to speak the languages of human beings and even of angels, but if I have no love, my speech is no more than a noisy gong or a clanging bell....

13: [11]When I was a child, my speech, feelings, and thinking were all those of a child; now that I am an adult, I have no more use for childish ways. [12]What we see now is like a dim image in a mirror; then we shall see face-to-face. What I know now is only partial; then it shall be complete—as complete as God's knowledge of me.

The King James Version

Revelation 12: [1]And there appeared a great wonder in heaven; a woman clothed with the sun, and the moon under her feet, and upon her head a crown of twelve stars: [2]and she being with child cried, travailing in birth, and pained to be delivered. [3]And there appeared another great wonder in heaven; and behold a great red dragon, having seven heads and ten horns, and seven crowns upon his heads. [4]And his tail drew the third part of the stars of heaven, and did cast them to the earth: and the dragon stood before the woman which was ready to be delivered, for to devour her child as soon as it was born.

The Good News Bible

Revelation 12: [1]Then a great and mysterious sight appeared in the sky. There was a woman, whose dress was the sun and who had the moon under her feet and a crown of twelve stars on her head. [2]She was soon to give birth, and the pains and suffering of childbirth made her cry out....

> [7]And there was war in heaven: Michael and his angels fought against the dragon; and the dragon fought and his angels, [8]and prevailed not; neither was their place found any more in heaven. [9]And the great dragon was cast out, that old serpent, called the Devil, and Satan, which deceiveth the whole world: he was cast out into the earth, and his angels were cast out with him....

THE KING JAMES VERSION

> REVELATION 21: [1]And I saw a new heaven and a new earth: for the first heaven and the first earth were passed away; and there was no more sea. [2]And I John saw the holy city, new Jerusalem, coming down from God out of heaven, prepared as a bride adorned for her husband.... [4]...and there shall be no more death, neither sorrow, nor crying, neither shall there be any more pain: for the former things are all passed away.... [18]and the city was pure gold, like unto clear glass...; for the glory of God did lighten it, and the Lamb of God is the light thereof. [21]And the twelve gates were twelve pearls; every several gate was of one pearl....[22]And I saw no temple therein: for the Lord God Almighty and the Lamb are the temple of it. [23]And the city had no need of the sun, neither of the moon, to shine in it: for the glory of God did lighten it, and the Lamb of God is the light thereof...[25]...for there shall be no night there.
>
> 22: [1]And he showed me a pure river of water of life, clear as crystal, proceeding out of the throne of God and of the Lamb. [2]In the midst of the street of it, and on either side of the river, was there the tree of life, which bare twelve manner of fruits, and yielded her fruit every month: and the leaves of the tree were for the healing of nations.... [13]I am Alpha and Omega, the beginning and the end, the first and the last.

It's hard to resist. Let's articulate some differences in how the English language is working in the Elizabethan and a modern translation.

LUKE 1:57:

a) BISHOPS' BIBLE (1568): "Elizabeth's time came that she should bee delivered, and she brought forth a son."
b) KING JAMES VERSION: (one draft) "Now Elizabeth's time was fulfilled that she should bee delivered, and she brought forth a son." Then the translators settled on "Now Elizabeth's full time came that she should bee delivered, and she brought forth a sonne."
c) NEW ENGLISH BIBLE (twentieth century): "Now the time came for Elizabeth's child to be born, and she gave birth to a son." (Nicholson 152)

Notice that King James' translators choose a double spondee, four longs in a row, "[Eliza]***beth's full time came***," reinforcing both Elizabeth's fullness and the magnitude of the moment. The modern New English Bible's version reads with one spondee, "***time came***," diminishing the moment and ignoring Elizabeth's own fullness.

The older "That she should be delivered" has a wonderful iambic rhythm, evoking perhaps rhythms of labor, reinforced by the active consonance (repetition of consonant sounds within words) of "***sh***e ***sh***ould," and the triple assonance (repetition of vowel sounds) of "sh***e***... b***e*** d***e***livered," also quite active. By contrast the modern version has a more stuttering rhythm, "child to be born," suggesting more the tension of birth, while effectively evoking both the gesture of the mother and the plosive nature of birth through the alliteration of "***b***e ***b***orn." (Plosive sounds, formed by the breath parting the lips, include *b* and *p.)*

"And she brought forth a sonne" continues the iambic rhythm of "that she should be delivered." The *b* of *brought* embodies the gesture of the mother, while *forth,* with its super-active *f*, takes the activity of the birth beyond the physical baby arriving just outside the mother, almost with the gesture of a gift to the larger world. By contrast the modern "and she gave birth to a son," settles for the physical fact of the action, a contracted consciousness by comparison.

When contemporary translations of the Bible are less grounded than the King James translation in images of the eye and in rhythms of the ear and less imbued with imagination and inspiration, the Bible generates less imagination and inspiration in those who experience it and, hence, in our culture at large. Although the English language in our time has over 500,000 words, a million if we including technical jargon—by far the largest of any language on Earth—one has to ask whether the spirit of the language is able to be as active as it was in Elizabethan England, whether in Shakespeare's fertilely expansive manner or in the King Kames Version and its fertilely focused manner. How can we quicken the activity of the spirit of the English language in our time? I will address this question in chapters on language in relation to adolescent development.

As we conclude our attention to the phenomenon of the King James Version of the Bible, it is fitting to remind ourselves of its rendering of the story of the tower of Babel.

> GENESIS 11: 1. And the whole earth was of one language, and of one speech.... 4. And they said to one another, Go to, let us build a city, and a tower, whose top may reach unto heaven.... 6. And the LORD said... 7. go to, let us go down, and there confound their language, that they may not understand one another's speech.... 9. Therefore is the name of it [the city] called Babel; because the LORD did there confound the language of all the earth: and from thence did the LORD scatter them abroad upon the face of all the earth.

In the language of the Bible, fallen humanity has been scattered in isolated misunderstanding ever since Babel—separated not only from the Creator, but also through limited language (the "babble") from one another as well. All the more extraordinary then is the picture of forty-eight scholars working together on sixty-five different texts in Hebrew, Aramaic, Greek, and English over seven years, rendering the Word of the Lord in a virtually seamless, seminal masterpiece, yet in a simplified language intended for everyone. Does any activity in the history of language and literature come closer to embodying the dynamic of the Holy Spirit as described by Paul in the New Testament Book of Acts?

> ACTS 2: 1.And when the day of Pentecost was fully come,
> they [the apostles] were all with one accord in one place.
> 2.And suddenly there came a sound from heaven as of a
> rushing mighty wind, and it filled all the house where
> they were sitting. 3.And there appeared unto them clo-
> ven tongues like as of fire, and it sat upon each of them.
> 4.And they were all filled with the Holy Ghost, and
> began to speak with other tongues, as the spirit gave
> them utterance.
> 5.And there were dwelling at Jerusalem Jews, devout
> men, of every nation under heaven. 6.Now when this
> was noised abroad, the multitude came together, and
> were confounded, because that every man heard them
> speak in his own language.... 8.and how hear we every
> man in our own tongue, wherein we were born? 9.Par-
> thians, and Medes, and Elamites, and the dwellers in
> Mesopatamia, and in Judea, and Cappadocia, in Pontus,
> and Asia, 10.Phrygia, and Pamphylia, in Egypt, and in
> the parts of Libya about Cyrene, and strangers of Rome,
> and proselytes, Cretes and Arabians, we do hear them
> speak in our tongues the wonderful works of God.

Considering that the spirit of the English language was able to inspire King James' forty-eight translators in a manner so akin to the workings of the Holy Spirit in Acts, one cannot help but wonder what role the King James Version of the Bible has played in the evolution of the English language and becoming the language of the globe—the closest presently to a language of all nations. The King James Version of the Bible is an epitome of combining imagination and inspiration. The translators honored the two poles of the Catholic eye and the Puritan ear, surrendering neither one nor the other, while melding a rare combination of richness and clarity. The great Judeo-Christian imaginations of the Western world are embodied in language whose rhythms allow imaginations to inspire in a more nourishing way than any other work of art in the English-speaking world.

On the one hand, Shakespeare, indeed Elizabethan literature in general, and on the other, the King James Version of the Bible, form a polarity that embodies the complementary ways that the spirit of a language can work. Shakespeare and his contemporaries at the Mermaid Tavern drew in everything possible, even from beyond the peripheries of their known world, through perhaps the greatest expansion of language ever (and hence consciousness) in just several decades. By contrast, the forty-eight scholars in their studies contracted and distilled, through a simplified center in equally potent language. Together both poles continue to be the closest language can come to the infinitely revitalizing nourishment of the Holy Grail.

Part II

Chapter 9

Lyric Activity in Metaphysical Poetry: John Donne

While in the early 1600s Elizabethan drama was certainly center stage, increasingly the King James Version of the Bible permeated the land. Almost imperceptibly, however, the spirit of the English language was working in quiet yet significantly different ways in the wings. The initial practitioner of the quiet craft led a surprising life.

The Life of John Donne (1572–1631)

In 1593, while the young actor William Shakespeare was just beginning to write plays, an even younger scholar, because he was Catholic, was unable to receive degrees for his studies at the universities of Oxford and Cambridge. As he began work at the Inns of Court in London, his older brother died in prison, having been arrested for sheltering a Catholic priest. The young man was able to enjoy life nevertheless, especially courting ladies, seeing plays, and writing a variety of verse. In time, through several kinds of conversions, John Donne would become known in his day as the most gifted preacher in London; he received his due value as a potent lyric poet only posthumously.

Queen Elizabeth had only recently regained for the crown the Protestant (Anglican) faith of her father, Henry VIII, after the death of her predecessor Queen Mary, a Catholic. John Donne was born in early 1572 in the Catholic family of a well-to-do London merchant, an ironmonger who died when John was four. It is not surprising, therefore, that images of metallurgy and alchemy appeared later in Donne's poetry. John's mother was a descendant of Sir Thomas More, who had resisted Henry VIII's emancipation of the English Church from Rome. Moreover, one of her uncles had been a Catholic martyr. The tensions of Protestant power were a constant influence in the family's life. John's mother's brother, Jaspar Heywood, translator of Seneca, was imprisoned for his role in a Jesuit mission to England. John's early teachers had been Jesuits. After John's brother Henry died of fever in prison for having hidden a priest, that Romanist priest was hanged and disemboweled before an eager crowd.

Although John had studied at both Oxford and Cambridge Universities, he received no degree, because he refused to sign the Oath of Supremacy, declaring the English monarch head of the Church of England. In his early twenties, John Donne worked long hours at the Inns of Court, studying law, languages and theology. The serious scholar of the morning was quite other at night. During the decade of the 1590s, the heyday of Elizabethan theater, young John appears to have assumed the persona of Jack the Rake, portrayed with large, floppy hat, undone lace collar, melancholy air, described by a contemporary as a great visitor of ladies, a frequent theatergoer, and a writer of conceited verses. Even in his twenties, Donne seems to have privately written elegies, satires, juvenilia, as well as some songs and sonnets, though some may have circulated among friends. His library included little poetry, but one contemporary poem he kept nearby until he died: Francis Bacon's popular poem "The World."

> The world's a bubble, and the life of man
> Less than a span,
> In his conception wretched, from the womb,
> So to the tomb;

Curst from the cradle, and brought up to years
With cares and fears.
Who then to frail mortality shall trust,
But limns on water, or but writes in dust...

Young Donne traveled in two naval expeditions to Cadiz and the Azores, and in 1598, at the age of twenty-six, he became private secretary to Sir Thomas Egerton, Lord Keeper of the Great Seal, and soon a member of Parliament. Donne's star was rising and he was an able individual of worldly promise. However, when he was twenty-nine, the year James assumed the throne, Donne fell in love with Sir Egerton's niece, Anne More, and eloped with the seventeen-year-old. His impulsiveness landed him in prison for a short while and barred him from meaningful employment for a long while. "John Donne, Anne Donne, Un-done," he wrote, having fallen from favor in the eyes of those in power. While his marriage appears to have been essentially sunny, his future in terms of worldly success was now cloudy.

John Donne, leaving his impetuous youth behind in his intellectual-soul stage of development, groped in several directions. It may have been when he was around thirty that Donne converted to the Anglican faith. In 1604, he became keenly interested in the appearance of new stars in the constellations of Serpentarius and Cygnus. He contemplated immigrating to Virginia, where the new colony of Jamestown was struggling. Although practicing law, he may also have written religious pamphlets for one employer, Thomas Morton, who later became Bishop of Durham. He wrote anti-Jesuit polemics that attracted the notice of the king, and he wrote some "Holy Sonnets." Nevertheless, by age thirty-five, he was still so poor, sick, and unhappy that he wrote a treatise on suicide, unpublished. A decade of financial misery was eventually alleviated somewhat by both the forgiving support of Anne More's father and the wealthy Sir Robert Drury's offer of part of his home to the Donnes. Moreover, King James recognized Donne's promise in spite of his struggles.

Finally, in 1615, at age forty-three, John Donne succumbed to increasing royal pressure to take the orders of ordination as an Anglican priest. He became royal chaplain, preaching to king and court. His patient, explaining tone as a preacher engendered popularity that soon brought him fame throughout London. Within two years of ordination, his wife Anne died at age thirty-six, having borne twelve children, six of whom were still living.

Two years later, John Donne was well-schooled in death and ready spiritually to preach at a ceremony, promising important births of several kinds, for the wedding of King James's daughter Elizabeth to Frederick, who would become King of Bohemia. Donne said to Frederick, "Be thou a new star, that to us portends / Ends of great wonder; and be thou those ends." In his "Marriage Song," written for their wedding, Donne portrays the joining of two phoenixes, and the marriage of the Sun and Moon—Rosicrucian imagery. Emanating from Christian Rosenkreutz, who was born in the mid-thirteenth century, Rosicrucian thinking was circulating strongly in Europe during the early 1600s. Its ideals include inspiring understanding of the human being in relation to the whole universe and, specifically, to seeds for future democracy. Frederick and Elizabeth hoped that their Bohemia would become a living embodiment of Rosicrucian ideals, but those hopes would soon be crushed by the Spanish Catholic Hapsburgs in the Thirty Years War (1618–1648).

In 1621, forty-nine, Dr. John Donne was appointed Dean of St. Paul's Cathedral. He declared that he would finally reject "the mistress of my youth, Poetry" for "the wife of mine age, Divinity." Eventually, his great sermons were published in ten volumes. He suffered a serious illness of an unknown nature, yet according to his friend and first biographer, Izaac Walton, in keeping with Bacon's poem "The World," John Donne

> sent for a carver to make for him in wood the figure of an urn, giving him directions for the compass and height of it; and to bring with it a board of the just height of his body. These being got, then without delay a choice painter was got to be in readiness to draw his picture, which was taken as followeth. Several charcoal fires being first made in his large study, he brought with him into that place

> his winding-sheet in his hand, and, having put off all his clothes, had this sheet put on him, and so tied with knots at his head and feet, and his hands so placed, as dead bodies are usually fitted to be shrouded and put into their coffin, or grave. Upon this urn he thus stood with his eyes shut, and with so much of the sheet turned aside as might show his lean, pale, and deathlike face...; and when the picture was fully finished, he caused it to be set by his bedside, where it continued, and became his hourly object till his death.

In 1631, at fifty-nine, the Dean of St. Paul's gave a sermon to King Charles I, entitled "Death's Duel." John Donne died not long after. The individual, John Donne, had navigated through various dangerous waters in his life, including dramatic ebbs and flows of fortune: deadly tensions between Catholicism and Protestantism, passions and love, social disgrace and poverty, numerous deaths in family, clarifying focus of faith, royal favor when King James recognized Donne's potential, then emerging in time to become the spiritual voice of London, all with hardly any public awareness of the reason we know him today: his poetry.

Donne's Poetry: Sound Work

How does John Donne work with language? As we shall see, he does so in a range of ways.

A Valediction: Of Weeping

Let me pour forth
My tears before thy face, whilst I stay here,
For thy face coins them, and thy stamp they bear,
And by this mintage they are something worth,
For thus they be
Pregnant of thee;
Fruits of much grief they are, emblems of more,
When a tear falls, that thou falst which it bore,
So thou and I are nothing then, when on a divers shore.

On a round ball
A workman that hath copies by, can lay
An Europe, Afric, and an Asia,
And quickly make that, which was nothing, all,
So doth each tear,
Which thee doth wear,
A globe, yea, world by that impression grow,
Till thy tears mixed with mine do overflow
This world, by waters sent from thee, my heaven
dissolved so.

O more than moon,
Draw not up seas to drown me in thy sphere,
Weep not dead, in thine arms, but forbear
To teach the sea, what it may do too soon;
Let not the wind
Example find,
To do me more harm, than it purposeth;
Since thou and I sigh one another's breath,
Whoe'er sighs most, is cruellest, and hastes the other's
death.

Three stanzas, each nine lines long, share the same form. The first line, bimeter, expands to three pentameters, followed by a contraction, two bimeters, swelling, expanding back out to two pentameters, culminating in the final heptameter.

The initial line, "Let me poure forth," serves as the concentrated source of the poem, the issuing forth of the speaker's tears. In the second line, "My teares before thy face, whils't I stay here," Donne the poet establishes the contrast between "my teares" and "thy face." Yet "my" and "thy" already share the *i* sound, and "I stay" echoes, in vowel-sound sympathy, "thy face," at the same time as differentiating their positions spatially. In the third line, "For thy face coins them, and thy stampe they beare," *thy* (her) shares *th* with *them* (his tears), and *thy* again shares *th* with "they," (his tears again), supporting the stated fusion between the two seemingly separate lovers. The *m* sounds in *them* and *stampe,* followed by *mintage* and *something* in the fourth line, reinforce the meeting, merging activity of the image of *mintage,* or coin bearing stamp, hence lover reflecting lover.

In lines five and six, the distilled couplet rhyme of *be(e)* and *thee* fuses the sound shared so far by *me,* "*teares,* and *heare,* culminating in *thee,* the transference from the original *me* to the beloved other, *thee.* This same *ee* sound, which evokes the clear transparency of the tear, allowing it to become a medium between the two lovers, reappears in line seven with a new sound in the poem, the almost explosive, wrenching, grunt-like *g* in *griefe. Griefe,* extending the *ee*, altering it with the plosive *g*, also anticipates with its *f*, the ensuing double *fall* and *falst* of the following line eight. The fall of the *teare,* his tear with her image on it, is the picture of the fall of their union, shattered in the final line, leaving only their separation. The very shape of the stanza mirrors both the content and some of the sound-patterns, expanding and contracting like the physical shape of a tear, reflecting in miniature the largeness opposite it.

Those two sounds late in the first stanza, which embody the speaker's grief, "thou falls," evolve into the keynote for the second stanza, "round ball."

> Fruits of much grief they are, emblems of more,
> When a tear f***all***s, that thou f***al***st which it bore,
> So thou and I are nothing then, when on a divers shore.
>
> On a round b***all***...

Expanding from the natural image of a tear to the analogy of an artificial, human-crafted round map, the poet evokes the worker's fashioning, crafting, through a sequence of ten *a*'s in the first quatrain:

> A workman that hath copies by, can lay
> An Europe, Afric, and an Asia,
> And quickly make that,...

culminating in the round, inclusive, sealing sound that frames the quatrain rhyme with *ball:* "And quickly make that, which was nothing, all."

In the repetition of the sound "all" is accomplished the notion of the whole universe being represented in a single, simple sphere. This second stanza's central bimeter couplet internalizes the end rhyme of the first stanza's central bimeter couplet "For thus they be Pregnant of thee;" with "each tear, Which thee," and then reinforces it in the new end rhyme, "So doth each tear, Which thee doth wear," implying, pre-suggesting, but refraining from saying, "sphere."

The second stanza then re-expands out into the appropriate, inevitable image, "globe," whose vowel sound, completely new in the poem, reinforces in both shape and sound the dominant image of the second stanza: "...globe...grow, overflow," culminating in "so."

So *doth* each tear,
Which thee doth wear,
A gl**o**be, yea, world by that impression g*row*,
Till thy tears mixed with mine do **o**verfl*ow*
This world, by waters sent from thee, my heaven dissolved *so*.

The "conceit" is that since not only the beloved's image (microcosm), but in fact the whole world (macrocosm), is reflected in his tear, if she were to weep tears, they would flood the world like Noah's flood.

O more than moon,
Draw not up seas to drown me in thy sphere,
Weep not dead, in thine arms, but forbear
To teach the sea, what it may do too soon;
Let not the wind
Example find,
To do me more harm, than it purposeth;
Since thou and I sigh one another's breath,
Whoe'er sighs most, is cruellest, and hastes the other's death.

The third stanza then pleads to her, with five *n*'s in the first two lines, reinforcing his request for her not to weep, drowning him. "...than moone...not...drowne...in." The fourth line includes a quadruple assonance of newly emphasized sound in the poem,

> but forbear
> t*o* teach the sea, what it may d*oe* t*oo* s*oo*ne;

The *u*, embodying the future he fears, sounds again in "t*o* d*oe* more harm," and rings as both the leading and central sound of the final line of the poem, "Wh*o*e're sighs most, is cr***u***ellest, and hastes the other's death." How fragile is this beholding of the other, and hence of the whole world, in oneself.

Distinctive Qualities of Donne's Poetry

People may like John Donne's poetry for a range of reasons. Some will enjoy the celebration of the arguments of seduction, the anticipation of sensual pleasures reflected in the language of "Elegy 19, To His Mistress Going to Bed":

> ...Off with that girdle...
> Your gown going off, such beauteous state reveals,
> As when from flowry meads the hill's shadow steals.
> ...Licence my roving hands, and let them go,
> Before, behind, between, above, below.
> O my America! My new-found land...
> ...Full nakedness! All joyes are due to thee,
> As souls unbodied, bodies uncloth'd must be.

Others will enjoy the refreshing, colloquial imperative in a number of poems:

> Off with that girdle...
> For God's sake hold your tongue and let me love...
> *The Canonization*

> Batter my heart, three-person'd God...
> *Holy Sonnet no.14*

In this colloquial imperative, the lyric takes both surprise and contemporary speech patterns from its cousin, the popular drama, as though the speaker were engaged in immediate, spontaneous, dramatic dialogue, right upon the stage.

Some love the ingenious extent to which a simplest image, such as a flea, can be penetrated, illuminated, expanded upon, so that it becomes a multidimensional symbol, working in this case as an argument for what one lover can offer another:

> Marke but this flea, and marke in this,
> How little that which thou deny'st me is;
> ....
> Just so much honor, when thou yields't to mee,
> Will wast, as this flea's death tooke life from thee.

There is an almost pervasive, omnipresent touch of humor, to be enjoyed even in the holiest of subjects. Irony and clever, intricate connection compose what became known as "wit." One delights in reason serving even the ridiculous, in ways that, though playfully stretched, remain "true," the quality of "wit" which T. S. Eliot characterizes in Donne's poetry as "the tough reasonableness beneath the slight lyric grace" (252). Modern scholar Louis Martz elaborates:

> Wit, in all the rich and varied sense that the word held in this era: intellect, reason, powerful mental capacity, cleverness, ingenuity, intellectual quickness, inventive and constructive ability, a talent for uttering brilliant things, the power of amusing surprise. (xx)

Another characteristic of Donne's poetry can be the strange, haunting power that a seemingly unpoetic image may have, such as "The Relique": "A bracelet of bright haire about the bone" in a grave. The bracelet of hair about the bone engenders a fantasy of the speaker and his sweetheart becoming, when the grave is dug up, objects of veneration, like Mary Magdalene and "I / a something else thereby," as though not daring to presume to articulate his implied analogy with Christ.

In this vein, some especially appreciate the Zen-like revelations that emerge through Donne's articulation of seeming contradictions, as in "Sonnet 14," when he says to God,

> ...for I
> except you'enthrall mee, never shall be free,
> Nor ever chast, except you ravish mee.

Meditation

Whatever one's preferences, and of course Donne enthusiasts love all these characteristics of his poetry, it is crucial to understand one primary and potent practice in relation to the character of John Donne's work with the English language. Although Donne's biography is rarely able to date his poems precisely, it is fair to trust that he was both familiar with and in fact practiced Christian meditation, in ways that informed his poetry.

The major articulator of Christian meditation in that era was none other than Ignatius Loyola, founder of the Catholic Jesuit order. An English priest, Edward Dawson, who lived in both Spain and England, published in English in 1614, *The Practical Methode of Meditation*, based on Loyola's *Spiritual Exercises.* Donne, originally Catholic, would certainly have been familiar with Loyola's Jesuit meditations. Although Donne eventually wrote polemics against Jesuit doctrine (*Pseudo-Martyr*), readers of Donne's poetry will recognize some familiar dynamics in Loyola's meditative modes.

One practice is an imagination of place: to imagine in the greatest graphic, sensory detail possible, the physical setting of one's object of meditation. Dawson elaborates on many nuances of each of the five physical senses. The effect is to incarnate one's attention to the reality of worldly context through disciplined, accurate imagination.

Then, the course of the meditation is essentially a threefold dynamic. 1) Memory: with the help of imagining place, one recreates the actual context as faithfully as possible. 2) Understanding: through elaboration, relationship to other realities via similitudes, the exercise of human reason, and eventually dialogue with self and God, one attempts to illuminate the subject with new, divinely inspired understanding. In Dawson's language, "we may help ourselves much to the framing of spirituall conceipts [concepts] if we apply unto our matter familiar similitudes" (Martz xxviii). 3) Will: in light of new understanding of the subject, one finds the way to live in accord with divine harmony. Our fruitful meditation will have led us to "spirituall conceipts, fit to move our Will to virtuous affections."

Readers familiar with Rudolf Steiner's *Intuitive Thinking as a Spiritual Path*) (or *The Philosophy of Spiritual Activity*) and *The Foundations of Human Experience* (or *Study of Man*) will recognize in Loyola's (Dawson's) threefold dynamic of meditation parallels to Steiner's threefold sequence of cognition: conclusion, judgment, concept: 1) Conclusion includes beholding the thing, the memory, the object of the exercise, as precisely as possible, recreating whatever elements of sensory experience compose the reality of the object—a focused, centering activity from outside. 2) Judgment includes the activity of considering, weighing, comparing the thing to other things or experiences, considering it perhaps from a variety of perspectives, perhaps even with other people, researching, finding what else one can know about it—a more horizontal, peripheral activity. 3) Concept, the subtlest of the three, includes trying to glean the essential concept of the object of the exercise—as though one could know it from within its center. In Donne's "A Valediction: Of Weeping," the first stanza (Loyola's "memory of place" or Steiner's "conclusion") focuses on the relationship between the speaker's tears and the beloved's face. The second stanza (Loyola's "understanding," Steiner's "judgment") compares the tear to the globe of the Earth. The third stanza (Loyola's "spirituall conceipt to move our Will," Steiner's "concept") realizes the fragility of each lover's existence in relation to the other.

Donne's Contribution

What is the nature of John Donne's contribution to English poetry? It can seem that in the course of his poetic life his attention scaled, sublimating from the sensual to the spiritual, from the full nakedness of woman to the glory of three-person'd God.

But biographers avoid so simple a picture, allowing that poems of sensuous and spiritual content may well intersperse chronologically. The "seducer" and the "struggling saint" may be not so separate after all, simply using varying language, whether sacred or profane, to explore actually similar subjects: the creature's relationship to the Creator and his beloved creation.

In the context of this book so far, we can remind ourselves that Donne's elder, William Shakespeare, thrived as a lyric poet within the confines of the sonnet. As a dramatic poet, Shakespeare outgrew the limitations of rhyming couplets, needing the possibilities of blank verse. John Donne the lyric poet is content to both play and work within the confines of rhyme. He enjoys both couplets and playing with ranges of combinations. I am inclined, considering Donne's keen use of reason and wit, to consider his poetry as a bit of a sigh, a bit of an in-breath, in the wake of the consciousness-soul expansiveness of Elizabethan poetry, as a slight ebbing, a slight contraction to a more rational-soul way, reminiscent of some of Chaucer's own wit.

> And in this flea our two bloods mingled be...
> Oh stay, three lives in one flea spare,
> Where we almost, nay more than married are.
> This flea is you and I, and this
> Our marriage bed and marriage temple is...
>
> "The Flea"

John Donne shares with medieval predecessors, Renaissance neo-Platonists, and even his contemporary Rosicrucians, the capacity to behold macrocosm in microcosm, still sustained in the context of the "Great Chain of Being." But he has a new capacity to see the object as thing itself, not as idea or category. This is a consciousness soul capacity: to behold the world of the senses in its own right, whether flea, bracelet of hair, or twin compass. He could look *through* an image, using it figuratively, but he could also look *to* it, seeing it itself. Then the application of reason, tempered, illumined through meditation, allows spirit to reveal sense in particularly elastic, fresh marriages of connection through extended metaphor. Samuel

Johnson noted in metaphysical poetry "a combination of dissimilar images, or discovery of occult resemblances in things apparently unlike.... The most heterogeneous ideas are yoked by violence together; nature and art are ransacked for illustrations, comparisons, and allusion" (I, 12–16).

It's as though Donne is practicing rational-soul activity, tempered through new consciousness-soul attention, enabled especially though the meditative penetration of his subject matter, not sublimating, transcending the physical world of sense, but immanently incarnating into, indeed illuminating it. Dryden first came up with the term, rightly recognizing Donne's poetry as "metaphysical" in quality, above, beyond the physical, not forsaking the physical, but reconnecting, enspiriting, redeeming it. Martz recognized that "poetry is metaphysical, then, when it seeks by complex analogies to find a central principle of being, within the bounds of a given situation" (xxv), such as, for example, a tear being analogous to the whole Earth, or a woman's unclothed body an America, a newfound land. One might characterize this "metaphysical" activity, this combination of rational (intellectual) and consciousness (spirit) soul activity, as requiring a particular combination of sensory perception guided by tough, tempered reason, yet exercising an almost sacred, even priestly, capacity, of imagination to reveal connections in the apparently disparate, though actually unified creation.

Although only four of Donne's poems were published in his lifetime, his lyric poetry has exercised, with almost homeopathic potency, a quietly concentrating influence, amidst the gloriously expansive, flourishing Elizabethan birth of English literature. "Donne may be considered an inventor of an attitude, a system of feeling or of morals.... Donne would have been an individual at any time and place" (Eliot 251,2).

To understand John Donne not only as primary but also as representative of lyric activity of his time, it might be helpful to include short biographical sketches of three other "Metaphysical" poets. The biographical sketches reflect something of the activity of the spirit of the English language at work in the lyric context.

Henry Vaughan (1621–1695)

During the English Civil War, Henry Vaughan and his twin Thomas had been active on the royalist side. Under Cromwell's protectorate, Thomas Vaughan had translated (as Eugenius Philalethes) a number of "esoteric" and Hermetic works from the continent, *Rosicrucian Manifestos*, specifically in 1652 Valentin Andreas' *Fama* and *Confessio*. Thomas Vaughan wrote *Anthroposophia Theomagica*. Samuel Butler, in his 1662 satire *Hudibras*, nicknames T. Vaughan *"Anthroposophus."*

Henry Vaughan published *Poems* (1646); "Olor Iscanus" (The Swan of Usk, 1651), and "Silex Scintillanus" (The Sparkling Flint, 1650, 1655). Henry Vaughan's poetry "can be regarded as a summation of the currents and influences which characterized seventeenth-century Freemasonry" (Baigent and Leigh 159). Freemasonry had its origins partially in the guilds of medieval "operative" masons who raised the Gothic cathedrals. In the mid-sixteen hundreds, Masonic lodges emerged throughout Europe, embodying esoteric lore strongly permeated by Rosicrucian ideals, "speculative" masonry, in which members were no longer moving actual stones. Henry Vaughn's poetry was the only "Metaphysical" poetry to be published significantly during the poet's lifetime.

In 1666, the Great Fire leveled eighty percent of old London, including more than eighty-seven churches. In 1685, the great architect Christopher Wren is alleged to have been Grand Master of Freemasonry in England, the crucial link between "speculative" and "operative" Freemasonry. It is significant that Rosicrucian notions influenced three of the four most memorable lyric poets: Donne, Marvell, and Vaughn, with the notable exception of Herbert. While the man actively influenced public life, their work as poets was essentially private, as though their poetic work was as intimate as meditation.

> My soul, there is a country
> Far beyond the stars,
> Where stands a winged sentry
> All skillful in the wars....

Leave then thy foolish ranges;
For none can thee secure
But One who never changes,
Thy God, thy life, thy cure.

"Peace"

Recommended Poems by Henry Vaughn: "The Retreat," "The World," "They are all Gone into the World of Light," "Peace," and "The Night."

GEORGE HERBERT (1593–1633)

The fifth son of a Welsh family, George Herbert lost his father at a young age. George's mother had been a friend of John Donne. Educated at Westminster School, George studied at Trinity College, where he was selected to be the public orator at Cambridge University. For two years, he served as a member of Parliament, reflecting a worldly, political orientation, similar in some ways to John Donne's.

George Herbert's life shifted inward and culminated in his late thirties. In 1629, at the age of thirty-six, he married Jane Danvers. The following year, George became rector of Bemerton near Salisbury. Most of his English poems were composed in these later years, "a constant attempt...to make poetry do the work of prayer and devotion" (Kermode and Hollander 1166). He prayed to God instead of invoking the muse.

Reverend George Herbert spent three years as "a learned, godly, and painful divine." He preached, prayed, rebuilt the church out of his own pocket, attended the poor, helped the sick, and sat by the bed of the dying, known as "Holy Mr. Herbert." In 1633, at forty, George Herbert died of consumption (tuberculosis). His poems were published posthumously in a book called *The Temple.* Like John Donne's work, George Herbert's poetic activity is private, memorably musical, spiritually meditative, with visually symmetrical originality; it only engendered such musically meditative poetic possibilities generations later, especially in T. S. Eliot and Elizabeth Bishop.

Lord, who createst man in wealth and store,
Though foolishly he lost the same,
Decaying more and more
Till he became
Most poor:
With Thee
O let me rise
As larks, harmoniously,
And sing this day Thy victories:
Then shall the fall further the flight in me.

Recommended Poems by George Herbert: "The Altar," "Easter Wings," "Affliction IV," "Mortification," "Decay," "Conscience," "The Collar," "Heaven," "Love III."

Andrew Marvell (1621–1678)

The son of a Yorkshire member of the Calvinist clergy, Andrew Marvell went to the Hull Grammar School and, at twelve, to Trinity College, Cambridge University, to study Greek and Latin in particular. In 1639, it appears that young Andrew, at age eighteen, temporarily converted to Roman Catholicism. At age twenty he lost his appointment to Cambridge, and while traveling in Europe a year later, came of age around the beginning of the English Civil War. By the end of the war, although he had been associating recently with King Charles' Royalists, his sympathies aligned with the victorious Parliamentarian, Anti-Royalist forces. "On the subject of a statue of Charles I, he wrote, 'It is such a King as no chisel can mend. Men...ought & might have trusted the King'" (Eliot 253). In the late 1640s, Marvell associated with a group of Parliamentarians with Rosicrucian sympathies, including John Milton, a vigorous civil servant whose later epic poetry we will explore in a following chapter.

In 1650, at the age of twenty-nine, Andrew Marvell served as tutor to Mary Fairfax, daughter of the Parliamentarians' leading general, who in fact turned command over to Cromwell. Lord Fairfax was devoting himself to translating hermetic, esoteric texts. Marvell wrote most of his lyric poetry during these several years at Appleton House, in the context of such esoteric studies. Paul Bembridge has shown how Marvell's best-known poem, "To His Coy Mistress," rings with echoes of the Rosicrucian document *Fama* (Bembridge 233–235). Marvell also served as tutor to William Dutton, Cromwell's future son-in-law.

> ...An hundred years should go to praise
> Thine eyes, and on thy forehead gaze,
> Two hundred to adore each breast,
> But thirty thousand to the rest.
> An age at least to every part,
> And the last age should show your heart...
>
> "To His Coy Mistress"

Beneath the witty and erotic catalogue of the beloved's fine physical features lies an elasticity of time in relation to space, a way of thinking able to move gracefully between macrocosm and microcosm, characteristic of Rosicrucian concepts.

In 1653, John Milton recommended Andrew Marvell for Assistant Latin Secretary to the new government, and by the age of thirty-six, Marvell was the Latin Secretary, serving as a colleague of both Milton and John Dryden. After Cromwell's death in 1659, Marvell served as member of Parliament for Hull and occasionally as secretary for English embassies in Russia, Denmark, and Sweden. During the Restoration of Charles II in 1660, Marvell may have been influential in saving Milton from imprisonment and even execution. By 1662, Andrew Marvell was serving as a member of Parliament in King Charles II's Restoration government, voting to disinter the body of Oliver Cromwell and behead it. As T. S. Eliot said, "Marvell was more a man of his century than a Puritan" (253). Andrew Marvell proved politically adaptable in dramatic shifts of political fortune, from the monarchy of Charles I to the parliamentarian dictatorship of Cromwell and later to the restored monarchy of Charles II. Of Andrew Marvell's poetry, Eliot said that it finds the proper degree of seriousness for every subject he treated, a capacity Eliot found lacking in Wordsworth, Shelley, Keats,

Hardy, and Yeats. Eliot especially valued Marvell's tough inspection of experience.

A bachelor of seemingly violent temper and perhaps secret homosexual proclivity, he died at age fifty-seven. Three years later, in 1681, his *Miscellaneous Poems* was published to little notice, but bearing the identifying mark of the Rosicrucians, "C Ros." The Rosicrucian document *Fama* had declared that "the word C. R. should be their seal, mark, and character" (Bembridge 231). The publisher, Robert Boulter, had already published the first edition of Milton's *Paradise Lost*, showing as well on page five the Rosicrucian sign, "C Ros." By now many scholars share the appraisal of Marvell's verse as the most major minor in English.

Recommended Poems: "A Dialogue between the Soul and the Body," "To His Coy Mistress," "The Definition of Love," "Horatian Ode on Cromwell's Return from Ireland," "On a Drop of Dew."

Metaphysical Poetry

In conclusion, the muse of lyric poetry worked in conjunction with the spirit of the English language in particularly quiet, yet seminal ways in England during the first half of the seventeenth century. Characteristics of what Dryden later called "Metaphysical" poetry include the fact that the contemporary English-speaking public was not aware of the poetry; Donne, Herbert, Marvell had published hardly a poem in their lifetimes. Henry Vaughan, indebted to Herbert, is an exception. His poetry shares a maturity of thinking powers, imbued with devotion to spirit. The poetry is playful, witty, and illuminating. A number of poets of the time reflect, in varying degrees, the influence of contemporary Rosicrucian streams of thought, including certainly Donne, Marvell, and Vaughan. In this context, the poets often work with images of the microcosm in some way embodying the macrocosm. A mercurial capacity for fresh metaphor reunites disparate elements of the fallen world. The subject of the poetry, whether explicitly "profane" or "sacred," often includes some version of the feminine beloved, in the form of woman or nature, versions of the ultimate feminine wisdom, the divine Sophia, revered by the contemporary Rosicrucians. In a way, the English lyric poetry of the seventeenth century had the effect of dew, to subtly, almost invisibly, freshen the world in the morning of a new era, with almost homeopathic potency. The image of a dewdrop (*Ros,* Latin for dew), appearing often in metaphysical poetry, was central to Rosicrucian iconography.

Chapter 10

The English Epic: Milton

HAVING SAVORED THE flourishing Elizabethan drama, and with an awareness of the comparatively quiet lyrical activity that followed, let us shift to a mood of elegy. The Globe Theatre burned down in 1613; William Shakespeare of Stratford died in 1616 (April 23, St. George's Day). In the 1630s and 1640s, Cromwell's Presbyterian and independently Protestant Roundheads soon shattered countless panes of medieval stained glass in cathedrals and churches around the country, and eventually beheaded the supposedly divinely chosen Catholic king, Charles I. Even more dramatic, from our point of view, than such an unimaginable gesture, in September 1642, the puritanical Parliament closed all theaters and theater troupes around the country, closing the doors to the muses of comedy and tragedy, known to the Greeks as Thalia and Melpomene.

Long after the birth of Greek drama, emerging from the temples of the Greeks to enter the amphitheaters of the classical world, the spirit of drama had eventually, essentially died in the degenerate Rome of bawdy sensationalism and coliseum blood spectacles. In the first several centuries after Christ, the simple Easter celebration in the Roman catacombs, with three choirboys as the three Marys speaking to the priest dressed as an angel, had born the seeds not only of the birth of Christianity but also of the rebirth of drama. As diametrically opposed to the extreme Roman debauchery sixteen hundred years earlier, drama was extinguished by the Protestant, Puritan impulse in austere, plain-clothed England of the 1630s to 1650s. The spirit of drama withdrew from the English language, never again to be as at home in it until perhaps the twentieth century. When Charles II was restored to the throne in 1666, drama was allowed once again in England's theaters. But when a Shakespearean tragedy such as *Lear* or *Macbeth* was performed, the ending would be changed to a happy one, with no real tragedy or catharsis of soul. It's as though the spirit of drama was allowed to be resurrected only in castrated form. Melpomene, the Muse of Tragedy, was allowed only in a sterile way.

The Muse of Lyric Poetry, known to the Greeks as Euterpe, was quietly active in poets such as John Donne, George Herbert, Andrew Marvell, and young John Milton. However, the silence in the theaters, the ebb tide of the departure of Drama, allowed a new tide to swell, to gather its momentum from the ages. Calliope, the Muse of Epic Poetry, was preparing, in the silence, to sound through the English language, as never before, as never since. She chose as her singer John Milton, a young poet who was earnestly serving in his good Puritan government.

Ancient Drama and Epic

Before we focus on Milton, let us discuss some characteristics of the classic epic, as one of the three original forms of literature. In ancient Greece, all three forms emerged at approximately the same time: Homer's epics around 700 B.C.E., Sappho's lyrics around 600 B.C.E., and Aeschylus' dramas around 500 B.C.E.

Whereas drama emerged from the mysteries of Persephone and Hades, of Dionysus, celebrating death and resurrection, the epic was inspired more by Artemis, the mysteries of birth and of the word. Although drama's original focal source was Eleusis, southwest of Athens, the epics sprang especially from the far-eastern shores of the Aegean Sea in the region of Ephesus. Tragedy and comedy were inspired by the muses Melpomene and Thalia, whose inspiration brought forth hundreds and hundreds of plays. The muse Calliope inspired a handful of epics. Although dramas were narrated through a combination of chorus and dialogue, epics were sung in the third person, describing what he, she, or they did. The lyric communicated a moment of experience, and the action of the drama traditionally explored a character's *katharsis* (purging/purification) during one day, at one place. The epic, however, followed the hero's journey or battle over vast expanses of space and long periods of time. Drama is intensive, all-consuming communication; epic is extensive, encyclopedic, embracing all geography, all the knowledge of the time. The audience in drama evolved from the initial group of priests and novitiates inside the temple, out into the open air of the amphitheater, where all levels of society were expected, even required initially, to watch—a democratic audience. The epics in contrast were sung in the courts, originally to an aristocratic audience.

The original dramas were typically sung-spoken, and hence even moved in a rhythm of u—u—u -, iambic trimeter, as in "*Outoi Synecthein*" (I am not here to hate, *Antigone*, Sophocles). This ascending, excarnating rhythm guided the human soul away from the forces of the Earth, so that the soul could exercise, through the limbs, the will to pursue the riddles of human destiny, just as Antigone discards past patterns and dictates, to honor her brother's death as she feels moved to do.

The original epics were typically sung in a rhythm of _uu_ uu_u / _uu _uu _u, dactylic hexameter, as in *andra moi ennepe musa, / polutropon hos mala pola* (Sing in me, O Muse, of the man of many turns), the opening lines of Homer's *Odyssey.* The epic might also be sung in the rhythm and meter of _u_u_u_u, trochaic tetrameter, as later in Longfellow's *Hiawatha*, "By the shores of Gitchee-goomee." These descending, incarnating rhythms enabled the all-knowing singer to communicate to the listeners earth-life as a revelation of the divine, to experience thought-pictures revealing the divine, rather than human actions on stage revealing human destiny.

The Life of John Milton (1608–1674)

What vessel could prove fit for the Epic muse, in conjunction with the spirit of the English language, to offer the Epic of English literature? In the late 1620s, an unusually able student of languages at Cambridge University won many prizes and few friends among students or professors. Observant and aloof, critical and merciless, he was so fine in appearance and writing style that he became known as "Lady." At the age of twenty-one, he wrote *On the Morning of Christ's Nativity*, recognized as one of the primary lyrics of the English language. However, decades of political activity and prose would ensue before John Milton would lose his sight and find his major inspiration.

John Milton was born to a middle-class Cockney family Dec. 9, 1608, in Cheapside, London. John's father had been disinherited when his Roman Catholic father found an English Bible in his room. Hence, he made his living as a scrivener and moneylender. He educated his boy passionately, preparing him for a life in the Protestant ministry, where he would be able to enjoy the pursuit of literature, indeed all fields of knowledge, for the rest of his life.

John enjoyed his schooling at St. Paul's in London. Father Milton provided extra tutoring in Greek, Latin, French, Italian, and Hebrew, so that, by the age of twelve, young John was hardly getting to sleep by midnight. In addition to the poetic influence of Spenser, two books had a major influence on Milton: Bacon's *Advancement of Learning*, and Sylvester's translation of *Du Bartas*, a French Protestant pseudo-epic on the creation.

In contrast to his harmonious experience at St. Paul's, sixteen-year-old John resisted, rebelled, and was resented at Cambridge University, aggravating both professors and fellow students. Essentially an observer with seemingly little humor, "Lady," the beautiful, fair-complexioned, gray-eyed youth with long brown hair watched his fellows' theatrical antics with disdain. He knew his was the finer work, the polishing, and the crafting of lyric verse, both in English and in Latin. He wrote five elegies of quality. When, on Dec. 25, 1629, the twenty-one-year-old wrote *Ode on the Morning of Christ's Nativity*, the lyric poet had been born.

While completing a Masters degree, he wrote the masterful lyrics, *L'Allegro* and *Il Penseroso*. He spent the rest of his twenties completing his poetic training more thoroughly than any other English poet, mastering all available poetic forms. However, as a nascent epic poet, he wanted simply to know everything one could about the world. "I take it to be my portion of in this life, joined with a strong propensity of nature, to leave something so written to aftertimes, as they should not willingly let it die" (Schmidt 234). He wrestled beyond the confines of lyric poetry in his court masque, *Comus*, and even in his elegy *Lycidas*.

Milton spent much of his thirtieth year in Italy, meeting Galileo and having his creative horizons expanded by the Italian Renaissance. Returning to London as a private schoolmaster in 1640, John Milton committed himself in *Reason of Church Government* on the one hand "not to make verbal curiosities the end (that were a toilsome vanity), but to be an interpreter and relater of the best and sagest things among mine own citizens throughout this island in the mother dialect" (Kermode and Hollander 1207). He started plans for England's Arthurian epic.

On the other hand, as political and religious turmoil intensified toward Civil War, Milton devoted his verbal abilities to numerous tracts in prose. He claimed that he wrote prose with his left hand, poetry with his right; four-fifths of his writings would be "left-handed." At age thirty-four, he married sixteen-year-old Catholic Mary Powell, who left him three months later, returning three years later to remain until her death in childbirth seven years later. He wrote tracts against censorship (*Areopagitica*), against the institution of bishops, supported divorce on grounds of disharmony rather than adultery, and articulated educational ideals inspired by both the Czech Comenius and the English scientist Francis Bacon. The only poetry he published was *The Poems of Mr. John Milton* in 1645.

During these years, Milton's circle of acquaintances included the philosopher Hartlib, the scientist Robert Boyle, the mathematician John Pell, the poet Andrew Marvell, and the founder of the first rotary clubs, Cyriack Skinner, all of whom worked actively with the Rosicrucian ideals articulated in Valentin Andreae's *Fama* and *Confessio*, which were circulating in those decades. These men devoted their energies to creating a new society. From 1649 to 1655, Milton served the new commonwealth under Cromwell as Secretary for Foreign Tongues to the Council of State. In 1649 shortly after the execution of Charles I, Milton's *Tenure of Kings and Magistrates* argued for the divine right of removing kings. *Defences of the English People* appeared in 1651 and 1654, and *The Ready and Easy Way to Establish a Free Commonwealth* was published in 1660.

At about age forty-three, Milton started losing his sight to the degree that by 1652, within a year, he was blind. Although he continued his government work for three years, his loss of sight allowed him to reconnect with his earlier sense of destiny as a poet. The ancient Greeks had a saying: "The lyric poet drinks wine; the epic poet drinks water," and John Milton in his forties finally took up with his right hand the cup of water of the epic poet. Having earlier imagined the Arthurian matter of Britain as the subject of his national epic, Milton found his scope expanding to portray nothing less than the Fall of all humanity, though from a distinctly English Protestant perspective. In the 1650s, he began dictating *Paradise Lost* to one or another of his daughters, often up to forty lines a day, otherwise spending his days walking, playing music, and being read to. In 1656, at age forty-eight, he married Katherine Woodcock, who died two years later, the same year that their daughter Katherine and Milton's leader Oliver Cromwell died.

In 1660, with the Stuart Charles II made king of England by parliament and the beginning of The Restoration, severe anti-Puritan laws were passed and Milton was forced into hiding that summer. Before being granted full pardon, he was arrested and briefly imprisoned at age fifty-two. In 1662, Milton married Elizabeth Minshull, who survived him. He first published *Paradise Lost* in 1667 in ten books, altering it into the classic epic of twelve books by 1674, the year he died at age sixty-six. In 1671, he had published *Paradise Regained* and *Samson Agonistes.*

A hundred and fifty years later, Samuel Taylor Coleridge wrote:

> My mind is not capable of forming a more august conception than arises from the contemplation of this greatest man in his latter days: poor, sick, old, blind, slandered, persecuted: "Darkness before and danger's voice behind," in an

> age in which he was as little understood by the party for whom, as by that against whom, he had contended, and among men before whom he strode so far as to dwarf himself by the distance; yet still listening to the music of his own thoughts, or, if additionally cheered, yet cheered only by the prophetic faith of two or three solitary individuals, he did nevertheless "argue not / Against Heaven's hand or will, nor bate a jot / Of heart or hope; but still bore up and steer'd / Right onward." (Schmid 239)

The English Epic

Could *Paradise Lost* have been written in rhyming couplets, or any rhyme scheme other than blank verse? Dante's *terza rima* (*aba bcb cdc*...etc.) served to evoke the tightly layered, nine-circled structure of each of the three domains, *Inferno, Purgatorio,* and *Paradisio* in the *Divine Comedy.* Yet, to evoke the "darkness visible," the "palpable obscure," the vast unmeasured spaces of both the abyss of the fallen angels and of the "vast vacuity," Satan travels through to the created world to foster the imagination beyond measure; could Milton have endeavored such an ambitious scope in any but the blank verse? Blank verse surrenders anew, at the end of each pentameter line, the sound structures rhyme provides. Calliope, the epic muse, can scarcely be confined in rhyme. As previously noted, blank verse allows the spirit of the English language to surrender some of its "soul," its musicality, to allow the ego of the reader the freedom to be more thoughtfully active, considering the spirit of the subject. The "sound transparency" of the English blank verse allows the spiritual soul, the consciousness soul, to be more independently, objectively active in its explorations of human experience.

> Of man's first disobedience, and the fruit
> Of that forbidden tree, whose mortal taste
> Brought death into the world, and all our woe,
> With loss of Eden, till one greater Man
> Restore us, and regain that blissful seat,

Sing, heavenly Muse, that on the secret top
Of Oreb, or of Sinai, didst inspire
That shepherd who first taught the chosen seed
In the beginning how the heavens and the earth
Rose out of Chaos; or if Sion hill
Delight thee more, and Siloa's brook that flowed
Fast by the oracle of God, I thence
Invoke thy aid to my adventurous song
That with no middle flight intends to soar
Above the Aonian mount, while it pursues
Things unattempted yet in prose or rhyme.
Paradise Lost (opening sentence)

In fact, at the end of each line Milton, the blind composer/poet/dictator, and we the readers stand, like Satan in Book Two, poised on the edge of the abyss with all possibilities before us, in terms of sound and, hence, in terms of sense.

...So eagerly the fiend
O'er bog or steep, through strait, rough, dense, or rare,
With head, hands, wings, or feet pursues his way,
And swims or sinks, or wades, or creeps, or flies."

With blank verse no rhyme dictates, or limits, any direction of thought the poet may wish to, or need to, pursue. Or, perhaps even more like Adam and Eve leaving Eden, at the end of *Paradise Lost*,

The world was all before them, where to choose
Their place of rest, and Providence their guide:
They hand in hand, with wandering steps and slow,
Through Eden took their solitary way.

Both Milton the poet and we the readers have what for some people, and especially for the rational-mind soul consciousness, would be an agonizing, unbearable freedom, but freedom that allows the consciousness to explore in any and all possible directions, therefore having the need to choose anew at the end of each pentameter line. Such freedom is necessary for any poet, according to Milton, undertaking the great epic of a language, as with Homer, as with Virgil (though not for Dante in his *terza rima*). Such freedom is especially needed by any poet daring to undertake so vast a subject as the original Fall from heaven, the Creation, and the Fall of humankind from Eden, particularly from a Protestant point of view. And hence such freedom may especially be called for early in the era of the consciousness soul. (The era of the development of the consciousness soul for all of humanity extends from the early 1400s well into the fourth millennium.) Such literature, written in blank verse, can serve to train the soul toward the freedom to act appropriately in the moment—action not dictated merely by previous patterns. This freedom is essential for the maturing consciousness soul.

Milton's syntax, or sentence structure, is rendered possible by the blank verse and serves the epic scope of *Paradise Lost*. In other poetry, the rhyming couplet trains our thinking to live in the scope of the two-line feeling (sentience) or thought (sentence). The openness of the blank verse allows Milton to begin his epic with a fifteen-line, single-sentence invocation that unfolds phrases and dependent clauses as Chaucer does, opening dimensions within dimensions within dimensions of thought, all anchored by the essential, unifying thought. In response to contemporary criticism of the lack of heroic couplets, Milton explained blank verse in his introduction to *Paradise Lost* as "the sense variously drawn out from one verse to another," a challenge that most of his contemporaries seemed to find difficult to sustain. Especially for modern Americans, who tend to think in action-snaps no longer than pistol shots or "sound bites," Milton's syntax, reinforced by the blank verse, exercises, stretches, and expands our thinking, over vast unrhymed lines, generating an increasingly epic capacity for sustaining extensive thought content.

The irony of the impact the *Star Wars* trilogy of films had on North Americans in the 1970s and 1980s is that, while *Star Wars* clearly was a response to a folk-soul starvation for epic content, the medium has been insidious in its effect. The short frames (one to three seconds) have dramatically shortened rather than lengthened the viewers' "thoughtful" attention span, transforming the orientation of much of the film industry, and hence contracting the attention span of the film-viewing folk, having an effect just the opposite of the epic.

Let us remember the original classic epic, in Homer's extended, descending rhythm, of the dactylic hexameter: __uu__uu_u // u__uu__uu__u. The rhythm is "descending" because the first beat steps strongly onto the earth. Rudolf Steiner spoke of it in the context of epics as a rhythm of birth, or incarnation out of the divine. The same is true of the other epic rhythmic foot, the trochee, _u, as in the following.

> By the shores of Gitchee-Gumee
> By the shining Big-Sea-Water,
> Stood the wigwam of Nokomis
> Daughter of the Moon Nokomis.
>
> LONGFELLOW, *The Song of Hiawatha*

Why is Milton's *Paradise Lost*, the great epic of the English language, neither in Homer's dactylic hexameter, nor in the epic alternative, trochaic tetrameter, but in iambic pentameter instead? u__u__u__u__u__. This rhythm, by contrast, steps lightly in the first syllable. It ascends; Steiner spoke of it as an excarnating rhythm. The dactylic hexameter guided humanity into the rational soul era, beginning in the eighth century B.C.E. During that era, reason is being born as a human faculty. Virgil, writing shortly before the time of Christ, the turning point of time, writes his *Aeneid* in dactylic hexameter. Dante wrote *The Divine Comedy* (c.1300 C.E., near the end of the intellectual soul era) in iambic pentameter, *terza rima*. The iambic rhythm originally informed ancient Greek dramatic poetry, the vessel for exploring riddles of human destiny. Does the evolution of the epic from descending dactylic hexameter into ascending iambic pentameter reflect an incarnation, a merging of divine into human activity, and even into human destiny? Did the divine descent allow the human being to begin to ascend?

Does the combination of iambic pentameter and blank verse reflect a final poise possible in the English language, a perfect consistency of the medium, prepared as it was, through Chaucer, and the Elizabethans, especially Shakespeare? Just about a lifetime after the spirit of the English language is giving birth to Milton's epics *Paradise Lost* and *Paradise Regained*, Daniel Defoe is writing *Robinson Crusoe* (1719) and Richardson *Pamela* (1740) and Fielding *Tom Jones* (1749). A novel form of literature is soon to be born in England. Does the blank verse of Milton's epic reflect a final stage before the spirit of the English language devotes its forces to this new form, the novel?

> Sing Heavenly Muse, that...didst inspire
> That Shepherd, [Moses] who first taught the chosen Seed,
> In the Beginning how the Heav'ns and Earth rose out of
> Chaos:...
> And chiefly thou O spirit, ...from the first
> Wast present, and with mighty wings outspread
> Dove-like sat'st brooding on the vast Abyss
> And mad'st it pregnant.
>
> book one, 5–22

Whom is the English, Protestant, epic poet John Milton invoking? Ultimately, all the hierarchies work under the coordinated influence of the Trinity: the Creator Father, the Son who underwent death and resurrection for all humanity, and the Holy Spirit. We have considered that, in terms of language, the Bible portrays the event of the Tower of Babel as embodying a turning point. When humanity tried to build a tower up to the heavens, God insured that people would not understand one another's language. The "one human tongue shattered into many." The Holy Spirit offers the antidote to perennial human misunderstanding. As noted in chapter 7 from the King James Bible, Acts 2: 1, forty days after the death and resurrection of Christ at Whitsun, the eleven disciples were gathered in an upper room. The Holy Spirit descended upon them in the form of a flaming tongue above each one's head. When the disciples went forth into the world, they had become able to understand the languages of whatever people they met. The seed had been offered for the "rejoining," the "remembering" of one human tongue, one language. Babel had been healed, made whole.

In the present book, we want to understand the workings of the spirit of the English language. From the Protestant Christian perspective, the Trinity precedes creation. "Before Abraham was, I am" (John 8:58) reflects Christ's eternal being. The Holy Spirit is that "Spirit of God" that "moved upon the face of the waters" (Genesis 1:2) before the Father-God Creator got to work. The Holy Spirit, often portrayed as a dove, is the divine entering the human, the immortal inhabiting the mortal, as embodied in the baptism of Christ at the River Jordan. "And Jesus, when he was baptized, went straightway out of the water, and lo, the heavens were opened unto him, and he saw the Spirit of God descending like a dove, and lighting upon him" (Matthew 3:16). For the Christian poet, the Holy Spirit becomes the Christian equivalent of the ancient Greek inspiring muse. For whom does this blind Christian poet speak, not sing, his epic?

Whereas the blind Homer originally sang his epics to courts of noble lords and ladies, blind Milton dictates his epic to be read in a printed copy, which, like the Protestant Bible itself, is available to be read by any literate individual, whenever and wherever one wishes. The Protestant epic of the 1600s in England has some of the democratic flavor of both the Protestant Bible in the vernacular and the newest form of literature just on the verge of birth, the novel. The implication of the Gospel's image of the tongues of flame is that, eventually, all would be able to understand all.

> And chiefly Thou O Spirit, that dost prefer
> Before all Temples th'upright heart and pure.
> Insruct me, for Thou know'st; Thou from the first
> Wast present, and with mighty wings outspread
> Dove-like satst brooding on the vast Abyss
> And mad'st it pregnant:...
>
> *Paradise Lost*, I, 17–21

The preferred temple of the Holy Spirit is anyone's "upright heart and pure."

Although Milton clearly invokes the Holy Spirit as his muse, William Blake, born a century after Milton was composing *Paradise Lost* and considering himself Milton's poetic disciple, nevertheless had a surprising perspective on Milton's muses. In his *Marriage of Heaven and Hell,* Blake wrote,

> ...in Paradise Lost Reason is call'd Messiah
> And the original Archangel, or possessor of the command of the heavenly host, is call'd the Devil or Satan, and his children are call'd Sin and Death.
> But in the Book of Job, Milton's Messiah is call'd Satan....
> in Milton, the Father is Destiny, the Son a Ratio of the five senses, & the Holy-ghost Vacuum!

> Note: The reason Milton wrote in fetters when he wrote of Angels & God, and at liberty when of Devils & Hell is because he was a true Poet and of the Devil's party without knowing it.

Blake, master of imagination, as we shall see later in chapter 11, felt Milton's Christ to be a reflection of the faculty of reason grounded in the five senses. It's as though Blake recognized Milton being the "Lady" of his university years scoffing at his fellows' theatrics, the "good" Christian poet, not allowing what the Greeks might have recognized as Dionysian influence when he, Milton, was attempting to portray Christ poetically. Blake the poet experienced Milton's poetic language as most vital and most inspired when portraying Satan and his fallen host. Hence, Blake's voice, in his own "Hell" in *The Marriage of Heaven and Hell,* claims Milton as being of the Devil's party, a way of paying tribute to the energy of Milton's imagination in the Satan sections of *Paradise Lost.*

Can we imagine that Milton, in spite of some of Blake's qualifications, invoked the Holy Spirit successfully to help sing the epic of the English language? Can we imagine the spirit of the English language, that archangel, to be working in conjunction with both Calliope, the ancient Greek muse of epic poetry, as well as, perhaps ultimately, the Christian Holy Spirit? It is not as though Milton's *Paradise Lost*, Protestant democratic though it may be, inhabits the imaginations and ear-memories of all English speaking peoples, which Shakespeare does to a substantial degree. Nevertheless, *Paradise Lost* remains the primary epic of the English language, having significantly influenced primary English poets, notably Blake in his epics (one even titled *Milton*), Wordsworth in his effort at a subjective epic, *The Prelude*, and recently Nobel Laureate Derek Walcott in the grand, extending syntax of his lines, and in his epic effort, *Homeros. Beowulf*, in old Anglo-Saxon, is our first English epic. Nevertheless, John Milton's *Paradise Lost* remains the most ambitious and accomplished epic in the English language, the largest in scope, the most universal in content, among the most distinct in language, the English epic most likely to remain a thousand years from now.

Emerson described the English language as being the sea into which pour all other languages as tributaries. Is not this image almost the complementary image of the Whitsun tongues of flame, enabling the apostles to understand peoples of all languages? If any language has been evolving in recent centuries to become, during this past half-century, the language through which different peoples are able to understand and communicate with each other, it is the English language. A human language is different from tongues of flame, but is it fair to imagine this English language inflamed, inspirited, inspired by the Holy Spirit? Milton invites it into his epic. I think we can experience such influence in universally accessible passages, such as Satan's encounter with Sin and Death. One can reasonably imagine that Milton, invoking the Holy Spirit into his epic, invites it to some significant degree into the work of the language as a whole, in conjunction with the spirit of the language, the particular archangel.

For example, Satan, solitary, leaving Pandemonium en route to the created world, arrives at the Gates of Hell:

> And thrice threefold the Gates; three fold were Brass,
> Three Iron, three of Adamantine Rock,
> Impenetrable, impaled before the circling fire,
> Yet unconsum'd. Before the Gates there sat
> On either side a formidable shape;
> The one seem'd Woman to the waste, and fair,
> But ended foul in many a scaly fould
> Voluminous and vast, a Serpent arm'd

With mortal sting: about her middle round
A cry of hell Hounds never ceasing bark'd
With wide *Cerberean* mouths full loud, and rung
A hideous Peal; yet, when they list, would creep,
If aught disturb'd their noyse, into her womb,
And kennel there, yet there still lurk'd and howl'd,
Within unseen....The other shape,
If shape it might be call'd that shape had none
Distinguishable in member, joint, or limb,
Or substance might be call'd that shadow seem'd,
For each seem'd either; black it stood as Night,
Fierce as ten Furies, terrible as Hell;
And shook a dreadful Dart...

Paradise Lost, II. 645-659, 666–672

So the Word evokes, through Milton, Satan's progeny: his daughter Sin, with whom he begets hellhounds, and his son Death, whom he battles. The spirit of the English language works with the lyric muse Euterpe to prepare young John Milton for his unique work with the epic muse Calliope. The same can be said of Milton's devoted yet courageously differing disciple William Blake.

Chapter 11

The Eighteenth Century and Blake

The Eighteenth Century

When the monarchy was restored in 1660, when Charles II was invited to resume the rule on the throne of England and the "Paradise" of the Civil Government was lost, surrendered, the theaters of England were allowed to reopen. The comic muse Thalia was allowed to be active once again in Restoration comedies such as Oliver Goldsmith's *She Stoops to Conquer.* However, Melpomene, the tragic muse, was permitted to sing only with clipped wings, blinded eyes and a muffled voice. When a tragedy was performed, a *Hamlet* or a *Lear* culminated with a happy ending, diminishing tragedy in the mood of restoration. The pendulum swing to monarchy was reinforced with a general interest in Rome, engendering a neoclassical, Augustan age in English Literature. Two major poets and expert translators of Greek and Latin, John Dryden and Alexander Pope, were masters of metrical perfection, verbal wit, and rhyming "heroic" couplets.

It seems that the epic muse Calliope gives each language one major work, usually relatively early in the development of that language. Greek received two, through Homer's *Iliad* and *Odyssey*; Latin received Virgil's *Aeneid*, Italian Dante's *Divine Comedy*, German *The Niebelunglied*, and English Milton's *Paradise Lost.* After Milton, Calliope could only be played with and satirized in English, as in Pope's mock epic, *The Rape of the Lock.*

And now, unveil'd, the *Toilet* stands display'd,
Each Silver Vase in mystic Order laid.
First, rob'd in White, the Nymph intent adores
With Head uncover'd, the *Cosmetic* Pow'rs.
A heav'nly Image in the Glass appears,
To that she bends, to that her Eyes she rears;
Th' inferior Priestess, at her Altar's side,
Trembling, begins the sacred Rites of Pride.
Unnumber'd Treasures ope at once, and here
The various Off'rings of the World appear;
From each she nicely culls with curious Toil,
And decks the Goddess with the glitt'ring Spoil.
This casket *India's* glowing Gems unlocks,
And all *Arabia* breathes from yonder Box.
The Tortoise here and Elephant unite,
Transform'd to *Combs,* the speckled and the white.
Here Files of Pins extend their shining Rows,
Puffs, Powders, Patches, Bibles, Billet-doux.
Now awful Beauty puts on all its Arms;
The Fair each moment rises in her Charms,
Repairs her Smiles, awakens ev'ry Grace,
And calls forth all the Wonders of her Face;
Sees by Degrees a purer Blush arise,
And keener Lightnings quicken in her Eyes.
The busy *Sylphs* surround their darling Care;
These set the Head, and those divide the Hair,
Some fold the Sleeve, whilst others plait the Gown;
And Betty's prais'd for labours not her own.

The situation of this epic, the eighteenth century equivalent of Helen at Troy, is Belinda in her boudoir, summoning, as Agamemnon leading the Greeks, all the instruments and beings involved in her war for beauty. In his *Essay on Man,* Pope said, "The Proper study of Man is Man." We can look at the pervasive rhyming couplets of Dryden and Pope as indicative of the soul-character of the time. What had first emerged in Chaucer's time as the culmination of the intellectual soul stage of development reappears three hundred to four hundred years later. After the incredible, unparalleled consciousness soul expansion through Elizabethan, especially Shakespearean, drama and Milton's epic, the language of the English poetry of the late seventeenth and early eighteenth centuries seems to suffer a perhaps inevitable contraction, even retraction, into a mode, a form, more characteristic of the reason-oriented rational soul. After all, the French thinkers Descartes ("I think: therefore, I am"), Voltaire ("If God did not exist, it would be necessary to invent Him... History should be written as philosophy"), and Rousseau, whose Social Contract offered modern humanity a way to create society without losing independence, especially generated celebration of the Age of Reason, the Enlightenment.

In England the Royal Academy of Science was able to work with full public support of both government and patrons. But by the end of its years as the "Invisible College" during Cromwell's regime, the Academy allowed no vestige of the Rosicrucian dimensions characteristic of many of its founding members such as Francis Bacon, John Dee, Robert Fludd, and even Robert Boyle. Sir Isaac Newton's rational explanations of the mathematically calculable paths of the planets, strictly according to the physical laws of gravity, strongly enhanced people's experience of the evacuation of the gods, or even of any being, from the clockwork machine of the universe.

Samuel Johnson shed the spark of his wit and the light of his reason on nearly everything, creating the English language's first dictionary. Jonathan Swift applied his satirical wit in *Gulliver's Travels.* The Scottish philosopher John Locke influenced many people's assumptions with *Tabula Rasa*, the notion that the human soul is a blank slate, informed fully by impressions from outside. This variety of influences combined into a new confidence in humanity's rational capacities. Into this general celebration of the light of human reason was born a different kind of light, a "holy" flame.

The Life of William Blake (1757–1827)

In 1778 in London, a young man asked an illiterate young woman, Catherine Boucher, after she listened to his tale of unrequited love, "do you pity me?" When she answered "yes," he intuited that she would become his lifelong soulmate, but he could not have imagined that she would become perhaps the most fruitful "helpmate" in the history of the arts. That same year, the twenty-one-year-old engraver's apprentice was acknowledged as one of the most promising of England's young artists, being awarded six years' free tuition at the recently formed Royal Academy, directed by the eminent painter Sir Joshua Reynolds. Little could Reynolds have imagined that, when William Blake was rescued from obscurity more than a century later, he would be remembered more as a poet than as a painter. Nevertheless, the promising young painter would do more than any artist ever to marry the image and the word; he would become the most spirited and spiritual disciple of the spirit of the English language.

Emmanuel Swedenborg, the Swedish seer and mystic, had written that the Last Judgement had been accomplished in the spiritual world in 1757, that the former Heaven and former Earth had passed away, and that all things had become new (Ackroyd 18). In London, at 7:45 p.m., Nov. 28, 1757, Swedenborg's eventual though temporary spiritual disciple, William Blake, was born, the third of seven children, to Catherine Hermitage and James Blake, a hosier, both of whom were dissenters, practicing their faiths independently of contemporary established religions. William said, years later, that there was "an angel at my birth" (Ackroyd 17). His baptismal font included carvings of the tree of life, of the serpent offering the forbidden fruit to Adam and Eve, of Noah, John the Baptist, and Jesus Christ.

Young William's head, perhaps large for a child, would remain unusually large as an adult. His large brown eyes, under a high, broad brow, were crowned by golden-red hair. A tough, vigorous boy with powerful shoulders, he remained short as a man of five feet, five inches. At the age of four, he saw God's face in the window, and began to scream. At the age of eight, he saw angels in the trees like stars. He saw angels among the haymakers. William's father, who initially threatened to beat him for lying, was so influenced by his wife Catherine's gentle sense that he did not send William to school, recognizing him as too sensitive. William's visions continued his whole life.

He spent much of his early youth wandering alone, both through London's "uncharter'd" streets and through the fields, streams, and woods of the city's rural outskirts. Young William had an early gift for drawing and verse, liking to hang them on the walls of his mother's room. At the age of ten, William was enrolled in the Pars Drawing School, where he began his lifelong tutelage under the line and color in the works of the three masters, Michelangelo, Raphael, and Dürer.

At the age of fifteen, William Blake formally began his seven-year apprenticeship with James Basire, traditional engraver and copier. In the spirit of the medieval guild, William was enrolled as "Apprentice in the Art and Mystery of his Profession." His contract required him "not to fornicate or marry,... not dice,... or haunt Taverns or Playhouses" (Ackroyd 42). In fact, right down the street from Basire's Engraving shop was the Freemasons' tavern, and directly across the street was the Freemasons' hall. While Blake does not seem to have become a Freemason formally, his work reflects profound absorption of primary Masonic imagery, most potently perhaps the compasses in his drawing of Newton and the best-known "Ancient of Days." Young William would have learned of Hiram Abif, skilled in any manner of engraving, the builder of the Temple of Solomon, and he would have learned of the ultimate engraver, God, carving the tablets for Moses. The Freemasons, having emerged in the mid-late 1600s, were increasingly permeating European culture, nurturing esoteric histories as background for energetic and innovative public works.

During his adolescence, learning the craft of engraving, William Blake trained his eye for truthful, accurate observation. He schooled his hand according to the lawfulness of line. Applying acid to copper, he was applying fire to matter. He worked long, hard, twelve-hour days. He stated, "I have a great ambition to know everything" (Ackroyd 56). When he returned to his room at night, he read, took notes, and practiced mirror writing, for every word appearing on an engraving had first to be etched in reverse on the copper plate. Blake deliberately practiced mirror writing, an activity Leonardo had employed naturally, reinforcing a reverse-image relationship to normal physical reality and strengthening William's already-common experiences of the spiritual world. Galway Kinnell said of Blake's mirror writing that it seemed to appear from the inside of the person.

The master Basire sent his apprentice Blake to spend months of drawing and engraving at Westminster Abbey, England's primary Gothic Cathedral. During his time there, young William witnessed a rare event that had a powerful impact on him. The tomb of King Edward I, who had died in 1307, was opened as part of the general interest in recovering England's pre-Norman past. The image of the perfectly preserved body of the leader of the English folk, dressed in robes of red satin embroidered with jewels and lined with damask and cloth of gold, fused past, present, and future in a lasting impression, leading to the red and gold that reappear often in both his paintings and poems.

The young draftsman-engraver gradually became a master of line, under the primary influence of England's own medieval Gothic tradition, an influence even more deeply reinforced in the nascent poet through the power of the myths of Atlantis and the lore of the Druids, which he learned as he delved into England's ancient past. In addition to reading whatever history he could, young Blake read Spenser, Shakespeare, Milton, Ossian, and Chatterton. Blake wrote, still in his adolescence, "The pure soul will... put a path into the heaven of glory / Leaving a track of light for men to wonder at" (Ackroyd 63). For young Blake, drawing a line was less shading and darkening than an earthly hint at a ray of light, complementing the soul-spiritual illumination of a line of poetry.

At the age of twenty-one, in 1779, William Blake experienced two dramatic developments in his life, outwardly and inwardly, professionally and romantically. The artisan Blake was recognized as a fine potential artist and granted a place in the Royal

Academy, which the painter Sir Joshua Reynolds had formed only shortly before. The Royal Academy was part of a national effort to generate an English artistic tradition. In the Greek atmosphere of the Academy, William found himself scorning Reynolds' sense of "general beauty," as well as Reynolds' emphasis on oil pigments, preferring both the line and watercolor of fresco. Nevertheless Blake thrived in the company of fellow young artists, such as Flaxman, Stothard, Cumberland, and Sharp, soon to become known in contemporary England.

The second major development for twenty-one-year-old Blake occurred at a family gathering at the Boucher home. William, suffering from unrequited love, was noticed by the host's eighteen-year-old daughter Catherine. Upon sharing with her his woe, he asked, "Do you pity me?" When she answered, "Yes," he said, "Well then, I love you." Within a year or so they were married. Not only did William teach Catherine how to read and to write, but he also taught her how to draw, engrave, and paint. Blake and his "beloved" embarked on one of the great artistic marriage-partnerships in all history. William Blake, son of Catherine, brother of Catherine, husband of Catherine, having received his primary engraving training in the Gothic cathedral of Westminster Abbey, in his original myths, later created Cathedron as the place where human forms, bodies, were woven on looms.

In his promising twenties, William Blake, in an unknowing echo of Shakespeare and the Mermaid Tavern, spent much time at Matthew's over green tea and lemonade with individuals such as Boswell, Swinburne, the neo-Platonist mathematician Thomas Taylor, and Joseph Johnson, Blake's first publisher, who also published Thomas Paine, Henry Fuseli, William Godwin and Mary Wollstonecraft. Blake left London only once. He saw eternity there, "a human awful wonder of God."

> In Great Eternity every particular form gives forth or emanates
> Its own peculiar Light & the form is the divine vision
> And the Light is his Garment this is Jerusalem in every man.

Whereas the adolescent had been disciplined through line, the artist in his twenties explored light in his drawings and paintings. Blake was becoming what John Ruskin later called "one of the finest colorists of his time." Yet professionally, William suffered two shades of disappointment in his late twenties. Josiah Wedgewood sent Blake's friend Flaxman to Italy for seven years, but Blake failed to earn such a sponsorship. And when, in 1786, Boydell commissioned a Shakespeare Gallery by contemporary artists, Blake was not among the artists invited. What had earlier been recognized as promise was now being passed over.

When William was thirty, his nineteen-year-old brother Robert, newly enrolled in the Royal Academy, began to die of consumption. For a whole fortnight, William sat with Robert. At the last minute, Blake beheld Robert's released spirit ascend heavenward through the "matter-of-fact ceiling . . . clapping its hands for joy." Then William slept for three days and nights. Thirteen years later, William wrote, "With his spirit I converse daily and Hourly in the Spirit. . . . I hear his advice" (Ackroyd 101).

Around the time of Robert's death, Blake had been pondering on how to unite painting and poetry, the image and the word. Blake had been studying Swedenborg's explorations of the spiritual world while developing his friendship with the Swiss writer and artist Henry Fuseli, gifted in visual embodiment of nonphysical experiences. Robert, after his death, revealed to brother William through their daily conversations a new process of relief etching, with the letter raised instead of cut into the copper plate. William considered this new process to be a suitable medium for revealing spiritual realities through both word and image.

First, with a camelhair brush William painted the words and images on the copper plate with a mixture of salad oil and candle grease, in backwards writing. Second, this mixture resisted *aqua fortis* (vinegar, salt armanack, baysalt, and *verte de griz* purchased from the local druggist), which bit into the copper plate for three to four hours, down to one tenth of a millimeter. Third, Blake rolled burnt walnut oil or burnt linseed oil onto the raised lettering, and then made an imprint on Whitman paper. Fourth, after a preliminary "wash" with glue and water, William hand-painted words and images with a "distemper" of water, color pigment, and glue, each copy becoming individually colored. Now, on a practical, outward level, Blake could produce and print his own books on his own press. Inwardly, Blake was becoming the first English poet since Spenser to single-handedly create his own mythological reality.

At the age of thirty-three, William and Catherine moved to a part of London called Lambeth, where their house on the Thames had ten rooms and a garden. While William spent much of the time communing with the dead, including brother Robert, monarchs, Michelangelo, the Angel Gabriel, and the ghost of a flea, Catherine had become his potent partner in the many disciplines of his multi-media labors, particularly the many stages of preparing engravings. One friend, receiving no greeting at the gate, the front door, or the dining room door, opened the back kitchen door, to find William and Catherine in the garden, under the tree, unclothed, reading Milton's *Paradise Lost*, where Adam and Eve are being enlightened by the Archangel Raphael, before the Fall. During those years William also loved reading the ecstatic Christian poet St. Theresa and was already replacing his interest in Swedenborg with the Swiss physician-alchemist Paracelsus and the German cobbler-mystic Jacob Boehme.

Blake was etching many songs of experience on the other side of palm-sized, copper plates he'd used for *Songs of Innocence*. Blake's Song of Innocence, "The Chimney Sweeper," reflects as background the fact that in England May 1 was the one holiday for the "climbing boys" or "lily-whites," when they weren't out calling in the streets from pre-dawn dark to midday. According to Peter Ackroyd (123), on the day of the festivities they whitened their faces with meal, covered their heads with white powdered periwigs, and wore clothes with white lace. They wore pieces of foil and bright ribbons and, on each cheek, had a patch of gold leaf. They paraded through the city banging brushes and climbing tools. On that day they were the lords of misrule, white and clean and beautiful. These boys were sold, between the ages of four and seven, at twenty to thirty shillings for a seven-year apprenticeship. The average chimney was seven inches square. It wasn't unusual for a twelve-year-old chimney sweep to be a cripple on crutches, three-feet-seven-inches tall, with hair like hog bristles, and head blackened and scabbed like a warm cinder. William Blake, in his *Songs of Innocence and Experience*, was becoming, as Galway Kinnell has said, the only poet in our language to call out against child exploitation, racism, prostitution, and poverty, and (except maybe early Donne) the only poet to celebrate sexual love. Although he wore a red Jacobin hat in 1790, in initial sympathy with the ideals of the French Revolution, Blake did not share the atheistic, rationalistic traits of Godwin, Paine, and other radicals. In these years he wrote what later became the preface to his epic *Milton*.

> I will not cease from Mental fight
> Nor my Sword sleep in my hand
> Till we have built Jerusalem
> In England's green & pleasant land.

Inspired equally by Milton and Durer, by Shakespeare and Raphael, Blake was becoming our first and perhaps only poet-prophet-painter, as, in *America a Prophecy*, *Europe*, and *Los*, he painted plates directly, without engraving, creating some of his most beautiful illuminations.

In 1800, William Hayley, "epic" poet and biographer of Milton and Cowper, invited William and Catherine to move to his cottage by the sea in Felpham's Vale, Sussex, the only time the Blakes lived outside London. Here, Hayley and Blake together studied Greek, reading Homer and the New Testament, Hebrew, and Italian, reading Dante's *Divine Comedy*. Although Blake had two paintings exhibited at the royal Academy at the time, he had to come to terms with the fact that he was not enjoying an outwardly illustrious career. Embarking on a series of sixty to eighty biblical watercolors, he wrote, "I am more famed in Heaven for my works than I could well conceive. In my Brain are studies & chambers fill'd with books & pictures of old; & those works are the delight and study of Archangels. Why, then, should I be anxious about riches or fame of mortality" (Ackroyd 218).

Along the shore one day, Blake saw "particles bright forming the shape of a man, expanding, like a Sea without a shore, the whole natural world becoming 'One Man.'" Another time, also along the shore, he saw spirits of ancient poets and prophets as "majestic shadows, grey but luminous, superior to the common height of men." In Blake's garden one day,

> there was a great stillness among the branches & flowers, and more than common sweetness in the air; I heard a low and pleasant sound...At last I saw a broad leaf of a flower move and underneath I saw a procession of creatures, of the colour and size of green & grey grasshoppers, bearing a body laid out on a rose-leaf, which they buried with songs, and then disappeared. It was a fairy funeral.

In addition to seeing social injustices clearly in the world around him, William Blake was capable of various kinds of vision, ranging from spiritual hierarchies, through the dead, to the kingdom of the elementals. (Ackroyd 228)

William and Catherine's seventeen-year honeymoon continued, as she devotedly helped him with engravings and paintings. Perhaps inspired by both Homer and Dante, William, in his mid-forties, began writing epic verse, initially *Vala*, later to become the never published *Four Zoas*. Two dynamics drew their three-year stint by the sea to a close. One was that the dampness made Catherine suffer acutely from rheumatism. The second was a consequence of the same choleric temper that had led adolescent Blake to throw a boy off the roof of Westminster Abbey. An inebriate dragoon, private Scofield, made a scene at Blake's gate; Blake picked him up by the lapels and propelled him a good fifty yards down the road. Scofield, pressing charges, accused Blake of having uttered condemning words of the English government, a serious, seditious charge of treason, in a time of Napoleon's ascendancy to power. An observer at the trial remembered that, as Blake uttered the word "False!...one only remembered his flashing eye" (Ackroyd 240). The dragged-out proceedings of his trial haunted Blake for two years, accentuating an already innate nervous fear, until he was acquitted. The experience, however, catalyzed their return to London in October 1803 and to a two-room apartment at 17 South Molton Street. With no garden, no trees, and no Thames, the Blakes essentially retreated to "Poverty Lane" for the next seventeen years.

When Blake was forty-seven, an exhibit of Old Masters, Dürer and Schongauer, Guliano Romano, and Michelangelo re-inspired Blake's "intellectual vision." After twenty years "as a slave bound in a mill among beasts and devils," as an artisan not an artist, Blake deliberately shed the influence of classical art, resuming a more native English style (Ackroyd 268). William undertook no commercial designs for the next eleven years. Still suffering from the aftermath of the trial, Blake began a series of nineteen watercolors of the Book of Job, an exploration that would grow over the years to seventy paintings and engravings. He did illustrations of England's own *Canterbury Tales*. He published, at the age of fifty, *Auguries of Innocence*, potent, seed-like proverbs, generative with prophetic wisdom.

The same year, 1807, he finished *The Four Zoas*, his primary mythic-psychological epic, exploring the mysteries of the human being. Initially, Blake had explored the duality, the contraries of Urizen (reason), the white-haired oppressor and Orc (desire), the young, fiery rebel. He discovered, lo and behold, that Orc tended to become Urizen, who then begat a new Orc, a dynamic trapped in a perpetual cycle. Blake began to realize that the only way for the human psyche to liberate itself from this trap was through the activity of imagination, eternal imagination, in its highest form called Urthona by Blake; in its human form, Los, portrayed as the blacksmith transforming fallen matter. In his myths, Blake developed a fourth being, Tharmas, associated with water. A century before Freud, Jung, and Rudolf Steiner, Blake was not only discovering this four-fold nature of the human being, but he was also discerning that, when the human I AM is not actively identifying, the human being is haunted by its abstracting "spectre," separating each of the four members from its own female emanation until, through imagination, the human being becomes reintegrated into one whole: Albion.

Simultaneously he had been working on his epic *Milton*, which was followed, over the length of a decade, by his work on *Jerusalem*.

Milton (4 copies)

The Microscope knows not of this nor the Telescope. They alter
The ratio of the Spectators Organs but leave Objects untouched
For every Space larger than a red globule of Mans blood
Is visionary and is created by the Hammer of Los.
And every Space smaller, than a globule of Man's blood, opens
Into Eternity of which this vegetable Earth's but a shadow.
The red Globule is the unwearied Sun by Los created
To measure Time and Space to mortal Men.

Jerusalem (5 copies)

All that has existed in the space of six thousand years
Permanent, and not lost nor vanish'd, all remaining still.
For everything exists & not one sigh nor smile nor tear,
One hair nor particle of dust, not one can pass away.

As we read more and more of his poetry, as we see more and more of his drawings and paintings, we should not forget that not only had Blake sung his *Songs of Innocence and Experience*, but also, it seems, throughout his life he continued to sing his poetic compositions, even his epics. This creator was continuously engaged multi-sensually. But when, in 1808, Blake mounted an exhibition of his works, the few people who came bought nothing. Catherine told a friend, "I have very little of Mr. Blake's company. He is always in Paradise." Her utmost devotion to her poet-painter-prophet mate is unparalleled in English literature. Some scholars think that, without Catherine, it is possible that none of Blake's works would have appeared. Together, the partners continued his explorations, in a variety of forms, lyric, panegyric, epic, dialogue, song, dramatic verse, in a variety of media, ink-wiping, white-line, black-line relief, reverse writing, full-page relief etchings, drawing, and painting. Friends visiting them at Molton Street found William and Catherine in threadbare clothes, with cold mutton for supper and no understanding of "holiday"; there was always the pleasure of work.

In Blake's early sixties, some young people who called themselves "the Ancients" began to appreciate the largely forgotten or ignored poet-painter, adopting him as their sage and mentor. John Varley and William Blake spent several deliberate nights, from 9 P.M. until to 4 A.M., summoning "visionary heads," which Blake would proceed to sketch. At the age of sixty-three, William moved with Catherine for the final time, to two rooms on the first floor of 3 Fountain Street, where at least they had the Thames "like a bar of gold' and Dürer's "Melancholia " on the wall. As Blake's health weakened, he continued the engravings of Job and the paintings of Dante's *Divine Comedy,* which some consider the best watercolors of the age. John Ruskin later considered, "In expressing conditions of glaring and flickering light, Blake is greater than Rembrandt." The accomplished engraver had become a master painter (Ackroyd 346).

Whereas the younger Blake had been sensitive in a way that made him often prickly with people, the elder sage rested in a kind, gentle manner. Children loved him, although he and Catherine never had their own. One of the Ancients remarked, "Blake and Coleridge, when in company, seemed like congenial beings, of another sphere, breathing for a while on our earth" (Ackroyd 361). Beset particularly with weakening gall bladder, sixty-nine-year-old William Blake spent his last months working on illuminations of the Bible and on Dante watercolors, which became suffused with brilliant, warm, golden colors akin to medieval illuminations.

In August 1827, the day of his death, William stopped his Dante work, which he had been trying to finish. He turned to Catherine, who was in tears. "Stay, Kate," he said; "keep just as you are—I will draw your portrait—for you have ever been an angel to me." When he completed it, he put it down, and then began to sing verses and hymns (Catherine called them songs of Joy and Triumph). He told Catherine they would never be parted. At 6 P.M., he expired "like the sighing of a gentle breeze." Richmond wrote, "Just before he died, his countenance became Fair, his eyes brighten'd and He burst out into singing of the things he saw in Heaven." Having been separated only two or three weeks in their forty-five years of marriage, Catherine said that after William's death, "he used to come and sit with her for two or three hours every day, talking, advising." She couldn't make transactions about selling any of his work "until she had an opportunity of consulting Mr. Blake." In October 1831, on her own death day, Catherine was calm and cheerful, "repeating texts of scripture and calling continually to her William, as if he were only in the next room, to say she was coming to him and wouldn't be long now" (Ackroyd 367, 368).

Most people have no idea of the number of fields in which Blake was a potent pioneer. William Blake, a good engraver, was one of the best colorists of the eighteenth century. He was one of the greatest psychologists, along with Shakespeare, Dickens, and Dostoyevsky, in all literature and one of the greatest individual myth-makers in all literature. As mentioned, Blake was the first poet in the English language to write against child exploitation, racism, and poverty. Galway Kinnell calls him the only prophet-poet in the English language. Kinnell also considers the concentrated intensity of Blake's short poems only to be matched in English by Emily Dickinson. In addition, Blake is one of the English language's few epic poets; his epics may become duly appreciated only in another century. Although he abhorred organized religion, Blake may be the most Christian poet in our language. And perhaps in the whole world, Blake is the artist who has most married image and word, painting and poetry, in the combined medium of his self-printed works. Hence, he is the spiritual grandfather of the "main lesson books" in Waldorf Education, as throughout their education Waldorf students create, as artfully as possible, their own books for each subject.

William Blake wrote the lyric poems most people associate with him, *Songs of Innocence and Experience*, mainly during his thirties, his intellectual-soul years. He wrote his prophecies, *America a Prophecy*, *Europe*, and *Los* during his late thirties, his consciousness-soul stage. He wrote his mighty epics, *Milton*, *Jerusalem*, and the *Four Zoas*, largely during his ripe forties, after his consciousness-soul stage, reaching far into the future. Of all of the poets of the English language, Blake was the man of most muses, the most selfless disciple of the Word, and the most original disciple of the spirit of the English language.

William Blake: The Poetry

One Song of Innocence, less known than most, is called *A Cradle Song.* This short poem weaves an entrancing lullaby with a simple, meditative texture of sounds, working almost more strongly than the imagery, the content:

A Cradle Song

Sweet dreams, form a shade
O'er my lovely infant's head;
Sweet dreams of pleasant streams
By happy, silent, moony beams.

Sweet sleep, with soft down
Weave thy brows an infant crown.
Sweet sleep, Angel mild,
Hover o'er my happy child.

Sweet babe, in thy face
Holy image I can trace.
Sweet Babe, once like thee,
Thy maker lay and wept for me,

Wept for me, for thee, for all.
When he was an infant small.
Thou his image ever see,
Heavenly face that smiles on thee,

Smiles on thee, on me, on all;
Who became an infant small.
Infant smiles are his own smiles;
Heaven and earth to peace beguiles.

The word *sweet* sounds six times in twenty lines, sometimes with *dreams* and sometimes with *sleep.* The "ee" sound, associated in the art of eurythmy with the planet Mercury, influenced by the god Mercury, the messenger between the Heaven and Earth, between gods and mortals, informs not only the opening stanza (sweet dreams, sweet dreams, streams, beams) but it informs all the stanzas. (Eurythmy is the movement art of visible speech and visible music, attempting to work objectively to reflect universal laws of spiritual science.) As the singing parent evokes the child's dreams in "silent, moony beams," in the opening stanza, the "i" resounds in the second stanza as the singer calls, "Angel mild, / Hover o'er my happy child." The "i" sound, which Rudolf Steiner associates with the moon, reflects the light of the Sun and evokes not only the angel's light over, and even within, the "child" in the second stanza, but also the sound intensifies in the middle stanza.

What has sounded in the "angel mild" and "my happy child" is reinforced in the middle stanza with "In thy face," and then, in what is essentially the mid-line of the whole poem, the *I* sounds in "I can trace," the adult speaker of the poem, presumably the parent of the child. The conscious adult knows, looking at the babe, that "once like thee, / Thy maker lay..." The "i" sound journeys, in the poem, from angel to child to adult, to the maker (Christ), culminating, in the final five lines, in a crescendo communion, a duet between Creator and infant, between Heaven and Earth, especially in the four-times-repeated *smiles*.

Blake carries *A Cradle Song* on four-beat lines, often with spondees, "Sweet dreams," crafting, with rhyming couplets, a meditative, entrancing lullaby. The consonant sounds most supporting this vowel activity, are above all the spirit-aspiring, sublimating *s*.

Galway Kinnell has said that Blake's "Infant Sorrow" is the first poem of the English language describing human birth. "A Cradle Song" reinforces the possibility that William Blake may be the greatest poet of incarnation in the English language, in the evocation of the texture, the tissue, the mood of new birth, and in the ultimate Christian sense of the divine becoming human. In that sense, as well as a number of others, William Blake may be the most Christian of poets in the English language.

The Clod and the Pebble

"Love seeketh not itself to please,
Nor for itself hath any care,
But for another gives its ease,
And builds a Heaven in Hell's despair."

So sang a little Clod of Clay
Trodden with the cattle's feet,
But a Pebble of the brook
Warbled out these metres meet:

"Love seeketh only Self to please,
To bind another to Its delight,
Joys in another's loss of ease,
And builds a Hell in Heaven's despite."

This simple song of experience reveals much of an essential dynamic in Blake's poetry, his craft, and, indeed, his worldview. The twelve-line poem is a study in symmetry. One of Blake's primary guidelines is "Without contraries is no Progression." It is not surprising that the teenage Blake—who had spent many of his free hours while apprenticed as an engraver, practicing mirror writing, and who as an adult wrote much of his poetry in reverse writing so it could be engraved in prints—would embody such symmetry in content and form. The Clod speaks in the first stanza in an alternating rhyme pattern: "please," "care," "ease," "despair," setting up the expected pattern of the whole poem.

In the middle stanza, the narrative voice of the poem concludes the Clod's song and introduces the Pebble's warble, breaking up the established symmetry of rhyme, precisely in the middle of the stanza, in the middle of the poem almost, one might say, at the mirror face. The rhyme starts as "Clay/feet," then changes to "Brook/meet" as the Pebble prepares to respond.

The Pebble's response mirrors the Clod's song almost precisely, replacing "not itself" with "only Self," starting with the same alternating rhyme, even with the same words, *please* and *ease*, yet altering the other sound from "care" and "despair" to "delight" and, in an intense, ever-so-slight twist, culminating with not "desp-air" but "desp-ite." Whereas the Clod challenged Hell's despair, the pebble champions Heaven's despite. Who wins? Neither. The contrary holds; the polarity holds sway; no judge comes down on one or the other.

Blake knows the kind of love, or identity, needed to regenerate spiritual humanity in the form of his mythical Albion. Blake knows the force and character of "My Spectre around Me Night and Day," the title of a short poem exploring the dynamic of the double. Blake, whom his wife Catherine said spent more time with the angels than with her, knows the power of the interfluence between the two worlds. Blake, the master artisan engraver, knows the precise relationship between two mirror images, and Blake, the creator of *The Marriage of Heaven and Hell*, knows the powerful, mysterious interplay between two seemingly opposite worlds, with each often wearing the face of the other. Never settle for Blake at face value.

From Blake's epic poem *Jerusalem*: *The Emanation of The Giant Albion:*

In every Nation of the Earth till the Twelve Sons of Albion
Enrooted into every Nation: a mighty Polypus growing
From Albion over the whole Earth: such is my awful Vision.

I see the Four-fold Man. The Humanity in deadly sleep
And its fallen Emanation. The Spectre & its cruel Shadow.
I see the Past, Present & Future, existing all at once
Before me; O Divine Spirit sustain me on thy wings!
That I may awake Albion from his long & cold repose.
For Bacon & Newton sheathd in dismal steel, their terrors hang
Like iron scourges over Albion, Reasonings like vast Serpents
Infold around my limbs, bruising my minute articulations

I turn my eyes to the Schools & Universities of Europe
And there behold the Loom of Locke whose Woof rages dire
Washd by the Water-wheels of Newton. black the cloth
In heavy wreathes folds over every Nation; cruel Works
Of many Wheels I view, wheel without wheel, with cogs tyrannic
Moving by compulsion each other: not as those in Eden: which

Wheel within Wheel in freedom revolve in harmony & peace.
WILLIAM BLAKE, *Jerusalem*, plate 15

Without paying close attention to this passage, let us simply observe that William Blake is not writing in the standard iambic pentameter of most English poetry at the time. Nor is he writing in the more usual four-beat line that constitutes much of his lyric poetry, which hearkens back partially to the Anglo-Saxon four-beat line influenced by his earlier experience in the Gothic cathedral of Westminster Abbey. In the timeless tradition of ancient ballads, the four-beat line may also have served him well. However, as the poet became increasingly the prophet, exploring the human psyche by clarifying complexities rarely made conscious before or since in poetry, he explored Christian mythological mysteries in original domains. He generated his own mythology, as no individual has perhaps ever done in poetry. William Blake changed, and he moved beyond the old sentient-soul four-beat line and even beyond the pentameter that had served Chaucer, Shakespeare, and Milton so well, so deeply, so vastly. Rather than hearkening back to the ancient Greek dactylic hexameter, Blake stretched to a new, essentially seven-foot line, to bear his epic explorations. "For Bacon & Newton sheathd in dismal steel, their terrors hang" (Ibid.)

In terms of content, it is crucial to understand that Blake wrestled into being an evolving clarity of understanding, through his prophecies and epics, of the fourfold human being, in its fallen form abstracted by its specter into separate faculties, each further abstracted from its own emanation until, through the activity of imagination, the human being can so identify with its fallen members, that it can reintegrate them into a re-spiritualized divine human form, the sleeping Albion, the spirit body rejuvenated, renewed. Blake's epics, unfamiliar to most readers, await attention. Yeats rediscovered Blake's lyric poetry after almost a century. Now, almost two centuries later, it may be time to rediscover Blake's epic poetry.

Chapter 12

Wordsworth

The Life of William Wordsworth (1770–1850)

An undistinguished young Englishman spent the dramatic year of 1792 in, of all places, France. For him, it was to be a year of crossing many borders. Having graduated from Cambridge University, he crossed the English Channel geographically into a French-speaking land. Politically, he witnessed and celebrated the revolutionary fervor of the people, the "democrats" struggling to overcome the aristocracy. Wordsworth felt that it was bliss to be alive in that dawn. Romantically, he fell in love with a French woman, even fathering a child. They intended to marry, but owing to both a lack of funds and the twisting political climate making it unsafe for any English person to remain in France, he was forced to return home, without sweetheart and child. The looming war between England and France prevented him from rejoining them. As a consequence, he realized that he would be unable professionally to fulfill his intention to become a minister. He lived in a cottage with his sister and wrote poetry. Little could anyone have imagined that, before long, William Wordsworth would revolutionize English poetry, eventually becoming Poet Laureate of England. Personal deeds and worldly events combined to force this young man to retreat from his imagined pulpit, enabling him quietly to cultivate an original relationship with the spirit of the English language.

William Wordsworth, one of four boys and a girl, was born April 17, 1770, in the Lake District of northwestern England.

His family had descended long ago from Viking invaders. At age eight, near the beginning of his schooling, he lost his mother. The four brothers boarded with a woman who nourished them well, and they wandered the hills and lakes. William read abundantly, as well, including, as he noted, Fielding's works, *Don Quixote,* and Swift's *Gulliver's Travels.* When William was thirteen and near puberty, the Wordsworths suddenly lost their father John, an attorney. Orphaned before reaching manhood, the brood of five supported one another as well as they could. From the age of seventeen until he reached twenty-one, he attended St. John's College, Cambridge University, reading in Greek, Latin, Italian, Spanish, French and English, while avoiding mathematics and generally experiencing an undistinguished academic career. The rough mannered, North Country man shone no light the aristocrats or university academics could recognize.

The summer of 1790, when William turned twenty, he fulfilled the pattern of many educated young English men, hiking the French and Italian Alps, 350 miles in two weeks, followed by two months of more leisurely wandering. Witnessing French revolutionary fervor from the periphery, William felt his own ideals kindled. He completed his degree at Cambridge in January 1791. When he returned the next year to France, he fell in love with Annette Vallon and fathered a daughter, Caroline. Political dangers and lack of money forced his return to England, without Annette and Caroline. Having assumed he would enter the clergy, he realized he would have to re-imagine his life. Wrought with conflicting loyalties between England and France, with guilt over Annette and Caroline, and paralyzed by the war, William had to battle mightily to wrest some sense of self from the confusion. As the French call for *liberté, égalité, fraternité* degenerated into the terror of the bloodthirsty guillotine, Wordsworth's political ideals cooled. In 1793, at twenty-three, he first visited Tintern Abbey, about which he would write five years later. During that period he spent time with the social theorist William Godwin and read Rousseau.

After a dying friend left him some income, William settled in Alfoxden, Somerset, southwestern England, with his sister

Dorothy, from whom he had long been separated, and devoted his energies to writing poetry. Nevertheless, it was his childhood Northumberland region, with its ancient Viking heritage, that permeated his voice. Hazlitt described him then as

> gaunt and don Quixote-like. He was quaintly dressed . . . in a brown fustian jacket and striped pantaloons. There was something of a roll, a lounge in his gait. . . . There was a severe, worn pressure of thought about his temples, a fire in his eye (as if he saw something in objects more than the outward appearance), an intense high narrow forehead, a roman nose, cheeks furrowed by strong purpose and feeling, and a convulsive inclination to laughter about the mouth, a good deal at variance with the solemn, stately expression of the rest of his face. . . . He sat down and talked very naturally and freely, with a mixture of clear gushing accents in his voice, a deep guttural intonation, and strong tincture of the northern burr, like the crust on wine. (Perkins 686)

In 1795, at age twenty-five, he met Samuel Taylor Coleridge, which began a fertile literary friendship. That year, too, a new legacy enabled Wordsworth to support himself more comfortably in Racedown, Dorsetshire. Hailing Wordsworth as "the best poet of the age," Coleridge moved nearby. Almost daily walks and talks led the two to engender a slender volume of poetry, *Lyrical Ballads*, initially published in 1798 anonymously when William was twenty-eight. Part of the catalyst for publishing the little book was to finance a trip to Germany for Wordsworth, Dorothy, and Coleridge. Not sharing Coleridge's ambition to go off and actually learn German, Wordsworth and Dorothy spent much time with each other, huddled by the hearth in the Hartz Mountains, leading Wordsworth to reflect on many scenes of his childhood among streams, rocks, trees, lakes, and hills. An impulse began to germinate to write a poem of epic scope, whose subject would be not a great hero on a great journey or fighting a great war, but, for the first time in the history of poetry, the journey of development of the poet himself. He would complete his first version of *The Prelude or, Growth of a Poet's Mind: Advertisement,* seven years later, in 1805, yet he would continue to revise it for the rest of his long life. Meanwhile, *Lyrical Ballads* was quietly selling and gradually altering the course of English poetry, especially through its emphasis on both immediate nature and contemporary speech as sources of poetry.

In 1799, he and Dorothy returned north and settled in Grasmere in the Lake District. Again, Coleridge settled nearby. The early years there yielded some of Wordsworth's best sonnets, which he added to the second edition of *Lyrical Ballads* in 1800, including his crucial preface, articulating his philosophy of poetry. Wordsworth declared his intention "to choose incidents and situations from common life, and to relate or describe them...in a selection of language really used by men." He stated his intention to use scenes and situations to explore and reveal the primary laws of human nature, chiefly regarding the manner in which we associate ideas in a state of excitement.

> I have said that poetry is the spontaneous overflow of powerful feelings; it takes its origin from emotion recollected in tranquility; the emotion is contemplated till by a species of reaction the tranquility gradually disappears, and an emotion, kindred to that which was before the subject of contemplation, is gradually produced and does itself actually exist in the mind. In this mood successful composition generally begins. (Perkins 329)

A prime example of poetry originating in emotion recollected in tranquility is "I Wandered Lonely as a Cloud."

> I wandered lonely as a cloud
> That floats on high o'er vales and hills,
> When all at once I saw a crowd,
> A host, of golden daffodils;
> Beside the lake, beneath the trees,
> Fluttering and dancing in the breeze.

Continuous as the stars that shine
And twinkle on the milky way,
They stretched in never-ending line
Along the margin of a bay:
Ten thousand saw I at a glance,
Tossing their heads in sprightly dance.

The waves beside them danced; but they
Out-did the sparkling waves in glee:
A poet could not but be gay,
In such a jocund company:
I gazed—and gazed—but little thought
What wealth the show to me had brought:

For oft, when on my couch I lie
In vacant or in pensive mood,
They flash upon that inward eye
Which is the bliss of solitude;
And then my heart with pleasure fills,
And dances with the daffodils.

In 1802, Wordsworth, at thirty-two, finally received his father's inheritance and returned with Dorothy to Calais, France, for the month of August to meet Annette Vallon and their daughter Caroline and to transfer guardianship officially to Annette. William, in spite of Dorothy's discomfort, would then be free that fall to wed Mary Hutchinson, a childhood friend from the Lake District. During that August, William, Annette, Caroline, and Dorothy often walked the beaches, perhaps generating imminent lines for Wordsworth's *Ode: Intimations of Immortality from Recollections of Early Childhood.*

Hazlitt said of Dorothy, whom he considered a better diarist than poet, "Her eyes were not soft, as Mrs. Wordsworth's, nor were they fierce or bold; but they were wild and startling." Although William remained quite close to Dorothy for some years, William's close brother John drowned in 1805, and his friendship with Coleridge began to deteriorate, breaking finally in 1810, when William was forty. Coleridge's decreasing physical health, afflicted partly by addiction to laudanum, an alcoholic mixture of opium, affected his emotional health adversely and strained the taciturn northerner's capacity for compassion. Wordsworth's great decade of poetry had been between the ages of twenty-seven and thirty-seven (1797–1807), when *Ode: Intimations of Immortality* was published. Wordsworth's greatest poetic fertility occurred essentially during his intellectual-soul years, enhanced richly through his connection with Coleridge. Afterward, religious conversion to the Church of England, as well as family crisis, may have diffused some of his poetic concentration. Two of William and Mary's five children died in 1812.

In 1813, at forty-three, Wordsworth's appointment as Stamp Distributor of Westmoreland reflected his growing recognition as a poet of national stature. Although less prolific, he enjoyed recognizing and encouraging younger poets. Shouldering the burden of Dorothy's physical and mental decline, including depression and instability, became increasingly difficult. Grasmere remained his primary home for the rest of his life. By 1820, when Wordsworth was fifty-eight, he and Coleridge reconciled and toured the Rhineland together.

In 1843, at seventy-three, in recognition of his venerable poetic accomplishments, William Wordsworth was chosen as Poet Laureate of England. Only after Wordsworth died in 1850, at the age of eighty, would his masterpiece, *The Prelude or, Growth of a Poet's Mind: Advertisement*, be published, one of the few candidates in the English language for an epic poem, after Milton's *Paradise Lost.* Wordsworth had always considered this long poem too personal to be published in his lifetime; he had thought of it as his "Poem to Coleridge." William Wordsworth and Samuel Taylor Coleridge were two brothers of the Word. Through them the spirit of the English language, and particularly the muse of lyric poetry, worked in one of the most fertile poetic partnerships the English language has known.

Wordsworth: The Poetry

Lines Composed a Few Miles above Tintern Abbey on Revisiting the Banks of the Wye during a Tour, July 13, 1798

Five years have past; five summers, with the length
Of five long winters! and again I hear
These waters, rolling from their mountain-springs
With a soft inland murmur.—Once again
Do I behold these steep and lofty cliffs,
That on a wild secluded scene impress
Thoughts of more deep seclusion; and connect
The landscape with the quiet of the sky.
The day is come when I again repose
Here, under this dark sycamore, and view
These plots of cottage-ground, these orchard-tufts,
Which at this season, with their unripe fruits,
Are clad in one green hue, and lose themselves
'Mid groves and copses. Once again I see
These hedge-rows, hardly hedge-rows, little lines
Of sportive wood run wild: these pastoral farms,
Green to the very door; and wreaths of smoke,
Sent up, in silence, from among the trees!
With some uncertain notice, as might seem
Of vagrant dwellers in the houseless woods,
Or of some Hermit's cave, where by his fire
The Hermit sits alone.

These beauteous forms,
Through a long absence, have not been to me
As is a landscape to a blind man's eye:
But oft, in lonely rooms, and 'mid the din
Of towns and cities, I have owed to them
In hours of weariness, sensations sweet,
Felt in the blood, and felt along the heart;
And passing even into my purer mind,
With tranquil restoration:—feelings too

Of unremembered pleasure; such perhaps,
As have no slight or trivial influence
On that best portion of a good man's life,
His little, nameless, unremembered acts
Of kindness and of love. Nor less, I trust,
To them I may have owed another gift,
Of aspect more sublime; that blessed mood,
In which the burthen of the mystery,
In which the heavy and the weary weight
Of all this unintelligible world,
Is lightened:—that serene and blessed mood,
In which the affections gently lead us on,—
Until, the breath of this corporeal frame
And even the motion of our human blood
Almost suspended, we are laid asleep
In body, and become a living soul:
While with an eye made quiet by the power
Of harmony, and the deep power of joy,
We see into the life of things....

In *Tintern Abbey*, written when Wordsworth was twenty-eight, the poet turned his attention from the familiar natural world, in order to explore the real subject of the poem, the continuing, evolving life of that initial sensory experience in the being of the poet himself. An effective crafter of lyric rhyme, Wordsworth turned to blank verse for this delicate, new interior exploration, unprecedented in poetry. Wordsworth composed *Tintern Abbey* by heart on a long walk with Dorothy, writing it down only at the end of the day in his lodging.

The title, subtitle, and opening lines have both the substance and tone of fact, natural fact, of unaffected human experience. "Lines," place: Tintern Abbey; time: "July 13, 1798." It is almost a scientist's log entry. "Five years have passed, five summers...winters." Initial sense impressions, " hearing...water, beholding...cliffs," quickly yield " thoughts." The cliffs he sees "connect the landscape with the quiet of the sky," an image prefiguring the interior experience soon to be yielded by the poet's reflections on the nature around him.

...Once again
Do I behold these steep and lofty cliffs,
That on a wild secluded scene impress
Thoughts of more deep seclusion; and connect
The landscape with the quiet of the sky.

In the present, the "hedge-rows" are quickly altered by art, a drafter's eye: "hardly hedge-rows, little lines / Of Sportive wood run wild." In his reflections, the initial sense experience of five years previous becomes the basis for his relationship to the natural world around him, the first level of his human experience.

In the second stanza of the poem, the poet/speaker realizes that those initial sensory impressions have resurfaced frequently during the preceding five years in the form of "sensations sweet / felt in the blood, and felt in the heart." What was initially physical, external, and experienced through the senses continued to live in altered form, in both the medium (blood) and the source (heart) of the life body as "sensations sweet," with a connotation of beneficence, or positivism. As sensation, the experience is hardly a conscious one, yet it offers a replenishing activity, recurring independently of external environment, senses, and stimulation "in lonely rooms, and 'mid the din / Of towns and cities." The second level of experience is vital, "internal," barely conscious, yet pleasing, affecting the soul.

Marking the third level of experience, Wordsworth notices that such sensations can pass from the blood and heart, "even into my purer mind," from the living physical substance into a more interior realm of being. In the purer mind they evolve from sensations into feelings, yet still not fully conscious. Whereas sensations were "sweet," these feelings give "pleasure." Yet the pleasure is "unremembered." How much of our soul life is colored with various feelings of which we are largely unaware as we carry on with our life in the time and place of the moment? We can imagine Wordsworth in London, experiencing feelings of pleasure, whose origin he may at best be dimly conscious of being in experiences of winds, water, cliffs, and hedges from five years earlier.

These feelings are not just incidental, extraneous minor indulgences, ribbon on the wrapping, icing on the cake. The poet/speaker is conscious in his research that these feelings in fact "influence," flow into, "the best of a good man's life." These barely recognized feelings of pleasure inspire us to deeds, generate action, make us capable of "little, nameless, unremembered, acts / Of kindness and of love." Not grand, monumental, nation-changing acts, but more like a stream overflowing and pouring into nooks and crannies here and there along its greater course.

Such feelings, arising from original sensory experience and generating action, create a "blessed mood, / ...In which the heavy and the weary weight / Of all this unintelligible world / is lightened." Such feelings are a source of a primary levity in life, offsetting the gravity of the world, the "burthen" of the unintelligible mystery.

We are led to the fourth level of experience by these "affections," these feelings, in a realm beyond even, or deeper within, the "purer mind" of the third level, beyond feelings and actions. Only when "the breath of this corporeal frame / And even the motion of our human blood / [are] Almost suspended," are we "laid asleep / in body, and become a living soul:" In a realm beyond physical senses, beyond sensation, beyond even feelings and actions, almost a death-in-life, with breath and blood stilled, something yet finer becomes possible.

> While with an eye made quiet by the power
> Of harmony, and the deep power of joy,
> We see into the life of things.

The culminating fourth stage of the journey through memory of the original sensory impression is articulated in a triple braid of diphthongs. Diphthongs, combinations of vowel sounds, are relatively new notes sounding on the scale of human expression in the English language, as noted earlier, emerging in the fourteenth to fifteenth centuries. The dominating sound of the culminating three lines of the experience is the diphthong "I," a combination of "ah" and "ee." "While...eye...quiet." On the one hand, evoking a physical sense organ, the eye, and, on the other hand, rendering it "quiet," the poet creates an effect in which the "I" sound—implying willy-nilly the "I" of the self—sounds three times in the line, goes quiet in the next line, yet resounds centrally in the final line, "life..."

> While with an eye made quiet by the power
> Of harmony, and the deep power of joy,
> We see into the life of things.

Only with the eye quiet can the "I" (we) "see into the life of things."

How is the eye made quiet? By the "power" of harmony, by the "power" of joy. The diphthong "ow," formed by combining "ah" and "o," is perhaps as surprising a sound as "power" is surprising as a concept associated with harmony and joy. The third diphthong, in "joy," is formed from "o" and "ee." The word *joy* meant, for Wordsworth and Coleridge, no shallow "happy" or spritely "gay" (See Coleridge's *Dejection: An Ode*). Joy embodied a power as deep as the source of a mighty fountain. These three diphthongs, grafted hybrid vowels in "eye," "power," and "joy" do extra, super-invigorating work compared to pure vowels, affecting a sea change of soul. This quieting is no simple surrender—no withdrawing, abstracting, transcending; on the contrary, it empowers a higher faculty, a super-seeing. "We see into the life of things."

Wordsworth embodies an act of intuition, not into "spirit" or essence, but into "life"; not through abstractions, universals, or generalities, but into the life of "things," that good old, inescapable, perennial, indestructible Anglo-Saxon word, embodying any mundane object in creation, yet ringing with the "ing" of *being*. Wordsworth is always the brusque descendant of Vikings from the North Country through the ways he wields the sword of the word.

In the spirit of blank verse, this delicate exploration of the evolving influence of the original sensory experience unfolds in a stanza of more than twenty-six lines in only two sentences: from "These beauteous forms..." (line 23) to "...Of kindness and of love" (36); then from "Nor less, I trust..." (36) through "...the life of things" (49).

> These beauteous forms, (23)
> Through a long absence, have not been to me
> As is a landscape to a blind man's eye:
> But oft, in lonely rooms, and 'mid the din
> Of towns and cities, I have owed to them
> In hours of weariness, sensations sweet,
> Felt in the blood, and felt along the heart;
> And passing even into my purer mind,
> With tranquil restoration:—feelings too
> Of unremembered pleasure; such perhaps,
> As have no slight or trivial influence
> On that best portion of a good man's life,
> His little, nameless, unremembered acts
> Of kindness and of love. Nor less, I trust, (36)
> To them I may have owed another gift,
> Of aspect more sublime; that blessed mood,
> In which the burthen of the mystery,
> In which the heavy and the weary weight
> Of all this unintelligible world,
> Is lightened:—that serene and blessed mood,
> In which the affections gently lead us on.,—
> Until, the breath of this corporeal frame
> And even the motion of our human blood
> Almost suspended, we are laid asleep
> In body, and become a living soul:
> While with an eye made quiet by the power
> Of harmony, and the deep power of joy,
> We see into the life of things.... (49)

Remembering Milton's appreciation of blank verse as "the sense variously drawn out from one verse to another," we can recognize that Wordsworth's use of blank verse here allows us to sustain our connection to the original sensory experience as it evolves though the four levels of experience, essentially the same yet altering its influence. One could even say that the extended blank verse, not allowing our minds to conclude, or close, each couple of lines, almost forces our consciousness to extend itself, openly evolving in the process. The iambic pentameter carries the ascending, heart-breathing rhythm of the experience. The open, unrhymed lines allow our minds to remain open through the whole of the exploration. The language becomes not simply a medium for communication, but as well a medium for transformation.

The rest of the poem *Tintern Abbey*, and indeed the rest of Wordsworth's poetry, offers many other dimensions. Yet, in a way, these two stanzas can serve effectively as a lens through which to discern essential ways in which Wordsworth worked with the spirit of the English language. First, in a way that interested Blake not at all (Blake was interested in nature essentially as revelation of spirit), in partnership with Coleridge, Wordsworth turned his attention in a new way to nature—not in the literary tradition of pastoral poetry, with its conceits. Rather, Wordsworth worked to overcome the Enlightenment's separation from Nature, the gap between subject and object, as natural science had been developing its ability to "know" the natural world "objectively." Wordsworth and Coleridge strove to look and listen to nature with an open mind, freshly observing not simply with the scientist's cold eye, but also with the open inner eye of the poet, allowing art (poetry) to be informed by "things" and by the laws that the conscious poet could experience actively in nature. In this sense, Wordsworth and Coleridge spearheaded in England the Romantic movement's healing of the Western world's alienation from nature. Second, Wordsworth was keen to find poetic diction that imitates not the language of previous poetry, but rather the intonations and cadence of the living speech of the time and people of place, people "rooted" in fields, woods, and streams.

Third, *Tintern Abbey* sounds a note that Wordsworth elaborates in his attempt at a long poem in English. A devout admirer of Milton, Wordsworth did not presume to write a second English epic, after *Paradise Lost*. However, he dared an undertaking that was courageous in a different way. Throughout the history of Western poetry, poems had a subject: journeys or battles (epic); the destinies of individuals and families (drama); love for another, traditionally a woman (lyric). In Wordsworth's *Prelude* the subject is not Greek, Biblical, Norse, or Arthurian; for the first time, a poem's subject was nothing other than the literal subject writing the poem, the development of the poet himself. The subject, always external previously, becomes internal. The self-awareness that Wordsworth applies to the levels of his own memory of one experience in *Tintern Abbey*, he turns to the larger scope of those incidents in his biography he can recognize as having influenced the development of his soul life as a poet.

Whereas Blake is constantly visionary, Wordsworth articulates in *The Prelude* (1805) that there are "in our existence spots of time/ Which with distinct pre-eminence retain/ A vivifying virtue." Coleridge wrote in *Biographia literaria* that Wordsworth's earlier poems reveal

> union of deep feeling with profound thought, the fine balance of truth in observing, with the imaginative faculty in modifying, the objects observed; and above all the original gift of spreading the tone, the atmosphere, and with it the depth and height of the ideal world..., of which, for the common view, custom had bedimmed all the luster, had dried up the sparkle and the dew drops (Richards 474).

Coleridge also said of Wordsworth in *Table Talk*:

> I think Wordsworth possessed more of the genius of a great philosophic poet than any man I ever knew, or, as I believe, has existed in England since Milton; but it seems to me that he ought never to have abandoned the contemplative position which is peculiarly—perhaps I might say exclusively—fitted for him. His proper title is *Spectator ab extra*. (July 21, 1832)

Coleridge recognized a distinct poetic kinship in Wordsworth and Goethe in their "peculiarity of utter non-sympathy with the subjects of their poetry. They are always, both of them, feeling for, never with, their characters" (Ibid., July 21, 1832).

Through Wordsworth the spirit of the English language found new sources, contemporary speech and actual living, not literary, nature. To see into the life of things, while exercising soul objectivity, is a capacity of the consciousness soul. To be *Spectator ab extra* ("spectator from outside"—think of Hamlet) is to experience life and the world from a consciousness soul perspective. To be able to think about one's thinking, about one's memory, is an activity of a next stage of development, what Rudolf Steiner characterized as spirit self. The attention is not just to the content, as in much twentieth century confessional poetry, but it endeavors to observe objectively the process.

Chapter 13

Coleridge

The Life of Samuel Taylor Coleridge (1772–1834)

In 1793, a brilliant young man returned to Cambridge University after a ludicrous misadventure. Having made quite a splash in a number of ways, including falling deeply into debt when he had first begun at Cambridge, he had sought to evade and perhaps solve his problems by enlisting in the cavalry under an alias. The notion, though romantic, was impractical: the young man, though brilliant, could not stay in the saddle. His older brothers had eventually to buy him out of the service. The rest of his university stint was somewhat like a summer storm, with unpredictable flashes of illumination, amidst broad patches of torpor.

Though a bumbler in the saddle, as a walker he was mighty. At the age of twenty-two, he set off on a five-hundred-mile walking tour. Passing through Oxford, he met young Robert Southey, a poet/scholar, with whom he envisioned an ideal new society in America. Although he failed to fulfill it, with unfortunate consequences for his own ensuing marriage, he inspired many English citizens to find new lives in America. Politically, he inspired audiences toward ending England's war with France. Theologically, he inspired audiences from the pulpit on Sundays. After one such sermon he walked forty miles to meet a young poet named William Wordsworth, initiating one of the most fertile friendships in literary history. Samuel Taylor Coleridge, perhaps the most brilliant mind in England in his day, became a kind of damaged archangel, a few of whose poems will always inform the English-speaking folk. Together, Wordsworth and Coleridge would help each other become primary poets, articulating a poetic revolution more profoundly successful than the French political one by which they had been initially enticed. This young man's omnivorous open-mindedness would lead him, through his many levels of work with the spirit of the English language—preaching, literary criticism, philosophy, theology, and poetry—to save the English people from their natural propensity for rational empiricism so they could be open to and for the possibilities of imagination.

Born Oct. 21, 1772, the youngest of ten children, to a county clergyman and his wife in Devon, young Samuel was large, fat, and black-haired, with grey, "astonishing" eyes. He soon became a little like the Biblical Jacob's Joseph, favored by the father, yet alone among the fold. "My Father was very fond of me, and I was my mother's darling—in consequence I was very miserable." In his second year he burned his hand reaching for fire in the fireplace, and spoke his first words, "Nasty Dr. Young," to the attending physician. When it was time for him to be inoculated, he refused to let his eyes be blindfolded, insisting on watching the doctor's lancet. At the end of his third year, he could read a chapter of the Bible. "So I became fretful and timorous, and a tell-tale; and the schoolboys drove me from play, and were always tormenting me, and hence I took no pleasure in boyish sports, but read incessantly" (Holmes 2).

"At six years old, I remember to have read Belisarius, *Robinson Crusoe*, and the strange tale of Philip Quarll, the English Hermit." Quarll spent fifty years on an island, at one point shooting with a homemade bow a large, beautiful sea bird, which he immediately regretted.

> And then I found the Arabian Nights' Entertainment...one tale of which (the tale of a man who was compelled to seek a pure virgin) made so deep an impression on me (I had read it in the evening while my mother was mending stockings) that I was haunted by specters, whenever I was in the dark—and I distinctly remember the anxious and fretful eagerness, with which I used to watch the window, in which

> the books lay, whenever the Sun lay upon them, I would seize it, carry it by the wall, & bask, and read. I was accustomed to race up and down the churchyard, and act over all I had been reading, on the docks, the nettles, and the rank grass. . . . (Holmes 7)
>
> So I became a dreamer, and acquired an indisposition to all bodily activity; and I was fretful, and inordinately passionate, and as I could not play at anything, and was slothful, I was despised and hated by the boys; and because I could read and spell and had, I may truly say, a memory and an understanding forced into an almost unnatural ripeness, I was flattered and wondered at by all the old women. And so I became very vain, and despised most of the boys that were at all near my own age, and before I was eight years old I was a character. (Holmes 11)

A precocious dreamer, he wandered much among the fields, streams, and streets outside London. He loved coming upon strangers and posing them unusual questions.

One night in his seventh year, he left the house in a rage over an older brother's taunting. He ended up spending a cold October night by a river, weakening his health from then on.

> I remember that at eight years old I walked with my father one winter evening from a farmer's house, a mile from Otter, and he told me the names of the stars and how Jupiter was a thousand times larger than our world, and that the other twinkling stars were suns that had worlds rolling around them; and when I came home he showed me how they rolled around. I heard him with a profound delight and admiration: but without the least mixture of wonder or incredulity. For from my early reading of fairy tales and genii, etc., my mind had been habituated to the Vast, and I never regarded my senses in any way as the criteria of my belief. I regulated all my creeds by my conceptions, not by my sight, even at that age. Should children be permitted to read romances, and relations of giants and magicians and genii? I know all that has been said against it; but I have formed my faith in the affirmative.

> I know no other way of giving the mind a love of the Great and the Whole. Those who have been led to the same truths step by step, through the constant testimony of their senses, seem to me to want a sense which I possess. They contemplate nothing but parts." (Letter to Poole, Oct. 16, 1797)

Young Samuel loved visiting the Pixies' Parlour, a sandstone cave beneath an old oak's roots overlooking the river, a mysterious place of goblins, ghosts and other folklore. He carved his initials there. He loved above all the river Otter itself, playing by it, in it, continuously moving, altering its form. And he loved a neighbor's spiral staircase. He later remembered, "the eye commanded the whole spiral ascent with the marbled pavement of the great hall from which it seemed to spring up as if it merely used the ground on which it rested. My readers will find no difficulty in translating these forms of the outward senses into their intellectual analogies" (Holmes 12).

At the age of nine, Samuel suffered a severe fever, during which his brother used to sneak up and read him Pope's *Homer.* When he asked his mother why the neighbor didn't come visit him, she said she feared catching the fever. Young Samuel replied, "Ah, Mamma, the four angels round my bed aren't afraid of catching it!" Those four angels, "Matthew, Mark, Luke, and John," he prayed to every night, in fervent belief, feeling even in later adult tribulations that they protected him (letter to Poole, Oct. 9, 1797).

One night that year, his father dreamed that death had touched him with his dart. The next night he died in his sleep, and young Samuel lost his strongest connection to his family. Later, reflecting on this loss, he wrote,

> When I was first plucked up and transplanted from my birthplace and family, at the death of my dear father, whose revered image has ever survived in my mind...Providence (it has often occurred to me) gave the first intimation, that it was my lot, and that it was best for me, to make of my way of life a detached individual, a *Terrae filius.*" (H. N. Coleridge 705)

After some time at a school in which Samuel knew his grammar better than his teachers, he lived for another while with an uncle in London.

> My uncle was very proud of me, and used to carry me from coffee-house to coffee-house and tavern to tavern. Nothing was more common than for a large party to exclaim in my hearing that I was a prodigy, etc., . . . so that while I remained at my uncle's I was most completely spoiled and pampered, both mind and body." (Holmes 24)

Nevertheless, he soon found a nourishing environment at Christ's Hospital School, and a lifelong intellectual companion, classmate Charles Lamb, who would later become a leading literary critic. There he might be among a swarm of friends, passionately discussing Greek tragedy. It was there he fell in love with a schoolmate's sister, yet unrequitedly. A successful scholar of the classics, he also plunged into medical studies, philosophy, and theology. In his final year, he was awarded substantial scholarships to university. Yet misfortune arrived and he lay long ill with rheumatic fever, his brother Luke died of fever, and his sister Nancy died of consumption.

At age nineteen he went to Jesus College, Cambridge University, where he began brilliantly, was dangerously active politically, yet soon became both bored and broke. "I became a proverb for the University of idleness" (Holmes 45). Eventually, to ease his debt, he withdrew and enlisted in the Light Dragoons under the alias Silas Tomkyn Comberbacke. Although he wrote powerful love letters for his fellow dragoons, Silas suffered from saddle sores and he kept falling off his horse, until his brothers came to the rescue, buying him out of the rest of his service. Returning to Cambridge, Coleridge wrestled unsuccessfully with his lifelong tendency to procrastinate in the face of necessary disciplines. He was known as one of the more brilliant, exciting, yet unpredictable characters at the university.

In the summer of 1794, twenty-two-year-old Coleridge's five-hundred-mile walk took him through Oxford, where he met the young poet, Robert Southey, who later became Poet Laureate of

England. Together they conceived a vision to create the ideal society in the new world of America, of course along the banks of the Susquehanna River. There would be twelve men and their mates. Coleridge named the new way of life "Pantisocracy." They would think in the morning, work the fields in the afternoon, and enjoy art together in the evening. Southey wished his mate to be Edith Fricker. When another of the twelve chose a Fricker sister, Coleridge followed suit, asking sister Sara to be his mate. Attracted to her as he was, he knew he did not love her. She turned out to be too similar to his usually baffled mother. In the fall of 1794, Pantisocracy was the talk of the whole university and the disdain of the Coleridge family. Coleridge withdrew from Cambridge after Christmas to devote himself to raising subscriptions to support Pantisocracy. Owing to foreseeable financial challenges and, from Coleridge's point of view, Southey's abandonment of the project, Pantisocracy was stillborn a year or so after conception. Yet the ideals of Pantisocracy, associated with young Coleridge, continued to inspire many English citizens to find new lives in the new world. Coleridge's marriage, misconceived, burdened him the rest of his life.

Coleridge's pamphlets, lectures, and sermons, calling for an end to war against France, generated his reputation as a political firebrand who could stir a crowd brilliantly, whether for or against his apparently Jacobin, democratic ideals. Whether suffering illness himself, or, as frequently happened, intensely and extensively nursing this or that seriously ill friend or acquaintance, Coleridge became familiar with thresholds of consciousness. He was often loved and adored by young admirers and had numerous exciting, close friendships.

In 1795, at age twenty-three, Samuel Taylor Coleridge preached a sermon in a Unitarian Church in Bridgewater, in southwestern England, on a Sunday morning. He knew that in the area there lived a young poet whose poetry interested him. After the service Samuel embarked on foot, walking the forty miles to Racedown, arriving late the next afternoon. Dorothy Wordsworth was working in her garden. She sensed a figure blocking the afternoon sun on the ridge. Then, wrote Wordsworth later, "He did not keep to the highroad, but leaped over a gate and bounded down a pathless field by which he cut off an angle" (Holmes 149). Introducing himself, Coleridge stayed for two weeks. Dorothy observed,

> He is a wonderful man. His conversation teems with soul, mind, and spirit. Then he is so benevolent, so good tempered and cheerful, and, like William, interests himself so much about every little trifle. At first I thought him plain, that is for about three minutes: he is pale and thin, has a wide mouth, thick lips, and not very good teeth, longish loose-growing half-curling rough black hair. But if you hear him speak for five minutes, you can think no more of them. His eye is large and full, not dark but grey, such an eye as would receive from a heavy soul the dullest expression; but it speaks every emotion of his animated mind; it has more of the poet's eye 'in a fine frenzy rolling' than I have ever witnessed. He has fine dark eyebrows and an overhanging forehead. (Holmes 149)

For a year and a half, Coleridge and Wordsworth saw each other almost daily, in Somerset, often walking the fields and moors, sharing observations, reflections, making studies of a particular stream over the days, hearing each other's poems, giving each other lines. Such daily studies of the stream, the rivulets feeding it, its meandering path down to the sea, noting varying effects of light on the water's surfaces, reflections of clouds, of starlight, always varying, responding to each contour of the land, altering appropriately, are likely sources of his later theory of organic form, in which the subject evolves organically. Coleridge's "conversation poems," such as *This Lime-tree Bower My Prison* and *Frost at Midnight*, are primary embodiments of this organic form of poetry, new in the history of poetry. Coleridge industriously recorded observations of nature, portions of overheard dialogue, and ideas in notebooks (160 over the decades), which became great sources for later poetry and prose. John Livingstone Lowes's *Road to Xanadu* traces all Coleridge's reading as sources of his poems, *Kubla Khan* and the *Rime of the Ancient Mariner.*

Coleridge admired Wordsworth profoundly. "Wordsworth is a very great man, the only man to whom at all times and in all modes of excellence I feel myself inferior." Yet Coleridge may have helped Wordsworth more than Wordsworth him. I. A. Richards thought that Coleridge "first truly showed Wordsworth how to become his own poetic self." Hazlitt later wrote,

> Coleridge has told me that he himself liked to compose in walking over uneven ground, or breaking through the straggling branches of a copse-wood; whereas Wordsworth always wrote (if he could) walking up and down a straight gravel-walk, or in some spot where the continuity of his verse met with no collateral interruption. (Holmes 196)

Biographer Holmes concluded that intellectually Coleridge was a huge river, while Wordsworth was a mighty rock (151).

When, in 1798, Hazlitt, one of the most astute critics of the time, walked far on a winter day to hear Coleridge preach, he offered his first-hand experience of Coleridge in the following:

> His voice "rose like a steam of rich distilled perfumes," and when he came to the last two words, which he pronounced loud, deep, and distinct, it seemed to me, who was then young, as if the sounds had echoed from the bottom of the human heart, and as if that prayer might have floated in solemn silence through the universe.... The preacher then launched into his subject, like an eagle dallying with the wind. From the distance of the pew, "there was to me a strange wilderness in his aspect, a dusky obscurity." (Holmes 178)

Later, close up,

> His forehead was broad and high, light as if built of ivory, with large projecting eyebrows, and his eyes rolling beneath them like a seas with darkened luster.... His mouth was gross, voluptuous, open, eloquent; his chin good-humoured and round; but his nose, the rudder of the face, the index of

> the will, was small, feeble, nothing-like what he has done. (Holmes 180)

On one trek, Coleridge hiked ninety miles round trip in two days. Coleridge seemed to strengthen as he strode, even climbing mountains, able to continue speaking as others were winded silent. Coleridge wrote Wedgewood, the china magnate:

> I devote myself . . . in poetry, to elevate the imagination and set the affections in right tune by the beauty of the inanimated impregnated, as with a living soul . . . what our faculties are & what they are capable of becoming—I love fields & woods & mountains with almost a visionary fondness—and because I have found benevolence & quietness growing within me as that fondness increased, therefore I should wish to be the means of implanting in others. (Holmes 186)

The day after the letter, the Wedgewood family gave Coleridge a lifelong annuity, so he resigned from the pulpit and spent his twenty-sixth year studying language and philosophy in Germany. Studying Kant, Hegel, and Schelling reinforced his earlier roots in Plato and Plotinus. As a result, Coleridge was instrumental in introducing German Transcendentalism to England. He later wrote to Wordsworth in *Table Talk*, "The pith of my system is to make the senses out of the mind—not the mind out of the senses, as Locke did." During this year spent in Germany, Coleridge suffered the death of his second son, infant Berkely, back in England.

Intrigued with folk customs, Coleridge included in his letters the first English description of the German customs of Christmas tree and "Father Christmas," which later, through Queen Victoria's German husband Prince Albert, permeated the English-speaking world. Through his studies of Lessing, Coleridge developed his understanding of poetry having power through a combination of clarity and obscurity. "Poetry gives mostly pleasure when only generally and not perfectly understood."

Returning from an exploratory visit to the Lake District with the Wordsworths, he observed out his carriage window in November,

> Starlings in vast flights drove along like smoke, mist, or any thing misty without volition—now a circular area inclined in an Arc—now a Globe—now from complete Orb into an Ellipse & Oblong—now a balloon with the car suspended, now a concave Semicircle—& still it expands and & condenses, some moments glimmering & shivering, dim & shadowy, now thickening, deepening, blackening." (Holmes 253)

Such an astutely observed impression may well have been the basis for his later understanding of the flexible nature of imagination. He later wrote in *Biographia literaria*,

> The poet, described in ideal perfection, brings the whole soul of man into activity, with the subordination of its faculties to each other, according to their relative worth and dignity. He diffuses a tone and spirit of unity, that blends, and (as it were) fuses, each into each, by that synthetic and magical power, to which we have exclusively appropriated the name of imagination.... It dissolves, diffuses, dissipates, in order to re-create; or where this process is rendered impossible, yet still at all events it struggles to idealize and to unify. It is essentially vital, even as all objects (as objects) are essentially fixed and dead.

After Coleridge returned from Germany, he moved first to London, where he wrote seventy-six articles in five months for the *Morning Post*, including sketches of important contemporary public figures such as Bonaparte, Pitt, Washington, Fox, and the Foreign Minister Lord Grenville. During this time he was inspiring friends such as Southey, Wordsworth, the scientist Humphrey Davy (later to become Director of the Royal Institution in London), and the social philosopher, William Godwin, a cadre powerfully embodying what one might call "the spirit of the time."

Godwin was married to Mary Wollstonecraft, whose daughter Mary would marry Shelley and write the novel *Frankenstein.*

Samuel Taylor Coleridge became remarkably influential in England in a number of ways, literary and other. Not only had young Coleridge innovated the organic form of the conversation poems; he had also rejuvenated the old popular ballad form literarily in the *Rime of the Ancient Mariner.* In addition, he infused the political tract in journalism with new literary flavor. In January, 1800, Coleridge "published a detailed verbal study of one of Lord Grenville's papers on the necessity of prosecuting the war with France, showing how minute errors in grammar and false figures of speech served to disguise illogical political and strategic thinking" (Holmes 262). (This was a type of political criticism popularized over a century later by George Orwell in his concept of "non-speak.") Coleridge showed, for example, how the misplacing of one verbal connective, "also," in a single sentence cast doubts on Grenville's entire analysis of the French military campaign in Europe. Such linguistic analysis in political speeches anticipated not only Orwell's analysis, but also the twentieth-century literary school of "New Criticism," focusing primarily on the work of the language in a particular text.

Coleridge's entrancing long poem *Christabel*, though incomplete and rejected by Wordsworth from the second edition of *Lyrical Ballads* (1800), nevertheless influenced Byron, Shelley, Keats (*Eve of St. Agnes*), Tennyson (*Lady of Shalott*), and the Pre-Raphaelites, evoking the power of the feminine mystique.

Coleridge moved eventually to the Lake District, only a thirteen-mile walk from the Wordsworths. He had fallen hopelessly in love with Sara Hutchinson, whose sister, Mary, Wordsworth would marry in 1802. His growing addiction to liquid laudanum, a common opiate medicine prescribed to him originally for a toothache, compounded unhappy marriage and unfulfilled love. The poet, in pain both physically and emotionally, remained the philosopher.

"The great Lock, as he was fond of calling the philosopher, had been turned; and the key, though in parts it might seem at times to have been cut and filed by Kant, was truly what he had learned long ago from Plato and Plotinus" (Richards). Coleridge, the perennial yet practical philosopher, had been hopeful in his twenties that new governmental forms were possible. In his thirties, Coleridge turned his faith and attention to the individual. Long before mountaineering became popular for its own sake, Coleridge was the first non-shepherd to do a solo ascent of Mt. Scafell. Coleridge was as well the first English person to write literarily about fell walking, virtually inventing what became a Romantic notion of walking the wilds with a kerchief-knapsack and a staff. In September 1803, Coleridge walked 263 miles in eight days, from Loch Lomond to Perth in Scotland. Coleridge also pioneered a new kind of nature writing: observation of objects with the subject, the first person, active in the experience.

> Am now...near Grasmere...traveling along the ridge I came to the other side of those precipices and down below me on my left—no-no-no! no words can convey any idea of this prodigious wilderness. That precipice fine on this side was but its ridge, sharp as a jagged knife, level so long, and then ascending so boldly—what a frightful bulgy precipice I stand on and to my right how the Crag which corresponds to the other, how it plunges down, like a waterfall, reaches a level steepness, and again plunges! —the Moon is above Fairfield almost at the full! —now descending over a perilous peat-moss then known a Hill of stones all dark, and darkling, I climbed stone after stone down a half dry torrent and came out at the Raise Gap. And O! my God! How did that opposite precipice look—in the moonshine—its name Stile Crags. (Holmes 281)

Coleridge's subjective experience generates participation in the objective observation.

At age thirty-two, he sought health in Malta for two years, returning worse. Separating then formally from his wife, he moved to London, working primarily as lecturer, critic, and editor. By 1810, age thirty-eight, he and Wordsworth quarreled, mending to some degree two years later. Degenerating further physically, socially, and poetically, Coleridge nevertheless gave successful lecture courses on Shakespeare and Milton, fortunately, since he lost his annuity due to war losses.

At forty-four, Coleridge, debilitated, moved into the house of the physician James Gillian for the rest of his life. Under such care, he was able to continue working, rarely as poet, but as critic, then theologian, and always as philosopher. Initially a Unitarian, Coleridge the poet, who thrived in the creative interaction between creator and creation, found that theologically he needed the corresponding threefold dynamic among Father (Creator), Son (creation/poem), and Holy Spirit (creative activity of imagination). Hence he had long ceased preaching in the stiflingly rational, monotheistic Unitarian circles.

He published *Statesman's Manual*, *Treatise on Method*, and *Aids to Reflection.* Among Coleridge's later ambitions was his intention to write a unifying philosophy, tying together all fields. The incomplete manifestation of this ambition, *Biographia Literaria*, contains some of his most important thinking. He may have been the most brilliant mind of his time in England. Friend of Sir Humphrey Davy, Coleridge had enormous scientific grounding in his philosophy. The law of conservation of matter confirmed his intuition that no energy is ever lost.

Philosophically, Coleridge's most important contributions to the maturing of the English-speaking mind may be his distinctions between Imagination and Fancy, and between Reason and Understanding. Although Coleridge bore painfully the failure of not completing the *Biographia Literaria,* he would be glad to know how seminal the two following distinctions have turned out to be for the evolving English, American, and hence modern mind.

Biographia Literaria: Imagination and Fancy, Chapter xiii:

The Imagination then, I consider either as primary, or secondary. The primary Imagination I hold to be the living Power and prime Agent of all human Perception, and as

> a repetition in the finite mind of the eternal act of creation in the infinite I AM. The secondary Imagination I consider as an echo of the former, co-existing with the conscious will, yet still as identical with the former in the kind of its agency, and differing only in *degree,* and in the *mode* of its operation. It dissolves, diffuses, dissipates, in order to re-create; or where this process is rendered impossible, yet still at all events it struggles to idealize and to unify. It is essentially vital, even as all objects (*as* objects) are essentially fixed and dead.
>
> FANCY, on the contrary, has no other counters to play with, but fixities and definites. The Fancy is, indeed, no other than a mode of Memory emancipated from the order of time and space; while it as blended with, and modified by that empirical phenomenon of the will, which we express by the word *Choice.* But equally with the ordinary memory the FANCY must receive all its materials ready made from the law of association.

In "Reason and Understanding," from *The Friend,* Coleridge characterized reason as "that intuition of things which arises when we possess ourselves, as one with the whole, which is substantial knowledge." In understanding however, "we think of ourselves as separated beings, and place nature in antithesis to the mind, as object to subject, thing to thought, death to life." This is abstract knowledge, or the science of mere understanding.

Coleridge recognized both imagination and reason as antidotes for the chasm between subject and object in the Age of "Reason," which would more suitably be called the Age of Understanding in Coleridge's language.

Although Coleridge the poet never could take wing later as he had in his twenties and early thirties, Coleridge the philosopher understood the poet's task mightily.

> The poet, described in ideal perfection, brings the whole soul of man into activity, with the subordination of its faculties to each other, according to their relative worth and dignity. He diffuses a tone and spirit of unity that blends,

> and (as it were) fuses, each into each, by that synthetic and magical power, to which we have exclusively appropriated the name of imagination. This power, first put in action by the will and understanding, and retained under their irremissive and unnoticed control, reveals itself in the balance or reconciliation of opposites or discordant qualities: of sameness, with difference; of the general, with the concrete; the idea, with the image; the individual, with the representative; the sense of novelty and freshness, with old and familiar objects; a more than usual state of emotion, with more than usual order; judgment ever awake and steady self-possession, with enthusiasm and feeling profound or vehement; and while it blends and harmonizes the natural and the artificial, still subordinates art to nature; the manner to the matter; and our admiration of the poet to our sympathy with the poetry. (chap. 14, *Biographia literaria*)

His contemporary Hazlitt said of him, harshly but accurately, "[Coleridge's] mind is (as he himself might express it) tangential. There is no subject on which he has not touched, none on which he has rested" (Hazlitt 37). His mind worked with the same synthetic mobility he attributed to imagination. Considered by many to be the most brilliant conversationalist of his day, Coleridge might stop by someone's home for an unexpected visit. Dinner and the evening would include dazzling discourse, mostly from Coleridge himself, in any number of directions. Afterward, as the hosts went to sleep, Coleridge might read in a number of books and periodicals. In the morning he could quote from any of them, almost verbatim. An omniglot, he was interested in everything. Through his passionate interests he soared high, too high. The fellow who had fallen too easily from his horse as a twenty-year-old fell too easily from the heavens of his contemplations, lacking a natural, self-preserving interior balance.

In November 1833, Samuel Taylor Coleridge composed his own epitaph.

Stop, Christian passerby!—Stop, child of God,
And read with gentle breast. Beneath this sod
A poet lies, or that which once seem'd he.
O, lift one thought in prayer for S. T. C.;
That he who many a year with toil of breath
Found death in life, may here find life in death!
Mercy for praise—to be forgiven for fame
He ask'd, and hoped, through Christ. Do thou the same!

Thirty years earlier, embarking for Malta by sea, Coleridge had written, "Death itself will be only a Voyage—a Voyage not from, but to our native Country." Finally, July 25, 1834, Samuel Taylor Coleridge, the long-suffering, damaged archangel, voyaged home, almost sixty-one years old.

In spite of their quarrels and Wordsworth's intimate experience of Coleridge's foibles, England's future Poet Laureate still considered him "the most wonderful man I have ever met" (Sisman 425). Most of Samuel Taylor Coleridge's enduring poetry he had written during the seven years between the ages of twenty-five and thirty-two, late in his sentient soul stage of development, and early in his rational/intellectual-soul stage.

Coleridge's Poetry

Coleridge the poet will probably always be remembered for two poems; the musically magical *Kubla Khan* and the spellbinding, initiatory ballad-tale, *the Rime of the Ancient Mariner.* There may be no more enchanting a concentration of lines (fifty-four) in English Poetry than *Kubla Khan.*

A damsel with a dulcimer
In a vision once I saw:
It was an Abyssinian maid,
And on her dulcimer she played,
Singing of Mount Abora.
Could I revive within me
Her symphony and song,
To such a deep delight 'twould win me,

That with music loud and long,
I would build that dome in air,
That sunny dome! Those caves of ice!
And all who heard should see them there,
And all should cry, Beware! Beware!
His flashing eyes, his floating hair!
Weave a circle round him thrice,
And close your eyes with holy dread,
For he on honey-dew hath fed,
And drunk the milk of paradise.

In the *Ancient Mariner,* Coleridge takes the traditional medieval form of the ballad and rejuvenates it, allowing stanzas to ebb and flow in length (number of lines), from the traditional four, to five, and six, according to the mood or need at that moment in the story of the poem.

Beyond the shadow of the ship,
I watched the water-snakes:
They moved in tracks of shining white,
And when they reared, the elfish light
Fell off in hoary flakes.

Within the shadow of the ship
I watched their rich attire:
Blue, glossy green, and velvet black,
They coiled and swam; and every track
Was a flash of golden fire.

O happy living things! No tongue
Their beauty might declare:
A spring of love gushed from my heart,
And I blessed them unaware:
Sure my kind saint took pity on me,
And I blessed them unaware.

The self-same moment I could pray;
And from my neck so free
The Albatross fell off, and sank
Like lead into the sea.

However, in terms of the evolving way the spirit of the English language works through poetry, let us look closely at *This Lime-Tree Bower My Prison.*

Both Shakespeare and Milton had found blank verse to be the necessary medium best serving their mightiest explorations. Wordsworth would use it the following year in *Tintern Abbey* to explore levels of memory, and later, at Coleridge's urging, Wordsworth used it to explore the whole becoming of a poet in *The Prelude*, the first interior "epic" poem. However, Coleridge, already in June 1797, at the age of twenty-five, used blank verse as the medium, not for a monumental task but for an almost casual reflection. The actual circumstance was that Coleridge's dear school friend and most sensitively helpful critic of his poetry, Charles Lamb, had just arrived for a long-awaited visit to the Coleridge home in Nether Stowey, in southwestern England. Coleridge's young wife Sara had accidentally spilled boiling milk on Coleridge's foot. Hence, Coleridge was unable to accompany Lamb, Sara, and William and Dorothy Wordsworth on a hike through his beloved Quantock Hills. However, the limiting reality of the biographical circumstance became a catalyst for the poet's expansive act of imagination. Coleridge, in his poem, begins to imaginatively accompany Lamb and friends through the terrain Coleridge has known through his senses so well.

> Well, they are gone, and here must I remain,
> This lime-tree bower my prison. I have lost...

The matter is not grand, the phrasing colloquial, conversational in tone, a reflective monologue initially. Then he starts to imagine in detail the roaring dell he had told them of.

> That branchless ash,
> Unsunn'd and damp, whose few poor yellow leaves
> N'er tremble in the gale, yet tremble still,
> Fann'd by the waterfall.

The triple assonance of the *a* in "th*a*t br*a*nchless *a*sh" evokes an agony in sound, reinforcing the solitary image of the tree, "damp," unsunn'd. Its malnourishment is reinforced by the quadruple spondee of "whose few poor yellow," slowing the line into an almost painful inertia of stillness, inactivity, these leaves that, deep in the dell, ne'er tremble from any breeze, are never literally inspired. (*Inspire* originally meant to blow or breathe.) Yet, even so, miracle of miracles, though not from the macrocosmic wind itself, a source comes from the waterfall, an unnatural wind generated from nature itself, an extra source of inspiration, analogous perhaps to ailing Coleridge being inspired nevertheless to write this poem, engendering an artistic fullness out of the natural emptiness.

As though recharged by his imaginative activity within the poem, the poet's imagination travels up from the dark, solitary dell out into the vast expanse of the hilly fields and meadows. The monologue itself expands, becoming an address, "thou gentle-hearted Charles," an intimate communication.

> Shine in the slant beams of the sinking orb,
> Ye purple heath-flowers! richlier burn, ye clouds!
> Live in the yellow light, ye distant groves!
> And kindle, thou blue Ocean!

The very natural elements of the scene inter-fuse: "shine . . . purple heath flowers! . . . burn, . . . clouds! Live in yellow light . . . groves! And kindle, thou blue Ocean!" The poet does not simply behold this interfusion of elements; he, through his imagination, commands it, in a series of five imperatives, exercising the secondary imagination, in imitation of the Primary imagination of the Creator.

The poem culminates in one of the most simple, powerful, yet primal images in all literature, drawn from his observations of nature, yet potentized again through Coleridge's imagination of the union of the particular and the universal.

> My gentle-hearted Charles! When the last rook
> Beat its straight path along the dusky air
> Homewards, I blest it! Deeming its black wing
> (now a dim speck, now vanishing in light)

had cross'd the mighty Orb's dilated glory

And, just in case the beauty of the particular were not sufficiently rendered:

or, when all was still,
Flew creaking o'er thy head, and had a charm
For thee, my gentle-hearted Charles, to whom
No sound is dissonant which tells of Life

In his *Biographia literaria*, Coleridge wrote, "The origin of metre . . . I would trace to the balance in the mind effected by that spontaneous effort which strives to hold in check the workings of passion." In his conversation poems, Coleridge crafted a combination of the emotionally restraining iambic pentameter, the open-endedness of blank verse's lack of rhyme, and the organically evolving subject in a conversational tone. From a larger perspective, in terms of the activity of the spirit of the English language, one can see Coleridge's conversation poems as the foot of a bridge, across the Atlantic Ocean via his later, prose *Table Talk* and *Aids to Reflection*, to two little-known Congregational ministers in New England (see chapter 21), through Ralph Waldo Emerson, and finally, fifty-five years later, to the emergence of the first genuinely American poet of the New World and hence the New (or Modern) Age, Walt Whitman, and "free verse" (see chapter 23). Coleridge's articulation of the flexible, dissolving, yet unifying nature of imagination, and hence of its organic, living quality, as embodied especially in his conversation poems, inspired Emerson's understanding of the imagination, which would in turn inspire Whitman's enactment of it in his organically evolving, flexibly forming poetry.

Chapter 14

Byron

The Life of George Gordon, Lord Byron (1788–1824)

In 1809, a young English aristocrat, upon coming of age, assumed his seat in the House of Lords and promptly left the country to see the world with a friend and four servants. They saw much of Spain and Portugal, sometimes traveling seventy miles a day on horseback. Sailing from Gibraltar and arriving in Sardinia, he became recognized as the best pistol shot in the area. He went to Missolonghi, Greece, where years later he would become the best known martyr of the Greek revolution against the Turks. The travelers saw major sites of the East, including Smyrna, Ephesus, Constantinople, and Troy, in present-day Turkey. The young Lord swam the Hellespont, from Europe to Asia. He wrote, "If I am a poet, Greece has made me one." During the travels he started a long poem called *Childe Harold*. One morning after he returned to England, he awoke to find himself famous. Before his death fifteen years later, George Gordon, Lord Byron would become to all of Europe an emblem of his era. He remains so two hundred years later.

George Gordon Byron was born lordless in London, January 22, 1788. His grandfather had been an admiral known as "Foul-weather Jack," after shipwrecking on the wild, bleak shores of southern Patagonia. His great-uncle, known as Wicked Lord, had killed a man in a duel. His father, Captain J. Byron, abandoned his mother, Catherine, shortly after George's birth, possibly because of his abhorrence of the baby's left clubfoot. Known as Mad Jack, the captain squandered Catherine's Gordon inheritance, visiting his wife on some Sundays, when debtors were safe. When George was three, his absent father died.

Growing up impoverished in Aberdeen, between the rivers Dee and Don, young George Gordon whiled away many hours reading the Old Testament, remaining uninterested in the New Testament. By age ten, he was avidly reading *The Arabian Nights*, Roman history, Latin, and much about the Turks and the Greeks. He compensated for his handicap with aggressive cricket, fierce boxing, and keen marksmanship with both pistol and archery. When George was ten, the fifth Lord Byron, George's great-uncle, "Wicked Lord," died without an heir, leaving George Gordon to become the sixth Lord Byron.

His new title led his mother Catherine to move him from a shabby Scottish flat into a palace, the Byron estate, Newstead, near Nottingham and Sherwood Forest. An obese, self-indulgent, hysterical woman, Catherine spoiled and neglected young George, once leaving him nine miles away with May Gray, a flighty, loose maid who seems to have seduced him at some point. Young George noticed that his new title and his new fortune brought him new respect from others.

From the age of thirteen to seventeen and a half, young Lord Byron endured a stormy time at Harrow School, where his reputation increased as a fighter, sharpshooter, skilled rider, and swimmer. He also experienced homosexual activity there, which was not unusual in English boarding schools and was perhaps understandable for a boy who lacked affection growing up.

In 1805, Lord Byron arrived at Trinity College, Cambridge University, with an entourage of one servant, a coach with four horses, two saddle horses, a groom, a valet, and a bulldog. He wore many rings, gold trim on his robe, a brooch on his shirtfront and an embroidered, black dress coat with his shirt open at the neck. He carried a stick and he kept a bear on a chain. He liked to keep his mistress disguised as a boy. He vacillated between bouts of excessive drinking and absolute abstinence. The poet had also been writing.

When his first collection of poems, *Hours of Idleness,* was harshly criticized by the *Edinburgh Review*, the young man responded with his satirical *English Bards and Scotch Reviewers*, in which couplets tactlessly ridiculed such contemporary poets as Scott, Wordsworth, and Coleridge. Having dared to taunt his poetic elders, the twenty-one-year-old Lord Byron presumed to assume his proper seat in the House of Lords. "I have taken my seat, and now I will go abroad" (Nichol 57). In classic English tradition, Byron embarked for a tour of Europe with his friend Hobhouse, the balancing influence in Byron's life. His tour abroad also included his valet and three additional servants.

They traveled on horseback in Portugal and Spain, sometimes seventy miles a day. From Gibraltar they sailed to Sicily and Sardinia, where Byron proved his outstanding ability as a sharpshooter. Revisiting terrain from his childhood reading and setting the stage for his future, Byron sailed from Malta to Missolonghi, Greece, which had been under Turkish rule for three centuries. The stature of the major sites they visited inspired Byron and a lieutenant to swim the Hellespont (or Dardanelles), from Europe to Asia, a formidable challenge. Greece was certainly the midwife to the birth of the poet, for during these travels he had started to pen the adventures of Childe Harold in Spenserian stanzas.

Within weeks of twenty-three-year-old Byron's return to England, his mother died during a hysterical fit over an upholstery bill. His friend Matthews drowned soon after. Newly alone in the world, Byron's life changed again with the publication of *Childe Harold's Pilgrimage* in February, 1812. "I awoke one morning, and found myself famous."

The Bacchanalian carnival life of George Gordon, Lord Byron began. Sir Walter Scott found him "full of fun, frolic, wit, and whim, as playful as a kitten." Byron had a notoriously handsome countenance, with fine blue veins, pale marble temples. He openly pursued a scandalous liaison with Lady Caroline Lamb, who memorably declared him to be "mad, bad, and dangerous to know" (Perkins 779). In time, perhaps to replace Hobhouse, his earlier friend and balance wheel, Byron was drawn to the wealthy and plain Anne Isabella Milbanke. A thoughtful scholar of philosophy, mathematics, classical literature, "Annabella" refused his initial proposal of marriage.

"'Lara' I wrote while undressing after coming home from balls and masquerades, in the year of revelry 1814" (Nichol 49). That year, too, Byron reconnected with his half-sister Augusta. Unencumbered by her worthless husband and three girls, Augusta and George enjoyed mutual delight, which soon had London sensing that taboos of incest had been burst. That year Byron confessed to Lady Melbourne, "I have been all my life trying to make someone love me" (Castle 1). To culminate the year of revelry, Byron proposed again to Annabella. This time she said yes.

During their marriage, Byron drank too much and indulged in tempestuous rages. He hated sleeping in a bed with another. Annabella thought he was going mad, and, owing to his unspeakable behavior, she sued for separation. During this interlude of scandal, a woman fainted simply at the sight of him while at a London ball. Another woman warned her daughter, "Don't look at him; he is dangerous to look at." Former lovers kept personal mementos of him as they would talismans.

Officially separated and virtually banished, in April 1816, twenty-eight-year-old George Gordon, Lord Byron left England, never again to see either his mother country or his sister Augusta, who had been appointed lady-in-waiting to Queen Charlotte. Augusta had a daughter, Ada, whom some considered to have been fathered by Byron.

That summer, Byron rented a chateau on Lac Leman, Switzerland, and spent time with Percy Bysshe and Mary Shelley (daughter of William Godwin and Mary Wollstonecraft), who were on their honeymoon. They toured Lake Geneva, visiting the Chateau de Chillon (*Childe Harolde,* Canto III). Mary Shelley's visiting stepsister, Claire Clairmont, enjoyed a liaison with Byron, which led to a child, Allegra. One stormy night, while in the company of their friend Dr. Polidari, they had a contest for creating ghost stories, one of the most fruitful nights in the history of literature, engendering Byron's strongest attempt at a drama, *Manfred,* as well as Mary Shelley's famous novel, *Frankenstein.*

By age thirty, 1818, Byron was in Venice, Italy, working on Canto IV of *Childe Harold*, as well as *Don Juan*, *Manfred*, and *Beppo*. He settled in near his "last passion," the hotheaded Countess Teresa Guicoli, eighteen-year-old third wife of a fifty-seven-year-old count. Her family, implicated for planning revolution, had been forced into exile. An English visitor wrote that Byron "could not have been more than thirty, but he looked forty. His face had become pale, bloated and sallow. He had grown very fat, his shoulders broad and round, and the knuckles of his hands were lost in fat" (Grosskurth 1). Drinking bouts and bulimic eating binges would be followed by starving diets of red cabbage washed down with cider or Rhine wine.

In the early months of 1822, Byron joined the Shelleys again near Pisa, staying in a marble *palazza* perhaps of Michelangelo's design, accompanied by his usual entourage of servants, monkey, bulldog, mastiff, peafowl, hens, and mistress, Countess Guicioli. Two months later, when Shelley brought his swarthy, former pirate friend, Edward John Trelawney, to the *palazza*, Byron's bulldog Moretto greeted them with a growl. Shelley retired with one of Byron's poems, while Byron and Trelawney played pool. Trelawney observed of the thirty-four-year-old,

> In external appearance Byron realized that ideal standard with which imagination adorns genius. In the prime of his life. Regular features, without stain of furrow on his pallid skin, shoulders broad, chest open, body and limbs finely proportioned...small finely furnished head, curly hair...airy and graceful appearance from massiveness and length of throat; you saw his genius in his eyes and lips. Nature could do little more than she had done for him, both in outward form and in the inward spirit she had given to animate it. But all those rare fits, to his jaundiced imagination, only serve to make his one personal defect the more apparent.... He brooded over that blemish as sensitive minds will brood until they magnify a wart into a wen. His lameness certainly helped to make him skeptical, cynical, and savage....

> He wore a tartan jacket (Gordon clan), blue velvet cap and gold band, long nankeen trousers strapped to his feet...he was thin at the time,...from a diet of cold potatoes and vinegar, biscuits and soda water....By starving his body, Byron kept his brains clear; no man had brighter eyes, or a clearer voice. (Armstrong 210)

Lady Blessington noticed a certain gaucherie owing to the concealment of his lame foot, and a bad and vulgar taste in dress and furniture. "Byron gave the impression of caring more of being a lord than of being a Poet." Trelawney was a little disappointed as Byron chattered of nothing and boasted of everything. Prepared to see a solemn mystery, he might quickly become bored with a rather dull farce. Nevertheless, when Shelley reentered the room, the two poets talked of poetry. "Byron invited criticism,...accepting, brilliantly defending, quoting extraordinarily." At such times, Trelawney felt he was seeing the real Byron, the author of *Childe Harold* and *Don Juan*. His friends experienced Byron as ever-changing, mercurial, protean. Frequently the three of them and others rode, drank, dined, and shot pistols (Armstrong 212, 213).

One evening while riding, Byron quoted Coleridge: "Gazing on the Western sky, / And its peculiar tint of yellow green." With a contemptuous sneer, Byron said, "Who ever saw a green sky!" Shelley remained silent, knowing Byron to be insensitive to halftones of landscape, as to subtle gradations of character. Trelawney said, "The sky in England is oftener green than blue." "Black, you mean," responded Byron. As soon as Trelawney quoted from *Don Juan,* however, Byron's good spirits returned (Armstrong 214,215).

Byron could suffer intensely. Years earlier he had quarreled with Claire Clairemont about their daughter Allegra; Byron had finally sent the four-year-old to a convent near Ravenna. In April 1822, Allegra Byron died of typhus fever. The sea was often a balm for Byron's pains. Trelawny observed, "As Byron swam, peace would return—the sea was Byron's Pool of Bethesda. Byron was at his best when swimming. He walked with a strange, tiptoeing gait. He swam like a fish" (Armstrong 241). Later, in July, after the corpses of storm-shipwrecked Shelley and friends had been found, Byron sickened, then, swam with Trelawney and another a mile out to sea and back. Byron wrote, "Shelley was without exception the best and least selfish man I ever knew." Byron, reflecting, said, "Death is welcome. I have no wish to live, but I can't bear pain. . . . Trelawney, don't repeat the ceremony you went through with Shelley (cremation)—no one wants my ashes" (Armstrong 287).

A year earlier, when Byron was thirty-three, a Greek revolt had begun in April 1821. Punishment had been severe; the Turks hanged Patriarch Reggorio in Constantinople, massacred 25,000 Greeks on the island of Chios, and carried off 45,000 more, while the Greeks indulged in their own savageries. In 1819, Byron had written in "The Isles of Greece" about one of his primary childhood interests: "I dreamed that Greece might still be free."

Neither Byron nor Trelawney felt admiration for modern Greeks, whom they considered "a dishonest, treacherous, and cowardly race," but both hankered to help—Trelawney wanting immediate action, Byron holding off for a plan. In the summer of 1823, Trelawney had the will; Byron had the means. He chartered a tub-like coal vessel, the *Hercules,* to carry horses, two cannons, arms, ammunition, one year's medical stores for a thousand men, cash, letters of credit, a wardrobe of military magnificence, Trelawney, doctors, and dogs. As they embarked, Byron said, "If things are farcical, they will do for *Don Juan;* if heroic, you shall have another canto of *Childe Harold*" (Armstrong 297).

They landed at Cephalonia, close to Ithaca by the mouth of the Gulf of Corinth and near Missolonghi, the site of his visit as a twenty-one-year-old. Initially, the poet was greeted more fervently than the would-be soldier. Of course, Byron said on arriving, "Let's have a swim. I hate antiquarian twaddle. Do people think I have no lucid intervals, that I came to Greece to scribble more nonsense? I will show them that I can do something better. I wish I had never written a line, to have it cast in my teeth at every turn" (Trelawney 110).

With Byron's magic name famous throughout Europe, word spread quickly among the marshes and lagoons of Missolonghi that "the delivering angel" had arrived. George Gordon, Lord Byron, celebrated his thirty-sixth birthday January 22, 1824, patiently and tactfully planning for an artillery unit and six hundred infantry, which he looked forward to leading in a brief white kilt, a *fustanella*. He wrote a poem, "On this Day I Complete My Thirty-sixth Year," which he concluded with the following two stanzas,

> If thou regret'st thy Youth, *why live?*
> The Land of honourable Death
> Is here:—up to the Field, and give
> Away thy Breath.
>
> Seek out—less often sought than found—
> A Soldier's Grave, for thee the best;
> Then look around, and choose thy Ground,
> And take thy Rest!
>
> (Byron's final entry in his last journal)

In February, Byron suffered a violent seizure, possibly a stroke. On April 9, Augusta sent him a silhouette of Ada, age eight. After riding in a thunderstorm led to chills and fever, a physician bled him, engendering delirium. The following April 18, he said, "I want to go rest now." The next day, April 19, 1824, "the restless heart rests." A terrific thunderstorm broke over Missolonghi. The Greeks crossed themselves. "The great man is gone" (Grosskurth 470).

When Trelawney arrived the next day, he waded through the streets to the house on the margin of shallow, shiny seawater. When he pulled back the black pall and the white shroud, Trelawney observed, "He was more beautiful in death than in life. Yet how often I had heard him curse that body." In contrast to Byron's express wishes, five doctors performed an autopsy, opening the brain and removing internal organs for souvenirs. When the body was shipped back to England, the Dean of Westminster Abbey refused its burial there. Friends could barely recognize the stitched up corpse, which was buried instead on the family estate in Ewstead. In Missolonghi, the Turks showed three thousand heads as a result of battle. Harold Nicholson wrote in *Byron: The Last Journey:* "Lord Byron accomplished nothing at Missolonghi except his own suicide; but by that single act of heroism he secured the liberation of Greece." In 1826, the Greeks established independence. Byron's death had catalyzed sympathetic support from European powers to aid the Greeks in their five-year-long struggle against the Ottoman Empire (Abrams 291).

Byron: The Poetry

Childe Harold's Pilgrimage: Canto IV

CLXXVIII

There is a pleasure in the pathless woods,
There is a rapture on the lonely shore.
There is a society where none intrudes,
By the deep Sea, and music in its roar.
I love not Man the less, but Nature more,
From these our interviews, in which I steal
From all I may be or have been before,
To mingle with the Universe, and feel
What I can ne'er express, yet can not all conceal.

CLXXIX

Roll on, thou deep and dark blue Ocean—roll!
Ten thousand fleets sweep over thee in vain;
Man marks the earth with ruin—his control
Stops with the shore; —upon the watery plain
The wrecks are all thy deed, nor doth remain
A shadow of man's ravage, save his own,
When, for a moment, like a drop of rain,
He sinks into the depths with bubbling groan,
Without a grave, unknell'd, uncoffin'd, and unknown.

In contrast to most lines of iambic pentameter in these Spenserian stanzas, the first line in stanza CLXXIX begins with the spondee, "Roll on," generating momentum. The next words recover the iambic rhythm, "thou deep and dark..." Yet "blue" is a strong stress, followed by the strong "O-"; and the final iamb has the weak syllable "-cean" linked to the preceding strong O, with the pause of the dash further separating it from the final strong "Roll!" The ocean is rhythmic, but not regular; its waves constantly alter their rhythm. The "o" sounds of Roll...Ocean-roll!" almost extend their embrace around the globe. When "ten thousand fleets sweep," with their own extending sound of "ee," it's surrounded by the ocean's "deep" and "thee," leaving their efforts "in vain."

In the next two lines, within six "feet" sounds a concentration of "th," as "Man marks the earth with...with the..." The "th" sounds evoke something of the substantiality of the Earth, where humanity has some control; yet immediately after that word, "control" rhymes with the ocean's "roll," the "o" is brought up short with the more abrupt "o" sound of "Stops," reinforced by the "t" and the explosive "p."

"Man marks" and his "ruin" have their limits. "...upon the watery plain / The wrecks are all...," brought down through the triple "d" of the Ocean's "deed doth." And the painful, quadruple short "a" of "shadow of man's ravage" is negated by "nor...," with one exception. When one dies at sea, "like a drop of rain," "drop" echoes the earlier "stops," the end of one's control. Human control of the terrain stops at the shore; control of oneself ends at the "drop," one's death, culminating "without a grave," in a series of seven negating "n" sounds: "unknell'd, uncoffin'd, and unknown."

Although George Gordon, Lord Byron continues to epitomize for many the Romantic era, as a poet he was a classicist in spirit, lamenting the fall of poetry since Pope's neoclassical mastery of the craft. Byron the man embodied rebellion against social mores and championed Greek independence. Through the almost-cavalier ease of Byron's poetic craft, the spirit of the English language was able to work more artfully than many may acknowledge. When Chaucer stretched from the old four-beat line to the pentameter line and established the pattern of rhyming couplets, he was both stretching and establishing parameters of a new, burgeoning consciousness. When Shakespeare and Milton dissolved the rhymes and explored through their more transparent blank verse, they took the emerging consciousness yet a step further, allowing the English language to surrender itself, even sacrifice itself, so that thinking could become more freely active. Byron, the social and political rebel, nevertheless remains a poetic aristocrat, resting securely in familiar old forms, playing with almost idle ease and impressive expertise, as though showing off dueling skills, whether with a sword or his beloved pistols. One might say that the spirit of the time takes Byron more seriously than does the spirit of the language. The character of Byron rises, etched romantically against the horizon of his time; consciousness however settles back, savoring pleasures of the oral palate, like good old brandy. The spirit of the English language smiles upon her spoiled boy, like a muse fondling her young lover, knowing he'll stay just to play.

Chapter 15

Shelley

The Life of Percy Bysshe Shelley (1792–1822)

In 1813, a blithe young man who had turned his back on God, and who had consequently been turned out of Oxford University, also turned his back on his nineteen-year-old wife of three years soon after she had given birth. While visiting the social theorist William Godwin, he fell in love with Godwin's daughter and eloped with her, turning his back on England as he came of age. In time, this gentle but burning soul would become recognized as a particularly winged lyric poet, before his untimely fall, like Icarus, into the sea. Although he disdained both God and society, Percy Bysshe Shelley would become one of the finest poetic apprentices of the spirit of the English language.

Percy Bysshe Shelley was born August 4, 1792, in Field Place, Sussex. The eldest child of a wealthy, aristocratic family, Percy grew up with his four younger sisters and baby brother in an estate richly inhabited for them by a number of characters, including the Old Dragon in St. Leonard's Wood, the headless Spectre, the Great Tortoise of the pond, the Old Snake that was the familiar of the garden, and the Gray Alchemist in the garret, all natural creatures transformed in the children's imaginations.

Fair and slight with long, bright hair and full blue eyes, young Percy ran, wandered, and rode a pony throughout his region, even exploring alone at night. On the one hand, he set fire to a stack of firewood, wanting "a little hell of his own," and taught his three-year-old brother to say "The Devil!" (Woodberry xv). On the other hand, his pockets always empty on his wanderings, he never hesitated to borrow servants' money to give to beggars. Though he had an attraction to the devil, he had what some would call Christian compassion for fellow creatures. From a young age, he had a strong longing to adopt a child, an unusual soul sentiment for a young boy.

This unusual individual had numerous atypical traits growing up. Studying Latin and Greek by the age of six, he was enrolled in the Sion House Academy at ten and Eton by age twelve. Throughout his life, he drew pines and cedars on manuscripts. At Eton, he stood apart from the whole school, "a being never to be forgotten," in the words of one peer. Once he stuck a fork through a boy's hand. It wasn't unusual for him to be surrounded by a ring of boys jeering, "Mad Shelley!" or, "Shelley, Shelley, Shelley!" (Ibid. xvii). He loved versifying in Latin as he boated. Chemistry was one of his favorite subjects, especially if it involved exploding a stump with gunpowder. Young Percy Bysshe Shelley, an original, fit no molds.

When he entered Oxford at eighteen, his fine-featured, delicate-complexioned, almost feminine head was unusually small, under its long, bushy hair. Wearing expensive but rumpled clothes with shirt collar open, making abrupt gestures, Shelley spoke in a voice capable of being either shrill, harsh, and discordant or low, soft, clear, distinct, and expressive. A vegetarian on principle, he was bored by set meals; he often nibbled on bread so that one could follow his trail by the bread crumbs. He had been inspired by William Godwin's *Political Justice*. Rationalist philosophers such as the British empiricist Locke, the Scottish naturalist Hume, and the French skeptic Voltaire were favorites. This Elf-King, Oberon, Adonis, Ariel could talk till dawn. One night, when Shelley would finally let his friend fall asleep at two in the morning, the friend thought, "What an extraordinary creature!...the grace of a young girl, the purity of a maiden who has never left her mother's side,...and nevertheless an indomitable force...the soul of a Benedictine monk, with the ideas of a Jacobin" (Maurois 214).

When young Shelley tried to publish a novel, *St. Irvine, or the Rosicrucian*, the publisher, Stockdale, considered it too dangerously subversive. Within a year Shelley was expelled from Oxford for writing and publishing a pamphlet, *The Necessity of Atheism*. Consequently, Shelley was "exiled" from his family to a penniless, friendless solitude in London. That same year nineteen-year-old Percy eloped with sixteen-year-old Harriet Westbrook to save her from suicidal despair at being sent off to boarding school. This act of will, not passion, was soon followed, in spite of his disapproval of the institution, by their marriage in Edinburgh. With Harriet's sister, Eliza, the young couple wandered, spending several months in the Lake District, often in the company of the older poet and future Laureate Southey, who saw in young Shelley much of himself and Coleridge in their fiery twenties. Then three months in Ireland working for Catholic Emancipation were followed by time in Lynnmouth, Wales.

As Shelley neared his twenty-first birthday, Harriet neared her due date. They returned to London where Harriet gave birth to Ianthe Elizabeth. Hampered by debts, he tried to free others from theirs, often borrowing to help another. That same year he met and fell in love with Mary Godwin, daughter of his hero/mentor, the social activist William Godwin and brilliant Mary Wollstonecraft. Shelley and Mary eloped to Europe, leaving Harriet in her second pregnancy, and ill with despair.

When the weary travelers returned to England, they remained gypsies, scorned for their social improprieties, while Shelley himself was often hiding from creditors. Although his father had essentially disinherited him, Percy's grandfather had bypassed his own son in favor of the eldest grandson, Percy Bysshe Shelley. In 1815 grandfather Sir Shelley died, making Percy's father second Baronet, but leaving most of the family fortune to Percy himself, allowing him to pay off debts and to help Harriet, Godwin, and others in need.

When, in 1816, Harriet committed suicide, Shelley and Mary were married, and twenty-four-year-old Shelley and George Gordon, Lord Byron, enjoyed an extended tour of Lake Geneva in Switzerland. Accompanying the honeymoon trip of Shelley and Mary Godwin was Claire Clairemont, Mary's stepsister. As they traveled, Shelley would sign, at the inns, in Greek, "lover of mankind, democrat, and atheist." As one of the other players in the famous stormy evening at Chamonix, in the French Alps, Shelley, along with Mary, Byron, Claire, and their good friend, Dr. Polidari, gathered. They challenged one another to write the spookiest ghost stories. The particular atmosphere of the evening, the fertilizing interfluence of the individuals, led to gestation, to germination, which in time yielded a story about vampires by Dr. Polidari, Byron's play, *Manfred*, Shelley's play, *Prometheus Unbound*, and Mary Shelley's novel, *Frankenstein*.

That evening catalyzed substantial work in two primary directions of the Western imagination. The image of the vampire, in some compelling way, embodies the experience of being bound to blood, of being unable to die, a kind of demonic version of eternal life, being trapped in one's past condition, at the expense of others' lives. Rudolf Steiner described such an orientation as influenced by Lucifer, the backward-hearkening face of evil. While the image of the vampire had already existed in the Western imagination, Mary Shelley generated its polar counterpart, the creature Frankenstein, created anew from formerly dead flesh and bone, recharged by the spark of lightning harnessed by a mere, though intelligent, man, Dr. Frankenstein. The creature embodied a future goal of modern science, that of human beings' ability to create life. The creature suffers agony over his imperfectly human semblance, suffers danger at humanity's inability to recognize some human essence within him, and becomes a destructive, vengeful force as a consequence.

The image of Frankenstein's monster has become an essential element of the Western imagination, an archetype of matter mastered by reason, with potential both to serve and to destroy humanity, an image of the earth-bound, future-oriented force of evil that the Book of Job calls "Behemoth," in contrast to the Luciferic "Leviathan," and to which Rudolf Steiner gave the old Persian name "Ahriman." In *Prometheus Unbound*, Shelley explored the aftermath of Aeschylus' portrayal in *Prometheus Bound* of what the Titan suffered for giving humanity the gift of fire, formerly belonging solely to the gods, and having his liver pecked by birds daily and restored nightly. The subject has similarities to the Biblical serpent's temptation of Adam and Eve, offering God-like knowledge of good and evil. For humans to have such god-like knowledge prematurely entails suffering as consequence. In *Manfred,* Byron's character makes a Faustian deal with Arimanes, a demon of the Earth; yet in dying, he accomplishes his independence. That single evening catalyzed major works of imagination that explore two faces of evil, contemporary versions of Leviathon and Behemoth, of Lucifer and Ahriman, substantially influencing the Western imagination.

By the time Shelley was thirty in 1822, the Shelleys had been drifting from one Italian town to another for four years. Although they found the warmth healthy and the scenery stimulating, Mary had lost two children; she distrusted Italian ways, and she suffered from Percy's love of solitude. In addition to Byron's entourage of servants, monkey, bulldog, mastiff, sea fowl, hens, and mistress, Countess Guiccioli, various friends joined the Shelleys in Pisa.

On his first visit, the tall, dark, pirate Trelawney was talking to Shelley's friend Edward Williams when he felt eyes from the dark passage. "Swiftly. Then gliding in, blushing like a girl, a tall, thin stripling held out both his hands." Soon profoundly affected by Shelley, the boyish Ariel, Trelawney wondered,...was "this mild-looking, beardless boy, dressed like a boy in a black jacket and trousers he seemed to have outgrown...the veritable monster at war with all the world, excommunicated by the Fathers of the Church, deprived of civil rights by a grim Lord Chancellor, discarded by family, denounced by rival sages of literature as founder of a Satanic school?"(Armstrong 206). Then he was gone. Their friend Jane Williams said of Shelley, "He comes and goes like a spirit; no one knows where and when" (Ibid. 207). Trelawney, perhaps unaware of William Blake, felt that no great poet had ever lived so entirely without applause. *The Literary Gazette* had dismissed Shelley's poem *Adonais* as a "mere collection of bloated words." As a consequence, Shelley's poems were forbidden fruit to publishers (Ibid. 208).

Trelawney felt that, if Shelley had one fault, it was that he worked too hard. "He would set to work on a pyramid of books, his eyes glistening with an energy as fierce as a gold digger who works at a rock of quartz, crushing through all impediments, no grain of pure ore escaping his eager scrutiny.... He had seen no more of the world than a girl in a boarding school, and his habit of brooding on his own thoughts, in solitude and silence, damaged his health of mind and body" (Ibid. 215). One morning, Trelawney left Shelley standing in front of the fireplace reading a book on the mantel shelf; Trelawney returned at night to find him still there, still standing, having forgotten to sit down, forgotten to eat the food that had been brought to him. Trelawney decided "the dreamy bard needed glimpses of rough life, pulling him away at times" (Ibid. 216).

Another time Trelawney was bathing in a deep pool in the Arno River. Shelley was ashore, watching the aquatic gymnastics that Trelawney had learned in the South Seas. Shelley asked, "Why can't I swim? It seems so easy." Trelawney answered, "Because you think you can't. Take a header off this bank, and when you rise, turn on your back; you will float like a duck." Shelley stripped, plunged, and, "lay there stretched on the bottom like a conger eel, not making the least effort to struggle or save himself." After Trelawney scooped him up from the bottom, Shelley said, "They say Truth lies at the bottom of the well. In another minute I should have found it, and you would have found an empty shell. It is an easy way of getting rid of the body.... Don't tell Mary—not a word. But it's a great temptation: in another minute I might have been in another planet" (Ibid. 216).

Another time, Trelawney found Shelley under a tree, gazing into the water. Next to him were two books, one by his favorite Greek dramatist, Sophocles, the other by Shakespeare. He'd been writing verses on a guitar, quoting Ariel to Miranda, "Take this slave of Music." Shelley, looking up, said to Trelawney, "When my brain gets heated with thought, it soon boils and throws off images and words faster than I can skim off. In the morning, out of the rude sketch, as you justly call it, I shall attempt a drawing. If you ask me why I publish what few or none will care to read, it is that the spirits I have raised haunt me until they are sent to the devil of a printer. All authors are anxious to breach their bantlings" (Ibid. 219).

Inspired by Byron's sailboat, the *Bolivar,* Shelley ordered a smaller, eighteen-foot open sailboat to be built, named the *Ariel.* That spring, the four-year-old Allegra, daughter of Clare Clairmont and Lord Byron, had died of typhoid fever in a convent in Ravenna. Two of Percy's dreams in late June gave Mary uneasy foreboding. One was of the dead child Allegra beckoning from the sea. In the second, a friend was calling, "Get up, Shelley, the sea is flooding the house and it is all coming down" (Ibid. 244).

On July 8, 1822, after depositing the visiting Leigh Hunts with Byron, Shelley set sail at 2 P.M. with his friend Edward Williams and a boy, from Leghorn to the bay of Levia. Trelawney and Captain Roberts were to accompany him in the *Bolivar,* but they were held up by bureaucratic paperwork. The *Ariel* soon entered a sea fog, with no breath of air in the harbor. In a heavy atmosphere, the sea was solid and smooth as a sheet of lead, covered only with scum. Then appeared a wind, drops of rain, and a furious thunderstorm that lasted twenty minutes.

Three days later the *Bolivar* sailed, having sent couriers as far up the coast as Nice. When a body was found on Viareggio, although its face and hands were fleshless, Trelawney recognized the tall, slight figure and the jacket with Sophocles in one pocket, Keats in the other. Three miles up the coast Williams was found, and several days later the third corpse. The bodies were temporarily buried where found. Because Italian law required everything on shore to be burned, owing to fear of plague, Trelawney convinced the widows of the Hellenic rightness of a funeral pyre. He fashioned an iron frame, with two boxes to gather ashes. A brass plaque stated their death by shipwreck. The classic ritual included incense, wine, honey, salt, and sugar. Williams' body, fish-eaten, yet with recognizable teeth and collar, burned in two or three hours. Afterward, Byron, Trelawney, and Shenley swam more than a mile out to sea; Byron sickened, and Shenley almost drowned.

At 10 A.M., August 16, 1822, Shelley's body was unearthed; the skull, unusually thin, broke to pieces. After three hours in a tremendous fire, the body separated, falling open at the breast, revealing the heart, likewise small. By 4 P.M., the body was fully consumed, much more slowly than Williams's had been. Yet, "the heart was still perfect...furnace red hot, the largest bones reduced to ashes and nothing distinguishable except the heart... 'It will not burn!'...a bright flame around it." Trelawney took Shelley's heart, an oily fluid flowing from it burning his hand. "During the whole ceremony, a solitary seabird had been crossing and recrossing the fire." When Trelawney gave the little black shriveled heart to Mary, she was repelled. Leigh Hunt took it then, and Mary later accepted it back in England. Percy Bysshe Shelley's ashes were interred in the Cemetery of Protestants in Rome, under the words, "*Cor cordium*," heart of hearts (Ibid. 256).

Shelley: The Poetry

In *The Cloud*, written when Shelley was twenty-eight, he creates an unusual rhyme pattern that suitably reflects the subject.

> I bring fresh showers for the thirsting flowers,
> From the seas and the streams;
> I bear light shade for the leaves when laid
> In their noonday dreams.
> From my wings are shaken the dews that waken
> The sweet buds every one,
> When rocked to rest on their mother's breast,
> As she dances about the sun,
> I wield the flail of the lashing hail,
> And whiten the green plains under,
> And then again I dissolve it in rain,
> And laugh as I pass in thunder.

His six twelve-line stanzas include an unusual alternation, both of rhyme and length. The first is a five-beat line, with an internal rhyme of the second and fifth beats, (*showers* and *flowers*). The alternating line is always a three-beat line, with an end-rhyme with the next (here the fourth) line (*streams* and *dreams*).

The third line (the second five-beat line) has its own new internal rhyme, (*shade* and *laid*) rhyming with no other lines. The long lines rhyme internally; a short line rhymes externally, only within itself, once. One could note the rhyme scheme as: aa, b, cc, b, dd, e, ff, e, gg, h, ii, h.

The form of Shelley's verse gathers an unusual momentum in the long, internally rhyming line: "I bring fresh showers for the thirsting flowers," then contracting, or releasing in the shorter line, as clouds themselves burgeon, gather, then bear, releasing, diminishing themselves, part of a larger rhythm of evaporation, coagulation, and then precipitation. "From the seas and the streams." The ever-new rhyme sound in each long line suggests both the uniqueness of each cloud, and the moving nature of clouds. The end-rhyme of two shorter lines (*streams/dreams*) suggests continuity, yet the change in every quatrain also suggests continuous movement.

Not only do rhythms within the scope of a stanza alter, but also the rhythms within the lines often alter. The long lines often stretch elastically between four-beat and five-beat length, as iambs alter into anapest.

> I ***bring*** fresh ***show***ers ***for*** the ***thirst***ing ***flow***ers,
> From the ***seas*** and the ***streams***;
> I ***bear*** light ***shade*** for the ***leaves*** when ***laid***
> In their ***noon***day ***dreams***.
> From my ***wings*** are ***shak***en the ***dews*** that ***wak***en
> A con***tin***uous, ***gen***tle ***alt***er***ing***.

Shelley explores a realm, indeed a material, an activity, above the world of immediate human experience. No one in 1820 had yet literally, in Joni Mitchell's words, "Looked at clouds from both sides." Through his attention from the Earth, through observation, through imagination, the poet is able to identify with the ephemeral essence of the cloud, in relation to the Sun, to the Moon, identifying its particular mediating activity.

> I am the daughter of Earth and Water,
> And the nursling of the Sky;

I pass though the pores of the ocean and shores;
I change, but I cannot die.
For after the rain when with never a stain
The pavilion of Heaven is bare,
And the winds and sunbeams with their convex gleams
Build up the blue dome of air,
I silently laugh at my own cenotaph,
And out of the caverns of rain,
Like a child from the womb, like a ghost from the tomb,
I arise and unbuild it again.

Shelley the atheist nevertheless gleans an eternal activity, in which, through his imagination, he participates, the rhythms and rhymes of his poem serving as a fitting instrument.

In Shelley's best-known poem, *Ozymandias*, one sound primarily informs the unusual experience evoked by the poem.

I met a traveler from an antique land, [a]
Who said: Two vast and trunkless legs of stone [b]
Stand in the desert, Near them, on the sand, [a]
Half sunk, a shattered visage lies, whose frown [b]
And wrinkled lip and sneer of cold command, [a]
Tell that its sculptor well those passions read, [c]
Which yet survive stamped on these lifeless things, [d]
The hand that mocked them, and the heart that fed: [c]
And on the pedestal these words appear: [e]
"My name is Ozymandias, King of Kings: [d]
Look on my works, ye mighty, and despair!" [e]
Nothing beside remains. Round the decay [f]
Of that colossal wreck, boundless and bare [e]
The lone and level sands stretch far away. [f]

As though emanating from the word *passions* in line 6, and reinforced in the heart of his name, *Ozymandias*, in line 10, the sound "a" permeates almost every line of the poem.

1) Traveler… an… antique land,
2) vast and…
3) stand…sand,

4) Half ...shattered...
5) And ...and...command,
6) ...that...
7) stamped...
8) Hand that...and ...that...
9) And...
10) Ozymandias...
11) ...and...
12) ...
13) ...that...and...
14) ...and...sands...

Shelley, combining traits of Petrarchan and Shakespearean sonnets, wrought a new form of sonnet to suit his subject. The first four lines begin with a traditional alternation, a-b-a-b, land...stone...sand...frown." The rhyme is standard. The slant rhyme of *stone* and *frown*, with the slightly painful shift to the diphthong, "Ouw," might warn us of something unsettling. But the next line continues, or extends the familiar pattern, command, so our pattern has become a-b-a-b-a, and we're probably subconsciously preparing ourselves for that alternating sequence through eight lines at least, the traditional opening eight lines, octet, of a Petrarchan sonnet. But no, the sixth line shifts into a new end sound, *read*, followed by *things* in line seven and *fed* in line eight. The poem has shifted in its rhyme scheme: a-b-a-b-a-c-d-c.

And what has been happening in the content of the poem? The poem has in the opening five lines moved from the speaker of the poem, "I," to the voice of the traveler, to his description, primarily external, of the wrecked stone sculpture. Line five starts to shift. The consonant sounds evoke the sculptural details in the stone. "And wrinkled lip and sneer of cold command." First the repeated short "i" vowel sound, "wr***i***nkled l***i***p," reinforced in the next line by "***i***ts," draws literally in, prepares us actually for an inwardness becoming revealed evoking the chisel cutting ***in*** to stone, through the cut, crafted features, evoked by the "k" of "wrin***k***led,...***c***old, and ***c***ommand." In line six, the poem moves overtly into the "passions," the soul life informing the stone semblance, during the slightly off-kilter triad of "...read /...things /... fed": c-d-c. "The hand that mocked them, and the heart that fed."

Line 9, the first of the traditional sestet in a Petrarchan sonnet, begins with a new end sound: "appear." Not the physical remains, not the evoked emotions, but now the actual words of the subject "appear," not sound. Perhaps surprising, the new end sound moves not forward into new terrain, but reaches back; *Kings* rhymes with *things* of line 7, linking the great capitalized title with the emotions of lines 6, 7, and 8 and with the mere things on which they're stamped. The next line, slant-rhyming with *appear,* has a slight shift forward, *despair.* And then the final quatrain sustains the new movement, *despair, decay, bare,* and *away:* e-f-e-f.

Shelley permeates his sonnet on the proud king's decayed, disappearing monument with the agonizing vowel sound of the harsh "a" of *shattered,* framing the picture of the wreck in a new rhyme scheme which lurches forward (a-b-a-b-a-c) and then backward (d-c-e-d), settling into a strange repose (e-f-e-f), as if surrendering to the lone and leveling sands of time.

Ode to the West Wind, perhaps the second most well-known of Shelley's poems, calls itself an ode, yet it consists of five sonnets, again in a new form, each sonnet using Dante's *terza rima* rhyming pattern for the four stanzas of three lines each, culminating, as did Shakespeare, with a rhyming couplet. The *terza rima*, which Dante used for his whole *Commedia divina,* alternated from the inside out: a-b-a, b-c-b, c-d-c, d-e-d, etc. Shakespeare, while alternating his sonnets' rhyme patterns within three different quatrains (a-b-a-b-c-d-c-d-e-f-e-f), concluded with a rhyming couplet (g-g).

> O Wild West Wind, thou breath of Autumn's being,
> Thou, from whose unseen presences the leaves dead
> Are driven, like ghosts from an enchanter fleeing,
>
> Yellow, and black, and pale, and hectic red,
> Pestilence-stricken multitudes! O thou,
> Who chariotest to their dark wintry bed

The winged seeds, where they lie cold and low,
Each like a corpse within its grave, until
Thine azure sister of the Spring shall blow

Her clarion o'er the dreaming earth, and fill
(Driving sweet buds like flocks to feed in air)
With living hues and odours plain abandoned hill:

Wild Spirit, which art moving everywhere;
Destroyer and preserver; hear, oh, hear!

In lines four and five, the combination of the vowel "a" and the consonant sound "k" evoke the repeated, pained, and edged turbulence of the loosed leaves, ("*a*nd bl*ack*, and pale, *a*nd") in a kind of frenzy before the wind, amplified by the repeated short "e" of "h*e*ctic r*e*d,... P*e*stil*e*nce" and the short "i" of "hect*i*c... / Pest*i*lence-str*i*cken." All three short vowel sounds, "a," "e," and "i," are shallow and constricted, suggesting a swirling activity, almost as though being beaten.

In stanza 3, Shelley evokes a quite different scene and mood, through the repeated "m" sounds of "su*mm*er drea*m*s...*M*editerranean" and the "l" sounds of "*l*ay, / *l*u*ll*ed, ...coi*l*...chrysta*ll*ine." The "m" sounds evoke a near merging of the Mediterranean Sea, the atmosphere of the season summer, and the mood and even medium of dreams. The "l" reinforces the living streaming of that sea's waters. Later in the stanza, the West Wind causes the Atlantic's powers to:

Cleave themselves into chasms, while far below
The sea-blooms and the oozy woods which wear
The sapless foliage of the ocean, know

Thy voice, and suddenly grow gray with fear,
And Tremble, and despoil themselves: oh, hear!

The "u" sounds of "the sea-bl*oo*ms and the *oo*zy w*oo*ds" suggest extending, even gently waving, undulating plant life below, to such different rhythms from plants on earth in air, and yet affected, directed nevertheless by this West Wind.

...4...
Oh, lift me as a wave, a leaf, a cloud!
...5...
Make me thy lyre, even as the forest is;
...Be thou, Spirit fierce,
My spirit! Be thou me, impetuous one!

Drive my dead thoughts over the universe
Like withered leaves to quicken a new birth!
And, by the incantation of this verse,

Scatter, as from an unextinguished hearth
Ashes and sparks, my words among mankind!
Be through my lips to unawakened earth

The trumpet of a prophecy! O wind,
If Winter comes, can Spring be far behind?

Does Dante's *terza rima* serve Shelley's exploration of the West Wind? When the dominant end sounds of a stanza (lines 1 and 3) surrender in the next stanza, allowing the initial middle end sound (line 2) to become the dominant end sounds in the next stanza (lines 4 and 6), is not the form echoing, reinforcing, and engendering the very relationship and activity that the poet ends up invoking in stanza 5: "Make me thy lyre...Be thou me...Scatter ...my words among mankind." Is not the particular poet asking to be enlarged, enhanced by the universal spirit? The "macro" is invited by the "micro" to allow and to help the micro to become, to affect the macro in the spirit of the unfolding *terza rima*. This invitation is the very gesture of inspiration. The rhyme pattern embodies the relationship of the poet to inspiration, of the poet to the West Wind. Greek and Latin scholar Shelley would know that the Greek word *pneuma* means breath, wind, and spirit, and that the Latin *spiritu* means both breath (inspire) and spirit.

Shelley, at the age of twenty-five, wrote his "Hymn to Intellectual Beauty," arising from his voyage with Lord Byron around Lake Geneva in Switzerland. Again, he fashioned a distinct form, seven twelve-line stanzas, each beginning with five lines of usually iambic pentameter, distilling into two lines of tetrameter, expanding back out into a pentameter, contracting back into three tetrameters, and usually concluding with a pentameter.

> The awful shadow of some unseen Power
> Floats though unseen among us, visiting
> This various world with as inconstant wing
> As summer winds that creep from flower to flower;
> Like moonbeams that behind some piny mountain shower,
> It visits with inconstant glance
> Each human heart and countenance;
> Like hues and harmonies of evening,
> Like clouds in starlight widely spread,
> Like memory of music fled,
> Like aught that for its grace may be
> Dear, and yet dearer for its mystery....
>
> v
>
> While yet a boy I sought for ghosts, and sped
> Through many a listening chamber, cave and ruin
> And starlight wood, with fearful steps pursuing
> Hopes of high talk with the departed dead;...
>   I was not heard—I saw them not—
> When, musing deeply on the lot
> Of life,...
> Sudden thy shadow fell on me;
> I shrieked, and clasped my hands in ecstasy!
>
> vi
>
> I vowed that I would dedicate my powers
> To thee and thine—have I not kept the vow?
> ...They know that never joy illumined my brow
> Unlinked with hope that thou wouldst free
> This world from its dark slavery,—
> That thou, O awful Loveliness,
> Wouldst give whate'er these words cannot express.

The sensitive, imagining boy who became an avowed atheist as an adult was nevertheless able, through his attention to the phenomena of clouds and wind, to experience in fact what Shelley called the "Spirit of Intellectual Beauty," embodying the activities of that spirit through dynamic textures of consonant and vowel patterns, through fitting rhythmic and rhyme forms and shifts. Shelley's proclaimed atheism reflected a courageous independence from religious and even spiritual tradition, an independence characteristic of an early consciousness-soul relationship to life, weaning the individual from assumptions. This inward freedom enabled Shelley to adapt what one might call intellectual-soul poetic forms, such as iambic pentameter rhyming couplets, in suitably flexible, fitting ways. However, Shelley the poet deferred, in his powerful tutelage to both the Muse of Lyric Poetry and to the spirit of the English language, to a mightier embodiment of spirit than his rational mind allowed. Percy Bysshe Shelley devoted his considerable poetic powers to the service of that unseen power he named "Loveliness" and "Intellectual Beauty."

Chapter 16

Keats

The Life of John Keats (1795–1821)

In 1816, an unusually short orphan passed his apothecary exam at London's Guys Hospital by cramming. Having decided to become a poet, he skipped his surgery exam and assumed sailor's pants and shirt as his poetic garb. Just as he came of age, the young man was introduced by his former schoolteacher to Leigh Hunt, through whom he met the painter Benjamin Robert Haydon, Charles Lamb, the critic William Hazlitt, Percy Bysshe Shelley, William Wordsworth, the painter Joseph Severn, the writer Charles Brown, the publisher John Taylor, and others. He would soon publish his first book, *Poems*, which, echoing Spenser and Hunt, was criticized by the Tories as belonging to the "effeminate" school of poetry. Undaunted, the young poet accepted a good-natured poetic challenge from Shelley, which he acknowledged losing. However, within two years he would experience the most fertile year any lyric poet is known to have had. Three years after that, John Keats died in Rome at the age of twenty-five, "his name writ in water." Never has the emergence of a person's individuality merged so intimately, so intensely, and so fruitfully with the activity of the spirit of the English language.

> O latest born and loveliest vision far
> Of all Olympus' faded hierarchy!

Like his favored Apollo in the Olympic Pantheon, John Keats was the youngest of the pantheon of Romantic Poets. He was born in London October 31, 1795, Halloween, the last night mischievous spirits run abroad before the serious Christianity of All Souls and All Saints days pulls sanctity to the hearth for the winter. Keats's grandfather, a good-willed glutton, owned the Swan and Hoop Inn. His daughter Francis Jennings, flirtatious, pulling her skirts up high at mud-puddles, possibly even a nymphomaniac, fell in love with the head hostler of the Swan and Hoop, an excellent horse rider named Thomas Keats. The eldest, and his mother's favorite, John was followed by two brothers, George, Thomas (a third died in infancy), and a sister, Frances Mary.

At the age of seven, with the threat of Napoleon invading England, John saw the British redcoats marching in the streets. For all of England, the navy was the great hope, and his uncle, naval Captain Midgely Jennings, was John's idol. John was sent to school at Enfield, where his parents thought he would receive positive encouragement without the caning typical of Harrow and Eton. Vivacious, athletic, not at all interested in books, John Keats, with his handsome red-gold curls and prominent nose, was the smallest boy in the school.

The next year, his father Thomas Keats, while riding "fast and most probably very much in liquor" (according to Keats's later guardian, Richard Abbey), fell off his horse and died (Bates 12). Two months later, Keats's mother married William Rawlings, a banker with little interest in Francis Keats and much interest in the Swan and Hoop. One month later, Francis Jennings Keats Rawlings left both Rawlings and her four children. Rumors soon placed her near Enfield, living with the Jewish merchant Abraham. At one point later on, Keats denied he ever had a mother. Alice and John Jennings, the careful, conservative, loving grandparents provided a reassuring haven for the four orphans.

At school, young John with his open spontaneity, became quite popular. After his father's death and his mother's abandonment, nine-year-old John became more wary and reserved. Like lame Byron, the excellent marksman, unusually short John Keats compensated for his size by becoming the boxing champion of his school. Boastful, proud, self-centered, and thoughtless, he tested his friends through boxing. Only his brother George could beat him.

When John was ten, their grandfather died, leaving the family with 13,000 pounds sterling, a good sum in those days. Three years later, John Keats lost his last familial father figure; his idol, Uncle Midgely Jennings, died of consumption, the first in an ensuing family concerto of consumption. In those years, one out of four Londoners died of the illness, now called tuberculosis. At age fourteen, John Keats was officially head of the family of four. Their legal guardian, Richard Abbey, took younger sister Fanny into the Abbey family and withheld the Keats children's inheritance. Later, at age twenty-one, Fanny sued Abbey for the family fortune and received it. It is not surprising that Francis Keats Rawlings reappeared, deathly ill herself with consumption. John, age fourteen, nursed his mother, cooked meals for her, read to her, gave medicine, and stayed up all night, guarding her door with a sword to protect her rest. After his mother died, John cried behind the Enfield office desk, to the embarrassment and sympathy of the headmaster and others. As had happened with Wordsworth, John Keats was officially orphaned at puberty.

Enfield saw a different Keats after his mother's death. Previously uninterested in books and outwardly oriented, John pulled inward and began to read extensively. As even his younger brothers George and Tom outgrew him, he remained "little Johnny Keats," barely an inch over five feet. John now had to be forced out of the library by the masters, back out onto the playing fields. He studied Latin but not Greek. His brother George wrote later of John's "nervous, morbid, temperament," suffering "many a bitter fit of hypochondriasm." His schoolmate Edward Holmes later remembered Keats "in passions of tears or outrageous fit of laughter—always in extremes" (Bates 17).

One who was sympathetic to the boy's grief was the headmaster's son, Charles Cowden Clark, a young teacher who befriended Keats, giving him books on the history of England, and copies of *The Examiner*, the journal edited by the poet-critic Leigh Hunt, who held court in jail for having criticized the king. Through Clarke, Sir Edmund Spenser's *Fairie Queene* was the first poetry to spark young Keats's imagination, with such phrases as "a sea-shouldering whale," as Keats later recalled in a letter. In his own first poem, *Imitation of Spenser*, he enjoyed, on the one hand, imitating Spenser's form, and on the other, fashioning fresh language, such as "silvering." Keats wrote of Clark, "You first taught me all the sweets of song, / The grand, the sweet, the terse, the free, the fine." The former boxing champion, once he shifted his focus to language, soon won all the related academic prizes at Enfield.

By the time Keats was fifteen, his guardian Richard Abbey apprenticed him to the surgeon, Thomas Hammond, with whom he learned to set bones, pull teeth, even give medical advice. One fellow apprentice experienced him as an idle fellow, always writing poetry. During those years, Keats read Dante, Shakespeare, and Milton. After four years, he succeeded in leaving Hammond's unpleasant tutelage to study at Guys Hospital, London. John Keats was the first to win the reward of serving as assistant to the surgeon, William Lukas. He immersed himself in bones, blood, vapors, and smells in the company of many bright young men. His second year, he became "dresser," in charge of surgeon's cases around the hospital. Although Keats the medical student identified too strongly with the patients, often feeling that he had failed his mother, his roommates found him arrogant as poetry became increasingly important to him. The urban world left Keats the poet malnourished, starving for the sensory impressions of nature, yet his capacities for observation were being steadily schooled. Detached, scientific objectivity enabled keen observation to combine with reason as the basis of often-intuitive diagnoses, a disciplined training for his later articulated "negative capability."

Swinging between outgoing energy and indolent despair, Keats wrote poetry about writing poetry. He declared his vow to succeed as a poet or to kill himself. When Keats decided to forgo medicine to "become a poet" among English poets, he enjoyed his outer poetic sailor garb until he became a poet inwardly.

In 1814, John Keats's grandmother died, the last bastion of stability in the family. At age nineteen John was ultimately responsible for the family of four. Initially overwhelmed, he considered the world his prison, with death as his only release. In fact, however, the three brothers supported one another vigorously during these several years, healthily, courageously finding their ways in the world.

In 1815, after Wellington defeated Napoleon, twenty-year-old John Keats observed a woman for half an hour at a peace celebration at Vauxhall. He fell in love with her, said no word to her, and never saw her again. The mystery of woman was to remain for him an elusive riddle.

In February of that year, after Leigh Hunt was released from jail, Keats gave Cowden Clarke a poem for Hunt, who loved it and was soon the first to publish a poem by Keats: "O Solitude! If I Must with Thee Dwell." After they later met, Hunt took twenty-one-year-old Keats under his wing, and John shifted from imitating Spenser to imitating Hunt. Through Hunt, directly or indirectly, young Keats met Charles Lamb, William Hazlitt (whom he heard lecture on Chaucer and Spenser), Percy Bysshe Shelley, and William Wordsworth. Exhibiting a real talent for friendship, Keats's fine eye caught the eye of the painter Joseph Severn, a keen observer of nature. The writer Charles Brown became a steady, supportive friend. The publisher John Taylor also developed interest in young Keats.

His first book, *Poems*, echoing Spenser and Hunt, was ridiculed by Tory critics when it appeared in March, 1817. The poet and essayist John Hamilton Reynolds was the first to support it. Although his famed contemporary Shelley was initially patronizing to Keats, a good-spirited wager between them led to Keats spending eight months writing the four-thousand-line *Endymion*. Keats readily acknowledged losing the bet to Shelley's *Alastor*, apologizing for his flawed poem, "a feverish attempt, rather than a deed accomplished" (Bates 169).

Having grown up suspended precariously between the two feminine poles of his attractive, affectionate, though unreliable mother Fanny and his older, more stable and reliable grandmother, Alice Jennings, John Keats lived at the age of twenty-two in a similar tension. On the one hand, Jane Cox entered his life like a leopard. She was so beautiful that he was not at all self-conscious. Yet he was not in love with her. On the other hand, brother George's sweetheart and then new wife, Georgiana, quickly became the most ideal, respected woman in John's life: disinterested and spiritual, like Socrates or Christ. Jane Cox offered physical attraction; sister-in-law Georgiana offered soul-spiritual sustenance.

In 1818, after two years of bounteous nourishment and exuberant growth in the literary life of London, Keats's personal life altered dramatically, leading to perhaps the most fertile year in any poet's life, somewhat like that of Rilke a century later, with a year yielding the *Duino Elegies* and the *Sonnets to Orpheus*. George Keats, after marrying Georgiana, moved to Kentucky, where he had bought part ownership of a steamboat. The loss of the two most dependable people in his life would lead to some of the most incisive literary letters ever. In one such letter of the time, addressed to his publisher's literary adviser, Richard Woodhouse, John Keats elaborated his experience of the transparency of a poet.

> What shocks the virtuous philosopher delights the cameleon Poet. . . . A Poet is the most unpoetical of any thing in existence; because he has no other Identity—he is continually in for—and filling some other body—the Sun, the Moon, the Sea and Men and Women who are creatures of impulse are poetical and have about them an unchangeable attribute—the poet has none; no identity. (Briggs 448)

This poet's "negative capability" Keats shares above all with Shakespeare, in their ability to selflessly inhabit and hence render the object of their poetry.

Although his youngest brother Tom was ill with consumption, John embarked with his friend Charles Brown on a walking tour of the northwestern Lake District and Scotland. Wordsworth happened not to be at home at Glasmere; however, Keats did look out Wordsworth's window to see his trees, his lake, and his mountains. Keats and Brown visited the tomb of Scotland's national poet, Robert Burns, and, in the cold rain typical of most of his trip, climbed Ben Nevis, which left Keats ill.

Weakened, Keats returned home to a double blow. He was hurt but not crushed by reviews criticizing *Endymion* (published April, 1818) for being too feminine in its language. To George and Georgiana he had written of his awareness that such criticism was temporal; he declared his confidence that he would be remembered among the poets after his death. He started *Hyperion* in a new, more masculine, epic voice. Second, and more urgent, he found Thomas in the last stages of consumption. As he had with his mother, and unknowingly like William Blake with his brother Robert, John spent the autumn nursing his younger brother. By the time John realized it was hopeless, as Thomas finally died in December 1818, Keats had probably contracted the illness himself.

Biographer John Murray noted that nothing prepares one for love so much as a long battle for the health of a loved one. The same may also be said of the long nursing of a loved one as preparation for poetic inspiration. That Christmas, twenty-three-year-old John Keats met and fell in love with eighteen-year-old Fanny Brawne. A flirtatious minx who enjoyed parties, Fanny nevertheless embodied both poles of the formerly distinct kinds of women in Keats's life. He appreciated that she loved him as a man, not as a poet. In a strange echo of Blake's threefold constellation of Catherines (mother, sister, and wife), Keats, in his final and only real love, completed his own threefold constellation of Frances/Fannys (mother, sister, and soon-to-be-fiancée).

Easily roused to jealousy, perhaps already suffering the low-grade fever of the family disease of which he was as yet unaware, Keats began his poetic *Anno Mirabile* by writing the short romantic narrative poem "The Eve of St. Agnes" January, 1819, inspired by one of Boccacio's stories. Mixing spiritual and physical in the festival of purity used for personal gain, Keats's picture of Porphyro sneaking into hostile quarters may reflect his own guilt at falling so in love with Fanny Brawne.

April yielded the sonnet "Bright Star!" It was followed by one of the most haunting and well-formed ballads in English poetry,

"La Belle Dame sans Merci," written in one day, and the first of the great odes, "Ode to Psyche." In May, during fifteen days at Charles Brown's house, Keats wrote "Ode to a Nightingale," "Ode on Melancholy," and "Ode to a Grecian Urn," as well as "Ode on Indolence." During those months, increasingly aware of his own growing consumption, he wrestled with feelings of hope, despair, and jealousy. Aware that, with the critical failure of his two books of poetry, he must figure how to support himself, he pondered whether he should be an apothecary or a journalist. In the summer, he wrote and struggled to sustain the epic style of *The Fall of Hyperion: A Dream.*

The autumn yielded the objectively toned, almost perfectly formed "Ode to Autumn," but as his illness and depression increased, Keats surrendered *Hyperion* as an epic, leaving it as a dream fragment. On October 16, he wrote to Fanny: "I should like to cast the die for Love or Death" (Bates 617). Samuel Taylor Coleridge, after meeting young Keats at this time, felt there was death in his hand.

On February 3, 1820, twenty-four-year-old Keats was caught outside a coach in chilling rain. Returning home with mounting fever, he suffered a violent hemorrhage. "Bring me a candle, Brown....I know the color of this blood; it is arterial blood. I cannot be deceived. That drop of blood is my death warrant. I must die" (Ibid. 636). Angered by talk of the afterlife, Keats was willing to acknowledge immortality in poetry, but not in religion. Fanny nursed him. February 13 he wrote, "How astonishingly, knowing I leave the world, I see the world around me." (Ibid. 637)

In July, 1820, when volume three, *Lamia, Isabella, The Eve of St. Agnes, and Other Poems* was published, reviews were finally favorable all around; nevertheless, sales to the public were not high. Hemorrhaging continued, and Keats decided to go to Italy alone so Fanny would not watch him die, though she wished to go with him. Joseph Severn, however, obtained a grant for painterly study and joined him on the journey. While both were sick the entire voyage at sea, Keats nevertheless entertained with puns. Because of a cholera outbreak, they were quarantined several extra weeks aboard ship off Naples.

By the time they completed their rough trip from Naples to Rome, Keats was too weak to accept Shelley's invitation to join him in Pisa. A specialist doctor confined Keats to his residence at 26 Piazza di Spania, submitting the poor patient to a regime of bloodletting, starvation diet, and, at the end, only milk. Always afraid Fanny would leave him, Keats initially opened none of her letters. Finally he did, loving her as an ideal. At home, his friend, the writer Charles Brown, and Fanny Brawne were in conflict as to whether they should join him in Italy. Keats pleaded to Brown to come." I'm leading a posthumous existence . . . stomach bad . . . we shall all die young." Brown did not follow (Ibid. 680).

At 4 P.M., February 23, 1821, twenty-five-year-old John Keats said to his loyal friend, "Severn, Aye, lift me up. I am dying. I shall be easy. Thank God I shall die easy." Keats did not die easily; by 11 P.M., he choked to death, "the phlegm seemed boiling in his throat" (Ibid. 696). The autopsy of the former medical student revealed his lungs entirely gone. The doctors couldn't imagine how he had lived the past two months. At his request, his epitaph in the Protestant cemetery in Rome read, above tufts of daisies,

HERE LIES ONE WHOSE
NAME IS WRIT IN WATER

Shelley, who had initially patronized the presumptuous young Keats, proceeded to write in his honor, *Adonais*, one of the great elegies in the English language.

> He has outsoared the shadow of our night; . . .
> He is made one with Nature: there is heard
> His voice in all her music, from the moan
> Of thunder to the song of night's sweet bird; . . .
> He is a portion of the loveliness
> Which once he made more lovely; . . .
> The soul of Adonais, like a star,
> Beacons from the abode where the Eternal are.

Keats's Poetry

Ode to Psyche

O Goddess! hear these tuneless numbers, wrung
    By sweet enforcement and remembrance dear,
And pardon that thy secrets should be sung
    Even into thine own soft-conched ear:
Surely I dreamt today, or did I see
    The winged Psyche with awakened eyes?
I wandered in a forest thoughtlessly,
    And, on the sudden, fainting with surprise,
Saw two fair creatures, couched side by side
    In deepest grass, beneath the whispering roof
    Of leaves and trembled blossoms, where there ran
        A brooklet, scarce espied:
'Mid hushed, cool-rooted flowers, fragrant-eyed,
    Blue, silver-white, and budded Tyrian,
They lay calm-breathing on the bedded grass;
    Their arms embraced, and their pinions too;
    Their lips touched not, but had not bade adieu,
As if disjoined by soft-handed slumber,
And ready still past kisses to outnumber
    At tender eye-dawn of aurorean love:
        The winged boy I knew;
    But who wast thou, O happy, happy dove?
        His Psyche true!

Keats brings to this first of the great odes, inaugurating his season of immortal poetry, his experiments to transform the rhyme patterns of the sonnet, exploring how, as David Perkins has noted, "to avoid what Keats called 'the pouncing rhymes' of the Petrarchan sonnet and the closing couplet of the Shakespearean kind, which Keats found 'too elegaic'" (Perkins 1182). During the weeks he worked on "Ode to Psyche," he also wrote his sonnet "On the Sonnet," with rhyme scheme a-b-c-a, b-d-c-a, b-c-d-e, d-e. The five stanzas of "Ode to Psyche" vary in number of lines and in rhyme scheme, according to what the particular content calls for, as poet Keats finds "Sandals more interwoven and complete / to fit the naked [and altering] foot of Poesy" ("On the Sonnet").

In the second stanza of "Ode to Psyche," as the speaker's eye rests on the scene he has espied in the forest, the rhythm slows, through a sequence of spondees, allowing details to emerge in an almost timeless unfolding.

> 'Mid hushed, cool-rooted flowers;....
>   Blue, silver-white...
> They lay calm-breathing...
>   ...tender eye-dawn of aurorean love

The long "u" sound of *cool,* with its extended consonantal "l," reinforced by its assonance with *rooted,* all require *cool* to be stressed. After the slow pace of the opening lines, the almost staccato iambic of line five: "Their lips touched not, but had not bade adieu" engenders an almost microscopic attention to the small space between their non-touching, yet still close lips, that intimate, tender space, "ready," full of potential, "past kisses to outnumber."

The power of this stanza occurs in part through a dynamic that it creates, perhaps more than any other stanza of Keats's poetry, and that he embodies, perhaps more than any other English poet except Shakespeare. The mood of the stanza and poem is certainly Greek. Various words of Greco-Latin origin reinforce the explicitly Greek atmosphere: *flowers, fragrant, Tyrian, embraced, pinions, adieu, disjoined, slumber, outnumber, tender, aurorean,* (and) *Psyche.* On the other hand, numerous words are of Anglo-Saxon origin: *mid, hushed, cool, rooted, eyed, Blue, silver, white, budded, calm, breathing, bedded, grass, arms, lips, touched, soft, handed, kisses, dawn, love, winged boy, happy, dove, true.*

But more important than the words themselves is a distinctive activity of language. One of the most distinguishing characteristics of our early Anglo-Saxon language is its use of "kennings," yoking together two words, usually concrete nouns, to form a third, new word. Examples include: *whale-path* (sea), *joy-wood* (harp), and *sky-candle* (Sun). Anyone speaking in a new language engages, necessarily and quickeningly in the activity of creating new words from existing, known ones. Our "Old Anglo-Saxon," right at the long-delayed beginnings of literacy in the ninth and tenth centuries, as noted in chapter 2, is in fact the youngest, freshest, and, hence, purest example of our literary language at work, forming itself.

Shakespeare, as expressed earlier, created many new words, such as *assassination, dislocate, indistinguishable, premeditated,* and *submerged*. Coleridge encouraged the formation of new words such as *esemplastic* to become aware of new experiences. Here, in "Ode to Psyche," young John Keats, as he is finally finding his potent, authentic poetic voice, exercises to a virtually unparalleled degree this Anglo-Saxon characteristic of "kennings"—forging words together to articulate new experiences. This stanza of eleven lines includes six word-yokings, "kennings": *cool-rooted, fragrant-eyed, silver-white, calm-breathing, soft-handed,* and *eye-dawn*. The first two, *cool-rooted* and *fragrant-eyed,* are in a construction familiar to speakers of modern English. The adjective *cool* normally modifies the noun *root*. Instead of saying "the flower with cool roots," a descriptive, but inert phrase, Keats turns the noun, the thing, into the past participle of the verb, *rooted,* reflecting activity, yet working as an adjective. Hence, in the most distilled language possible, in just three words, or five squeezed into three, the one word *flowers* is both *cool-rooted* and *fragrant-eyed,* rendered from bottom to top. The past participles, the verbed nouns, embody the usually unnoticed, slow-motion activity of the plant world, evoking as well, through the two original adjectives, *cool... fragrant,* the temperature, the moisture, the very air the plants breathe.

The stanza's most familiar example of kenning, *silver-white,* simply combines two adjectives to articulate a more distinct shade of color. The effect of *calm-breathing,* however, is unusual. *Breathing* is a present participle, a verb working as an adjective, modifying *they*. Instead of saying "calmly breathing" or "breathing calmly," Keats, by dropping the adverbial "-ly" and yoking *calm* to the front of *breathing,* distills the calm, one might say, into breathing with one beat less. Keats has named a distinct kind of breathing and, to do so accurately, has in fact created a new word: *calm-breathing. Soft-handed* works like *cool-rooted* and *fragrant-eyed,* with *soft* as the adjective yoked to *handed,* the noun turned into past participle of its verb form, both contracting the description and dynamizing the effect.

The final kenning in this stanza of "Ode to Psyche" is in a way the only pure kenning, in the original Anglo-Saxon sense. *Eye-dawn* is composed of two yoked nouns. *Eye* is not transformed into an adjective, not altered into *eyed, eyeish, eyian,* etc. The first line of the stanza had ended with *fragrant-eyed.* Here, *eye* remains *eye.* Why is *eye* even needed? Anglo-Saxon *dawn* is the point, reinforced by the Greek *Aurorean,* with its mythic overtones. The word *tender* requires something more intimate, more microcosmic, than simply the "dawn" of nature and the "Aurora" of myth. *Eye,* metaphorically identical to *dawn,* since both open, draws the activity to a human scale, while narratively anticipating Psyche opening her literal eye to forbiddenly behold her divine visitor.

Moreover, we can not avoid remarking that, as twenty-four-year-old Keats is enjoying and suffering his own dawn of love with Fanny Brawne, he is also finally experiencing the confidently awaited dawning of his own "I" as a poet. The phrase "At tender eye-dawn of aurorean love" is one of the freshest inventions in the language. Several stanzas later, the "i" sound of *eye* is stated explicitly, five times in one line: "I see, and sing, by my own eyes inspired." It is a veritable manifesto, a clarion call, almost a rooster-crowing, followed by a sevenfold repetition:

> Thy voice, thy lute, thy pipe…
> thy shrine, thy grove, thy oracle, thy heat

which then culminates in the essential statement, Keats's equivalent to Christ saying, "I am the way, the vine, the bread, the life," etc., except that Keats uses the future tense in a sixfold crescendo of commitment.

Yes, I will be thy priest
...shall those,...shall be...will I...will never...shall be

In "Ode to Psyche," a subject that one might consider "feminine," the awakening of the soul through love, Keats is certainly able to evoke a mood "tender," even feminine. But this newfound poet is able to do so through this "masculine," Anglo-Saxon blacksmithing of suitable new language to fit the frame. Remember, Blake's mythic blacksmith, "Los" (*Logos*), embodies the most highly active human imagination. Think of the energy, heat, and force needed to hammer and twist iron into new shapes.

This Anglo-Saxon activity of forming new words, combined with the gravity and pace of the sequence of spondees, reflects a new "masculine" force in Keats's poetry. (See the chapter 11 on the eleventh grade, language-generating consciousness.) A person, a poet, who generates new words also generates new consciousness, in oneself and anyone who reads or hears that language. This combining and yoking of words is powerful; this marrying of two to create a new third requires and quickens an activity of imagination, to intuit what, between the two, lives unified and anew. This joining activity engenders, gives birth, to new words and hence to new consciousness.

We can note that, at twenty-five, Shakespeare had just begun to write, while Milton had produced but a few short works; Spenser was still unknown, and, by his mid-twenties, Browning had written only *Pauline* and *Paracelsus*. We should also keep in mind that, in his short six years of writing, Keats changed and developed as much or more than many poets who lived to write for two or three decades.

John Keats's poetry always bears particularly sentient traits. Not a poet of intellect, Keats wrote poetry that tends to be like rich fruit, with thought buried deep within sensual imagery and tone, like seeds within the flesh of fruit. Yet the gesture of his mature poetry, in which the poet is so transparent as to allow the experience to speak for itself, is a hallmark of activity of the maturing consciousness soul.

Reflections on Romantic Poetry

Let us step back and reflect on the activity of the spirit of the English language that has come to be known as Romantic Poetry, while reminding ourselves of the context. Those poets responded to the eighteenth century Enlightenment, the Age of Reason: the clockwork universe engendered by Newton's mathematical calculations of the orbits of the planets and the influence of gravity; Locke's picture of the human soul as *tabula rasa*, an empty slate to be filled by sensory impressions; natural science and its growing emphasis, thanks to seventeenth-century Galileo, on measure, weight, and number as the basis for knowledge of reality of the physical world; and the Industrial Revolution, as it began to alter the "natural" rhythms of human work.

William Blake responded first, during the last decades of the eighteenth and beginning of the nineteenth centuries, to challenge the Age of Reason. His was a voice crying in the wilderness, in lyric, prophetic, and epic poetry, with the most potently spiritual and the most directly sociopolitical poetry of the language thus far. Uninterested in nature, the physical, fallen world, he explored the soul-spiritual world as it manifests outwardly and inwardly, socially and spiritually. He recognized the crucial role of the imagination as the faculty needed to reintegrate and re-spiritualize a dead, fragmented world.

In the second generation, Wordsworth and Coleridge, from 1797 through the first decade of the 1800s, in one sense shifted the activity of poetry in the English language in the direction of *roman,* the French word for novel. While the prose novel oriented itself in contemporary space and time, Wordsworth's and Coleridge's lyric poetry drew from rhythms and patterns of contemporary speech and nature as they experienced it directly, rather than as inherited through previous literature. Through attention to nature, Wordsworth in particular explored memory and the development of the poet as the subject of the poem, catalyzing a revolution in poetic self-awareness. Coleridge strove in his art to imitate the formative forces in nature, recreating in words the dynamics the Creator created through the Word.

Coleridge recognized imagination as the human equivalent of the Creator's activity, capable of integrating and reconciling opposites, fusing polarity within unity, and reuniting subject and object.

In the third generation of "Romantic" poets, during the second and third decades of the nineteenth century, Bryon, Shelley, and Keats inherited from Wordsworth and Coleridge the primacy of imagination as tool and nature as material. Whereas Byron's life captured the imagination of the Western world as the embodiment of the newly emancipated individual, the romantic hero, his poetry spoke to people more through its accessibility, technical mastery, and wit. Shelley, the avowed atheist of the six, nevertheless listened to the rhythms of the natural world with such sensitivity as to recreate them, inspired. While he scorned God the creator, he lent himself to the "Spirit of Intellectual Beauty." One reason Keats's poetry is so appreciated is his sentient-soul capacity to let language recreate sentient experience, and his distinctly consciousness-soul "negative capability" to write like an open eye, without imposing his feelings or preconceptions.

What was the relationship of the spirit of the English language to the muses of the original three forms of the human story, epic, drama, and lyric, during the late 1700s and early 1800s? Blake's epics may become better known in the future; Wordsworth's *Prelude* remains an important turning point in Western consciousness, though not widely read. When some Romantic poets (Coleridge, Byron, Shelley) tried to write dramas, they failed. Essentially, however, only the lyric muse was able to be active through the Romantic poets. Through the Word reuniting with the world, or created nature, humanly active imagination was able to heal a rift between subject and object, offering ways to reintegrate human experience in a world where the material (*mater*-mother) had become increasingly separated from the spirit.

The three elder poets, Blake, Wordsworth, and Coleridge, had to wrestle in the Age of Reason, as Jacob with the angel, to claim the validity of imagination and embody it through their poetry. They lived long lives, like Odysseus. The younger poets,

Byron, Shelley, and Keats, who inherited imagination's legitimacy, burned brilliantly and died young, like Icarus or Achilles, implying a need to temper the soul, becoming wiser in the ways of the world. Whereas the eighteenth century offered much apparent human progress in philosophy, natural science, and the birth of modern democracy, from a larger perspective it is possible to see the Enlightenment as an in-breath, an ebb, after the great birth in Elizabethan literature, the generation of the new consciousness soul. Seeing the Age of Reason as somewhat of a return to an intellectual-soul orientation, one can recognize the labor of the Romantic poets, indeed the English language itself, as fusing a renewed health and vitality in the language and, hence, consciousness of the English-speaking peoples, preparing them for the impending, rending influences on consciousness in the twentieth century.

Chapter 17

Elizabeth Barrett Browning

The Life of Elizabeth Barrett Browning (1806–1861)

In the late 1820s, a physically weak, young woman would often ride her donkey over the Malvern Hills of Gloucestershire and Herefordshire to spend a week helping old and blind Mr. Boyd with his life's project of memorizing eight thousand lines of ancient Greek, while his poor wife and daughters, too, needed the young poet's help. Consequently, she devoted substantial portions of her early twenties to reading aloud almost all ten plays of Euripides, most of Aeschylus, some of the New Testament, all in Greek, as well as several books of the Old Testament in Hebrew. As a teenager, she had been aware of the deaths of the three most inspiring poets of her time: Keats, Shelley, and Byron. Her own several poems that had been published, including one on the death of Byron, had all been anonymous. *An Essay on Mind, with Other Poems* sold fifty copies in Newcastle. The title poem endeavored to survey developments in history, science, metaphysics, and poetry from classical Greece to the present. As a twenty-year-old, she had spent six months writing "The Development of Genius," which her father advised her to burn.

Within a year after coming of age, she would lose her mother and, hence, assume responsibility, with her father, for her ten younger siblings. As a young woman, Elizabeth Barrett sacrificed her own emerging individuality to serve another, sacrificing her work in English for an aural education in Greek and Hebrew poetry. Such sacrifice at the time nevertheless eventually enhanced her work and ways with the spirit of the English language. This frail, young Elizabeth Barrett would come to be nominated by the Atheneum in 1850, upon the death of William Wordsworth, to become the next Poet Laureate of England. Although Tennyson was chosen, she was the first woman poet in the Western world since Sappho to receive such recognition.

Elizabeth Barrett's family had its roots in the New World. As far back as 1655, the Barretts had been leading planters on the Caribbean island of Jamaica, living in the Great House on Cinnamon Hill. Her great grandfather Edward married an orphan, "Trippy." Their daughter Elizabeth (Elizabeth Barrett's grandmother) married Charles Moulton, who fathered three children with her before wandering off to New York to sell slaves, and to England to father children with various mistresses. Edward Barrett would include his daughter Elizabeth's sons in his will only if they changed their names to Barrett. Young Edward Barrett Moulton Barrett entered Trinity College, Cambridge University, at age twenty, soon marrying twenty-four-year-old Mary Graham Clarke, of wealthy Newcastle merchants.

On March 6, 1806, Elizabeth Barrett Moulton Barrett was born, with oval face and receding chin. Three years later, Father Edward bought Hope's End, "a Turkish House, minarets and domes, spires and crescents," including twenty bedrooms with marble fireplaces, in the Malvern Hills of Gloucester (Taplin 6). Elizabeth was shy, intensely studious, and precocious, but cheerful, affectionate, and lovable. As the rooms filled eventually with eleven children, Elizabeth planned charades and plays with nearest brother Edward and the others. As Father Barrett gardened, supervised farms, served as sheriff, and led Bible and missionary societies, Elizabeth ("Ba") and Edward ("Bro") often accompanied him. Nevertheless, too frail to chase over the hills, Elizabeth spent much of her time studying Greek, Latin, and French. "Books and dreams are what I lived in—and domestic life only seemed to buzz gently around, like bees about the grass" (Ibid. 9).

By age four-and-a-half, Elizabeth the reader was enjoying the histories of Greece, Rome, England, as well as Pope's *Homer*, *Paradise Lost*, and Shakespeare. By age nine, Elizabeth wrote what she called an epic, and the next year various tragedies, French and English, which they used to act in the Nursery. The child Elizabeth longed to escape from the nursery, dress up in men's clothes, and become Byron's page. When a tutor arrived at Hope's End for Bro, Ba insisted on joining them. The twelve-year-old's classical reading included Homer, Plato, Horace, Xenophon, Ovid, Virgil's *Aeneid*, Dante, Racine, and Molière. She explored *Historical Display of the Effects of Physical and Moral Causes on the Character and Circumstances of Nations* and Douglas's "Essay on Certain Points of Resemblance Between Ancient And Modern Greeks." However, metaphysics was her greatest delight. She felt exhilarated by Locke. By age thirteen, she was devouring Tom Paine's *Age of Reason*, Voltaire's *Philosophical Dictionary*, Hume's *Essays*, as well as Mary Wollstonecraft.

Although her father discouraged "the other side," relatively recent fiction such as *Tom Jones*, Elizabeth loved the last canto of Byron's *Childe Harolde's Pilgrimage*, feeling that modern authors were, in fact, superior. The twelve-year-old writer had fashioned an "epic" in four books, *The Battle of Marathon*, "Pope's Homer done over again, or rather undone" (Ibid. 10). When her father published 250 copies privately, she dedicated it to him. At this age, her religious experience was "not the deep persuasion of the mild Christian but the wild visions of an enthusiast" (Ibid. 9).

Elizabeth the fifteen-year-old reader was saturating herself in the more contemporary worlds evoked in Washington Irving's *Sketchbook*, Scott's *Monastery and The Abbott*, Shelley's *Prometheus Unbound*, and Byron's *Don Juan*. After *New Monthly Magazine* published two poems on Greece by young Elizabeth Barrett, she spent almost a year in bed at a spa hotel in Gloucester, suffering from nervous disorders catalyzed by measles, for which she received many medicines, including opium. Elizabeth the teenager was already beginning a lifelong pattern of paying the price to her health for the extraordinary excesses of Elizabeth the precocious reader, when as a little child she could have been running, playing, generating the health of the physical instrument she would need to use the rest of her life.

She suffered from too much of the lamp. No doubt, had she read less as a child, she would have suffered less physically as an adult. Physically she paid the price for the benefits she later reaped poetically.

During her solitary life in Gloucester, her main companionship was daily letters from home. Perhaps the distance provided perspective on Elizabeth's father, "one of those tyrannical, arbitrary, puritanical rascals who go sleekly about the world, canting Calvinism abroad, and acting despotism at home." Unlike her then-unknown kindred spirit in Amherst, Massachusetts, Emily Dickinson, who noted that her father smiled once, Elizabeth remained able to appreciate her tyrant father's "elastic spirit and merry laugh" (Ibid. 19). Nevertheless, after Elizabeth returned home and Bro went off to school, she loved to read about Greece and Italy as she wrestled with depression. In her notebook, she wrote sixteen pages on Locke's *Essay Concerning Human Understanding*, while reading Kant, Berkeley, and Hume, working to develop her thinking through the most demanding philosophers influencing her time.

On June 30, 1824, the London newspaper *Globe and Traveller* printed eighteen-year-old Elizabeth's "Stanzas on the Death of Lord Byron," on one of her earliest heroes, with neither her name nor her initials. In fact, over the span of time arching the adolescence of the nascent poet rang the rhythm of the deaths of the three great young poets of her era: Keats when she was fourteen, Shelley when she was fifteen, and Byron at eighteen. Although the poets' untimely deaths were all dramatic, young Elizabeth certainly felt her life was not. "As to stories, my story amounts to the knife-grinders, with nothing at all for a catastrophe. A bird in a cage would have as good a story" (Ibid. 16). When on March 25, 1826, twenty-year-old Elizabeth published *An Essay on Mind, with Other Poems* with no name or initials, the title poem of eighty-eight pages surveying history, science, metaphysics, and poetry included eighteen pages of prose notes on Plutarch, Cicero, Bacon, Herodotus, and others. During the six months before turning twenty-one, she wrote "The Development of Genius," which her father considered "a lamentable waste of time,...I would not read over again what I have read for fifty pounds....I advise you to burn the wretched thing" (Ibid. 24).

As she approached the age of twenty-one, two older men entered her life. Livedate Price, a friend of Wordsworth, became her informal mentor for several years. As well, a blind, mediocre poet, Hugh Stuart Boyd, moved nearby. Having written to her about her "Essay on Mind," the forty-seven-year-old eventually invited twenty-two-year-old Elizabeth to ride her donkey across the Malvern Hills. Over the next four years she visited frequently, sometimes staying a week at a time. Helping Boyd memorize more than eight thousand lines of Greek, his wife and daughters welcomed Elizabeth's partnership. Over the years, she read aloud to him in Greek most of Aeschylus and Euripides and one or two books of the Old Testament in Hebrew. Although Elizabeth's twenties proved quiet in terms of her poetry, she inadvertently received a combination of classical as well as oral and aural training, perhaps unequaled in English poets. Her voice and her ear were being nourished, dripping wet, in the wellsprings of Western verse.

Meanwhile, Elizabeth's family life was changing. When Mrs. Barrett died, twenty-two-year-old Elizabeth was left with major responsibility for the brood of eleven, down to four-year-old Octavius. When cousins in Jamaica took land and slaves, the family fortune shrank; Bro and Sam had to come home from public school, while the other six brothers never went. In 1831, after The Great Slave Insurrection in Jamaica, Hope's End was seized and sold to pay debts.

After the Barretts moved to Sidmouth, Devonshire, the Boyds, not surprisingly, moved nearby. Elizabeth never set foot in the Malvern Hills again. During this time of anxiety, Elizabeth read the books from Genesis to Malachi in Hebrew, all the *Aeneid* in Latin, two plays of Euripides again, Italian novels, and Mme. de Stael's *Corrine*, a strong influence on Elizabeth's later *Aurora Leigh*. When Parliament abolished slavery in 1834, Elizabeth was deeply joyed, relieved of guilt as well as income. At twenty-seven, she published *Prometheus Bound* [translation of Euripides] *and Miscellaneous Poems*, again anonymously, which she later referred to as a frigid, rigid exercise.

When Father Barrett finally moved the clan to apartments in London, twenty-nine-year-old Elizabeth initially felt like a nun, walled up and away from life, but eventually, through her reading, she discovered the London of Fletcher, Shakespeare, and Chaucer. The tradition of English literature redeemed for her London's contemporary urban oppressiveness. Although Boyd, his wife having died, moved again nearby, their friendship faded, and two new ones emerged. John Kenyon, a schoolmate of Robert Browning Senior and friend of Southey and Wordsworth, knew Lamb and Coleridge. Kenyon introduced still young Elizabeth to the elder Wordsworth. "Must literary genius have moral qualities?" she asked him. Absolutely, he responded; Burns and Byron had "weakness of moral faculty" through "want of genius, not redundancy of it." Elizabeth found him kind, though undistinguished looking (Ibid. 59).

Kenyon also introduced Elizabeth to the well-known playwright, Mary Russell Mitford, and they soon became closest of friends. Mary greatly valued Elizabeth, "a slight, girlish figure, very delicate, with exquisite hands and feet, a round face, with a most noble forehead, a large mouth, beautifully formed, and full of expression, lips like parted coral, teeth large, regular, and glittering with healthy whiteness, large dark eyes . . . a dark complexion, with cheeks literally as bright as the dark China rose, as profusion of silk, dark curls. . . . Her talk, delightful as it was, had something too much of the lamp—she spoke too well" (Ibid. 61). During these early years in London, Elizabeth published a number of poems anonymously in *Annuals*, *Friendship Offerings*, and *The Book of Beauty*. Lady Caroline Lamb and Mary Russell Mitford highly praised her romantic ballads. On June 6, 1838, thirty-two-year-old Elizabeth Barrett published *The Seraphim, and Other Poems*, finally in her own name.

Poetry had been comparatively silent in England. Keats, Shelley, and Byron had died dramatically in the 1820s, as well as Blake, to virtually no notice. Coleridge had died in 1834, and Wordsworth was relatively inactive. Alfred Tennyson and Robert

Browning were still known only to small groups. Exploring what for her were the sublime uses of poetry and what she felt was the solemn responsibility of the poet in her poem, "The Seraphim," Elizabeth felt that "all my tendencies toward mysticism will be called into terrible operation by this dreaming upon angels." She recognized the book to be, "with all its feebleness and shortcomings and obscurities . . . yet the first utterance of my own individuality" (Ibid. 65). When the book was published in New York and Boston in 1841, one reviewer acknowledged Elizabeth Barrett as "a 'true poet' whose verse could not be read without a consciousness of love and holy thought" (Ibid. 71).

However, as her poetry gained popularity, at home and abroad, her health worsened. Her almost ever-present cough and bilious fever degenerated in her early thirties into spitting of blood, loss of voice, shattered nervous system, headaches, insomnia, fits of weeping, palpitations of the heart, forcing her in fact to spend much of the years at Torquay, by the sea, away from her family and London. Whereas the teenager had lamented her life being as undramatic as a bird in a cage, the maturing woman craved rest, not excitement. The doctor prescribed brandy and opium. And Elizabeth was soon, in her weakened state, to experience almost more drama than she could bear.

Thirty-three-year-old Elizabeth Barrett suffered three severe emotional blows within less than a year. First, her doctor died. Then, after twenty-eight-year-old brother Sam died in Jamaica, she was on the verge of nervous collapse. Four months later, beloved Bro drowned sailing with two friends and a boatman. For three months Elizabeth suffered occasional delirium and what she called absolute, hopeless madness, times when she could neither pray nor weep. She referred to the inner tears that scalded in her brain and said she felt "too near to God under the crushing of His hand" (Ibid. 79).

Although she felt quite alone and unprotected, she regained the will to live, moving back to London with a dog named Flush, given to her by Mary Mitford, later immortalized in Virginia Woolf's novel *Flush*. For the next five years, between the ages of thirty-four and thirty-nine, Elizabeth stayed mostly in her room on the fourth floor at 50 Wimpole Street. Her windows were sealed tight and her life confined to books, thoughts, and dreams; she lived in the company of busts of Homer and Chaucer and portraits of Wordsworth, Carlysle, Tennyson, and Browning. Opium both treated and mistreated her. "My amreeta draught, my elixir—because the tranquilizing power has been wonderful" (Talpin 89). Sleep did not come readily to her except through what she called a red hood of poppies. Yet the aftermaths of opium no doubt increased her natural propensity for depression and spells. Her only real antidote for the antidote was...poetry. "If it were not for this poetry which I feel within as a destiny to be worked out, I think I should wish to die tomorrow" (Ibid. 89). Little did she know that her poetry was soon to lead her to another reason to live.

Because the notion of any change gave her headaches and insomnia for days, both before and after an "event," only her family and four others friends were part of her routine: the author John Kenyon, Miss Mitford, G. B. Hunter, and Nelly Boardman. When in March 1842 Robert Browning read Elizabeth Barrett's article in *Atheneum* on the Greek Christian poets, he wrote to her, asking to pay a visit. She refused. Although Father Barrett was too attentive, a stubborn, cold tyrant, he was not the reason for her refusal. Nor was any lack of respect for Robert Browning. Elizabeth felt the highest praise for both Tennyson and Browning. "I am very fond of Tennyson. He makes me thrill sometimes to the end of my fingers, as only a true poet can." A few decades later, Emily Dickinson, similarly confined to her family home, would write, "If I feel physically as if the top of my head were taken off, I know that is poetry." For ten years, ever since having read his poem *Paracelsus*, Elizabeth had been "a great hero worshipper of Robert Browning," in whose writings she felt "the palpable presence of poetic genius everywhere." The reason for Elizabeth's refusal had more to do with her limits of being able to cope with actual human beings, combined with her inability to even imagine the potential for an actual romantic relationship (Talpin 95).

During these years, she traveled in her mind to France through travel books and by immersing herself in George

Sand, Victor Hugo, and Balzac. She remained rooted, however, in daily readings of the Bible and her English poets such as Shelley and Keats. Wordsworth she considered "a poet-hero of a movement essential to the better being of poetry. . . . Not one has swept the purple with more majesty than this poet." This future writer of *Sonnets from the Portuguese* considered Wordsworth's sonnets in particular the finest in the land. His moral tutelage certainly contributed to her shift of perspective on her childhood hero, Byron. "His poems discovered not a heart, but the wound of a heart; not humanity, but disease; not life, but a crisis" (Ibid. 103).

In 1844, at thirty-eight, Elizabeth Barrett published *Poems* to much critical praise, along with some complaint of false rhymes. The most thorough review came from the United States. Perhaps the most brilliant American critic of the time found in Elizabeth Barrett's verses "a happy audacity of thought and expression never before known in one of their sex. She had done more, in poetry, than any woman, living or dead. She had surpassed all her poetical contemporaries of either sex (with a single exception)" (Ibid. 137). Edgar Allen Poe was implying that the exception was Tennyson.

In mid-December 1844, Robert Browning returned from Italy and read Elizabeth Barrett's Poems. The sonnet "Past and Future" affected Browning on first reading "more than any poem he had read." It begins,

> My future will not copy fair my past
> On any leaf but Heavens. Be fully done
> Supernal Will!

In her "Lady Geraldine's Courtship," he found the most generous recognition he had yet received from a fellow poet.

> or from Browning some "Pomegranate,"
> which, if cut deep down the middle,
> Shows a heart within blood-tinctured,
> of a veined humanity.

On January 10, 1845, Robert, four months short of thirty-three, wrote in his first letter to thirty-eight-year-old Elizabeth, "I love your verses with all my heart. Into me has it gone, and part of me has it become, this great living poetry of yours." Elizabeth herself wrote, "I had a letter from Browning the poet last night, which threw me into ecstasies—Browning, the author of *Paracelsus*, and king of the mystics" (Ibid. 139). Ecstatic though she may have been about words from the poet, she felt that with her ill health and lack of vitality how could she even contemplate meeting the poet himself? "All the life and strength which are in me, seem to have passed into my poetry" (Ibid. 145). Any room in her heart had been either controlled by her father or delighted in and lost with Bro. Elizabeth had lived in seclusion, whereas Robert had traveled widely, associating with many in the public eye. "You are Paracelsus," she wrote to him, forestalling, "and I am a recluse, with nerves that have all been broken on the rack, and now hang loosely—quivering at a step and breath" (Ibid. 150).

Months later, however, on Tuesday, May 20, between three and four o'clock in the afternoon, Elizabeth Barrett cordially received Robert Browning at 50 Wimpole St. That night, she wrote, "I liked him much. Younger looking than I had expected," an interesting observation from a woman whose primary adult male companions had been, one might say, elderly father figures. In his second letter to her, Robert wrote, "I could not sleep night after night... Nothing was between the knowing and the loving." Elizabeth however skeptically dismissed this fast fall as "a mere poet's fancy, a confusion between the woman and the poetry" (Ibid. 151–152).

Nevertheless, weekly visits continued throughout the summer. When Robert declared his love a second time August 30, Elizabeth replied that she had nothing but "anxiety and sadness" to offer. Her wish to go to Pisa, Italy, for the winter was thwarted by Father Barrett, who allowed no sibling to go and declared her too weak to go alone. In mid-September, Robert said that, although he had little money, it would make him "supremely happy" for them to join lives. During three weeks of inner conflict, Elizabeth knew that Robert loved her as her father never had. On

September 26, 1845, she responded, "Henceforth I am yours for everything but to do you harm. None, except God and your will, shall interpose between you and me...nothing has humbled me so much as your love.... You see from above and I from below" (Ibid. 159).

Her father, perhaps sensing unconsciously some change in his daughter, estranged himself somewhat from her. Browning nevertheless continued his weekly visits. She commented helpfully on thirteen of his poems in *Dramatic Romances and Lyrics*, published in November 1845. During the winter, she felt at times confounded by discrepancies between the visitor and the letter-writer, to whom she felt closer. His "Luria & a Soul's Tragedy," published April 13, 1846, fueled her anxiety about whether he pitied or idealized her. With Robert's persistence, Elizabeth recommitted, knowing that Father Barrett, at the slightest hint of their romantic developments, would forbid all visits and burn all letters. To make possible some change by summer, Robert insisted that Elizabeth get outside for the first time in four years and strengthen herself.

In late May 1846, Elizabeth Barrett went for a walk in Regent's Park and climbed back up the stairs unaided. In June, Elizabeth asked to wait a year, but Robert pushed to leave for Italy before September. On July 22, Elizabeth wrote, "You shall see some day in Pisa what I will not show you now. Does not Solomon say that 'there is a time to read what is written'?" (Ibid. 243). Her unsuspecting friend, the art critic Mrs. Jamison, urged Elizabeth to travel with her to France and Italy in September. In early September, Elizabeth's dog Flush was bizarrely kidnapped and recovered within days.

Wednesday, September 9, Robert sent a note that they must be married directly, Saturday, and go to Italy. Thursday, Elizabeth responded, "I will act by your decision." Friday, Robert paid his ninetieth and final visit. Saturday, September 12, 1846, the rest of the Barrett family went to the sea. Pale as death, forty-year-old Elizabeth Barrett took a cab to Marleybone Parish Church. "We parted, as we met, at the door of Marleybone Church." The Brownings planned their wedding announcement, and agreed not to meet again until their departure from England a week later (Ibid. 178).

The following Saturday, with the unsuspecting Barrett family again at the sea, Robert and Elizabeth Barrett Browning, Flush, and their friend Wilson journeyed to Southampton, boated to Rouen, and traveled by carriage to Paris for desperately needed rest, recuperation, and a rendezvous with Mrs. Jamison. Elizabeth paid her respects to Georges Sand, the French novelist. ("Thou large-brained woman and large-hearted man..." Schmidt 460). There Elizabeth received a letter from Father Edward Barrett Moulton Barrett. "You sold your soul for genius...mere genius." The fanatical family man disinherited his daughter and never saw her again. But the newlyweds did receive letters of support from friends (Taplin 183).

Their journey took them through Avignon, where Laura inspired Petrarch's 365 sonnets, then to Genoa and Pisa, finally settling in Florence. After her first miscarriage, Elizabeth resolved, in bitterness at both her father's and her brothers' ire, never to live in England again. During their several years in Florence, Elizabeth was inspired especially by Raphael's Madonnas. She was able to reduce her morphine. She shared with the American sculptor Hiram Powers an interest in spiritualism and Swedenborg's teachings. Suffering her second miscarriage in spring, 1848, she greatly sympathized with Italy's temporarily aborted struggles for independence from Austria that summer.

Finally, March 9, 1849, forty-three-year-old Elizabeth Barrett Browning gave birth to Robert Wiedman Barrett Browning, whom they nicknamed "Pen." That summer, a frequent visitor was Margaret Fuller, the Marchesa d'Ossoli, perhaps the most brilliant American woman of the time, a Goethe scholar and fellow "transcendentalist" of Emerson, Thoreau, Alcott, and company in Concord. As Margaret foresaw, she and her child drowned just off the coast of America on their return home.

One morning in the summer of 1849, Robert was sitting at the breakfast table in Bagni di Lucca. "Three years after it had been twined," Elizabeth first placed "that wreath of sonnets" on Robert. Unbeknownst to Robert, Elizabeth had written forty-four sonnets during their most unusual courtship, completing the rough draft before their wedding. Now, three years after, surprised, Robert read them, deeply touched. They decided to slip them in under some sort of veil. She, of olive hue, thought she looked Portuguese; he called her '"My Portuguese." Her Portuguese poem, "Catarina to Camoens," had moved him to tears before he met her. She had taken more pains in the composition of those sonnets than in the rewriting of any of her earlier poems. For example, number 16 had undergone five stages of revision. In the forty-fourth sonnet, 50 Wimpole St., Sept. 1846, the image of flowers comes to represent the sonnets themselves (Ibid. 234).

> Yet heres eglantine,
> And heres ivy!—take them, as I used to do
> Thy flowers, and keep them where they shall not pine.

Robert Browning's poetry had, during those years, failed to receive much recognition, as he was overshadowed by his wife's reputation. After Wordsworth died in April 1850, the Atheneum recommended Elizabeth, not Robert Browning, as Poet Laureate, though Tennyson was the final choice. That summer, forty-four-year-old Elizabeth suffered her fourth miscarriage, losing a hundred ounces of blood in twenty-four hours. *November 1 Poems* was published, including revisions from 1838 and 1844, *Sonnets from the Portuguese*, and a translation of *Prometheus Bound*.

When Father Edward Barrett died in 1857, he had not communicated with the three children who had dared to marry, disinheriting Elizabeth, Alfred, and Henrietta. That year Harriet Beecher Stowe, whose novel *Uncle Tom's Cabin* was soon to help start the Civil War and end slavery in the United States, was a frequent visitor to the Brownings. Elizabeth's destiny, certainly in terms of rises and falls of family fortune, and possibly even in terms of her Portuguese-hued skin, had also been strongly connected to the issue of slavery, an institution she abhorred. Her dark skin suggested the possibility of African blood mixed among the generations of plantation owners. *Aurora Leigh* was Elizabeth's most widely known poem. Robert always spoke of Elizabeth as "the poet"; he was "the clever person by comparison."

June 29, 1861, fifty-five-year-old Elizabeth Barrett Browning, mother of Pen, died in Robert's arms in Casa Guidi, Florence. In addition to the wife and mother she had never imagined becoming, she had become the most recognized female poet in the Western world since Sappho.

Elizabeth Barrett Browning: The Poetry

While Elizabeth Barrett Browning was a master of a whole range of literary styles and forms, and while *Aurora Leigh* was her most popular poem during her lifetime, a hundred and fifty years later she is known for those secretly composed and most rewritten sonnets, as she will probably continue to be. While the lines, "How do I love thee? Let me count the ways" have become part of the English-speaking frame of reference, we will focus on sonnet XXIX.

> I think of thee!—my thoughts do twine and bud
> About thee, as wild vines, about a tree,
> Put out broad leaves, and soon there's nought to see
> Except the straggling green which hides the wood.
> Yet, O my palm-tree, be it understood
> I will not have my thoughts instead of thee
> Who art dearer, better! Rather, instantly
> Renew thy presence. As a strong tree should,
> Rustle thy boughs and set thy trunk all bare,
> And let these bands of greenery which insphere thee,
> Drop heavily down, burst, shattered, everywhere!
> Because, in this deep joy to see and hear thee
> And breathe within thy shadow a new air,
> I do not think of thee—I am too near thee.

The subject of the sonnet is the keynote, "I," and its object is "thee." The diphthong evoking one's individuality, "i," resounds four more times simply in the two opening lines of the sonnet: "m*y* thoughts do tw*i*ne as w*i*ld v*i*nes." Yet the serenely reaching long "ee" sound of the object sounds twice more in those first two lines: "About th*ee*...about a tr*ee*." The "i" sounds wrap around the "ee" sounds, as the thought-vines wrap around the beloved-tree. The effect is reinforced by the three-fold repetition of the stretching diphthong, "ou," in "Ab***ou***t leaves, ab***ou***t a tree, / Put ***ou***t broad leaves." Line 3 ends with the beloved's sound, *see*, negated by *nought*, while by the end of the first quatrain the lover has subsumed that sound into her own green.

Yet the second quatrain reaffirms the beloved, through direct address, "O my palm-tree," negating her own sound, "I will not have my thoughts, while re-sounding his yet again, instead of thee / Who art dearer." In a gesture not typical of male sonneteers preceding her, Elizabeth Barrett then charges the beloved to "Renew thy presence," offering her sound to him. "As a strong tree should, /Rustle thy boughs and set thy trunk all bare." The rush of airy "r" sounds—**R***enew, presence, strong,* t**r**ee*,* **R***ustle, tr**u**nk, ba*r*e, g*r*eenery, insphe*r*e*—both precede and embody the trees rustling. Her thoughts of him, with an excess of his sound that she has made hers, "these bands of greenery which insphere thee," have so smothered him that she urges him through his rustling "to drop...down," with the doubly descending "d," her thought-vines, so that they be "burst, shattered," reinforced by the explosive "t" sounds and the final falling "d."

In two preceding sonnets, Elizabeth Barrett placed the same diphthong, "ou," in almost exactly the same position in the poem. In sonnet XXV, the middle word of the ninth line, the opening line off the closing sestet, is *thou*, italicized, the first sounding of that diphthong in the poem. Sonnet XXVI begins with the line "I lived with visions for my company." Then the middle word of the closing line of the octet is *THOU,* capitalized, sounding for the second time in that poem. Then "THOU didst come." In sonnet XXIX the word *boughs* appears as the third word of the ninth line, the opening line of the sestet. The diphthong had sounded three times earlier in the first two lines (*about, about, out*) and yet it strongly echoes the pivotal effect of the thou in the preceding sonnets, reinforcing the tree of thee, in this particular sonnet.

> Yet, O my palm-tree, be it understood
> I will not have my thoughts instead of thee
> Who art dearer, better! Rather, instantly
> Renew thy presence. As a strong tree should,
> Rustle thy boughs and set thy trunk all bare

The problem, articulated in the first eight lines of this twofold Petrarchan sonnet XXIX, is that she, the lover, has loved him, the beloved, too smotheringly, at least with her thoughts. Remember, a Petrarchan sonnet typically poses a question or problem in the first eight lines, followed by an answer or solution in the final six lines (see chapter 6). The solution she offers him, in the first word of the final sestet, is for the tree to "Rustle thy boughs." While the rhyme scheme starts to shift appropriately, from the a-b-b-a-a-b-b-a pattern (*bud, tree, see, wood, understood, thee, instantly, should*) of the first octet, into a new sound (*bare*), this particular sonnet alters the traditional Petrarchan pattern of the sestet. In sonnet XXIX, the solution needs to reaffirm and celebrate the most important sound in the whole poetic experience. The new end-sound, *bare,* of line 9 is followed at the end of line 10 by the familiar *thee,* the original object of the preposition in the first line, now clearly emerging as the subject of the whole poem.

In fact, the sonnet culminates in an almost ecstatic celebration of the beloved. After the tenth line enjoys "these greenery... insphere thee," the twelfth line resumes a fourfold crescendo, "deep see hear," culminating in no less than, of course, *thee.* And in the final line, the lover makes her final sacrifice: "I do not think of thee—I am too near thee." She ends the poem by negating her opening statement. She places her final "I" right next to "thee—." And she lets the endnotes of the poem ring resoundingly, "near thee."

The pattern of the sestet has been c-b-c-b-c-b (*bare, thee, everywhere, thee, air, thee*). The first b-rhyme was *tree,* and four of the final five were *thee.* Indeed *thee* sounds seven times in the whole sonnet. Too much? Or, like Lear's "no, no, no, no, no," a rarely appropriate tolling that works.

Through Elizabeth Barrett Browning, the lyric muse Euterpe, was able to be more extensively active through a Western woman than any time since Sappho herself. Through her rich tutelage in other languages—Hebrew, Latin, French, and especially ancient Greek—the spirit of the English language was able to work in a variety of ways and forms. Through her relationship with her husband, the poet Robert Browning, the two were able to fertilely quicken the activity and the capacities of the English language.

Chapter 18

Robert Browning

The Life of Robert Browning (1812–1889)

In 1833, a young man, who some years before had left university early to return homesick to his mother, declared his independence from his seven-year apprenticeship to the poetry of one of the great poets of the era, Percy Bysshe Shelley. At age fourteen, he had discovered the recently deceased Shelley's work, all of which his mother bought for him. As a twenty-one-year-old, he published anonymously a long poem, *Pauline*, in which he evinced his devotion to Shelley and his poetry, including his "conversion" to vegetarianism and atheism. He wrote of having recognized "a need, a trust, a yearning after God." Although no copies sold, critics acknowledged the anonymous author as a legitimate poet. John Stuart Mill wrote that he had never seen such "morbid self-consciousness." Devastated by the general response, the young man resolved never to bare his soul again, but only to let others speak through his verse. How would Robert Browning, overshadowed much of his life, emerge eventually in the minds of some scholars as not only "the other Victorian poet," but also as one of the most important forefathers of modern poetry? This individual's dedication to the spirit of the English language was clear from the start and throughout his adult life as he tried and discovered various new forms of poetry.

Like the love of his life, Elizabeth Barrett, Robert Browning was of West Indian background. Robert's paternal grandmother, Margaret Tittle, of St. Kitts and Jamaica, had died giving birth to her son Robert. Robert Browning Senior, the poet's grandfather, had many children, sending his son Robert to work the Tittle plantation in St. Kitts. While there, Robert developed a hatred for the slave system in the West Indies and returned, to his father's astonishment and rage. Young Robert wanted to devote himself to art, but like many young men he was pressured to conform to his father's views; like his father, Robert Browning endured the Bank of England for fifty years to support his family. His avocations, however, were his real interests: art, literature, and collecting six thousand books.

In 1811, Robert Browning married Sarah Anna Wideman, a gentle, supportive woman, musically talented and of mixed Scottish and German parentage, with a "distinctly evangelical Christianity" of the Congregational denomination. On May 7, 1812, their son Robert Browning was born in Camberwell, a green pleasant town south of the Thames in London. His birth was soon followed by that of his sister Sarianna. In the atmosphere of his father's library, young Robert felt that his father seemed to have known Paracelsus, Faustus, and Talmudic personages personally. Robert began drawing at an early age and produced verses at six, convincing his family that he was a poet. Initially educated at home in Hebrew, Greek, and Latin, from ages eight to fourteen, Robert boarded on weekdays at the Peckham School. When he was twelve, his father, unlike Elizabeth Barrett's, was unable to publish his first collection of poems, which Robert himself later destroyed.

At age fourteen, Robert Browning discovered Percy Bysshe Shelley's *Queen Mab.* After his mother immediately bought all Shelley's works for him, Robert began his adolescent, apprentice-like, seven-year study of Master Shelley. At one point, he devilishly preached his atheism to orthodox young Sarah Flowers, who recovered from the shock to write the hymn "Nearer, My God, to Thee." To pursue further studies in Greek, Latin, and German, sixteen-year-old Robert enrolled at the University of London, where he enjoyed dancing, riding, boxing, and fencing, but withdrew before the year's end owing to extended homesickness. "He had never willingly spent a night away from home." The tender bond between Robert and his sweet mother was potent. "There was always a great delight to me in this prolonged relation of childhood." Whereas Elizabeth Barrett had an extremely overbearing father, Robert Browning had an overly understanding mother (Taplin 141).

At the age of twenty-one, in March, 1833, Robert Browning published anonymously his poem *Pauline*, telling of the spell Shelley had cast on him, inspiring his vegetarianism and atheism. Perhaps parallel to grandfather Robert's influence over father Robert to work in a bank, son Robert may have been influenced by his mother Sarah Anna to reclaim some religious reality—or Robert, coming of age, may have actually been reclaiming, independent of Shelley, his own spirituality, voicing "a yearning after God." *Pauline* sold no copies. Overly sensitive to Mill's observation of acute self-consciousness and to the general lack of response, young Browning resolved never again to "lay my soul bare...only [to] make men and women speak" (Ibid. 142). The following year, 1834, Robert traveled to St. Petersburg with the Russian consul general, perhaps contemplating a career in the diplomatic service.

A year later, however, Robert Browning published *Paracelsus*, which he later felt was a failure. Nevertheless, reviews were good, even from Carlysle and Wordsworth; one even placed Browning with Shelley, Coleridge, and Wordsworth. In May 26, 1836, Wordsworth toasted Browning as he had Elizabeth Barrett's *Seraphim & Other Poems*, eventually introducing him to many writers in London. At twenty-five, his first play, *Strafford*, lasted only five nights at Covent Garden, not designed effectively enough for the stage. At the time, a contemporary observed that Browning was "slim and dark, and very handsome, and—may I hint it—just a trifle of a dandy, addicted to lemon-coloured kid-gloves and such things...but full of ambition, eager for success, eager for fame, and what's more, determined to conquer fame and to achieve success."

The next year Robert took his first trip to Italy, including Venice and Padua, exploring, reaching for material and for inspiration. His long poem *Sordello* was unsuccessful, although Elizabeth Barrett thought it was "like a noble picture with its face to the wall just now—or at least, in the shadow." When in the early

1840s several more of his plays failed, Robert became depressed, despairing of ever fulfilling his ambitions as a playwright (Ibid. 143–144).

Having, like Elizabeth Barrett, mastered the forms of romances in particular, Browning's vow in his early twenties to let men and women speak would lead him a step further in the original spirit of Romance. The "Romance" languages were distinguished from the classical Mother tongue, Latin, as being the derivative languages, since they were written not in the literary Latin but in the living, contemporary language of the people, evoking the flavor of the folk. Robert Browning's vow was not to bare his soul in his poetry. However, his restraint in one direction propelled him more strongly in the other direction. He took the general impulse to write in the language of the people to a new, qualitative degree of intensity.

What was the context for Robert Browning's evolution of new poetic form? Generally speaking, it is fair to say that the muses of Tragedy and Comedy, Melpomene and Thalia, had not inspired great dramatic poetry in England since Elizabethan Drama in the late 1500s and early 1600s. Cromwell had silenced them completely by closing all theaters, forbidding drama. With the Restoration of King Charles II in 1660, theaters reopened, with safe celebrations of wit, reaching their heights perhaps with Sheridan in his play *The Rivals* and Goldsmith in his play *She Stoops to Conquer*, both of whom had been touched by Thalia, the muse of Comedy. But tragedy, in the neoclassical "Augustan" Age was considered simply unbearable. If a *Hamlet* or *Lear* were to be performed, the ending would be changed to something sweet, sentimental, and safe. The English folk soul in the late 1600s could not bear the potent *catharsis* of tragedy.

By the late 1700s, early 1800s, a time when Euterpe, the muse of lyric poetry, was most active in England, great lyric poets, Byron (*Manfred*), Shelley (*Prometheus Unbound*), and Keats (*Lamia*) had tried to write great dramas, and failed. None of their efforts have continued to nourish people. The dramatic muses failed them. During the 1830s and early 1840s, an ebb tide showing little evidence of the activity of any muse in England, young Robert Browning tried to write dramas, in verse. Some opened in theaters, for short runs. All failed. Though inspired by both Shakespeare's ear for voice and his dramatic spirit, Browning lacked his scope for allowing all of humanity to be reflected in the range of a play's characters. Discouraged, Robert retreated from his ambition to let others speak to each other through his poetry. However, he did not surrender. He focused his energies on allowing one character to speak. Robert Browning became master of the dramatic monologue.

In 1841 thirty-three-year-old Tennyson met thirty-year-old Browning. Although Tennyson's musical ear suffered from Browning's consonantal percussion, the two maintained respectful friendship for each other, with Browning liking Tennyson's work better than Tennyson did Browning's. From the age of thirty to thirty-five, Browning worked on a series of experiments in sound and sense, which were collected in *Bells and Pomegranates*. He wrote his final drama, thereafter directing his dramatic inclinations in other forms: "dramatic romances and lyrics." In 1842, *Dramatic Lyrics* appeared, revealing his new form of lyric poetry: self-sustained dramatic monologue. He explained that the poems were "for the most part Lyric in expression, always Dramatic in principle,... utterances of so many imaginary persons, not mine." In time Browning developed his mastery within the shorter radius, a more intimate stage, of a "polylogue" among the various aspects and conflicts of one character, rather than among several characters (Schmidt 456).

Now, at thirty-two, Robert realized that his poetry was still read by only a small intellectual circle. The formerly ambitious poet retreated to Italy in 1844, especially Naples and Rome, recognizing a more nourishing environment there. When he rejoined his parents in England, he found Elizabeth Barrett's *Poems*. When he wrote his first letter to her in January 1845, he had never been in love. As thirty-nine-year-old Elizabeth's heart had been occupied by her father and brother, so thirty-three-year-old Robert's had been tended by his mother. His three friendships had been with women interested in literature and the arts. His courtship of the invalid Elizabeth over a year culminated in their secret marriage and equally secret departure for Italy.

She was the poet people came to see; he was sometimes referred to as "Mrs. Browning's husband." She was the real poet; he called himself "the clever one by comparison" (Taplin 351). When he was thirty-seven, Robert's mother died, which grieved him almost as much as Elizabeth's death would more than a decade later. That same year, he received one morning the packet they ended up calling *Sonnets from the Portuguese*, perhaps the greatest literary gift a male poet had received from a woman in the history of the Western world. In addition, that year, 1849, his formerly semi-invalid Elizabeth, after two miscarriages, finally gave birth to their son "Pen."

It was six years later, 1855, when his signature masterpiece, *Men and Women*, appeared. It included fifty-one poems, lyrical and dramatic, many with imaginary voices, embodying action through character, revealing a crucial moment in the history of a soul. Elizabeth's *Aurora Leigh*, of course, sold better. However, the bequest to the Brownings by their longtime friend, John Kenyon, of eleven thousand pounds made their living more secure and compensated for Elizabeth's earlier disinheritance by her father. Robert Browning was then forty-three years old.

In June 1861, long after everyone, above all Elizabeth herself, imagined she would have succumbed, she died in Robert's arms in Casa Guidi, Florence, Italy. The fifteen-year, fairy-tale romance was over. Prince Charming had rescued Sleeping Beauty from the Wimpole Street castle of thorns, and it appears that they did in fact live happily ever after, enjoying one of the richest literary marriages ever. Her death, however, relieved Robert of Elizabeth's vow never again to live in England. Forty-nine-year-old Robert and thirteen-year-old Pen returned to London, England, where he set up a new home and prepared the final edition of Elizabeth's poems. His fifteen years in Italy, soaking up historical characters and settings, continued to be the primary source of the material for his poems, which were rarely set in England in the present. English Browning had little interest, poetically, in T. S. Eliot's later formulation, "There are other places... / But this is the nearest, in place and time, / Now and in England" (*The Four Quartets*). Even after he returned to live in England, Browning the poet continued to be interested in places and times other than contemporary England, predominantly Italy.

After Browning published *Dramatis personae* in 1864, he concentrated for four years on an epic work in four volumes, twenty-one thousand lines of verse. *The Ring and the Book*, twelve extended dramatic monologues that explore a seventeenth-century Roman murder in various voices and points of view, became a best seller. The fifty-six-year-old poet who had begun as a scarcely noticed solitary, and who had then rested for years in his wife's shadow, was now a celebrity, a lion of London. He was amused, flattered, and embarrassed by the formation of the Browning Society. His fame rivaled that of Tennyson. He dined with friends and at clubs, enjoying port and conversation, while speaking exuberantly of anything but his own poetry. During this period of his life, in 1882, Browning, who had left the University of London fifty-four years earlier because of homesickness, was awarded an honorary D.C.L. degree from Oxford University.

After twenty-eight years in England, seventy-six-year-old Robert Browning died at his son's house in Venice, Italy, on December 12, 1889. He was buried at Westminster Abbey among England's great poets. Ten years later, that correspondence with Elizabeth Barrett was published.

ROBERT BROWNING: THE POETRY

In *The Bishop Orders His Tomb at Saint Praxed's Church, Rome: 15__*, published in 1845 when Browning was thirty-three, the dying bishop sounds the keynote of the poem, echoing Ecclesiastes and Proverbs: "Vanity, saith the preacher, vanity!" One of the tensions in the poem breaks up the rhythm of the third line: "Nephews—sons mine . . . ah God, I know not! Well—." Instead of the usual iambic pentameter, the initial trochee, "Nephews," is followed by the dash, then the spondee of "sons mine," followed by the pause of an ellipsis, leading finally to a pair of iambs, "ah God, I know." The line ends though with, "not! Well—," a kind of emphatic, interrupted, yet also extended spondee. The tension, of course, lies in the initial habitual pose of addressing his "nephews," acknowledging them however on his deathbed as actually "sons mine." And their mother is immediately identified as the envy of Gandolf, an emotion motivating the whole scene.

Although fellow clergyman Gandolf had managed to snatch the best site for his tomb—"he graced his carrion with, God curse the same!"—the bishop will outdo him in splendor. The nine columns he imagines will be, "peach-blossom marble all, the rare, the ripe / as fresh-poured red wine of a mighty pulse." The "p" and "b" sounds of "***p***each-***b***lossom mar***b***le . . . ***p***oured . . . ***p***ulse" evoke the round stateliness of the columns, while the airy "r" sounds of "ma***r***ble . . . ***r***a***r***e . . . ***r***ipe . . . f***r***esh-pou***r***ed ***r***ed" reinforce the effect of the peach-blossom color wafting above the tomb.

When he tells his sons of his buried treasure, the lump of lapis lazuli, the bishop describes it as "Big as a Jew's head cut off at the nape, / Blue as a vein o'er the Madonna's breast." The effect shocks; the juxtaposition of the analogies of the casual savagery of "a Jew's head cut off" and the delicate, though almost profane, intimacy of the blue vein of the Madonna's breast is intensified by sound mating in the two lines. *Blue* echoes *Jew; vein* echoes *nape,* with the added horror of imagining open veins and arteries at the cut-off nape. *Breast* echoes *head.* And the vowel in *off* approaches the middle vowel in *Madonna.* The vowel sounds twist the two such different lines into an intensified intimacy with one another. Who knows how the bishop obtained his long-buried lapis lazuli?

The Christian Bishop imagines a bas-relief in bronze, with Pans and Nymphs, and, of course, "the Saviour at his sermon on the mount, / Saint Praxed in a glory," but even more "of course" for this father-bishop, "one Pan / Ready to twitch the Nymph's last garment off." He indulges in an utterly materialized imagination of his afterlife at the tomb.

> And then how I shall lie through centuries,
> And hear the blessed mutter of the mass,
> And see God made and eaten all day long,
> And feel the steady candle flame, and taste
> Good strong thick stupefying incense-smoke!

The rapturous hymn ascends on four lines of smooth iambic pentameter, then almost smothers to a halt with four stressed beats in a row: "good strong thick stup-..."

Returning to his reality, he, lying on his tomb, starts to become the sculpture he imagines.

> I fold my arms as if they clasped a crook,
> And stretch my feet forth straight as stone can point,
> And let the bedclothes, for a mortcloth, drop
> Into great laps and folds of sculptor's-work

As the bishop recognizes his sons' ambivalence, he bargains, lowering his expectations from black basalt to pistachio-nut green jasper. Acknowledging, "Evil and brief hath been my pilgrimage," he tries to force them to make the tomb all in lapis by threatening to give all his villas to the pope instead of to them. Then, almost like Satan looking at his offspring Death in book two of Milton's *Paradise Lost*, Browning's bishop recognizes,

> ... Will ye ever eat my heart?
> Ever your eyes were as a lizard's quick,
> They glitter like your mother's for my soul.

The reptilian image of the lizard, with its echoes of the serpent in Eden, is reinforced by the repetitions of the narrow, short "i," quickly spoken, in "W*i*ll... l*i*zard's qu*i*ck... gl*i*tter..."

Acknowledging their greed—after all, they are his sons—the bishop surrenders his dreams, realizing that, rather than for basalt, marble, jasper, or lapis, he may have to settle for "gritstone, a-crumble!" Surprisingly, he manages to bless them, "Well, go! I bless ye," before settling into his final watch to see if Gandolf, that cursed brother of the cloth who in life so envied him his beautiful woman, may be leering at his impoverished tomb. The bishop, in his dying scene, has managed to embody most of the Seven Deadly Sins—certainly lust, greed, wrath, envy, and pride.

Of his ancestors, Robert Browning shares Chaucer's interest five hundred years later in a range of characters telling a number of stories. However, Browning's scope tends, in spite of the extensive length of *The Ring and the Book*, to be more lyrical, more concentrated. With Shakespeare, Browning shares a fresh exuberance of language, especially from the Anglo-Saxon stream, although his subject matter tended to be Italian.

> Fee, faw, fum! Bubble and squeak!
> Blessedest Thursday's the fat of the week.
> Rumble and tumble, sleek and rough,
> Stinking and savory, smug and gruff...
>
> (*Holy Cross Day*)

As mentioned earlier, Browning was unable to sustain the universal scope of the bard's Globe Theatre that reflected all humanity. Like John Donne, Browning shares the surprise of dramatic opening lines, an enjoyment of rough-hewn lingo, and the intrigue of exploring universal elements in microcosmic scenes. With his former master Shelley, Browning continued to share the ideal of Intellectual Beauty as a source of inspiration, though Browning became more interested in what one might call a *chiaroscuro*, the interplay of light and dark in complex characters. What Robert Browning had failed to do in drama through many characters, he become able to do, especially in the dramatic monologue, by retreating to a single character. The modern poet Randall Jarrell, in *Poetry and the Age*, recognized that "the dramatic monologue, which once had depended for its effect upon being a departure from the norm of poetry, had now become in one form or another the norm," thanks largely to Robert Browning.

Some found his poetry too prosy. Tennyson, with his musical poetry, was uncomfortable with Browning's consonantality. Gerard Manley Hopkins complained of Browning's "Broad Church" way of talking, like "a man bouncing up from the table with his mouth full of bread and cheese and saying that he meant to stand no blasted nonsense" (Ford 930). Yet in this sense Browning was a descendant of Wordsworth, who had striven to enable lyric poetry to reflect the rhythms of the language contemporary people speak. In this stream, as well as in his poetry's reflection of incomplete illuminations, Robert Browning, more than any other Victorian poet, became the most influential immediate ancestor of such modern poets as Ezra Pound, T. S. Eliot, and Robert Lowell.

In Ancient Greece, the whole polis had experienced the *katharsis* of soul engendered by the tragedies, and whereas all levels of society experienced the mysteries of human nature in Shakespeare's Globe Theatre, Robert Browning explored with new concentration the complexities of individuality, allowing the dynamic of the poem to course through voice and contradictions of character. Through Browning, the English language reached to reflect complexities of individuality, enabling readers to become more conscious of such complexities and overlapping dimensions in one soul. Through Browning in particular, the long-slumbering muse of tragedy, Melpomene (and Thalia of comedy to a lesser extent) was awakened and invited into a new partnership with Euterpe, the lyric muse, the reigning muse of English poetry in the nineteenth century. Hence Browning fashioned a tool that could take the soul, the domain of Drama, and penetrate it with the concentration of the Lyric, the traditional province of the individuality. With the individual "I" illuminating the soul more consciously, modern humanity can take a substantial step forward in the development of its consciousness soul, its ability to be objectively aware, not only of the world, but also of its soul as it becomes increasingly individualized.

Reflection on the Brownings

During their lives together, Robert continued to defer to Elizabeth as the recognized poet, he being just the "clever one." Only after her death in 1861 did Elizabeth's Sonnet XXIX begin to fulfill its gesture, its offer and its wish. Posterity has allowed the "straggling green... vines" of much of Elizabeth's poetry, with the exception of the Sonnets, to fall away, as masterful, yet not unique contributions to the evolution of English poetry, and hence of English consciousness. By contrast, the work of Robert Browning stands revealed, palm-tree–like, as upholding a strong, particularly individual contribution to English poetry, and hence to the consciousness of those in the English-speaking world. The traditional subject reaches to overcome, to conquer the object of the love poem. Elizabeth Barrett offers and sacrifices herself to the beloved, a more "feminine" gesture. What Elizabeth accomplished in her sonnet, and was unable to accomplish sufficiently during the years of their marriage, she appears to have accomplished poetically, supporting his scarcely apparent development, as he has emerged as the enduring poet. Yet her role in the evolution of English poetry may become more clearly recognized. However posterity regards their work individually, Robert and Elizabeth Barrett Browning remain the most poetically fertile union in the history of literature.

Chapter 19

Tennyson

The Life of Alfred, Lord Tennyson (1809–1892)

In 1830, when a young Englishman won Cambridge University's Chancellor's Medal for his poem "Timbuctoo," his dear friend Arthur Hallam declared him "promising fair to be the greatest poet of our generation, perhaps the century." That same year, the young man wrote out the manuscript for a book of his poetry, lost it in the woods one night, and then rewrote the whole manuscript from memory. In a glen, with no thought of romance, he saw his future wife, asking her if she were a dryad. A doctor informed him that he had a traveling clot in his brain and could die at any moment. With his friend Arthur, the twenty-one-year-old traveled that summer to the Spanish Pyrenees to aid in a rebellion that soon failed. For the rest of his life, the Englishman would wear a Spanish sombrero and cape. When he returned to England, Alfred Tennyson was too sick to return to Cambridge University. Eventually, however, his name would become synonymous with his era, the Victorian Age. More than any twenty-one–year-old since Milton, Tennyson was recognizable as having a potent partnership with the spirit of the English language.

During the 1700s, Alfred Tennyson's great grandfather had moved his family down from York to Lincolnshire and married a wealthy blue blood from a family of difficult temper. Their son George had lost his mother at age five and grew up overbearing with his friends and a bully with his submissive wife Mary

Turner and family. Their eldest son George Clayton, an awkward, twitching six feet tall, suffered from fits of epilepsy. He was eclipsed in his parents' eyes by his younger brother Charles, and after George complained once too often of his disfavor, his father disinherited him, forcing him into the church.

The inherited, difficult temper was not easy to transcend, yet the family strove, fashioning its own eccentric texture. Rector George Clayton Tennyson, a man of imagination, passion, and increasing melancholy, married one of the beauties of Lincolnshire, Elizabeth Fytche, "one of the most angelick creatures on God's earth" (Richardson 17). Together, they brought eight boys and four girls into the world. The fourth, Alfred Tennyson, was born at Somersby Rectory, August 6, 1809. When he was baptized two days later, he suffered convulsions. On Sunday, Rev. George would deliver a finely balanced sermon that few parishioners could understand. The rest of the week, he would sleep into the late afternoon and then play the harp. Extremely sensitive to noise, the rector, who was generally genial to the outside world, could be black in mood at home. Little Alfred wondered if in heaven he might be permitted to make a little noise. His mother Elizabeth read poetry aloud and loved animals. After Alfred tamed an owl from his bedroom window, it liked to sit on Mrs. Tennyson's head. Local boys would beat dogs outside her window, knowing she would give them coins to stop. When the rector George walked, Elizabeth rode in a donkey chair pulled by the family Newfoundland dog.

Young Alfred bore the looks and passion of both parents, as well as the gloom of his father and the piety of his mother. The first poetry that moved the precocious boy was his own. At age five, stretching his arms in a gale, Alfred proclaimed, "I hear, I hear strange voices in the wind" (Ibid. 16). When, by age six, he could repeat the four "Odes of Horace" by heart, his father put him in Louth Grammar School, run by a sadist; one boy had to stay in bed for six weeks after a thrashing. The masters were brutally sarcastic bullies with the boys. As an adult, Alfred refused ever to go down that street again. "The only thing I learned was the phrase '*ponis desilientae aquae,*' the sound of water leaping down from on high" (Martin 30). Some of his best poetry would later evoke the sound of water, as well as the look of plants.

At age eight, "I remember making a line I thought greater than Campbell, Byron, or Scott, I rolled it out and was greatly moved by it: 'with slaughterous sons of thunder rolled by the flood.' Great nonsense, of course, but I thought it fine" (Ibid. 21). One Sunday, too sick to go to church, Alfred's brother gave him a slate with a challenge to write a verse about a flower. Some time after he covered both sides, perfectly metrical, he declared, "I mean to be famous" (Richardson 17).

When eleven-year-old Alfred, who was no keen scholar, was allowed to leave grammar school, he blossomed at home in the library of twenty-five hundred books, under the tutelage of Rector Tennyson. Alfred soon produced a manuscript with the modest title, *The Poetry of Tennyson, the Lyrical Poetry of Tennyson, and the Prose Writings of Tennyson.* Alfred first met King Arthur as he read Malory's fifteenth-century *Morte d'Arthur.* At age thirteen, he wrote an epic of four to five thousand lines in David Scott's octosyllabic mode, mingled with heroic couplets, perfectly metrical. Then, at fourteen, he began a drama, also perfectly metrical.

By this time ten servants were helping his inefficient Mother Elizabeth run the household. Outside the library, the rector's growing drinking of alcohol was aggravating his epilepsy. Alfred seemed at times the virtual head of the house. Though full of cultivation and taste, the children were simple-minded, simple-hearted, unworldly. They fished, fenced, acted plays and told stories. Charles and Alfred would walk on opposite sides of the hedge, composing poetry and shouting lines at each other.

Although Alfred, son of the harp-playing father, showed an early gift for musical timing in language, he lacked interest in regular time. One morning in the woods at four o'clock, Alfred greeted a fisherman, "Good day." "Poor fool," the fisherman responded; "thou doesn't know whether it be day or night"(Richardson 19). However, Alfred was absorbing the colors of the Lincolnshire land, and later he would "pull up the tubers of the Lincolnshire dialect and let them go into his lines, smelling freshly of the soil"

(Richardson 19). Another night, fifteen-year-old Alfred ran weeping through the woods, carving "Byron is dead," in sandstone.

Of the twelve children, Alfred most resembled their father in stature, features, walk, voice, and a huge head. Alfred also shared the "black blood" of his father. When the rector's moods were worst, Alfred would run through the night to the churchyard and throw himself on a grave, wishing he were dead. Like Walt Whitman's brood of siblings across the ocean, Alfred's whole family struggled with the challenge of living healthily in the world of time and space, usually without success. Eventually, one brother would become totally insane, one suffered incapacitating mental illness, one was an opium addict, one severely alcoholic, and the rest suffered at least one severe mental breakdown each.

Seventeen-year-old Alfred feared becoming like his father. As the rector's fits increased in frequency and intensity, the weekly *petit-mals* of epilepsy (associated in the contemporary Victorian minds with excessive sexuality and masturbation) included verbal abuse and threats of physical violence. Alfred created his own antidote. He found a way to generate a "waking trance . . . through repeating my own name to myself, . . . 'till consciousness and individuality itself seemed to dissolve and fade away into boundless being—and this not a confused state, but the clearest, the surest of the surest, utterly beyond words—where death was an almost laughable impossibility" (Martin 28, 29).

At age eighteen, Alfred's education at home culminated with a book, *Poems by Two Brothers*, most by Charles, some by Alfred. Alfred was relieved to leave the storm-fest of home for Trinity College, Cambridge University. He stood over six feet tall, with a broad chest, heavy legs, swarthy complexion, dark hair with a flash of chestnut, deep-set, hooded eyes, and a beautifully modeled nose above a sensuous mouth. These fine features on a rugged body made quite an impression. "That man must be a poet," observed one fellow student. Another recognized "the Hyperion shorn of his beams in Keats's poem, with a Pipe in his mouth." A professor wrote to Alfred's father, "I have got the third of the Tennysons in my room; he is an immense poet" (Richardson 19).

The huge youth who kept a snake and enjoyed smoking pipes and arguing attracted the attention of a number of young men with particular potential. In 1820, a Cambridge Conversazione Society had been formed to debate contemporary problems. By the late 1820s, the group, calling themselves The Apostles, included Black Jack Kemble; Richard Trench, future archbishop of Dublin; R. Milnes, later author of *Life, Letters, Literary Remains of John Keats;* Spedding, a later editor of Bacon; Lushington, who would become Rector of Glasgow University; and Thompson, a Greek scholar. Every Saturday night, The Apostles met, discussed essays, smoked, drank coffee, and ate anchovy sandwiches. They considered themselves the pride of Cambridge. "I often wonder what we have done to deserve being gifted, as we are, so much above those cursed idiotic Oxford brutes" (Richardson 20). Although Tennyson resigned after five meetings, not finding the group conversation easy, The Apostles had drawn out Tennyson the conversationalist in a multitude of fascinating ways. Generally, it was Alfred's experience that the professors "profess to teach / And teach us nothing, feeding not the heart," Cambridge nevertheless fired his intellect and touched his heart (Martin 68).

The next semester, Arthur Henry Hallam entered Cambridge University and Alfred Tennyson's life. One of four surviving of eleven children, Arthur's father had sent him from Eton to Cambridge, claiming that he wanted to get Arthur away from Gladstone (future Prime Minister of England) and other Oxford friends. In Italy, the wealthy Hallam had fallen in love after Eton with an older English girl, who stayed in Italy when Arthur returned to England for Cambridge. Alfred quickly found himself "falling in friendship." When Alfred Tennyson won the Chancellor's Medal for "Timbuctoo," Hallam considered him "promising fair to be the greatest poet of our generation, perhaps the century" (Richardson 22).

William Wordsworth, visiting his brother, Master of Trinity College, reported, "We have a respectable show of blossom in poetry (six years after Byron's death). Two brothers of the name of Tennyson, in particular, are not a little promising" (Richardson 22). Tennyson, then twenty-one, copied out his complete manuscript for *Poems, Chiefly Lyrical*, lost it in the woods one night, and then rewrote the whole manuscript from memory. Such was the capacity for both creativity and memory in the young poet. Nevertheless, the young man, so vitally inhabited by poetry, learned from a physician that he had a traveling blood clot and could die at any time.

That summer in 1830, Alfred Tennyson and Arthur Hallam traveled through France with money and ciphered instructions for Spanish rebels in the Pyrenees. Alfred began wearing a Spanish cape and sombrero, which would continue for the rest of his life. The "revolution" aborted, its two leaders captured and shot, Tennyson and Hallam returned in September. Although the would-be revolutionaries were disillusioned, the poet had been actively gathering impressions. "An artist ought to be lord of the five senses" (Martin 120). Alfred, however, was too sick to return to Cambridge.

During visits to his dear friend, Arthur fell in love with Alfred's sister Emily. Mr. Hallam, however, forbade him to see her until he came of age. Although Alfred was so devoted to Arthur that there was no room in his life for any woman, he did catch his first glimpse of his future wife strolling in a glen. "Are you a Dryad or an Oread wandering here?" he asked her (Richardson 22). The next year, Rector George Tennyson died of drugs, alcohol, epilepsy, and possibly typhus. Few relatives attended the funeral. Alfred slept in his father's deathbed, but, he later said, "a poet never sees a ghost" (Martin 132).

When Arthur Hallam came of age, he spent five weeks at Somersby, with Alfred and Emily. After Tennyson and Hallam traveled the Rhine in the summer, Alfred remained essentially homeless for the next eighteen years, circulating among family and friends. Because Alfred composed most of his poems orally, much blew away in his ever-present smoke. Friends had to urge him to write them down. Hallam sneakily wrote down "Lotos-Eaters." Owing to his weak eyesight, which occasioned a monocle, much of his poetry renders either large distances or minute detail, with little of the mid-range, such as human faces. In December 1832, Alfred Tennyson's *Poems* was published. When, months later, the poems were given a cold, critical reception by Edward Bulwer-Lytton and others, Alfred suffered extreme headaches, fear of insanity, and thoughts of suicide.

On September 15, 1833, Arthur Henry Hallam, age twenty-two, died in Vienna of cerebral thrombosis. Before news of his death reached the Tennysons, young Mary and Mathilde Tennyson saw at Somersby a "tall figure, clothed in white, down the lane, through the hedge where there's no gap" (Martin 182). Emily Tennyson grieved, collapsing for a year. Alfred Tennyson did not go to the funeral, but the day he found out about Arthur's death, he started writing verses, which would grow over the next seventeen years to become *In Memoriam*. On October 20, he wrote "Ulysses." Alfred Tennyson grieved for fifty-nine years, ever aware of Arthur Hallam's spiritual presence.

Alfred and Emily were not alone in their loss. Gladstone wrote that Hallam "was a spirit so exceptional that everything with which he was brought into relation during his shortened passage through this world, came to be, through this contact, glorified by a touch of the ideal." Henry Alford, later Dean of Canterbury, wrote,

> I do not remember anything for many years which has distressed me so much.... It seems, indeed, a loud and terrible stroke from the reality of things upon the fairy building of our youth.... I long ago set him down for the most wonderful person altogether I ever knew.

Alfred described "a gentleness and purity almost virginal in his voice, in manner and, countenance, and the upper part of his face, his forehead and eyes, wore angelic radiance they must still wear in heaven. On Arthur Hallam's brow and eyes this heavenly light, so fugitive in other faces, rested habitually." Allowing for inflationary temptations of eulogy, it is clear that Arthur Henry Hallam had been an unusual individual, and an unusual presence in people's lives, with quality even angelic (Richardson 26).

While Emily collapsed and Alfred wrote, other Tennysons were beginning to show signs of tenuous connections to the world. Young Edward, who would weep for days, was finally sent to an asylum in York. Brother Septimus suffered similarly. Sister Maud found help in a healthier local asylum, where patients took walks and played games. Alfred's friends would take grieving Alfred to the Lake District, where he composed *Morte d'Arthur.* Friends urged him to publish, but young Tennyson was wary of further critical attacks. Contemplating larger, long-term possibilities, he realized that, except for *King Arthur,* most of the big subjects had been done. John Stuart Mill, beginning a slowly growing, positive recognition of the young poet's worth, acknowledged Tennyson's power to create scenery symbolically reflecting human feeling.

When in 1836 his brother Charles married Louisa Sellwood, best man Alfred fell in love with a bridesmaid, the Dryad he had encountered in the woods six years earlier: sister Emily Sellwood. "O happy bridesmaid, make a happy bride!" He knew then that he "would break stones on the road" to have Emily Sellwood as his wife, shy, a bad-backed invalid though she was.

The twenty-eight-year-old poet was gradually gaining significant recognition. Along with Gladstone and Carlyle, Thackeray the novelist admired the fine-featured, shaggy-headed man who swam in tranquil chaos and tobacco smoke. Seeing that Tennyson smoked a small briar pipe nine hours a day, Elizabeth Barrett pondered to Mary Russell Mitford, "The smoke is said to be so essentially Tennysonian that he couldn't be supposed to rhyme without it" (Richardson 35). Whereas teenaged Alfred had instinctively developed a mantra to protect his own sanity from his father's insanity, Tennyson in his twenties may have instinctively found tobacco smoke to be an addiction that protected him in wreaths of smoke, serving his work in the world and doing less harm than other Tennyson addictions.

The next year, Alfred Tennyson and Emily Sellwood became formally engaged. "There is the glory of being loved, for so have we laid great bases for Eternity" (Richardson 35). Yet, his brother Charles's marriage with sister Louisa was wrecking, mainly because of Charles's old opium habit. Skeptical of Alfred's ability to support a family financially, father Sellwood forbade Alfred and Emily two years later from continuing any correspondence. Although Mrs. Tennyson offered to supply the necessary funds for marriage, Alfred, partially out of fear of failure in supporting himself as a poet, and as well declaring it "not right, in such a large family," refused (Richardson 35). The engagement was broken.

> ...we two rose
> There-closing like an individual life—
> In one blind cry of passion and of pain,
> Like bitter accusation ev'n to death
> Caught up the whole of love and utter'd it,
> And bade adieu forever.

Although his love life disappeared, the aura of his personality continued to grow. Whereas Elizabeth Barrett led a secluded life at 50 Wimpole Street, Alfred led a very full social life. Barrett, however, had heard of him, with an unduly large head and fathoming eye, smoking and composing poems all day, and losing many for neglecting to write them down. Tennyson had the air of a "bandit genius." Novelist Thackeray was impressed by his great big yellow face and growling voice, his manliness and simplicity of character. This poet, whose tobacco jar held two gallons, who drank tea from a bowl not a cup, who drank port by the bottle, was of heroic mold.

After ten years of public silence, the poet caught up with the personality. May 14, 1842, thirty-three-year-old Alfred Tennyson published two volumes of *Poems*. By the end of the year, it had merited twenty reviews. Edgar Allan Poe wrote, "I am not sure that Tennyson is not the greatest of the poets" (Martin 267). *The Edinburgh Review* declared, "He is called to take a lofty station among English poets of the ages. The poetry...never merely didactic or ceasing to be poetry...expresses throughout a tone of high and just moral feeling" (Richardson 39). Dickens told Forster,

> I have been reading Tennyson all morning on the seashore. Among other trifling effects, the waters have dried up as they did of old and shown me all the mermen and mermaids,

> at the bottom of the ocean; together with millions of queer creatures, half-fish and half-fungus, looking down into all manner of coral caves and seaweed conservatories." (Richardson 40)

Elizabeth Barrett valued "a higher degree of philosophical thought…the poet being divine as I always felt him to be" (Richardson 40). Miss Mitford wrote, "I prefer him to any poet of the age" (Richardson 41). England, having endured more than a decade of drought of poetic silence, felt nourished by one poet at least, since Barrett and Browning were only looming. After thirty-seven-year-old Elizabeth Barrett met thirty-four-year-old Alfred Tennyson in 1843, she wrote, "When I think of the most gifted men in England, I always think of Tennyson long and long before I get down to Dickens" (Richardson 41). She would have loved to know that a visitor had found Tennyson with Homer and Elizabeth Barrett on his table. William Wordsworth, two generations older, invited the poet to dine with the words, "Come, brother bard, to dinner" (Richardson 42). Although some thought Tennyson should already succeed Southey as Poet Laureate, Wordsworth was selected.

After Tennyson published his third volume of *Poems,* Arthur Hallam's father recommended that Queen Victoria award thirty-six-year-old Tennyson a pension of two hundred pounds per year. Because Alfred had lost most of his money in water-treatment schemes with sister Maud's doctor, this honor was particularly timely and fortunate. When *The Princess* appeared in 1847, Ruskin considered the piece on the Alp rare among all poetry. The following year Ralph Waldo Emerson met Tennyson, observing plain strength, general sanity, confidence-inspiring power, and good humor. Tennyson continued however often to suffer low spirits, aching for Emily, grieving for Arthur. He often wept as he read poems aloud. Nervously aware that Bulwer-Lytton was working on an Arthurian epic, Tennyson's own Arthurian work continued to germinate during a western tour to Tintagel.

When in 1848 Alfred Tennyson asked Emily Sellwood for her hand in marriage, she said no. By the next year, when he asked again, Alfred was drinking a bottle of wine a day. The next year, 1850, was to prove to be a year of fruition for Alfred Tennyson, man and poet. Begun seventeen years earlier, after Arthur Hallam had died, *In Memoriam* was published anonymously. England nevertheless recognized its author.

Although Elizabeth Barrett Browning was also considered, Tennyson was invited to become Poet Laureate of England. On June 13, forty-one-year-old Alfred Tennyson and thirty-seven-year-old Emily Sellwood married, twenty years after he had first seen her in the wood and thirteen years after they had first become engaged. "The Peace of God came into my life before the altar when I wedded her" (Martin 334). His worst depressions and melancholy receded. Alfred felt profound respect for Emily's religious feeling. After Hallam, Emily was the individual whose instincts about his poetry he trusted most. Though often ill, she had a will of steel. After their first son was born dead, the ageing mother gave birth to two more boys, Hallam and Lionel.

In relation to *In Memoriam*—although Charlotte Brontë, later Paul Verlaine and others, wondered how deep grief could yield such abundant verse—England experienced that "Tennyson did not merely lament the loss of Arthur Hallam; in his spiritual odyssey, he had known all the doubts and fears, all the misery and hopes that were peculiar to his age.... To a generation of doubt, of faltering faith, it revealed facets, and confirmed deep, abiding faith, after all" (Richardson 58). Thomas Hardy and many others, suffering personal loss, found replenishing consolation in *In Memoriam*. "I have written what I have felt and known, and I will never write anything else," said its author (Richardson 61). What had been written out of potent personal pains ripened and transmuted sufficiently to become a universal book of consolation. It is fair to say that the spirit of Arthur Hallam, through Alfred Tennyson's word-work, touched the nation.

In universities, Tennyson was in the air throughout the 1850s. From 1853, he lived well on an estate on the Isle of Wight, finally enjoying his family life. "Friend and Laureate of the Queen," Alfred Tennyson soon emerged, along with Victoria, as one of the names associated with his age. He grew to a stature of feeling responsible for his people in his time.

> Few English poets have so identified themselves with the age with which they lived as Tennyson. He had focused into a shining point existing feeling and thought, he had reflected the common perplexities, achievements, and aspirations. His influence was felt in all the arts of the Victorian era.... He inspired their painting, sculpture, music, comic operas, poetry. He followed their theological feuds, recorded their scientific discoveries. He tried to influence their politics, he determined to set their moral standards. He reflected his age; his age reflected him. (Richardson 287, 13)

In 1884, at age seventy-five, Alfred finally accepted, after two previous refusals, his appointment as a baron, becoming Alfred, Lord Tennyson. Michaelmas Day, September 29, 1892, eighty-three-year-old Tennyson went for his last drive in a carriage. On October 3, Alfred asked for Shakespeare's *Cymbeline.* October 4: "Where's my Shakespeare; I must have my Shakespeare." On October 5, he recited from *Cymbeline* a speech of Posthumous to Imagen that had always moved him to tears. "Hang there like fruit, my soul, / Till the tree die!" Then, "Hallam, Hallam." Then he whispered to Emily, "God bless you, my joy."

Tennyson's doctor later wrote, "On a bed a figure of breathing marble, flooded and bathed in the light of the full moon through the oriel window; his hand clasping the Shakespeare which he had asked for but recently, and which he kept by him to the end; the moonlight, the majestic figure as he lay there drawing thicker breath irresistibly brought to our mind his own Passing of Arthur." At 1:35 AM, October 6, 1892, Alfred, Lord Tennyson died peacefully. He had devoted much of his poetic energies to the Arthurian matter in *Idylls of the King* and other poems, and was guided in his adult life by the spirit of his friend Arthur Hallam (Martin 581).

Tennyson: The Poetry

In Memoriam
A. H. H.

[As context for section L]

I

I hold it truth with him who sings
    To one clear harp in divers tones,
    That men may rise on stepping-stones
Of their dead selves to higher things.

But who shall so forecast the years
    And find in loss a gain to match?
    Or reach a hand thro' time to catch
The far-off interest of tears?

Let Love clasp grief lest both be drown'd.
    Let darkness keep her raven gloss:
    Ah, sweeter to be drunk with loss,
To dance with Death, to beat the ground,

Than that the victor Hours should scorn
    The long result of love, and boast,
    "Behold the man that loved and lost,
But all he was is overworn." ...

V

I sometimes hold it half a sin
    To put in words the grief I feel:
    For words like nature half reveal
And half conceal the Soul within.

But, for the unquiet heart and brain,
    A use in measured language lies;
    The sad mechanic exercise,
Like dull narcotics, numbing pain.

In words, like weeds, I'll wrap me o'er,
    Like coarsest clothes against the cold.
    But that large grief which these enfold

Is given in outline and no more....

XLIX

From art, from nature, from the schools,
    Let random influences glance,
    Like light in many a shiver'd lance
That breaks about the dappled pools:

The lightest wave of thought shall lisp,
    The fancy's tenderest eddy wreathe,
    The lightest air of song shall breathe
To make the sullen surface crisp.

And look thy look, and go thy way,
    But blame not thou the winds that make
    The seeming-wanton ripple break,
The tender-pencill'd shadow play.

Beneath all fancied hopes and fears
    Ay me! the sorrow deepens down,
    Whose muffled motions blindly drown
The bases of my life in tears.

L

Be near me when my light is low,
    When the blood creeps, and the nerves prick
    And tingle; and the heart is sick,
And all the wheels of Being slow.

Be near me when the sensuous frame
    Is rack'd with pangs that conquer trust;
    And Time, a maniac scattering dust,
And Life, a Fury slinging flame.

Be near me when my faith is dry,
    And men the flies of latter spring,
    That lay their eggs, and sting and sing,
And weave their petty cells and die.

Be near me when I fade away,
    To point the term of human strife,

And on the low dark verge of life
The twilight of eternal day.

LI

Do we indeed desire the dead
Should still be near us at our side?
Is there no baseness we would hide?
No inner vileness that we dread?

Shall he for whose applause I strove,
I had such reverence for his blame,
See with clear eye some hidden shame,
And I be lessen'd in his love?

I wrong the grave with fears untrue:
Shall love be blamed for want of faith?
There must be wisdom with great Death:
The dead shall look me thro' and thro'.

Be near us when we climb or fall:
Ye watch, like God, the rolling hours
With larger other eyes than ours,
To make allowance for us all.

Stanza L, like most of the whole poem, consists of four stanzas of four lines each. In each stanza, the outer lines rhyme, and the inner lines rhyme: a-b-b-a. The lines are usually, like the first one, iambic tetrameter, a four-beat line. "Be near me when my light is low." The strongest sounds of the opening line are the opening three vowels in the plea, "B*e* n*ea*r m*e*." The speaker addresses the departed Arthur with commanding plea through the "ee" sound, which has long been associated with Hermes, or Mercury, the messenger between the gods and human beings. The strongest consonant sound in the opening line is the liquid "l" of "*l*ight is *l*ow."

In the second line, the usual rhythm alters dramatically into a halting anapest and a long, an anapest and a long: short-short-long-long. "When the blood creeps, and the nerves prick." The initially summoning *ee* is pulled into "creeps," and the "l" sounds of "*l*ight" and "*l*ow" congeal in "b*l*ood." Although the blood slows, the nerves quicken, evoked through the assonance of the narrow, short "i" in "pr*i*ck," and "t*i*ngle" and "s*i*ck," in "And tingle, and the heart is sick." And the "l," echoing down through "ting*l*e," now expands in the final line of the stanza, almost hauling the line to a stop, with the double "l" of "a*ll*," then the double "ee" of "wh*ee*ls" and its "l," then "being" extending before "slow": "And all the wheels of being slow."

The second stanza, like each in this section XLIX, begins with the same incantatory "Be near me." The "s" sounds in "*s*en*s*uou*s*" evoke the almost sizzling activity of the senses at the doorways between our outer and inner worlds. By the time of this second line of the second stanza, there has been a gentle buildup, scarcely noticed in the first stanza, of a series of four "ands," an apparently innocuous sound that nonetheless intensifies in "r*a*ck'd with p*a*ngs that conquer trust." This avalanche of assonance embodies an agony that is concentrated further in the next line, "*A*nd Time, a mani*a*c sc*a*ttering dust," the effect of which is accentuated further by the alliterative series of hard, cutting "c" sounds: "*c*onquer . . . mania*c* s*c*attering." The stanza culminates in the line "And Life a fury slinging flame." Now not only the narrative speaker (Tennyson) but also all Life resonates with the narrow "i" of the first stanza, with the recurrent "ng" giving "sli*nging*" double, whip-lashing intensity. Although Tennyson resists the old Anglo-Saxon three-beat alliteration by saying, "Fury slinging flame," instead of "fury flinging flame," he achieves as raw an evocation of fiery sound through the preceding "Life, a fury slinging flame."

In the third stanza the "f" sounds of "Life," as "a *F*ury slinging *f*lame," re-sound in "faith" that has become dry, and in those who have become "flies." These human flies "sting and sing," echoing Life's "slinging." The previous stanza's agonizing intensity of "rack'd . . . pangs . . . maniac scattering" disperses again to a more innocuous "And . . . and . . . th*a*t . . . and . . . and . . . and . . . *A*nd." The "i" of the first stanza's "My l*i*ght" and the second stanza's "T*i*me" and "L*i*fe" now re-sound in "m*y* . . . dr*y* . . . fl*ie*s . . . and d*ie*," a definite shriveling of context in meaning.

The summons in the fourth stanza refers to "when I fade away," the only pure sounding of that simplest, most mysterious diphthong in the English language, the sound only *I* can call myself. And it is followed by the triple assonance of the long "a": "f***a***de ***away***." The rhythm alters in the third line: "And on the low dark verge of life," with three longs in a row: "low dark verge." The "i" sounds again in the two internal lines' rhyme of "strife" and "life." Then in a mysterious transmutation it sounds twice more in the ephemeral word, "twilight," almost evaporating, bidding adieu, yet the final sound of the stanza and the whole section L is "day," that long "a" of the earlier "f***a***de aw***ay***;" yet this is an "eternal day," a light beyond fading.

It feels fitting that the a-b-b-a rhyme scheme would work for this poem by one man infused, enthused, by another his whole adult life, from the age of twenty-one, to his dying words. At its heart, this poem, *In Memoriam*, explicitly invites the other to "be near me," embodying in its form the constant presence of one within the other, of one surrounding the other, of Arthur around and within Alfred. Why did this master of multitudinous forms (*Locksley Hall* is even in octameter couplets) find the four-beat tetrameter the fitting vessel of the seventeen-year exploration of *In Memoriam*? Perhaps this descendant of Yorkshire stock retreated in his grief to the relief of the old northern four-beat line, allowing an intimacy of reflection and soul-spiritual exploration, without the alliterative, outward orientation of that old Anglo-Saxon sentient-soul line. Tennyson, like Dante, suffered the loss of a beloved one so that he listened in ways that allowed the lost love to guide the poet through his personal grief into a work of universal resonance, ringing with what Wordsworth called "the still sad music of humanity." Perhaps the other name for that era, in addition to "Victoria," should be "Arthur" (Hallam).

Master of measured language, the ultimate troubadour of English poetry, Tennyson was able to sing/write almost any kind of song in any kind of meter, of form, with perhaps the finest musical ear of any of our English poets. The whole tradition of English poetry culminated in Alfred, Lord Tennyson. The spirit of the English language celebrated a recapitulation of its musical activity throughout the thousand years, from Alfred the Great (the time of *Beowulf*) to Alfred, Lord Tennyson, a retrospective in the museum of Tennyson's poetry. After all, "Alfred" means, in old Anglo-Saxon, one counseled (*rede*) by the elves (*alf*). For some modern sensibilities, Tennyson's mastery of measure included too much of "sad mechanic exercise." From a modern perspective, Tennyson may be the nightingale in the twilight, the last poet singing from the other side of the riptide dividing the tradition of English poetry from the modern era, beginning in the twentieth century. The spirit of the English language had, through the medium of Tennyson, concentrated all the musicality it had surrendered over the centuries, the four-beat alliterative verse of the Old Anglo-Saxon, the rhyming couplets in iambic pentameter of Chaucer's Middle English, the blank verse of Shakespeare and Milton, the whole range of poetic forms, into a celebration, a last festival of the English language's sacrificed musicality, a celebration of composure, of composition, before the imminent fragmentation of the twentieth century.

Chapter 20

GERARD MANLEY HOPKINS

THE LIFE OF GERARD MANLEY HOPKINS (1844–1889)

IN 1865, A bright young man who had won many poetry prizes in secondary school, and who had been studying with some of the finest minds of his times at Oxford University (Jowett, Pater, and Ruskin), took a fateful walking tour in western England. Along the way, he met his first Roman Catholic priest. Within a year, he was taken into the Roman Catholic Church. The young scholar willingly paid the university fines each week as a Catholic going to Mass. Within another year, he completely gave up his gift of writing poetry to pursue his spiritual quest. Although he would hardly be published in his short life, the Jesuit priest Gerard Manley Hopkins would potently influence the landscape of modern poetry, more perhaps even than the world-renowned Alfred, Lord Tennyson. Hopkins, upon coming of age, gave up not only his individuality but also his connection to the activity of the spirit of the English language in poetry. What was lost was later found, at least in terms of poetry.

By the time Gerard Manley Hopkins arrived on July 28, 1844, as the first-born of an eventual eight, the tide of Romanticism had ebbed for more than a decade. Elizabeth Barrett Browning had just published *Poems* to great acclaim; Robert Browning remained comparatively in the background; Alfred (not yet Lord) Tennyson had well emerged from his decade of silence; and Thoreau was planting beans on Walden Pond.

While Gerard's mother Kate read German and had musical and literary tastes and his Aunt Annie was a painter and musician with an interest in archeology, Gerard's father Manley ran a marine insurance business in London. Manley was a writer, of not only the *Manual for Marine Insurance,* but also some verse, an unpublished novel, and a history of Hawaii, for which exotic kingdom he served as the Consul-General in London. The elder Manley was a High Anglican Sunday school teacher with a wide range of interests. In 1854 at the age of ten, when the university students were at the peak of reading and writing Tennysonan poetry, Gerard Manley Hopkins went to the Highgate School, north of London. Later, the twentieth-century poet John Betjeman would be a student there, and a certain transplanted Yankee, T. S. Eliot, would become a master there. One of Gerard's friends was Ernest Coleridge, Samuel Taylor Coleridge's grandson. A dreamy boy and a fearless climber of trees, "Skin," as Gerard was called, was sporty, clever, and generally popular, yet willing to suffer peer ridicule for reading from the New Testament each night, since he had promised his mother to do so.

A firm-willed teenager with ascetic inclinations, to share the suffering of sailors and to test human endurance, Gerard took a bet to abstain from liquids for a week. Seeing his blackened tongue and weakness, the heavy-handed headmaster punched the boy, and by the time Gerard was eighteen, his fury at the injustice of the headmaster had grown. "I was driven out of patience and cheeked him wildly, and he blazed into me with his riding whip." Later, looking back, Hopkins wrote that, like so many nineteenth-century English schoolboys, "the truth is I had no love for my schooldays and wished to banish the remembrance of them" (Bergonzi 4). Meanwhile, Gerard had been writing poetry at Highgate. By the time he graduated, he had a collection of handsomely bound prize-books, including a gold-medal prize for Latin verse. One schoolboy poem, *Winter with the Gulf-Stream*, was one of the few poems published in Hopkins's lifetime.

At the age of nineteen in April 1963, Gerard Manley Hopkins went to Balliol College at Oxford University. He loved the medieval atmosphere and the shapes of the buildings in the golden, afternoon light. He loved a panorama of dimensions there. He loved the concentration of young men ardently devoted to plain living and high thinking, the intellectual atmosphere so fearless and free, Ritualist, Traditionalist, Positivist, Materialist, all eager to advance respective views, yet all ready to listen with courtesy to their opponents. Young Hopkins himself had delicate features, carefully brushed hair, high forehead, prominent nose, and his mouth sensuous yet closed in firm, assertive line, a somewhat girlish manner.

Oxford University in the 1860s was strongly imbued with the Thirty-nine Articles of the Anglican Faith. Chapel was compulsory, and all professors were celibate clergy in the Anglican stream. Henry VIII had formed the Anglican Church in the early 1500s so that he could divorce his Spanish Catholic wife and be free to marry someone who might bear him an heir. The price, excommunication from the Roman Catholic Church, was paid willingly by Henry and, hence, willy-nilly, the English people. Three hundred years later, three streams were recognizable within the Anglican Church. The Low Church was Evangelical. The Broad Church was, one might say, modern, with a more worldly orientation. The High Church, valuing especially the richness of ritual, leaned most strongly in the direction of the former dear mother, the Catholic Church. While Gerard was reading for a bachelor of arts in classics, enjoying canoeing on the Cherwell, and social breakfasts of several courses of fish, eggs, and meat, plus the exclusively male world of good friendships and small, after-dinner wine parties in the evening, he nevertheless found himself inclined increasingly toward the High Church.

Gerard thrived as a scholar, inspired by great professors: Benjamin Jowett, the translator of Plato; Walter Pater, the non-Christian professor of aesthetics; and John Ruskin, professor of art, through whose influence Gerard spent measureless time sketching while patiently observing rocks, trees, and clouds. "The time was late and the wet yellow woods / Told off their leaves along the piercing gale." A keen reader of contemporary literature such as Dickens, Thackeray, and George Eliot, Gerard in his undergraduate years wrote many poems, narrative, dramatic, sonnets, songs, ballads, experimenting in a range of styles, imitating Shakespeare, Keats, Browning, Christina Rosetti, and William Morris. "The present fury is the ash, and perhaps barley and two shapes of growth in leaves and one in tree-boughs and also a fine conformation of fine-weather cloud." With one of his friends in particular, Robert Bridges, Gerard enjoyed both mastering poetic meter and experimenting adventurously.

Yet beneath the surface of Gerard's inspiring, genial, literary life at Oxford, a different, strange tide was swelling. Gerard exchanged poems with another friend, Digby Mackworth Dolben, who, at the age of fifteen, had been expelled from Eton for crossing himself and going to Catholic services. Well tutored, Digby had nevertheless been accepted to Oxford at the age of eighteen, and at the age of nineteen, he drowned. Gerard, at the age of twenty, started *A Little Book for Sins*. At the age of twenty-one, in June of 1865, he was on a walking tour in western England when he met his first Roman Catholic priest. In September, the young adult Hopkins resolved to enter the Catholic Church against much resistance from parents, professors, and friends. October 21, 1866, Father Newman, later to become Cardinal, received Gerard Manley Hopkins into the Catholic Church. Gerard's final year at Oxford included, on the one hand, paying fines each time the university office took the names of those Oxford students attending Catholic mass. On the other hand, Gerard Manley Hopkins graduated with a first-class degree, by far the best student in first class.

It turns out that, as he fulfilled his Catholic odyssey, Gerard had written poetry during those years with the intention of burning it later. One is called "Heaven-haven":

> I have desired to go
> Where springs not fail,
> To fields where flies no sharp and sided hail
> And a few lilies blow.
>
> And I have asked to be
> Where no storms come,
> Where the green swell is in the havens dumb,
> And out of the swing of the sea.

Another, "The Habit of Perfection," begins with these stanzas:

Elected Silence, sing to me
And beat upon my whorlèd ear,
Pipe me to pastures still and be
The music that I came to hear.

Shape nothing, lips; be lovely-dumb:
It is the shut, the curfew sent
From there where all surrender come
Which only makes you eloquent.

The young, twenty-two-year-old poet, choosing the haven dumb, elected silence, wrote no more poetry for nine years.

Within two years, which included a walking tour in the Swiss Alps, this young man had decided not only to become a Catholic, but also to become a priest and, to top that, a Jesuit. In England of the 1860s and 1870s, all other professional doors were now closed to him. The twenty-four-year-old began to prepare for priesthood, a process that would culminate in ordination at age thirty-three.

During his two-year probationary novitiate, Hopkins continued his intense attentions to the created world, recording journal entries:

> Chestnuts as bright as coals or spots of vermilion,... the other evening after a very bright day, the air rinsed quite clear, there was a slash of glowing yolk-colored sunset.... In May, One day, when the bluebells were in bloom I wrote the following. I do not think I have ever seen anything more beautiful than the bluebells I have been looking at. I know the beauty of our Lord by it. Its inscape is mixed of strength and grace, like an ash tree. (Ibid. 63)

Hopkins experienced the creation as a revelation of the Creator, but of that same Creator who incarnated into our creation. In fact, Hopkins created a new word, *Inscape*, for what one might call spirit in nature. A recent writer on Hopkins, R. K. R. Thornton, has clarified:

> If the picture that makes a whole and single thing out of an area of land is a landscape, then what makes up a single thing out of its inner nature would be its inscape. Experiencing the Creator in the inner nature of a thing affects the observer. There is a force (instress) that makes natural things the way they are (shapes their inscapes) and there is a power (instress) that this shape has to affect the beholder. In addition to the two kinds of instress, inscape can also work as a verb, to inscape, meaning to grasp the form, the design, unique to an entity. (Ibid. 64)

Having sacrificed his active poetic expression of such experience, Hopkins nevertheless both clarified and intensified his reflections about such beholding of creation.

In August 1870, at the age of twenty-six, Hopkins culminated his novitiate by taking vows of poverty, chastity, and obedience. He embarked on his three-year philosophate, studying philosophy and mathematics, all in Latin. In the harsh, bleak beauty of the moors, the rain, the light of Stonyhurst two hundred miles north of London, he continued to observe his experiences of the creation.

> The ash tree growing in the corner of the garden was felled. It was lopped first. I heard the sound and looking out and seeing it maimed there came at that moment a great pang and I wished to die and not see the inscapes of the world destroyed any more. (Ibid. 68)

An old Jesuit brother said of him, “Ay, a strange young man, crouching down that gate to stare at some wet sand. A fair natural ’e seemed to us, that Mr. ’opkins” (Ibid. 68).

Whereas before becoming a Jesuit, he had viewed Aristotle as the end-all and be-all of philosophy, Hopkins became especially interested in the forteenth-century Scottish, Franciscan philosopher Duns Scotus, the Subtle Doctor, who explored the tension between general nature and the particular individuality of a person or thing. Thisness, the *haeccitas* of incarnation, is the mystery Hopkins located through his word *inscape*.

After completing the philosophate, Hopkins became Professor of Rhetoric, teaching Latin, Greek, English, and some French to novitiates for a year in Roehampton. In lecture notes, he wrote the following:

> Poetry is speech framed for contemplation of the mind by the way of hearing or speech framed to be heard for its own sake and interest even over and above its interest of meaning. Some matter and meaning is essential to it but only as an element necessary to support and employ the shape which is contemplated for its own sake. (Ibid. 76)

Here, in the mid-1870s, Hopkins articulates an attitude that anticipates Symbolists and Modernists, with meaning supporting the sound shape of the poem (and hence the experience), rather than sound serving meaning.

At the age of thirty, Hopkins moved to St. Bamos in north Wales to begin the final three-year phase of training, the theologate, additionally learning Welsh, reading friends' poems, and commenting on them. In December 1875, a tragedy opened a door that had been sealed for him. A mighty storm wrecked the Deutschland on a Thames estuary shoal. No rescue attempts were possible; it took twenty-four hours for the ship to break up. Sixty drowned, including five Franciscan nuns exiled from Germany by a law against religious orders. When the Rector of St. Bennos sought someone to write about the disaster, Hopkins realized that his sacrifice of his gift, having lasted well beyond seven years, was no longer necessary.

The story of the wreck, his first poem in nine years, unfolded in a manner reflecting Ignatian meditative techniques, with layer upon layer of the experience evoked vividly (see chapter 8 about the meditative practices developed by Ignatius Loyola, founder of the Jesuit order of the Catholic Church). However, the ear of the once and future poet had been even more active than the eye. During his long season of silence, Hopkins, who valued composing music as a purer art than writing poetry, "had long had haunting my ear the echo of a new rhythm which now I realized on paper" (Ibid. 82). In his meditation on the wreck, the

Deutschland becomes a type for all humanity, culminating in the revelation, of course, of the Creator behind the storm, behind all, as in stanza 32:

> I admire thee, master of the tides,
>
> Of the Yore-flood, of the year's fall;
> The recurb and the recovery of the gulf's sides,
> The girth of it and the wharf of it and the wall;
> Staunching, quenching ocean of a motionable mind
> Ground of being, and granite of it; pást áll
> Grásp Gód, thróned behínd
> Death with a sovereignty that heeds but hides, bodes but abides;...
>
> 34
>
> Now burn, new born to the world
> Double-naturèd name,
> The heaven-flung, heart-fleshed, maiden-furled
> Miracle-in-Mary-of-flame,
> Mid-numberèd He in three of the thunder-throne!
> Not a dooms-day dazzle in his coming nor dark as he came;
> Kind, but royally reclaiming his own;
> A released shówer, let flásh to the shíre, not a líghtning of fíre hard-húrled.

Hopkins marked the stresses, to assure that the reader heard his new rhythm. *The Catholic Monthly* agreed to publish the poem, then rescinded its offer. No one understood *The Wreck of the Deutschland.* No one had read poetry that sounded like this, ecstatically fresh-fashioned, disdaining familiar habits of phrase and regular syntax.

But the seal had been broken. Gerard Manley Hopkins was writing poetry again, in Welsh, in Latin, in English. At age thirty-three, Hopkins experienced, not a crucifixion, but an *annus mirabile,* like that of Keats in 1819. The year 1877 yielded "God's Grandeur," "Starlight Night," "Spring," "The Windhover," "Pied Beauty," "Hurrahing in Harvest," and "The Lantern out of Doors." Yet his audience for these sonnets celebrating the sacramental remained select; he had only three readers: his university friend Robert Bridges; R. Watson Dixon, friend of Pre-Raphaelites such as William Morris and the Rossettis; and Coventry Patmore. After "The Loss of the Eurydice" was rejected in 1878, Hopkins gave up trying to publish. Some have rightly wondered how the course of modern poetry might have been affected if that poem had been accepted.

As the poet trumpeted, breaking his silence with a fanfare, the priest was stuttering. In March of the poet's *annus mirabile,* the priest gave a practice sermon that began well and then lost its way. After passing his theology exams in July, he received the orders of sub-deacon, deacon, and priest in September 1877. As a man, Hopkins was likable; as a scholar he was brilliant and broadly knowledgeable; as a pastor, his high-strung personality, a combination of fragile health and eccentric individualism, made the robes fit uncomfortably. His sermons were sometimes above his congregation.

As a novice priest, Gerard Manley Hopkins did stints at Sheffield, London, Oxford, near Leigh, Liverpool, Glasgow, until on August 15, 1881, at the age of thirty-seven, he took his final vows in the Society of Jesus. During a year and a half at Stonyhurst teaching Greek and Latin to bachelor of arts candidates, he played piano and learned Anglo-Saxon. He said he had read little of Whitman, "Yet, I always knew in my heart Walt Whitman's mind to be more like my own than any man's living. He is a very great scoundrel. This is not a pleasant confession. And this makes me more desirous to read him" (Ibid. 112). Whereas Tennyson's poetic musicality was the epitome of Apollonian form and measure, the Jesuit Priest Hopkins recognized that as poets he and democratic Walt Whitman later shared an unusually ecstatic, Dionysian relationship to language, although in quite different ways.

At the age of forty, Gerard Manley Hopkins began the final chapter of his short life as a fellow of the Royal University of Ireland and a professor of Greek at University College, Dublin, lecturing and examining students. As he settled into what he called the third remove, separated from his family, from England, and even from the Catholic Church in England, he underwent a mental and spiritual crisis, which yielded what are referred to as his terrible sonnets. He wrote to his friend Bridges, "I think that my fits of sadness, though they do not affect my judgment, resemble madness. Change is the only relief, and that I can seldom get" (Gardner 202). At age forty-two, he wrote, "Accounts of the First Punic War have sweated me down to nearer my lees and usual alluvial low water mudflats, groans, despair, and yearnings" (Bergonzi 127).

Considering the possible Egyptian origins of Greek civilization, he also worked on a book on Pindar and the theory of rhythm and Dorian measure. "I believe that I can now set music and meter both of them on a scientific footing, which will be final like the law of gravitation" (Ibid. 143). By December 1887, at age forty-four, "I am at work on a great choral fugue. I can hardly believe it. Such verse as I do compose is oral, made away from paper, and I put it down with repugnance" (Ibid. 144). For Hopkins, poetry was almost primarily musical, usually composed while walking. During his own sentient-soul stage (ages twenty-one to twenty-eight), Hopkins had sacrificed his gift of poetry. He reclaimed the gift and wrote his most memorable poems in the ripeness of his rational-soul stage (ages thirty to thirty-five). In a certain way, in his consciousness-soul stage (thirty-five to forty-two), Hopkins moved beyond poetry to music.

Early in 1889, Hopkins became quite ill, diagnosed finally with typhoid fever, which included severe peritonitis. With his parents present from England, Gerard Manley Hopkins received the Last Rites. On June 8, he died—his last words, "I am so happy, so happy."

The close circle of his loved ones mourned him as son, brother, friend. Others remembered Gerard Manley Hopkins as a knowledgeable member of the Society of Jesus, a Professor of Greek, a brilliant, eccentric scholar, an amateur composer, and a devoted but ineffective priest, but least as a poet. Except for his close friend Robert Bridges, later to become Poet Laureate of England. It was Bridges who first published Hopkins's poetry, in an anthology in 1917, and in his own right in 1918.

Hopkins: The Poetry

God's Grandeur

The world is charged with the grandeur of God.
It will flame out, like shining from shook foil;
It gathers to a greatness, like the ooze of oil
Crushed. Why do men then now not reck his rod?
Generations have trod, have trod, have trod;
And all is seared with trade; bleared, smeared with toil;
And wears man's smudge and shares man's smell: the soil
Is bare now, nor can foot feel, being shod.

And for all this, nature is never spent;
There lives the dearest freshness deep down things;
And though the last lights off the black West went
Oh, morning, at the brown brink eastwards, springs—
Because the Holy Ghost over the bent
World broods with warm breast and with ah! bright wings.

"God's Grandeur" behaves structurally like a traditional Petrarchan sonnet. The first octet, with rhyme scheme a-b-b-a-a-b-b-a, poses a problem, which the ensuing sestet, c-d-c-d-c-d, solves, or resolves. Yet both the words and the rhythms belie their Latinate/Italian framework. In the whole sonnet, only thirteen words have more than one syllable. Akin perhaps to each original utterance having creative power in God's creation of the world, Hopkins's words work, each syllable imbued with the power of the Word.

The opening line, beginning with the expected iambic (u_) feet of the world is charged, is immediately charged with the rhythm shift of two ensuing anapests (uu_), with the grandeur of God, extending the scope of the original and generally assumed iambic rhythm. The opening line breaks open with the alliteration of the guttural "g" sounds of *grandeur of God,* while shimmying with variations of a triple assonance in the open "ah" of *charged*. The flatter "a" of *grandeur* and the almost more focused "o" of *God,* are all variations of the open sound. "The world is charged with the grandeur of God."

Rhythmically the second line behaves like flame, extending, recoiling back on itself, then extending further. It will flame out (uu_u), like shining (u_u) from shook foil (u_ _). The consonantal texture of flame sounds, "f" and "sh", braids, alternating: "flame... ***sh***ining ***f***rom ***sh***ook ***f***oil." The third line's alliterative "g" sounds "gather to a **g**reatness" on the momentum of the opening "**g**randeur of **G**od," further amplified by the assonance of "***oo***ze of ***o***il," a phrase onomatopoetically evoking the swelling oil.

> It will flame out, like shining from shook foil;
> It gathers to a greatness, like the ooze of oil

The whole momentum is broken perfectly, not at the end of the line, as one might expect, but suddenly in the first syllable of the next line, "Crushed." Almost like oil splattered into drops, the monosyllables follow: "Why do men then now not reck his rod?" Amidst the repetition of "men then," and the strange disjunction of "then now," four "n" sounds elaborate the negative of *not.* Instead of saying to heed his counsel or obey his command, Hopkins contracts the Anglo-Saxon *reckon* into the verb *reck,* and uses the Hebrew biblical image of the rod (what God commands Moses to use, both as serpent-proof to Pharaoh and in parting the Red Sea). "R***e***ck" triples the assonance of "m***e***n th***e***n," and it subliminally evokes the more familiar wrecks, which people in fact are doing by not heeding God's will. "Crushed. Why do men then now not reck his rod?"

"Generations," the only four-syllable word in the poem, sets up the almost infernal endlessness of the triple repetition: "Have trod, have trod, have trod." "T***r***od," echoes the alliteration of "***r***ecks ***r***od," yet the "t" twists and the "d" tamps down the normally airy "r" into "trod." The next two lines form the aural counterpoint to the sounds of "God's grandeur" (flame... shining from shook foil) earlier in line two.

> And all is seared with trade; bleared, smeared with toil;
> And wears man's smudge and shares man's smell: the soil

Men are "S***ea***red,... bl***ea***red, and sm***ea***red," an assonance that levels out in the next line to "w***ea***rs and sh***a***res." The "s" of

"*S*eared" becomes messy with "***sm***eared, ***sm***udge, and ***sm***ell," a sizzling yet sticky consonant combination.

In the final line of the octet, the "f" sound, which evoked the grandeur of God in line two, is negated: "nor can *f*oot *f*eel." "Is bare now, nor can foot feel, being shod."

The octet as a whole embodies a decline. In terms of rhyme scheme, *God* and *rod* in the first quatrain have fallen to *trod* and *shod* in the second. God's "shine like foil" and "ooze of oil" have settled to *toil* and *soil,* bare soil, yielding nothing, no longer reflecting God's Grandeur. That is a problem for humankind, originally God's gardener, then, the laborer of the earth after the Fall. Humanity has beaten the world barren.

> And for all this, nature is never spent;
>   There lives the dearest freshness deep down things;
> And though the last lights off the black West went.
>   Oh, morning, at the brown brink eastward, springs—
> Because the Holy Ghost over the bent
>   World broods with warm breast and with ah! bright wings.

Yet, in the sestet the alliteration of "***n***ature, ***n***ever," and the triple assonance of "n*e*ver sp*e*nt" reinforce the proclamation of something deeper than bare soil. Since the subject, the human world, is exhausted, the grammatical syntax of line 10 allows the sentence to begin essentially with the verb *lives.* "There lives the dearest freshness deep down things;" "D*ea*rest" and "d*ee*p" resurrect the vowel activity of "s*ea*red, bl*ea*red, sm*ea*red" (l.6), yet now driving that "ee" sound literally down. And in the heart of the line, between *dearest* and *deep,* emerge two familiar sounds from line two, having evoked God's grandeur so effectively: "*f*res*h*ness," echoing, resurrecting now freshly, the "f" and "sh" of the second line's "flame...shining from shook foil." "And though the last lights off the black West went."

In line 11, the central alliterations of "*l*ast *l*ights" is balanced by the spread assonance of "*a*nd l*a*st bl*a*ck," with its somewhat painful vowel, that flattened "a." However, the strongest sound experience in the line is the consonant/vowel repetition at the end: "***We***st ***we***nt." The double "w" works almost like wings flying away. Yet the effect probably obscures our awareness that *went* is the only pure past tense in the poem, a fact brightened by the way in the next line, after the sound "at" almost marks the margin between fading light and fading night, the morning brings the ever-present tense, *springs*.

> Oh, morning, at the brown brink eastward, springs—
> Because the Holy Ghost over the bent
> World broods with warm breast and with ah! bright wings.

Although the world is "bent" (past participle), the Holy Ghost broods in an eternal present. And, although the West may be black and the world bent, nevertheless that morning "at the ***b***rown ***b***rink... ***b***ecause the Holy Ghost over the ***b***ent / world ***b***roods with... ***b***reast and... ***b***right wings," a sequence of seven enfolding "b" sounds reinforces the eternally protective gesture of the Holy Ghost. The protective "b" is complemented by the active "w" in the fivefold sequence of "***w***orld... ***w***ith ***w***arm... ***w***ith... ***w***ings. The completely unexpected "Ah!" interjects the spirit-brightness of the Holy Spirit's wings, echoing that original threefold variation in the first line: "ch***a***rged... gr***a***ndeur... G***o***d."

As the musician Hopkins listened to the influence of *instress* in *inscapes,* the poet Hopkins heard what he called "Sprung Rhythm." Essentially this sensitive composer found himself rehearing an ancient rhythm, really a beat from the Old Anglo-Saxon, the original source of our English (*Anglish*) language. Hopkins, professor of Greek and Latin, reached back to a time before the French-speaking Normans brought the southern, Greco-Roman influence in 1066 to gradually merge with the northern, Teutonic stream. The spoken French of the new nobility then did more than the Latin of clerics and clerks to bring that southern stream into the newly hybridized living English language (see chapter 3).

The four underlying characteristics of the Old Anglo-Saxon poetry include: 1) a four-beat, or four-stressed, line; 2) three beats of which were alliterated; 3) flexibility of the number of unstressed syllables among the four stressed ones; 4) and no end rhyme.*

* See chapter 2 for an elaboration of these.

Hopkins's ear reaches for that four-beat line, emphasizing the stresses, and embracing the flexibility of unstressed syllables. He embraces, too, the consonantal density of the Old Anglo-Saxon without the law-dictated triple alliteration per line. It is as though Hopkins evokes the glory of God's physical creation through the consonantal intensity of the old Anglo-Saxon, drawing out a fresh, sentient-soul relationship to the created world. While reclaiming the near-primal four-beat pulse (evoking the heart-beat) of the old line, he enjoys a new, quite modern independence of arrangement, a new freedom of consciousness, that invites and allows him freedom of sound arrangement, so concentrated and inspired that it's almost independent of sense. His intensely squeezed or extensively extended sequences of similar sounds evokes a musical experience, almost pure in its own right, virtually independent of sense and anticipating twentieth century symbolists and imagists in poetry, as well as the surrealists in the visual arts. Some of his poems do with sound what Picasso's cubist paintings and Dali's surrealist paintings do with images, yet within the confines of disciplined forms of sonnet and with a Jesuit's concentrated meditative approach.

One can imagine the spirit of the English language experiencing a joy of rebirth through the rawest, most intensely exhilarating activity of language since Shakespeare. This almost ecstatic yet disciplined trilling evokes precisely the devoted discipline of a disciple—a disciple of Christ, of the Word. This potently pre-modern poetry celebrates, evokes, quickens, and hence engenders the dearest freshness deep down things. While Hopkins liberates the English language from rational behavior to a greater extreme than the Romantic poets ever imagined, he does so in the service of life, eternal Life. Hopkins's poetry, anticipating many of the possibilities of modern poetry, at the same time offers the antidote to what Eliot later articulated in the *Wasteland:* "A heap of broken images, fear in a handful of dust," a picture of modern fragmentation.

While with one ear Hopkins reaches back to the four-beat line, much twentieth-century poetry has in fact been settling into four-beat lines, even down to recent rap and hip-hop. We saw how the eighteenth-century rhyming couplets reflected a rational-soul ebb tide, after the consciousness-soul expansion of Elizabethan England. Is it possible that this essentially sentient-soul, four-beat rhythm reflects a kind of ebb after the more consciousness soul-expanding iambic pentameter of the last four hundred years—an ebbing, nevertheless, in which such an intuition is possible of the dearest freshness, deep-down things, perhaps gathering forces for a next stage of consciousness-soul development? Hopkins may be rejuvenating our language especially, resurrecting the fallen world, revealing, inviting, and even recharging the spirit in matter, the Word in the world. It's as though what the Romantic poets accomplished in so many ways—reuniting subject and object, humankind and nature, above all through *imagination*—Hopkins accomplishes through *inspiration,* allowing the Word of the Creator to breathe life into Hopkins's creations, and hence into our creation. In the process, he gleans the dearest freshness, deep-down things as an act of *intuition*.

It is as though Tennyson and his poetry had embodied and epitomized the whole tradition of English poetry in a twilight culmination, whereas Hopkins, reaching back to the Old Anglo-Saxon dawn of the language and literature, wrote in a manner more prescient of a new era of poetry. The spirit of the English language is often active in a potent polarity. We have seen that Shakespeare's unmatched expansiveness was balanced by the King James biblical translation's reduced concentration of language. Tennyson, the public's poet of Victorian England, was balanced by the private, silent, unpublished Hopkins's distilled, potent poetry. So, across the ocean, not at the twilight but at the dawn of a new nation, Walt Whitman, the public's poet of the post–Civil War United States of America, was balanced by private, unpublished Emily Dickinson's gem-like flame.

Chapter 21

Eleventh Grade (Ages 16–17)

In the relationship between language development and child development, eleventh grade is the key year in the Waldorf curriculum. Think of this emerging, maturing soul, or astral body, having recapitulated in the ninth and tenth grades the physical and "etheric" stages of development as a basis for healthy soul development. Now, in eleventh grade, the unfolding soul is ripening and coming into its own; the soul is finally ready to live and act in its own substance and medium.

Historically, the eleventh grade usually moves from Rome through the Middle Ages and the Renaissance. Especially when eleventh grades tend to spend valuable time with Wolfram von Eschenbach's *Parzival* and Dante's *Divine Comedy*, each in translation, it is fortunate and indeed crucial for students to be able to spend not days but weeks in Middle English with Chaucer's *Canterbury Tales*. First, let the students remember the experience of speaking and living in the four-beat, alliterative Old Anglo-Saxon verse of *Beowulf* (discussed in chapter 2). What does it mean for them to then expand to Chaucer's iambic pentameter, in rhyming couplets, freed of the consonantal repetition?

> Whan that Aprill, with his shoures soote
> The droughte of March hath perced to the rote
> And bathed every veyne in swich licour
> Of which vertu engendred is the fleur...

They can, as eleventh graders, be even more conscious of differences in qualities than they could be in tenth grade. However, what does it mean for them, for weeks, maybe even six, to speak, hear, and read aloud during the day in school and silently at home at night the language of Chaucer's Middle English? They write character sketches or dialogues in Middle English; they perform scenes for classmates in Middle English. Here is one example of a contemporary teenager's tale told in Middle English.

The Drownynge Tale

WHYLOM, there was a vagrante and a thief
Cleped Noah who maketh much mischief
And known through all the regne for scoundrelrye.
He slepen only with women who be
y-wedded or abide in nunnerye,
none other wold he goine with to lye.
He hadde blonde curls and slender handes,
But with them he had killed many mannes,
And stolen many rynges and gilded stitche
If he hadde not alle lose, he wolde be riche.
Once in the sprynge as alle camme to be,
As smalle brooken firste flowen free
As people love and laugh and are happye,
Noah was restynge high up in a tree.
Nexte the port where shippes come to lande,
Where drunken sailors know not how to stande,
He saw with his eyen a ladye faire,
So prettye that he coulde not brake his staire,
So that he soon forgotten where he be,
And fallen heedlong from that highe tree.
He thought, "It matter not upon my heed,
If she a nonne be, or if y-wedde!
Alas!" thoght he, "this longynge that I feel!
I wol hir thak about the lendes weel."
He follow'd 'til she cometh to a shippe
That sailed to the sandes of Egypte.
Right then he thogt he wolde a sailor bee.
He wolde floghten the seven sees, pardee.
The master of the shippe with redde face,
Tolde Noeah that he hadde a place,

To swepen decks above and down baylow,
And kaypen shippe taydye evermo.
The ladye dere, his lemmin and his lyf,
That he woude surely make as his wyf,
Cam on the shippe and goed into hir room;
Our Noah shiver'd and he almost swoon'd.
… After three dayes out of hir romme she came,
He played his loote, and tryed to synge a songge,
But for his happynesse he coude noght speke,
And out cam only pips and little squeke.
His face turned red, he grabb'd hir hand,
"Alack my der, make me an happy man!"
"My love I graunt, but on one condicioun,
that we are wed in proper tradicioun…"
Right at this time ther cam a thonder-dent
And stronge wind that maketh mastes bent.
It threwe Noah right out of the shippe
The shippe falter'd too and floght no more,
And sinked to the sandye ocean floore.
As Noah sank, his bodye on hirs felle;
One coude say this waye was just as welle,
As they together sank unto their dome,
y-wedded they wer withoutte tradicioun.
Forever they woude together lye dead
As theire flesh becayme fishes' bread.
Alive, short tyme together did they spende,
But dead they lye together to no ende.

SETH WULSIN, GMWS, 2000

Eleventh graders immersing themselves substantially in Chaucer's Middle English experience:

1) What linguists acknowledge and what any of us can recognize as our grandfather/grandmother tongue (see chapter 4).
2) An extended, expanded consciousness made possible by the five-beat line, as opposed to the four-beat Old Anglo-Saxon. For seven centuries now, since the 1360s, this

iambic pentameter has been the primary vessel in English poetry of the early stages of the consciousness soul.

3) Still a grounding, active sounding of consonant sounds—for example, *Knicht* as opposed to the modern "knight" (nite). These pronounced consonants, some of which will become silent later in the fifteenth and sixteenth centuries, continue to ground the twenty-first–century eleventh grader, the speaker and the hearers, in the sounds of, and hence the soul experience of, the physical world.

4) Nevertheless, a released, liberated consciousness, no longer hammered or chained down to the relentless repetition of the consonantal alliteration. Not only does the line include a whole extra "foot" (rhythmic sound unit), but the words themselves, with a higher proportion of Latin and French origins, are allowed to sound a richer variety of vowel sounds with more range and freedom. Richer vowel range allows and generates interiorizing of the language and consciousness of the language user—joys and sorrows, love and hate, lust and chastity, pride and humility, and so on. Chaucer's language, in fact, guides its users from a more physical, vital language (consciousness reflecting the outer world) to a growing soul-conscious language, reflecting a more interior world. While the lingering Anglo-Saxon words ground the speaker in outward action amidst the things of the physical world, the proportion of Latinate, French–based words in Chaucer's Middle English language makes abstraction, conception, naturally more possible than did the Old Anglo-Saxon.

5) A quickening, wakening, wondering, yet ordering attention to sound and sense, as the ear works with the rhyming couplets (see chapter 4). The growing minds of the students experience the narrative development in neatly ordered pairs of lines. The musicality of the language in general, reinforced by the recurring end rhymes, reinforces the experience of a world-universe that resounds with harmony and order, echoing the lingering medieval experience of dwelling within the Ptolemaic universe of concentric planetary spheres, with Earth at the center,

and all in its proper places, in proper relation. The modern, third-millennium eleventh grader can benefit from a certain intellectual certainty, a firm fiber of mind, at this stage of development. The texture of the language is reliable, dependable. One line ends with a certain sound; the next line is bound to conclude with a similar sound, hence in some manner "concluding" that thought development, even when the narrative continues in the ensuing lines. The pace of development is predictable, dependable, reassuring, and hence strengthening, steadily exercising, steadily developing not only the story, but also the minds of those reading, speaking, listening, or even writing in these rhyming couplets.

6) From a larger, macrocosmic point of view, eleventh graders immersing themselves substantially in Chaucer's Middle English experience not only an underlying echo of the Old Anglo-Saxon sentient soul qualities (chapter 2), but they also experience in a more primal way, in their own English language, recapitulation of an intellectual-soul relationship to the world, through their language and thinking. Chaucer was living and writing right at the culmination of the intellectual-soul stage of humanity's development, having begun around 700 B.C.E with ancient Greek literature and philosophy, maturing through the Romans, and culminating in the Medieval Scholastic philosopher-theologians, which included Nominalists and Realists. Linguistically and literarily, Chaucer's iambic pentameter, with rhyming couplets, offers the modern teenager direct access to a frame and medium of mind and ways of thinking that aim confidently to understand the world, rationally discerning right and wrong, good and evil, true and false. The form, the manner, the tissue of Chaucer's literary language bears, even engenders, an intellectual-soul relationship to the world. Some of the content, especially distinction of character (chapter 4) already invites and quickens some of what Rudolf Steiner calls experience of the spiritual soul, or consciousness soul.

What does it mean that, in the early third millennium, eleventh graders in North American Waldorf schools, attempting to write Chaucer's Middle English in iambic pentameter, tend to fall into a four-beat line? Why does the contemporary poetry of the streets, both rap music and spoken-word poetry, tend to be uttered in four-beat lines, also heavily alliterative and rhymed, and with a heavy preponderance of Anglo-Saxon words? Are we falling back into a sentient-soul experience? Are the adolescents rising toward their own sentient-soul experience in their twenties? Is most rap music created by those in their twenties? Is this contemporary, four-beat, alliterative phenomenon a larger ebb, instinctively attempting to rejuvenate the West's first wave of barren consciousness-soul experience?

Modern teenagers will emerge in their third-millennium lives with more confidence and inner freedom if, by living through the development of their own language, they have been able to live in an intellectual-soul frame of mind and make that substance part of their own developing minds. Then, the study of the Renaissance later in the eleventh grade year will be better prepared, and actually even accomplished, by new mind qualities born through the work with Chaucer's language.

Any literary scholar familiar with Waldorf education and child development is likely to grasp comparable connections between tenth graders and Old Anglo-Saxon, as well as between eleventh graders and Chaucer's Middle English. The next stage of linguistic development, however, is less known in general and raises particular questions in trying to understand child development. During the fifteenth and early sixteenth centuries, little literature was written in English, while the language itself underwent some of the most dramatic changes in the history of languages (see chapter 5). What might such a "slumber" and substantial change in terms of the development of English language and literature suggest, macrocosmically, about possible corresponding soul-development in the sixteen- to seventeen-year-old eleventh grader?

Remember, four vowel sounds moved forward when they were spoken: *Nahme* to *name; ston* to *stone; ruf* to *roof; swet* to *sweet.*

What does it suggest that a vowel, formerly sounded deep within the chamber of the mouth, now sounds further out, closer to the lips, closer to the threshold between and the inner and outer worlds? What does it suggest that certain consonants, formerly sounded, become silent in the spoken word, yet remain visible in the written word as a kind of ghost of consciousness (*knicht* to *knight*)? What are implications of the formerly sounded final "e" going silent, sacrificing its sound into the rest of the word, allowing the primary vowel sound in the word to become long: *rote* instead of *rot, pole* instead of *pol?*

What becomes possible when two formerly distinct vowel sounds, "ahh" and "uu," combine to create a new multi-textured soul experience in the diphthong, "au," as in *round, bound,* even *sound.* What does it mean for a soul to be able to sustain two soul experiences simultaneously, in a blend? Some people even hear three sounds, including "ahh," "oh," "uu." Similarly, what does it mean for a soul to be able to sustain a comparable blend, creating the sound absolutely new to the English language and hence to the English-speaking consciousness, "ai" from "ahh" and "ee"? Again, some can even hear three sounds in the diphthong "ahh," "ay," "ee" (*fiv* to *five*).

Considering such questions, let us step back for a moment, to a larger perspective; let us imagine the genius, or the spirit or even the archangel, of the English language, laboring during this outwardly silent interlude, altering, transforming fundamental vowel sounds for the speakers of the English language. This transformation of the language was occurring during the late Middle Ages and early Renaissance, at the beginning of the stage of humanity's evolution devoted to developing the spiritual (consciousness) soul, extending from c.1400 to c.3500.

Why were these new sounds emerging in the English language just before the splendid awakening of renaissance of Elizabethan literature, most essentially, the plays of Shakespeare, whom Harold Bloom speaks of having created the personality of modern humanity, and whom Rudolf Steiner speaks of having charted the course for the development of the consciousness soul?

Corresponding to this, what may be occurring in the developing soul of an eleventh grade teenager? What stage of "slumber" does an inarticulate junior endure as soul substance changes to allow a new relationship to certain language sounds and, hence, to enable new kinds of consciousness? The typical journeys explored in eleventh grade, whether that of Parzival, Dante, or Hamlet, involves the hero leaving the familiar world (old consciousness) and journeying out into some kind of death-threatening wasteland and enduring trials of initiation in which one's former identity is no longer important. It is as though the shift of vowel sounds from deep in the throat forward, toward the outer world, prepares the English-speaking folk for outer explorations of the new world and the globe as a whole and, more important, for questions such as: To be or not to be? Does such language development suggest these inner transformations occurring subtly in eleventh graders, reorienting them toward venturing further into the world and voyaging more daringly and knowingly into the uncharted waters of the human soul?

Those experienced in teaching teenagers know that it is almost inescapable for every junior to experience some dark night of the soul and becoming lost in relation to the former sense of self, often feeling more alone than ever before and even dancing with death. Dante goes into and through the world of the dead. More than ever before or after, thoughts of suicide, whether "to be or not to be," have to be taken seriously and be met with immediate help.

Imagine what it means to the solo-voyaging junior when a mysterious inner transformation allows and even fosters a new experience of these same vowel sounds in such a way that the newly charged language gives the student new capacity to move into the outer world and to move more consciously into the many, often mysterious, realms of the inner world. More specific, there is a mysterious gelling, new resonance, clearer sounding than ever before in the student's life, as though a note were sounding at last, so that the student has a new connection to the sound "ai," through which, unlike the French *je* or the German *Ich*, English speakers voice the mysterious name of one's own individuality:

"I." While our understanding of human development points to the age of twenty-one as the time when people usually experience individuality in a more enduring manner; the growing, immanent emergence of the slowly surfacing individuality, the ego, or "I AM," profoundly affects the way a student's emerging, developing astral body is harmonized and shaped, ideally, in harmony with the individual's whole being.

It is as though the student, lost for a time as a "nobody" in the immeasurable, seemingly lawless realms of the astral wasteland, hears the call of "ai," or "I," which has the effect of summoning and ushering the nascent individuality into harmonizing the astral forces with the physical and life (ether) bodies, refertilizing the former wasteland to allow the seeming *inferno* to become *purgatorio* in its gradual move toward *paradisio*.

After immersion in Chaucer's Middle English, as students work with Shakespeare's language, these historically new vowels dawn in the soul with fresh potency, though twenty-first-century students may barely be conscious of it until the teacher helps the students to become so (chapter 6). Imagine the students' confidence growing while becoming aware of the whole new array of soul sounds available historically, now renewed developmentally for humanity and for Shakespeare in particular and, even more particularly, for students as tools for exploring the mysteries of heart and mind. Imagine, as the seventeen-year-old wonders, often in silent agony: When will I ever feel that I'm pulling my life together or feel I'm making sense of life? How quickening, how charging, and how encouraging it must be to hear this new sound, almost as though for the first time, *I*, "ai," like the ultimate tuning fork, ultimately enabling one to harmonize the various members of one's being.

Imagine what it's like for the eleventh grader to enjoy the artful play of Shakespeare's rhyming couplets and then, with Shakespeare, to step and stretch beyond their limits, shedding the rhythmic lawfulness of absolute certainties, yet the absolutely demanding confines of that second, repeated end rhyme. The soul of the junior experiences, for the first time historically, the horizon of the next line opening up completely in sound possibilities.

As the musicality of the English line surrenders, recedes, and sacrifices itself progressively from the alliteration of the Old Anglo-Saxon to the rhyming couplets of the Middle English, now to the blank verse of Shakespeare and soon after, Milton, what does the teenager experience? In a certain way, it is as though the spirit of the language is sacrificing some of its own astrality (musical substance) to allow greater freedom for the individual to think, to explore realms of consciousness. Hence, eleventh graders often find themselves, later in the eleventh grade, with new courage to venture into terrains such as "the bourne from which no traveler returns" (*Hamlet*, III, 2).

The texture of the language may seem paler, less substantial than in earlier centuries and earlier stages of soul development, although the variations of vowel coloring, while subtler, are actually far more extensive. The student may feel less buoyed by the language, yet more liberated from the language through its self-sacrificing gesture to grope toward concepts whose essence lives beyond the limits of language. Eleventh grade students may experience their role in the family, class, or school as less familiar and clear, feeling less buoyed by the community's definitions of them, yet these very sounds of the English language, newly sounding in Elizabethan England and newly resounding in the eleventh grader's maturing astral body, may enable that student to listen better to another's language, to think more effectively into another's way of thinking, to imagine more clearly another's world, and ultimately to identify better with and recognize the other's I AM, whatever the person's role, culture, or context.

Whereas tenth-grade students experienced the different stages of language development, eleventh graders, reviewing that and immersing themselves more fully in the languages themselves, can start to become more aware of the implications of those language developments. The very act of becoming conscious in the eleventh grade of the altering character of the English language means that the students, by thinking about their language, are taking the first step toward being able to think about their thinking, the crucial activity for becoming independent and freely self-aware.

Even the Shakespearean sonnet (chapter 7), through its very form, implies to eleventh graders a development from the twofold, dialectical form of the Petrarchan sonnet, which appeared at the culmination of the rational soul stage of humanity's development, to a threefold and even fourfold character of the explorations in a Shakespearean sonnet. Students can experience and recognize that the culminating couplet (in contrast to Chaucer's continuous, relentless couplets), coming as it does after three quatrains each with different end sounds, serves in fact as a way to conclude the altering, wandering exploration of the whole sonnet. In a similar way, the "I," or I AM, can pull together and integrate the three seemingly different quatrains, which are in fact harmonious parts of the whole sonnet. The form of the Shakespearean sonnet is an external confirmation of the quickening activity of the English language's new diphthong, "ai," or *I*. Of course, eleventh graders are not directly aware that the Shakespearean sonnet embodies and reflects the way the I AM is increasingly wakeful and working actively to harmonize and integrate the three members of the individual student's being, the physical, ether, and astral bodies.

Let me not to the marriage of true minds 116
Admit impediments. Love is not love
Which alters when it alteration finds
Or bends with the remover to remove:
O, no! it is an ever-fixed mark,
That looks on tempests and is never shaken;
It is the star to every wandering bark,
Whose worth's unknown, although his height be taken.
Love's not Time's fool, though rosy lips and cheeks
Within his bending sickle's compass come;
Love alters not with his brief hours and weeks,
But bears it out even to the edge of doom.
If this be error and upon me proved,
I never writ, nor no man ever loved.

WILLIAM SHAKESPEARE

DEATH OF A DOVE

A mourning dove lay on a frozen stone.
Her body jolted with fiery singeing pain;
Her frail grey wing was broken to the bone;
Down tender breast there ran dark crimson stain.
Her tiny bright black eye was brimmed with fright;
In quivering body thumped heart loud and wild;
The jagged, ripping arrow snatched her flight
And struck her down, a thin, weak, helpless child.
Lo!...Deep white warmth caressed the thrashing heart...
Cool wing-tips brushed burned breast with crystal dew...
And to her sobbing silence, fresh wind blew...
As broken heart and soul did gently part...
Lo! Shining star, leave wings of grey and sigh;
Take wings of light, and to sweet heaven fly!

HILARY PHARR GMWS, 1998

The students' year should not end with Shakespeare. Yes, the Elizabethan language has awakened soul faculties and "I" activity; yes, the language has enabled the literature to explore far afield, outwardly and inwardly, but let us not forget that Hamlet has been left in his tragedy, in certain ways still "a quintessence of dust" in "a sterile promontory." Historically, the alienation between subject and object in the early stages of the era of the consciousness soul was reinforced by the mechanization of the universe through Newton's theory of gravity and the pervasive attitudes in the Age of Reason during the 1700s. Eleventh graders need the Romantic poets to help them reunite with the world and heal the rift between subject and object. Reading, analyzing, and writing in imitation of the Romantic poets can all help the eleventh graders to:

1. Incarnate into the contemporary present through active eye and paying attention to particulars in nature.

> ...and there my friends
> Behold the dark green file of long lank weeds,
> That all at once (a most fantastic sight!)

Still nod and drip beneath the dripping edge
Of the blue clay-stone.
COLERIDGE, "This Lime-tree Bower My Prison"

2. Incarnate into the contemporary present through the ear, listening to the human voice and the living speech around us for rhythms and phrases to inform our poetry.

"What, you are stepping westward?"—"Yea."
...The voice was soft, and she who spake
was walking by her native lake:
The salutation had to me
The very sound of courtesy:
Its power was felt;...
WORDSWORTH, "Stepping Westward"

3. Imitate in one's imagination, the ways of the life forces in nature, in terms of allowing one's poetry to proceed "organically," as in Coleridge's conversation poem, "Frost at Midnight."
4. Be aware that the subject of a long, epic poem can, for the first time in human history, take as its subject not an outer journey or battle, but rather, as in *The Prelude*, the inner journey of the subject writing the poem, the poet—how Wordsworth became a poet. Consciousness of self in becoming.
5. Likewise, in shorter lyrics, the subject of the poem can be the poet's own memory of an experience in nature, becoming conscious of how that experience in nature at one time has continued to affect one's being, on various levels over time, as in Wordsworth's "Tintern Abbey." Students, having largely turned their attention outward in high school writing assignments, are now ready to regard their own soul experience as subject, objectively.

Hemlock

The cold, wet, rotten weather struggles to keep
me in, but out I run, frowning at the chill.
The dripping sky's a muted gray; the grass
is brown, My eyes adjust to the brightness of
the dull sun. In the garden beside the house
an early March bouquet of sturdy flowers
Has pushed up through the brown debris,
tricked into thinking it's warmer, safer
to be alive than it really is. My frown
relaxes as I stroll though the wet
dead grass toward the stump.
It's big and flat,
this stump, the centerpiece of our moderate yard.
And once upon a time it was a tree.
Now its cracked and gnarled surface lies
overgrown with fungus, moss, dead weeds.
I put my foot on it and slip away.
It was an amazing tree, taller than
the house. It shaded the whole yard
with its far reaching, low fir branches.
It was a home to birds, squirrels, insects
and us. I was a bird, a squirrel, a lost
child on an abandoned island, a bat,
a snake, a grown-up in its branches.
My dolls slept peacefully for weeks
In its strong boughs. I climbed
A bit, or lay below, staring up,
up through the needles, nests and cones
To the robin's egg sky. Its dry,
grassless floor was soft and warm, and I
was small, but powerful; I knew that it was mine.
But then one winter it grew brown…
I cried the day that it
was cut. For the squirrels, birds, and fungus,
but really for the loss and fear of change.

Now the Hemlock's gone. In summer
The grass is green, the apple trees grow fruit,
the doves and cardinals have found other
homes. And I've gone on to different
places. The yard can now house parties,
tag, frisbee-runs and badminton.
And you
my little friend, who follows me as I
pace dreamily about, are too young to
Remember. Even I forget. The other trees
are stonger; they now have light, and you
will play in them. There'll be another
home for you, for dolls and dreams.

Abigail Chapin, GMWS, 1998

6. Help students become conscious of and practice what Keats called the poet's gift of "negative capability," the ability to become independent of one's soul disposition in order to experience the "other" as truly as possible and to let the "other" speak through one, the poet.

To bend with apples the moss'd cottage trees,
And fill all fruit with ripeness to the core;
To swell the gourd, and plump the hazel shells
With a sweet kernel; to set budding more,
And still more, later flowers for the bees,
Until they think warm days will never cease,
For summer has o'er-brimmed their clammy cells.

John Keats, "Ode to Autumn"

Through the work with the language of the Romantic poets, the eleventh grader has healed the rift, accomplished the reunion between humanity and nature, between subject and object, between spirit and matter. The real birth, in the New World, will now become possible.

PART III

Chapter 22

ALTERATION OF THE EARLY AMERICAN MIND

THE BIRTH OF AMERICAN LITERATURE

ALTHOUGH THE ORAL tradition of Native American culture has been rich for ages, it was only in the mid-1820s that Sequoyah created the first Native American alphabet in Cherokee. Written stories therefore emerge as Native American Literature primarily in the twentieth century. While Native American culture has influenced European-American culture more subtly than most people realize, this exploration will focus on the emergence of a stream of written literature in America.

When one thinks of the Spanish settling in St. Augustine, Florida, in the 1580s, and of the English Pilgrims settling in Plymouth, Massachusetts, in the 1620s, it is perhaps astonishing to find little literature in North America in the 1600s. While an image such as Governor Winthrop's City upon a Hill, from his lay sermon, certainly dominated the imaginations of the early Puritans, the poet, Anne Bradstreet, writing in Boston in the 1640s and 1650s, was an exception:

THE FLESH AND THE SPIRIT

In secret place where once I stood
Close by the banks of lacrim flood,
I heard two sisters reason on
Things that are past and things to come.
One Flesh was called, who had her eye
On worldly wealth and vanity;
The other Spirit, who did rear
Her thoughts unto a higher sphere.

In one poem, to her book, she writes:

I cast thee by as one unfit for light,
Thy visage was so irksome in my sight;

Anne Bradstreet writes uncomfortably, almost guiltily, in a discouraging environment. Generally, seventeenth-century New England fostered no drama, little poetry and no fiction; the most creative word work was sermons and letters. Why so little literature in the New World? The settlers established geographic independence from the Old World with an ocean between. They secured religious independence while frequently being intolerant of others' religious independence. In addition, they were preoccupied with survival, clearing wilderness, forming various relationships with the Native American peoples. The religion of most northern settlers puritanically discouraged, even forbade, the arts as temptations of the devil.

American literature of the 1700s? In the first decades, one minister in the little western town of Northampton, Massachusetts, secretly wrote poetry, which Thomas Johnson discovered in a Yale library and published in 1939. Edward Taylor's "Preface of God's Determinations Touching His Elect" shows some potent word work, with spiraling repetitions, including a bold, sevenfold sequence of *nothings*.

Oh! What a might is this! Whose single frown
Doth shake the world as it would shake it down!
Which All from Nothing get, from Nothing All:

Hath All on Nothing set, lets Nothing fall.
Gave All to Nothing Man indeed, whereby
Through Nothing man all might Him Glorify.
In Nothing then embossed the brightest Gem
More precious than all preciousness in them.
But Nothing-man did throw down all by Sin,
And darkened that lightsome Gem in him
That now his Brightest Diamond is grown,
Darker by far than any Coalpit stone.

During the first half of the century, most literary energy was devoted to sermons. Two polarities generated much of the tension and energy of the Great Awakening of the 1730s and 1740s. While one stream of the Congregational and Presbyterian churches, led by Rev. Chauncy of Boston, felt all religious consideration should remain within reason, Jonathon Edwards, also from Northampton in the "wild west," led those eager to fan the passions beyond reason. Edwards, in his sermon "Sinners in the Hands of an Angry God," did not hesitate to go so far as to proclaim that the God who holds you over the pit of Hell, much as one holds a spider or some loathsome insect over the fire, abhors you and is dreadfully provoked. In the other polarity of the mid-eighteenth century, Edwards defended the Calvinist doctrine of predestination against the insidious but irresistibly spreading Arminian doctrine of free will.*

As the Great Awakening subsided by the 1750s, the settlers were consumed with their struggles for economic, legal, and political independence. The literary energy of the nation fighting to be born was distilled into two documents: *The Declaration of Independence*, July 4, 1776, and the *Constitution*, 1789. The first articulated the spirit of the new nation; the second articulated the form of the new nation. It is as though the political thinkers of the time worked with their rational minds and their imaginations, in accord with each other, with the spirit of the English

* Jacobus Arminius (1560–1609), a Dutch minister and divinity professor, founded the anti-Calvinistic school in Reformed Protestant theology. Methodists remain committed to Arminian theology, and Arminianism itself has become one of the dominant theological systems in the U.S.

language, and with the being of the new nation, in a mighty labor to fashion a conceptual body which would allow the new nation to form and to grow in a balanced way, honoring both the individual and the democratic mass, working toward executive, legislative, and judicial interaction, restraint, and support.

At this time in world history, the great ideals of the French Revolution, *Liberté, Egalité, Fraternité,* exploded into terrorizing and bloodshed, begetting within ten years the opposite of those ideals: Emperor Napoleon. Thus one has to imagine the quality of concentration, imagination, and clear thinking that allowed a number of individuals in the raw, uncultured, frontier nation of the United States to find the words to embody ideas that would allow them to live healthily in what has become the longest enduring democracy in world history. Not many poems, stories, plays, and novels have been written during the labor of birth. What a great, future-engendering labor that was. Nevertheless, long after geographical and religious independence, it was to be a whole lifetime after the declaration of economic, legal, and political independence, a whole lifetime later, that the new United States of America finally called for and began to articulate artistic independence.

Before considering that call for literary independence, let us first note the American frame of mind in relation to language during the late 1700s and early 1800s. *The Declaration of Independence* and the *Constitution*, perhaps two of the best offerings of the age, were fashioned during the height of the Age of Reason, The Age of Enlightenment. To understand the mind being born, we must understand the mind of England, the mother. Literarily, following the unparalleled expansion during the 1600s of Elizabethan drama, the works of lyric metaphysical poets, and such epics as Milton's *Paradise Lost*, England settled back into an Augustan Age in the 1700s, characterized as a reflection of Rome and epitomized by the skillful wit of Dryden and Pope. The rhyming couplets that fourteenth-century Chaucer had initiated and thrived in, and that Shakespeare and Milton had both outgrown, reappeared during the Age of Reason as a retreat to intellectual-soul mentality, in which one filters experience of the world through reason. Dryden and Pope mastered the rhyming couplets. The only possible epic at the time was a mock epic: Pope's *Rape of the Lock*. At the same time, in 1755, Dr. Johnson published the first dictionary of the English language. Johnson, in his *Rasselas*, warns against the hunger of the imagination, which preys on life, interfering with seeing things as they actually are.

Dr. Johnson's celebration of prose coincided with the emergence of the new form of literature, the novel, in the late 1600s and the 1700s. Novels such as Daniel Defoe's *Robinson Crusoe* and *Moll Flanders*, Henry Fielding's *Tom Jones*, Richardson's *Pamela and Clarissa*, generally portray and explore middle-class characters making their rational and emotional ways through contemporary society, in which human nature functions in the context of the normal laws of both linear time and three-dimensional space. However dynamic the characters and stories may be, the stage is limited. Lunatics, tragic lovers, poets, and certainly supernatural gods are outside the scope of the essentially rational English novel of the 1600s and 1700s.

The Royal Academy of Science had been maturing, tempered strongly by Galileo's discovery of the motions of the physical planets in our solar system, confirming theories of Tycho Brahe and Copernicus, about the Sun as the center of our universe, by Descartes's distinctions between matter and mind, by Newton's demonstrations of humankind's ability to calculate the course of the planets through the heavens mathematically, according to the laws of gravity. For many, Newton's clockwork universe marked the shift, as Heaven, or the heavens, started to become simply space.

In America in the late 1700s and early 1800s, theological thinking was also very rational. For those who feel a little confused about the religious origins of the American mind, perhaps a sketch summary would be helpful. The primary source of the early American mind (of New England settlers) was John Calvin (1509–1564), a major Protestant leader, in Geneva, Switzerland. His beliefs in the universal priesthood of all believers, the importance of faith over good works, and in predestination, influenced, especially, the Huguenots in France, the Presbyterians in Scotland, and the Puritans in England. The original Puritans in America considered themselves Congregationalists, compatible with Presbyterians, as more Scots poured into the colonies. In the Boston area in the 1700s, the Unitarians became a dominant influence, or stream. Believing in one God, denying the divinity of Christ, oriented toward social actions, inspired by John Locke, the Unitarians felt the Calvinist emphasis on human sinfulness to be inconsistent with reason. Eventually, the Unitarians split from the Presbyterians in 1805 and, led by Rev. William Ellery Channing, formed the American Unitarian Association in 1825. The Catholic culture of Maryland in these early centuries does not seem to have contributed in any significant way to the changing American mind, which eventually gave birth to American literature.

It is fair to characterize the general American theological mind at the end of the nineteenth century as earnest, thoughtful, rational, relatively literal in relation to the Bible, cautiously extending beyond reason to allegory, viewing an image in the Bible or in nature as a type for a spiritual truth. A good example of this frame of mind appeared in Charles Frazier's recent novel *Cold Mountain*, which portrays the attitude of a Civil War wife toward nature and God. Ada is venturing through the Blue Ridge Mountains; her husband Monroe has been away in the war for several years.

> After a time, they crossed a black creek, stepping with care on the dry backs of humped stones. Ada looked at the way the creek was seizing up with a thin rim of bright ice along its banks and around rocks and fallen trees and nubbles of moss, anything that hindered the flow. In the center of the creek, however, the fast water ripped along as always.

Where it ran shallower and slower, then, were the places prone to freezing. Monroe would have made a lesson of such a thing, Ada thought. He would have said that the match of that creek's parts would be in a person's life, the type of which God intended.

All God's works are but elaborate analogy. Every bright image in the visible world is a mere shadow of a divine thing, so that Earth and Heaven, low and high, strangely agree in form and meaning because they are in fact congruent:

> Monroe had a book wherein you could look up the types. The rose—its thorns and its blossom—a type of the difficult and dangerous path to spiritual awakening. The baby—come wailing to the world in pain and blood—a type of our miserable earthly lives, so consumed with violence. The crow—its blackness, its outlaw nature, its tendency to feast on carrion—a type of the dark forces that wait to overtake mans soul.
>
> So Ada quite naturally thought the stream and the ice might offer a weapon of the spirit. Or, perhaps, a warning. But she refused to believe that a book should say just how it should be construed or to what use it might be put. Whatever a book said would lack something essential and be as useless by itself as the gudgeon to a door hinge with no pintle. (Frazier 298)

Ada recognizes that her husband's book of equivalencies lacks something essential. Frazier's representation of Monroe's mind in the Blue Ridge Mountains of the 1850s probably works as a fair characterization of the bent of the American mind in New England in the early 1800s.

Whereas the Unitarians were emerging in Boston, the Congregationalists remained dominant in Connecticut, feeling, as their name implies, neither the need for a priest as a mediator between God and human individuals, nor the need for a hierarchy of bishops to direct the church, instead trusting the people of the congregation to carry the word, or spirit of God.

In the 1820s and 1830s, two young American Congregationalists struggled to reconcile their inner experience of the divine with the language available to articulate that experience. In their frustration, each independently found himself reading Samuel Taylor Coleridge's philosophical notes, *Aids to Reflection*. Coleridge's little book almost single-handedly catalyzed a linguistic evolution, if not a revolution, in the American mind. The two young Congregationalists, James Marsh and Horace Bushnell, are similar in several ways. Through Coleridge's influence, both were pioneers beyond the thinking of their time, though they managed to remain within the boundaries of the Congregational Church. They nevertheless went in a different directions from each other.

How did Coleridge's thinking affect their thinking? Back in England during the 1790s, the young poet-preacher Samuel Taylor Coleridge, fourteenth and favorite child of a minister, had assumed he would become a Unitarian minister, until the poet in him felt too stifled by Unitarian one-sided thinking. The artist in Coleridge felt dynamically the interrelationship of poet, poem, and inspiration, to the degree that the theologian in him became a Trinitarian, experiencing absolutely the parallels between the triad of poet, poem, and inspiration, on the one hand, and that of Father, Son, and Holy Spirit on the other. Coleridge experienced the poet as corresponding to the Creator-Father; the poem, or creation, to the Son, who incarnated into mortal flesh; and inspiration to the Holy Spirit, moving between creator and creation like the breath of God into the clay of Adam and as the tongues of flame among the apostles.

A keen philosophical thinker, Coleridge was also an astute observer of nature and a close friend of scientists such as Joseph Priestly, who discovered the properties of several gases, especially oxygen. What poet/philosopher/theologian Coleridge realized was that, if the divine Creator is immortal and limitless, then his living creation, too, has its limitless, unpredictable dimensions, beyond the grasp of the measuring human mind. Thus humanity, the primary creature, made in the image of the Creator, could conceivably use words in ways that reflect the infinitely mobile, multidimensional capacity of the original Word to create the living world. Coleridge wondered, if the spirit is multidimensional and endlessly vital, does not our language need to be correspondingly multidimensional, endlessly vital?

As a result of Coleridge's influence, the human language that will be able to do justice to the living spirit will not simply be rational exposition, nor will it simply be an almost arithmetic allegory such as rock equals steadfastness. No, the human language that will reflect the divine spirit, in kind, will be quickening and suggestive, with layers of meaning coexisting, facets simultaneously reflecting and symbols suggestive in numerous directions—a language luminous, numinous, not fixed but flowing, as the imagination of the ultimate I AM flows.

Now, let us return to the Unitarian influence. As Philip Gura has said, Ralph Waldo Emerson, Bronson Alcott, Theodore Parker, Elizabeth Peabody, and other Transcendentalists who became concerned with the problem of language (albeit in different degrees) were nurtured within the cocoon of the Unitarian Church. The Unitarian religion was based on John Locke's empiricist philosophy. Just as Locke viewed the soul as a tabula rasa, a blank slate to be filled with impressions, Locke viewed language, echoing the medieval nominalists, as an arbitrary group of signs arranged for external convenience. Elaborating upon Locke, the Scot Thomas Reid and fellow Common Sense philosophers valued observation of the world through the senses, experiencing language, therefore, as a reflection of the human particulars of time and space, not reflecting any eternal reality. Such attitudes, rooted in Locke, elaborated by the Scottish Common Sense philosophers and promulgated through the Unitarian Church, powerfully imbued Harvard, Yale, and Princeton during the early 1800s.

By the 1820s, though, some Harvard students were becoming excited by Kant and Coleridge, who articulated a knowing that precedes experience. One young Vermonter studied Divinity in Andover and Cambridge, Massachusetts, publishing, in fact, an edition of Coleridge's *Aids to Reflection* in 1829. James Marsh wrote an essay exploring how an emerging modern sensibility resulted from a new interrelationship of faith, reason, and imagination. Marsh saw the Enlightenment's emphasis on logical rationality leaving faith weakened. He felt Coleridge's understanding of imagination to be the key to healing the spiritual anemia of early nineteenth-century America. Coleridge, reflecting on recent church history, recognized:

> Too soon did the Doctors of the Church forget that the heart, the moral nature, was the beginning and the end: and that truth, knowledge, and insight were comprehended in its expansion. This was the true and first apostasy—when in council and synod the divine humanities of the Gospel gave way to speculative systems, and religion became a science of shadows under the name of theology, or at least a bare skeleton of truth, without life, or interest, alike inaccessible and unintelligible to the majority of Christians. (Coleridge 530)

Through Coleridge's acknowledgement of the crucial validity of the feeling life, Marsh experienced that the will's well-springs of faith could be rejuvenated, just as reason could be illuminated with the greater vitality of higher Reason, a faculty limited not to the mere human mind, but capable of shining with the light of the Creator. Hence one's language, rather than being a collection of labels stuck on the things of the world, could in fact bear the things of the world with such an artful care that they reveal the spirit of their creator. The language of theology could in fact vitally reflect the living spirit.

James Marsh became a Congregationalist minister, and in 1826 the wise trustees of the University of Vermont invited him to become president of their university. As president and professor, he devoted the rest of his life to establishing a college curriculum based on a Coleridgean foundation. Partially through Marsh's interests and efforts to heal the rifts between America's Calvinists and Unitarians, Coleridge's *Aids to Reflection* became, as Perry Miller said, the book that was of the greatest single importance in forming the Transcendentalists' minds.

Horace Bushnell, a generation younger than James Marsh, was a country boy who had carded wool with his father. When he arrived at Yale, he realized that he had no language with which to express his religious experiences. Reading Coleridge's *Aids to Reflection*, Bushnell found that writing became, to a considerable extent, the *making* of a language and much more than going to dictionaries. He became aware of how the second, third, or thirteenth sense of words, all but the physical first sense, belong to the empyrean and are given, as we see in the prophets, for inspiration. As early as 1839, he published his *Preliminary Dissertation on Language*. During the ensuing decade, he continuously strove to develop language shimmering with inspiration, like that of the prophets, language enspirited, enthused, vibrant with multidimensionality beyond the limitations of logic, in short, language which was like life.

Bushnell's collection of sermons, *God in Christ*, published in 1849, articulates a Logoism in the forms of things, so that things serve as types of images of what is inmost in our souls, because God, the universal Author, stands expressed everywhere. Bushnell experienced that, rather than being embroiled in the logical battles between the Unitarians and the Trinitarians, rather than being locked into Swedenborg's arithmetical one-to-one correspondences, people need to accept that the things of the world reflect only imperfectly the spirit of the Creator of that world. In the same manner, the words of our language only reach toward accurately reflecting, or doing justice to, both the world and the creator.

> But [said Bushnell], through the activity of the Logos in human language, our language was in fact constantly improving upon itself by multiplying its forms of representation. As form battles form, and one [word] neutralizes another, all [their] insufficiencies are filled out, the contrarieties liquidated, and the mind can then settle into a full and just apprehension of the pure spiritual truth. (Gura 63)

Bushnell articulated that Truth is not two-dimensional but spherical, to be apprehended through a multiplicity of forms. In short, Horace Bushnell, the Congregational theologian, experienced that, just as the human being is but an image of the Creator, so human language is but an image of the original Word. However, as such, human language could, and indeed should, glow with symbolic multiplicity of meaning, of connotation, of immeasurably limitless impossibilities, as anything living in fact is.

James Marsh and Horace Bushnell, while liberating language from the flat, rational equation of logical limit, maintained a flowing multiplicity of language permeated with the image of the Judeo-Christian Creator. They strove to activate language through the activity of imagination, imitating in kind, though not degree, the imagination of the infinite I AM as it is presently active in the creation. One could say that, through imagination's rescue of language from the limits of rationality, Marsh and Bushnell were attempting, with Coleridge as a guide, nothing less than the rejuvenation of American Protestantism, which was the dominant frame of mind in the still-new nation. From another perspective, these two good ministers began the process of galvanizing the American mind out of the Age of Reason, which, in its distilling clarification, had served so well the conceiving of the United States of America. Nevertheless, long after the separate geography had assured religious freedom and a lifetime after political and legal independence had been accomplished, these two men experienced that the American individual was not yet in fact spiritually free within the confines of the religious mind of the time. Because American theology had become trapped in what one might call a rational-soul eddy, these two Congregationalists recognized, experienced, the imagination as the medium that might allow the Christian to experience the spirit at the time, in time, the spirit of the time, as fully, as vitally, as human language can allow.

If the influence of Calvin can be seen as a taproot of early American consciousness, perhaps it is time to acknowledge Coleridge's crucial role as a light that led leaf to flower, in what Van Wyck Brooks called the flowering of New England, and in what F. O. Matthiessen called the American renaissance, in the extraordinary gift to world literature, within a couple of decades, of the works of Emerson, Thoreau, Hawthorne, Melville, Poe, Whitman, and Dickinson, long after geographical, religious, political, legal, and economic independence. It is also time to acknowledge the role of two little-known Congregational ministers, James Marsh and Horace Bushnell, in bringing that light to America, helping to make possible the way our American artists could think, imagine, and write beyond the confines of the Church. Marsh and Bushnell helped the early American mind to alter, so that Hawthorne's scarlet letter could evolve, could mean variously, so that

Melville's doubloon in *Moby-Dick* could be read so many different ways by so many different people, so that Whitman's *Song of Myself* could resonate so universally.

The spirit of the English language nourished the early European settlers of North America mainly through the King James translation of the *Bible* and through Bunyan's *Pilgrim's Progress.* Amid the pressures of physical survival, the spirit of the language was rarely courted, at most within the narrow confines of puritanical religious dictates. In general, the English language was harnessed practically to the linear tasks of reason with a small *r,* Blake's "mind-forg'd manacles." The two monumental exceptions, for which the spirit of the English language may have sacrificed most of its forces in eighteenth-century North America, were the *Declaration of Independence* and that most vibrantly universal, extraordinarily humanity-serving of documents, the *Constitution* of the United States of America. In the early nineteenth century, through the influence of Coleridge especially, the spirit of the English language in America began to become liberated from the confines of the European Age of Reason, so that it could enhance human creativity literarily with flexible, vital imagination and freedom, as it had enhanced human imagining governmentally decades earlier.*

* This chapter originally appeared in *The Riddle of America.*

Chapter 23

Poetry in American Prose: The Novel

Typically, the early English novel, born during the Age of Reason in the late 1600s and 1700s, dwelled neither in memory of the past nor in imagination of the future. Think of Fielding's *Tom Jones*, Richardson's *Moll Flanders*, or even Defoe's *Robinson Crusoe*, in which, although Crusoe marks the days, he focuses on the present moment. Typically as well, the world of the early novel is the familiar, known world of three-dimensional, physical space. Moreover, it is typically England. Even in *Robinson Crusoe,* the footprint on the sand belongs not to a god or some supernatural being, but to "Friday," a human being. The characters are familiar and middle class, with an occasional criminal, but no lunatics, mad lovers, or poets; in other words, it has no characters going far beyond the bounds of normality. The early novel sanely orients its frequently newly literate, mostly middle-class readers in their contemporary world.

However, by the early-mid 1800s, the English novel had in a way exhausted its material, its too sane, rational, prosaic, even materialistic limits. From what realms could new life enter the form of the novel? From the two raw, uncouth, sprawling worlds of savages and wilds, of many peoples, one to the east and one to the west: Russia and America. Within three decades, the 1850s to 1870s, from Russia came Gogol's *Dead Souls*, Turgenyev's *Fathers and Sons*, Tolstoy's *Cossacks*, *War and Peace*, and *Anna Karenina*, and Dostoyevsky's *Crime and Punishment*, *The Idiot*, *The Possessed*, and *The Brothers Karamazov*. The United States brought forth Hawthorne's *Scarlet Letter* and *The House of Seven Gables*, Melville's *Moby-Dick*, and Poe's stories.

What distinguishes these works from the previous, typical English novels? George Steiner has pointed out that the new form of the human story, the prose novel, was rejuvenated, even resurrected, through infusion of the spirit of the three original forms of literature: the epic, the drama, and the lyric. This book, *The Spirit of the English Language*, focuses on poetry not prose, and on English not Russian, but it attempts to glean the activity of the English language spirit as it works in poetry of the English language. Hence, one could say that the seasoned muses of epic (Kalliope), drama (Melpomene-tragedy and Thalia-comedy), and lyric poetry (Euterpe) come to the rescue of the waning, new prose form, the exhausted, prematurely aging novel, contributing their spirit and influence to infuse the novel with new life.

Epic, Drama, Lyric

The epic, as in Homer's *Iliad* and *Odyssey*, typically tells the story of an aristocratic hero engaged either in a great battle or in a long journey. The epic, originating in the West around Ephesus (in modern Turkey), extends over long periods of time (ten years at Troy) and great distances (the whole known world of the Mediterranean). The epic, in fact, includes an almost encyclopedic knowledge of the whole known world. The human adventure is supported or thwarted by many levels of beings participating, including supernatural gods and elemental beings of water and fire. The epic was usually sung in the third person narrative: "Then the soldiers swarmed over the beaches..." (*Iliad*). The poet simply reports the events, as an invisible narrator.

The drama, with its birth in the Dionysian mysteries at Eleusis, originally portrayed characters struggling with fate, the action concentrated in one day and in one place—for example, Oedipus's palace at Thebes. The gods, embodying the action completely in Aeschylus's early *Prometheus Bound*, have receded by the time of Sophocles' *Oedipus* to the background influence of Apollo's oracle of Delphi, still pulling the strings of destiny though. The story is told not in the third person, but in the dynamic, immediate dialogue of the first and second person, "I and you," communicating to each other, amplified by the chorus.

The lyric, mothered forth (as far as our written records of Western literature show) by the Greek poet Sappho, is essentially the song of oneself. The "I" sings, using images of nature to express in a moment a short version of a feeling or experience: "Swallow, swallow, Pandion's daughter of wind and sky, why me / why me?"

Among the many beauties, dimensions, and powers of Melville's *Moby-Dick* is the fact that the prose is permeated with epic, dramatic, and lyric passages.

> I. In old Norse times, the thrones of the sea-loving Danish kings were fabricated, saith tradition, of the tusks of the narwhale. How could one look at Ahab then, seated on that tripod of bones, without bethinking him of the royalty it symbolized? For a Khan of the plank, and a king of the sea, and a great Lord of Leviathans was Ahab (chapter 30, "The Pipe," p.130).

This is an example of epic prose, reaching high and broad, evoking kings, khans, and Lords, of several cultures, the whole sea, and even the mythic Leviathan.

> II. MALTESE SAILOR: Me too; where's your girls? Who but a fool would take his left hand by his right, and say to himself, How d'ye do? Partners! I must have partners!
>
> SICILIAN SAILOR: Aye; girls and a green!-then I'll hop with ye; yea, turn grasshopper!
>
> LONG-ISLAND SAILOR: Well, well, ye sulkies, there's plenty more of us. Hoe corn when you may, say I. All legs go to harvest soon. Ah! Here comes the music; now for it!
>
> AZORE SAILOR [ascending, and pitching the tambourine up the scuttle]: Here you are, Pip; and there's the windlass-bitts; up you mount! Now, boys!

> [The half of them dance to the tambourine; some go below; some sleep or lie among the coils of rigging. Oaths a-plenty.]
>
> AZORE SAILOR [dancing]: Go it, Pip! Bang it, bell-boy! Rig it, dig it, stig it, quig it, bell-boy! Make fire-flies; break the jinglers!
>
> PIP: Jinglers, you say?-there goes another, dropped off; I pound it so.
>
> CHINA SAILOR: Rattle thy teeth, then, and pound away; make a pagoda of thyself.
>
> FRENCH SAILOR: Merry-mad! Hold up thy hoop, Pip, till I jump through it! Split jibs! Tear yourselves!
>
> TASHTEGO [quietly smoking]: That's a white man; he calls that fun: humph! I save my sweat.
>
> OLD MANX SAILOR: Wonder whether those jolly lads bethink them of what they are dancing over. I'll dance over your grave, I will-that's the bitterest threat of your night-women, that beat head-winds round corners. O Christ! To think of the green navies and the green-skulled crews! Well, well; belike the whole world's one ball, as your scholars have it; and so 'tis right to make one ball-room of it. Dance on, lads, you're young; I was once. (chapter 40, "Midnight, Forecastle," p. 176).

This selection provides an example of dramatic prose, even set in explicit, dramatic script, involving a cast of characters, the action evolving through their direct, colloquial dialogue with each other.

III. Some days elapsed, and ice and icebergs all astern, the Pequod now went rolling through the bright Quito spring, which, at sea, almost perpetually reigns on the threshold of the eternal August of the Tropic. The warmly cool, clear, ringing, perfumed, over-flowing, redundant days were as crystal goblets of Persian sherbet, heaped up, flaked up, with rose-water snow. The starred and stately nights seemed haughty dames in

> jeweled velvets, nursing at home in lonely pride, the memory of their absent conquering earls, the golden helmeted suns! For sleeping man, 'twas hard to choose between such winsome days and such seducing nights. But all the witcheries of that unwaning weather did not merely lend new spells and potencies to the outward world. Inward they turned upon the soul, especially when the still mild hours of eve came on; then, memory shot her crystals as the clear ice most forms of noiseless twilights. And all these subtle agencies, more and more, they wrought on Ahab's texture." (chapter 29, "Enter Ahab; to Him, Stubb," p. 127).

This is an example of lyric prose, in which images of nature, the days and nights, quicken the language, revealing, reflecting human emotion, mood.

These original, primary forms of the human story have informed the novel, the "new" form of literature, infusing its prosaic world of contemporary, linear time and three-dimensional space with the flavor, even the spirit, of epic, dramatic, and lyric language. Rudolf Steiner spoke of the epic, with its origins in Ionian Greece, especially Ephesus, as particularly serving the birth of the culture of a people, not just reflecting but even engendering the life patterns, the rhythms, right down to the breathing (as in dactylic hexameter) habits of a people. He speaks of the epic quickening and engendering the life forces (esoterically, the ether body) of a singer, the audience, the whole folk, and hence even today, the reader. *Time* magazine, July 26, 2004, reported recent medical studies confirming this insight. Of three patient groups, the one speaking dactylic hexameter daily ended up with better health (both circulatory and respiratory) than either the group performing random speech exercises or the group with standard medical treatment. The dactylic hexameter rhythm of _ uu _uu _u \\ _uu _uu _u permeates Homer's epics, as in *andra moi ennepe musa*, \\ *polutropon hos mala pola* (Sing in me, O Muse, of the man of many turns), the opening lines of Homer's *Odyssey.*

In a similar manner, Rudolf Steiner speaks of the language of drama serving to quicken, exercise, and develop the soul body (or astral body) of a developing people, as together the *polis* (whole human community) struggles, through conflicts in relationships to find and fulfill their destinies. Dramatic passages help quicken, strengthen, and awaken the reader's soul, the astral body. Steiner speaks of lyric poetry exercising the individuality: the I AM both of the singer/writer and of the listener/reader. Delphi, with its worship of Apollo and its motto, "Human being, know thyself," was especially the source of lyric inspiration in the West.

The muses of epic, dramatic, and lyric poetry are working with the spirit of the English language in epic, dramatic, and lyric passages in *Moby-Dick*, not only rejuvenating the literary form of the novel, but more essentially awakening and artfully quickening the reader's own life body, soul body, and individuality. The explicitly clear poetic influence in *Moby-Dick* becomes generally possible in English prose, as well as in Russian and other languages, from the mid-nineteenth century on.

Conversely, we have seen how Shakespeare wove prose into some of his dramas (see chapter 7). And we have seen how some of the metaphysical poets informed their lyric poetry with colloquial language more typical of drama (see chapter 8). We have seen, too, how Shakespeare, Milton, and some of the Romantic poets used blank verse, shedding restrictions of rhyme, almost reaching toward prose (see chapters 7, 10, 12, 13).

We are about to see in the following chapter where Walt Whitman takes modern consciousness in terms of the mysterious threshold, almost even the shoreline, or better, the interfluence between poetry and prose. The general character of twentieth-century poetry in English is, in fact, influenced substantially by the prose of the novel.

Chapter 24

WHITMAN

THE LIFE OF WALT WHITMAN (1819–1892)

IN 1840, a former American country boy, whose formal education had finished at age ten, worked at the *New York Aurora*. As a boy, the sight of a sail on the horizon had inspired in him the desire to write. Although he loved to loaf and observe, this young reporter now sailed the teeming streams of life in the city. He knew and loved all aspects of this bustling city: the docks, with fresh fish and arriving dignitaries; the streets, with their criminals, police, politicians, and people from the whole globe; the churches, courts, concert halls, Shakespeare, and the operas of Rossini and Verdi. At the age of twenty-one, his eye, ear, voice, and pen served to reflect as truly and vividly as possible the multitudinous dimensions of this vital new city. Although there were signs of character in the dashing young man with his finger on the pulse of the times, there was scarcely a clue of any poet in the reporter who would, within a year, become editor in chief of the *New York Aurora*. No one could guess that he, Walt Whitman, would become one of the most radical pioneers in the history of poetry, the father of American poetry, and one of the primary generators of the new American consciousness. Whitman's emerging individuality used words initially to reflect the world, not yet to creatively transform the quintessential activity of the spirit of the English language.

Walt Whitman was born May 31, 1819, in Huntington, Long Island, to an illiterate mother, Louisa van Velsor, of Dutch descent and an itinerant carpenter father, Walter, of Quaker descent. From both parental streams, Walt inherited a combination of concrete humanitarianism on one hand and mystical abandon on the other. The second child of ardent American Democrats, Walt had siblings named Jesse, Mary Elizabeth, Hannah, Louisa, Andrew Jackson, George Washington, Thomas Jefferson, and Edward.

The threshold between this world and the other was not easy to keep clear in this Whitman family. Jesse, suffering from syphilis, died after years in an insane asylum. Hannah, Walt's favorite sister, married an artist in Burlington, Vermont, and suffered from spells of drunkenness and paranoia. Andrew Jackson Whitman became a drunkard, married a loose woman, and died of tuberculosis at age thirty-seven. The youngest, Eddie, was an epileptic of low mental acumen. Later, Walt's natural enjoyment of friendship with Eddie would become the inspiration for the radical transformation of a mental institution in Hamilton, Ontario, where the bars were removed and inmates took daily walks and played baseball with the local fire department.

Papa Walter became a carpenter, breaking the chain of five generations of farmers. A nonreligious Quaker, a Jeffersonian and Jacksonian Democrat, his two heroes were Tom Paine and the Quaker Elias Hicks. When Walt was five, Lafayette, the celebrated hero of the Revolution, picked him up and gave him a kiss. While the family moved eleven times, son Walt remained indifferent though affectionate toward his father, worshipping instead his stable, persevering mother.

A country boy before he became a man of the city, Walt enjoyed a childhood on Long Island composed of green cornfields, flourishing orchards, and fishing and crabbing. After a swim, young Walt loved to declaim Shakespeare and Homer's *Iliad* to the surf and the gulls. He liked to read Dante in the wood by the shore. In his early boyhood, the sight of a ship passing under full sail aroused his first impulse to write. Biographer Van Wyck Brooks recognized that for Walt the shore, where water married land, symbolized the blending of the real and the ideal. Walt later felt the need to write a book expressing this liquid theme. The poetic form he eventually evolved in his late thirties was oceanic: verses recalling waves, rising and falling, scarcely two alike in length or measure.

Owing to young Walt's curiosity, he loved to broaden his horizons reading Sir Walter Scott's novels and *Arabian Nights*. Age ten was his final year of public school education. The next year, Walt's family moved for the eleventh time, this time to Brooklyn, where he was apprenticed to a lawyer.

At age twelve, Walt began his seminal apprenticeship to a printer, an old master who described Washington and Jefferson, who had run messages across the river for Aaron Burr, and who often saw the widow of Alexander Hamilton. As a teenager, Walt himself watched Andrew Jackson "driven through Brooklyn streets in big-brimmed white beaver hat, white hair, piercing eyes behind spectacles" (Brooks 127). Adolescent Walt learned his craft as a printer, while being imbued with the lives of major founding fathers of the American Democratic Republic.

An overgrown youth, Walt was good-natured, clumsy, slovenly, and inclined to loaf beneath the apple trees, yet eagerly writing much for the newspaper. "Abstemious in youth as in age, young Walt never smoked or drank, never 'dissipated,' liked cheap, simple fare" (Ibid. 130). "He seemed [in person] oddly bisexual, his body being large and sturdy but [with] little muscle beneath [the[soft feminine flesh" (Chase 39).

Following a lifelong pattern of ebbing and flowing, Walt retreated at age seventeen from the city to teach for a year in rural Long Island. However, the teeming hustle-bustle of American city life drew him back. By age twenty-two, with an eye and an ear for anything in any domain of the city, Walt Whitman had become editor of New York's *Aurora* newspaper. The country boy had become a dandy, sporting a frock coat, tall hat, a cane, and flower in the lapel, with a carefully nurtured and trimmed beard. Tall, graceful, and neat, he had fresh pink skin and a lounging air. Like Socrates, Walt had an unusual capacity for standing still, to ruminate. Walt liked to loaf; he "felt like a god walking the Earth." And he loved the Indian name, *Manhattoes*, "the place encircled by swift and sparkling waters" (Brooks 122).

In his role as newspaper editor, Walt often met important personages as they entered the port and showed them the city. On Broadway, he had seen John Quincy Adams and Henry Clay. He heard public talks by Fenimore Cooper and often Daniel Webster. He loved and studied oratory; he declaimed in the woods and on the shore. He reviewed many performances of Shakespeare's plays. He loved opera, especially Rossini and Verdi. Van Wyck Brooks considered the three primary influences on Walt's still latent poetry to have been the three O's: ocean, oratory, and opera.

By 1846 at age twenty-seven, Walt had become editor of the *Brooklyn Daily Eagle*, New York's most important Democratic newspaper. He reviewed Coleridge, Goethe, Ruskin, Carlyle, and Georges Sand. He read Emerson and Margaret Fuller. His newspaper prose so far revealed no clues of the future poet, but he was used to speaking to the people, to the city, hence, by eventual extrapolation, to America and the world at large. He wrote of the scintillating surfaces of the world. As one of the masses, he wrote of and for the masses. He became a civic figure himself.

Decades later, looking back on *Leaves of Grass*, Walt Whitman wrote, "The book arose out of my life in Brooklyn and New York from 1838 to 1853, absorbing a million people, for fifteen years, with an intimacy, an abandon, probably never equaled" (Bucke 67). For this chronicler of the city, his primary passion was the politics of the people. Biographer Kowenhaven describes editor Whitman as "A Jeffersonian Democrat, an idealist, a violent patriot, a humanitarian, a reformer, an ardent defender of progress and a fighter for democracy who knows that democracy has to be fought for." Walt Whitman spent his twenties soaking up the world in almost all senses, sensual, sentient, yet, as far as we know, not sexual.

> As Whitman himself intrinsically knew, his poetic genius would not be liberated by a startling experience, by a ravishing dream, by a vision of God, or by love for a man or woman. It would be self-liberated like leaves of grass,

> slowly,...fully patiently, and in due time after its long dormancy. (Chase 36)

Nevertheless, at age twenty-nine, editor Walt Whitman let go of his role as watcher of the many worlds of the city. He and his brother Jeff set out to see the actual country of the United States of America, the idea of which he already loved so well. Their seven-month journey took them through Wheeling, West Virginia, down the Ohio River to Cincinnati, down the Mississippi River to New Orleans, back up to Hannibal, St. Louis, Milwaukee, Chicago, LaSalle, Cleveland, Mackinac Island, Lake Michigan, Lake Huron, over to Buffalo, Niagara Falls, and back down the Hudson River.

No one knows for sure, but many are the implications that Walt did experience some kind of sexual awakening, some kind of introduction to, initiation into, the power of Eros in, of all places, the sentient center of the North American continent, New Orleans. Whatever may have happened in particular to Walt in New Orleans, it is clear in general that the mighty rivers, the many forms of untamed wilderness, the varied kinds of peoples, both native and "settling," all combined in a potent catalyzation, a still subterranean awakening of forces in recorder-observer Walt.

Although the Walt who returned in September 1848 resumed a familiar role as editor of Brooklyn's *Freeman* newspaper, he resigned within a year. Something deeper, as yet unknown to him, was stirring within. Like his kindred spirit, Coleridge, worldly Walt was becoming disillusioned with the limitations of politics. However, in slow-brewing Walt, the poet was yet to emerge.

During his early thirties, Walt rose late, did some printing, some freelance writing; mainly he read and wrote a lot. Between ages thirty-two and thirty-five, in a long-awaited rapprochement, Walt joined his father carpentering. The young, dapper dandy of his twenties was becoming the "quiet, slow-footed, grey-bearded working man" (Ibid. 41). His lunch bucket always included something to read: Homer, Sophocles, Epictetus, The Bible, Shakespeare, or essays by Emerson.

Many times Walt reread George Sands's *La Contesse de Ruddstat*, which portrays a seer-poet. In 1847, at age twenty-eight, Walt wrote, "I cannot understand the mystery, but I am always conscious of myself as two—as my soul and I: and I reckon it is the same with all men and women" (Ibid. 42).

The key catalyst had been published back in 1844, Emerson's essay "The Poet," when he called for the American poet who would "chaunt our own times and social circumstances," and, like Dante, dare "to write his autobiography in colossal cipher, or into universality." Whitman later told one of his admirers that, if he had not read Emerson at the right moment, *Leaves of Grass* might never have been written. Whitman later reflected that he had been simmering, simmering, and that Emerson had brought him to a boil. Although no one realized the import at the time, one of Walt's simmering sputterings marked one of the major revolutions in the history of poetry, one of the major moments in the evolution of consciousness.

In 1855, at the age of thirty-six, a certain former journalist anonymously published his first notebook of poetry. The nameless photograph of the author on the frontispiece, was described by the *New York Herald Tribune* as "in garb, half sailor's, half workingman's, . . . a 'wideawake' perched jauntily on his head, one hand in his pocket and the other on his hip, a certain air of mild defiance, and an expression of pensive insolence on his face which seems to betoken a consciousness of his mission as the 'coming man.'" The only other clue to the authorship appeared in section 24 of *A Song of Myself:* " Walt Whitman, a cosmos, of Manhattan the son . . . " The seasoned journalist, Whitman himself, penned an anonymous, exceedingly favorable review, one of the few that did not dismiss the work as a batch of formless obscenities. He also sent the book to none other than the nationally known Ralph Waldo Emerson. Emerson responded with a letter several weeks later, one of the great responses of all time to an unknown author.

Emerson, having written to Carlyle of the strange "American poem," "a non-descript monster which had yet terrible eyes and buffalo strength," finally gambled on sending a letter July 21, 1855, to Mr. Walter Whitman, care of the publisher.

> Dear Sir, I am not blind to the worth of the wonderful gift of *Leaves of Grass*. I find it the most extraordinary piece of wit & wisdom that America has yet contributed....I give you joy of your free & brave thought....I find incomparable things said incomparably well....I find the courage of treatment, which so delights us, & which large perception only can inspire. I greet you at the beginning of a great career, which yet must have had a long foreground somewhere, for such a start. I rubbed my eyes to see if this sunbeam were no illusion; but the solid sense of the book is sober certainty. It has the best merits, namely of fortifying & encouraging.

In June 1857, age thirty-eight, Walt Whitman penned to himself a resolution: "The Great construction of the new Bible. Not to be diverted from the principal object—the main life—the three hundred and sixty-five....It ought to be ready in 1859" (Ibid. 110). Whitman's *Song of Myself* contained fifty-two sections, the number of weeks in a year. But to go so far as every day of the whole year, it would be the yearbook of the people, containing one gathers, a poem for each day—"a kind of saints' calendar of democracy" (Ibid. 111). *Leaves of Grass* never achieved just that form, but it certainly continued to grow, democratically welcoming more and more poems through the editions over the years. Some scholars even think that Whitman deliberately made some of the language more prosaic, and hence more democratic, in ensuing revisions.

In Walt's room in Brooklyn in 1857, there were only two engravings, one of Silenus and one of Bacchus. Walt Whitman indeed became democracy's Dionysus. Water-drinking teetotaler that he was, he exhorted Americans to celebrate everyone and every thing in this new world, intoxicated with the American spirit. T. S. Eliot recognized Whitman's prodigious faculty "in making America as it was... into something grand and significant,...of transmuting the real into the ideal" (Eliot 206–207).

When cannons fired on Fort Sumter on April 12, 1861, Walt Whitman was forty-two years old. In the next two years, in the context of the raging Civil War, he wrote twenty-five historical sketches for Brooklyn newspapers. After a visit to Horace Greeley's farm with Bronson Alcott and Henry David Thoreau, Thoreau wrote of Walt:

> A remarkably strong though coarse nature, of a sweet disposition, and much prized by his friends. Though peculiar and rough in his exterior, his skin (all over) red, he is essentially a gentleman...essentially strange to me...he is very broad but, as I have said, not fine....He told us that he loved to ride up and down Broadway all day on an omnibus, sitting beside the driver, listening to the roar of the carts, and sometimes gesticulating and declaiming Homer at the top of his voice. (Harding 373,375)

Inspired as he was by the ancient war of Troy, Walt was moved by his contemporary war not to fight but to help in hospitals. When in December 1862 Walt's brother George was wounded in Fredricksburg, Walt moved down to Virginia and Washington.

The man who had given his soul's attention for fifteen years to all dimensions of the city, the man who had expanded beyond his imagination in his seven-month tour of this continent, that same man gave his soul's forces to the injured and dying of the nation's Civil War. By the end of 1864, Walt Whitman had made 600 hospital visits. He saved hundreds of lives. He wrote thousands of letters home for soldiers. He saw eighty to a hundred thousand wounded and sick soldiers. The worldly dandy had become the Christlike carpenter/poet in his thirties and the good gray nurse in his forties. Whereas Emerson had become the voice of the nation and Lincoln its leader, it was really through his war poetry that Whitman became the poet of the nation, especially through his elegy for Lincoln, "When Lilacs Last in the Dooryard Bloom'd," as well as "O Captain, My Captain." Galway Kinnell has noted that "Drum Taps" may be the only war poetry since the *Iliad* actually about the soldiers.

Exhausted by his wartime tending, Walt suffered a partial stroke. By 1868, his work had started to make a strong impression in Europe, Germany, and France and with Rosetti and Swinburne in England. For the first time in his life, Walt Whitman finally owned his own home.

In Camden, New Jersey, the good grey Poet died on March 26, 1892, at age seventy-one. Like his then unknown mate, the mother of American poetry, Emily Dickinson, as well as the other poetic "WW," William Wordsworth, Walt wrote his greatest poetry within a span of about seven years, from around 1854 until 1861. While he continued to write, revise, and publish in nine continuously expanding editions of *Leaves of Grass* for the rest of his life, his keenest contributions come from that seven-year period, from about thirty-five to forty-two, his consciousness-soul stage of development. In that period, the United States of America finally found the poet that Emerson had called for, back in 1844. It is fair to conjecture that the vitality with which Walt Whitman was generating an American consciousness in his early editions of *Leaves of Grass*—the very vitality he gave during the Civil War to thousands of young men whom Walt believed were both preserving and renewing America as a democratic union.

WHITMAN: THE POETRY

In the context of the evolving language of English literature, why did it take so long for the "United States of America" to give forth its own poets, centuries after settling, and a lifetime after the *Declaration of Independence*? What are the traits of the poetry of the childless Father of American poetry, in the 1850s and 1860s?

As Walt begins his song, in the meter of the times, the meter of the age, he reaches, expands and extends beyond it, toward and even beyond the classic hexameter of Homer's original epics' verse. Homer's dactylic hexameter had rested in the balanced relationship between blood and breath, three pulse beats within one breath, the new breath being taken on the fourth pulse, during the *caesura* (pause).

Andra moi ennepe, Musa polutropon hos malla pola
Plankthe epei Troyes, hieron ptolietron eperse

(Sing in me O Muse, of the man of many turns, who
many ways
Wandered when he had sacked Troy's holy citadel.)

Spoken, Homer's line consisted of two trimeters, a hexameter. Actually, including the breathing pauses, Homer's line was an octameter, two tetrameters. Homer's line rests on the universal 4:1 relationship between blood and breath. Such is the character of the meter that had guided Western humanity into incarnation during the last 2,500 years.

Walt Whitman endeavored in his poetry to "construct the great Bible the 365 the democratic." Right away, he consciously connects with his own respiration, his breathing.

Song of Myself, Section 2

...The smoke of my own breath,
Echoes, ripples, buzz'd whispers, love-root, silk-thread,
crotch and vine,
My respiration and inspiration, the beating of my heart,
the passing of blood and air through my lungs,...

Yet, by this time in evolution, the form he finds is not the general, universal form of the dactylic hexameter, which Homer had sustained through forty-eight books of the *Iliad* and the *Odyssey*. He finds an individual form, according to the ebb and flow of his particular breathing and heartbeat, in response to the particular situation of the poetry, varying not only poem by poem, not only section by section, not only stanza by stanza, but varying line by line. As a boy, Walt Whitman used to run on the beach, declaiming Homer to the wind. In his thirties, while working with his father as a carpenter, he used to have *The Iliad* (or Shakespeare or Emerson) in his lunch pail. And as a grey-haired poet Walt still liked to declaim Homer down Broadway, right behind the bus driver. Blind Homer's ancient yet timeless rhythms so permeated Walt's life that their very saturating fullness may in fact have freed him to recognize and articulate new, varying rhythms in life.

However, in March 1850, when Walt was thirty-one, external events galvanized an internal reorientation, revolution. Trying to save the Union, in January Henry Clay had introduced a compromise program, including a strong fugitive slave act. Calhoun wanted a country with two presidents, two vetoes. On March 2, Walt Whitman wrote his last rhymed poem (of his youth), the "Dough-Face Song," attacking southern politicians: "We are all docile dough-faces / they knead us with the fist." On March 7, Daniel Webster, also trying to save the Union, decided to support the fugitive slave law. On March 22, democratic journalist Walt Whitman, boiling at what he considered to be Webster's betrayal of the ideals of freedom for all, abandoned all the propriety and pattern of rhyming, regularly metrical verse, and passionately penned America's first poem in free verse, the literary equivalent of what Emerson had called "the shot heard round the world." This little poem, although of course no one realized it at the time, sounded the beginning of modern poetry, a revolution as profound literarily as the American Revolution had been politically. The poem "Blood Money" appeared in the *New York Herald Tribune*, casting Daniel Webster as Judas.

> Of olden time, when it came to pass
> That the beautiful god, Jesus, should finish his work on earth,
> Then went Judas, and sold the divine youth,
> And took pay for his body.

When Shakespeare, increasingly throughout his plays, and Milton, consistently in *Paradise Lost*, wrote in blank verse, each had stood, at the end of each line, somewhat like Satan himself in *Paradise Lost*, on the border of Hell, of Pandemonium, having to embark into the "palpable obscure" (see chapters 6 and 9). Each poet chose the oblivion, free—and this is the almost unbearable agony—free to move in almost any direction with the thought of the line, because unfettered by, undirected by, the sounds of the end rime. In the seventeenth century, Shakespeare and Milton had been great enough poets, brave enough souls, to dare, to need, to embrace such awe-ful freedom as the lack of end rime in order to express the vast or deep scope of their subject matter. However, such a new courageous freedom, such latitude of possibility of thinking, was nevertheless sustained by the iambic pentameter, by regular meter and rhythm, u_u_u_u_u_, whatever direction the thought content might take.

> ...so eagerly the fiend
> O'er bog or steep, through strait, rough, dense, or rare,
> With head, hands, wings, or feet pursues his way,
> And swims or sinks, or wades, or creeps, or flies:
> (*Paradise Lost*, John Milton, book II, ll.945-950)

By the middle of the nineteenth century, in the raw, uncultured, independent New World of the United States of America, one poet was ready to take a step even further. Walt Whitman's poem, *A Song of Myself*, begins, for example with the lines,

> I celebrate myself, and sing myself,
> And what I assume you shall assume

The first line is classic iambic pentameter, the familiar standard of English poetry. The second is iambic pentameter (unrhyming) as well, with several variations. Off we go, in blank verse? The third line, however, "For every atom belonging to me as good belongs to you," expands beyond to a line of seven feet. The next recedes to three feet,

> I loafe and invite my soul,
> I lean and loafe at my ease observing a spear of summer grass.

Then its sequel expands out to seven feet (or strong beats) again. Extending or reaching a line length beyond the contemporary pentameter toward and even beyond Homer's original hexameter, may be a reach toward Homer's epic pace, sustained regularly by its connection to the human blood and breath. However, Whitman flows beyond that hexameter to heptameter, in a sequence of three seven-foot lines, ebbing then in the next line to trimeter.

My tongue, every atom of my blood, form'd from this soil,
this air,
Born here of parents born here from parents the same,
and their parents the same,
I now thirty-seven years old in perfect health begin,
Hoping to cease not till death.

Three lines later, Whitman may expand out to nine feet. The lines change in length not according to any predetermined patterns from the past.

Creeds and schools in abeyance,
Retiring back a while sufficed at what they are, but never
forgotten,
I harbor for good or bad, I permit to speak at every
hazard,
Nature without check with original energy.

Whereas Shakespeare and Milton stood alone at the end of each line of blank verse, free to proceed in their thinking, Walt stands alone at the end of each line, free to proceed not only in his thinking, but also in his feeling, in the rhythm of breath and blood which not only accompanies, but in fact, bears the thinking. Walt, in his "free verse," is able to adjust both the rhythm and the length of each line appropriately.

Although Coleridge had wanted the poetic mind to be able to find its course "organically," as a river or tree might, adapting as it proceeded, he valued regular meter as the restraint on emotion, engendering power in the poem. Even in Coleridge's "This Lime-Tree Bower My Prison" and "Frost at Midnight" in 1797 to 1798, as the subject matter shifts and flows, the meter, the blank verse, steadily sustains the experience (see chapter 12).

American Walt, in the 1850s, so frees himself, not only of anticipated rhyme, but also of metrical length of line, that not only does no pattern sustain him from line to line, but, for the first time in the history of Western poetry, the poet is also free to find the words, the rhythm, and the length of the line that fit the experience as it is in that moment, independent of the previous and the next moments. For the first time, the verse can meet the moment as it is. What potential for vibrantly fresh verse; how difficult, as poet, to remain attentive in verse to what the vibrantly fresh moment actually calls for. The poet Galway Kinnell has said of Whitman's almost existential freshness of language, "It is as if each line had been pressed while still wet upon a part of reality, and then taken into the poem bearing its contours" (Poet House, New York: March, 1992, Hundredth Anniversary of Whitman's Death).

Such consciousness, unbound by one's feelings, not determined by preconceptions, epitomizes the unfettered, objective quality of the mature consciousness soul. The individuality of the poet strives to express appropriately the individual character of each moment. One could say that in *Song of Myself*, the *I* of the lyric finds itself in the *they* of the epic.

Whitman's "Free Verse": Possible Exercises:

1. Let students hear and then speak some rhyming couplets (Chaucer, Shakespeare, or Pope). Then let them hear and then speak some blank verse, (Shakespeare, Milton, or even Wordsworth or Coleridge).
2. Speak five to eight lines of Whitman's *A Song of Myself*. Have them repeat after, line by line. What do they hear, notice? What are impressions?
3. Have them try to walk each line, stepping according to the strong and weak beats.
4. Have the students spread out, stop and close their eyes; each should think of some, any, particular experience, picturing it and feeling it. Eyes open, each student should walk a line, silently, any direction, with whatever number and any combination of short and long measures, (weak and strong), pausing at the end of the line. Then, picturing a next aspect of the experience, walk the next line, in whatever direction, whatever rhythm and length seems appropriate for evoking that stage of the experience, and again, for at least four or five lines. What is the effect of having this wide latitude, vir-

tually 360 degrees of possibility, and any length for each line, and any rhythm for each line, at the same time as having the varying lines be part of a unified whole?

5. Have the students write about that original experience, now putting words on paper, for each line, according to what the evolving nature of the experience seems to call for. Work on them further at night. The next day, share the experience of writing that way. Hear the pieces. Share observations, impressions. What are the possibilities, the opportunities, of writing in this "free verse?" What are the burdens, the responsibilities, perhaps even the cost, of writing in this apparently limitless, super-free way? What kind of consciousness is possible, in fact, what kind of consciousness is required to write in such a manner?

Chapter 25

Emily Dickinson

The Life of Emily Dickinson (1830–1886)

In the year 1851, in the still quite new United States of America, the still-unknown Walt Whitman had just started working on what would become *Leaves of Grass*. Ralph Waldo Emerson was on his annual lecture circuit. Henry David Thoreau wrote his "Essay on Civil Disobedience" as he continued to rework his journals to publish *Walden* three years later. Nathaniel Hawthorne published *The Scarlet Letter.* Herman Melville published *Moby-Dick*. That year, too, Edgar Allan Poe and James Fenimore Cooper died.

Two years earlier, a young woman in western Massachusetts had written, "Awake ye muses nine, sing me a strain divine, / Unwind the solemn twine, and tie my Valentine!" Two years before that, when the headmistress of her academy had asked all girls who wanted to be saved to rise, she alone had remained sitting. She did not return the following year. Although this young woman showed early signs of inner independence, and although she read widely, when she turned twenty-one, there was little sign of the poet who would become one of the most concentratedly potent in the English language. How did Emily Dickinson become one of the first female poets of enduring recognition and the "mother" of American poetry? This recalcitrant individual would become one of the keenest disciples of the spirit of the English language.

In the wide-open, mountain-ringed valley of the Connecticut River in northwestern Massachusetts, Emily Dickinson's grandfather helped found Amherst College in 1814 as a Congregational antidote for the grave errors, mostly Unitarian, spreading like a disease from the radical Harvard College back east in Cambridge. Mr. Dickinson had mortgaged and lost his home to do so and left to teach in Ohio for a time.

His son Edward, a thin, austere, punctilious, strict Calvinist, practiced law, brought the railroad and the telegraph to town, repurchased the Dickinson family home, and served as treasurer of Amherst College until his death in 1874. Edward and his wife Emily lived in the stately, red-brick "Homestead" on Main Street and had three children: Austin, Emily (born Dec. 10, 1830), and Lavinia. "The others worship an eclipse every morning whom we call Father," wrote young Emily (Sewall 333). Father Edward was said to have laughed on one occasion. Austin, Emily, and Lavinia had fun when "the ancient people" were away. One night they ran outside in their bloomers to ring the church bell, so that the village could see the Aurora Borealis.

As a child, Emily was a delightful sprite, a great mimic, often the center of attention. When her father thought she was too witty, he left the table. She loved picnics, walks in the hills, and "sugaring-off" parties. Emily knew the haunts of wildflowers in the valley, scrambling alone through forests with her big dog Carlo. An expert cook, Emily baked bread and boiled father's puddings, but her father didn't like her working in the garden. At age fifteen, Emily still could not tell time, and she didn't dare ask her father to teach her.

Father allowed her to read only Shakespeare, hymns, and the Bible. Brother Austin smuggled her the Brontës, Coleridge, Keats, the Brownings, Ruskin, Irving, and Hawthorne. She loved Dickens. She read Emerson's poems. From age fourteen on, Emily referred to Shakespeare in quotations more than any other source except the Bible. Although the Amherst community in general was skeptical of Mr. Shakespeare, Emily later wrote in a letter to her dear sister-in-law Sue, "Aside from you, I learned more from Shakespeare than from any one alive." Indeed her fresh fashioning of language may have been primarily a quickening gift from Mr. Shakespeare.

At first, Emily went to Amherst Academy, where students studied all classical subjects and the sciences. The teenager was quite pleased with her development: "I am growing handsome very fast indeed!"—expecting to become "the belle of Amherst when I reach my seventeenth year" (Ibid. 371). She then had a year at Mt. Holyoke Female Seminary, where there were three groups: the Christians, the Hopers, and the No-hopers. When one morning the headmistress asked all the girls to rise who wished to be Christians, it was Emily alone who refused.

In 1854, Edward Dickinson served in Congress in Washington. Twenty-four-year-old Emily joined him there for seven weeks, charming his companions and him with her delight and wit. On the long journey home, it seems one of the primary emotional shocks in Emily's life occurred. During the two weeks the Dickinsons spent in Philadelphia, though clues are slight, Emily seems to have fallen deeply and, of course, hopelessly in love with a married man of the clergy. At home, Emily refused to join the church, to father Edward's distress.

Emily, who a decade earlier had anticipated becoming the Belle of Amherst, began to retreat. She wrote, "Constant interchange wastes tho't and feeling, and we are then obliged to repair and renew—there isn't the brimfull feeling which one gets away." When visitors came to the Dickinson Homestead, Emily would usually "elf it," often disappearing. Sometimes a visitor would receive a message: "Tonight the crimson children are playing in the West," or "The lawn is full of south and the odours tangle, and I hear today for the first the river in the tree" (Brooks 318). Sometimes Emily would lower a basket of goodies and a letter or a poem, with an oleander blossom or dandelion. "Whenever I spoke, people said 'what' to me" (Sewall 667). She sent poems to friends, to heal with a "balsam" effect. Children loved her, because she listened to them (Brooks 318).

In 1856, when Austin married Sue, Emily became less close to her red-haired, art-and-music-loving brother, and grew closer to her new sister, Sue. At age twenty-six, Emily heard, on one of his many lecture circuits, Ralph Waldo Emerson speaking on rural life. Emily wrote that it "was as if where dreams come from" (Sewall 468). Emerson was in fact welcomed just next door, where Austin had built a warmer Italianate villa.

Another frequent visitor to Austin's house between 1858 and 1862 was Samuel Bowles, a journalist with the *Springfield Republican.* Bowles was known across the country as a fighter for honest politics. Biographer Sewall has written, "He was out of her reach in every way, professionally, domestically, morally. And she out of his reach, had she seen him clearly, in matters of the mind and spirit." Nevertheless, thirty letters, fifty poems, and possibly the "Master" letters suggest that she must have been deeply in love with him—the second time her heart was marked. Nevertheless, the relationship appears to have thrived largely in Emily's mind.

In April 1862, thirty-two-year-old Emily noticed an appeal in *The Atlantic*, the most enduring monthly magazine in the still-young nation. An editor named Thomas Wentworth Higginson had been thinking of the contents, authors (Margaret Fuller, Emerson, Thoreau, Hawthorne, Bronson Alcott, etc.), and influence of the short-lived but seminal *Dial*, published in Concord, Massachusetts, back in 1840 to 1844. Higginson called for "new genius.... Charge your style with life. Tolerate no superfluities.... There may be years of crowded passion in a word, and half a life in a sentence." Higginson, who became a colonel in the nation's first African American regiment, had supported the bold actions of John Brown in Harper's Ferry, yet Higginson certainly did not consider Walt Whitman to be the American genius he sought—unlike Emerson, who had recognized Whitman (see chapter 23). He felt Whitman should have burned *Leaves of Grass.* Higginson, clearly not from Amherst, felt "we should have more radicalism in our religion,... more religion in our radicalism," but not Whitman's radicalism in our poetry.

In time, Higginson received a little letter, unsigned, declaring, "I made no verse, but one or two until last winter." That year she wrote 366 poems, about one a day. Deferentially, the letter asks, "If you were not too occupied to tell me if my verses breathe..." In fact, she asked him to be her "Master." In a separate envelope, he found enclosed four poems and the signature "Emily Dickinson." Higginson noted that the poems had "curious power,...only dashes,...little rhyme" (Brooks 322).

Introducing herself a little further to Higginson, she wrote, "I...am small, like the wren, and my hair is bold, like the chestnut burr; and my eyes, like the sherry in the glass that the guest leaves"(Ibid. 323). "For Poets, I have Keats, and Mr. and Mrs. Browning. For Prose, Mr. Ruskin, Sir Thomas Browne, and the Revelations....For several years my lexicon was my only companion" (Sewall 532). She loved her dictionary and *Elementary Geology,* as well as *Jane Eyre*, *Middlemarch*, and Elizabeth Barrett Browning's *Aurora Leigh.** Emily valued both Hawthorne and Harriet Beecher Stowe, author of *Uncle Tom's Cabin* and friend of Elizabeth Barrett Browning. Emily considered Elizabeth Barrett Browning's books her "kinsmen of the shelf."

Over the years, Emily at times sent poems to Thomas Higginson to find out if they were clear. "If I read a book and it makes my whole body so cold no fire could ever warm me, I know that is poetry. If I feel physically as if the top of my head were taken off, I know that is poetry. These are the only ways. Is there any other way?" (Brooks 322). *Atlantic* editor Higginson was encouraging, but he felt her poems should be adapted to fit the forms of the time. Emily continued to ask him for advice, but she never honored his suggested changes. "When I try to organize, my little force explodes," she explained to him. "My own words so chill and burn me." Yet she later wrote him, "You were not aware that you saved my Life." Higginson and Emerson felt that Helen Hunt Jackson was the best woman poet in America. Helen Hunt Jackson, knowing Emily, knew otherwise. Emily did not know. Of the United States' few poets, she read especially Emerson and Longfellow. In 1862, Emily wrote of Whitman, "I never read his Book—but was told that he was disgraceful" (Sewall 543). Her

* Contemporaries Emily Dickinson, unknown, and Elizabeth Barrett Browning, nominated for England's Poet Laureate, shared some striking similarities biographically. Each had domineering fathers and suffered crippling shyness, combined with extraordinary poetic powers. See chapter 16.

manuscripts often show six possibilities for one word. In a world where "the divine madness" she felt stirring in her was hardly understood, much less welcomed, Shakespeare was a never-failing sustenance for the slim majority. In certain moments, she felt she needed nothing else. "Why clasp any hand but this?" (Ibid. 700).

Finally in 1870, when Emily was forty, her "Master," Thomas Wentworth Higginson, visited her. She placed two daylilies in his hand. "These are my introduction," she whispered. "Forgive me if I am frightened. I never see strangers and hardly know what to say" (Brooks 323).

Emily often wore white, with a cameo pin, often with flower in hand. She "flitted quick as a trout" when she was disturbed. She said of a visiting scholar, "He has the facts but not the phosphorescence of learning" (Ibid. 324). With her sister Lavinia, Emily tended a small conservatory housing ferns, jasmines, lilies, and heliotropes. She used a small watering pot with a long, slender spout. In winter, she sometimes sat up all night to keep the flowers from freezing. She wrote on sheets of notepaper, which she sewed together, rolling and tying bundles with thread or ribbon, and tucked them away in drawers of her bureau. She spent much time solitary in her red-curtained alcove, keeping company with portraits of Carlyle, Elizabeth Barrett Browning, and George Eliot.

When Emily was forty-four in 1874, her father Edward Dickinson died. The following year, Mrs. Dickinson suffered an incapacitating stroke. During these years, a frequent visitor at the Homestead was Judge Otis Phillips Lord from Salem. When Emily was forty-seven, Mrs. Lord died. Emily wrote love letters, and seemed to live with hope for her love number three, stalled however by her mother's lingering invalidity. By the time Mrs. Dickinson passed away, in Emily's fifty-second year, Lord himself was ill, and he died of a stroke two years later.

By the spring of 1886, age fifty-six, Emily herself lay ill and dying with Bright's disease (kidney failure). "Audacity of Bliss," she wrote to Higginson, "said Jacob to the angel, 'I will not let thee go except I bless thee.' Pugilist and poet, Jacob was correct."

Ever shy, she allowed the doctor to examine her only from a distance, through a partially opened door as she walked back and forth. In May, Emily wrote to Higginson, who was ill himself, "Deity–does he live now? / My friend—does he breathe?" To her young cousins she wrote her last note: "Little Cousins, Called back. Emily" (Sewall xxviii).

Thursday, May 13, Emily suffered convulsions, and slipped into unconsciousness. On Friday, the death rattle began. On Saturday, May 15, her brother Austin wrote, "The day was awful. She ceased to breathe that terrible breathing just before the whistles sounded for six" (Ibid. xxviii). On Tuesday, Susan Dickinson wrote the obituary on the editorial page of the *Springfield Republican*. At the funeral, Thomas Wentworth Higginson noted that she looked thirty, with no gray hair or wrinkle, and perfect peace on her beautiful brow.

In Emily's room, sister Lavinia found a box in which she was stunned to discover more than nine hundred poems stitched into forty little booklets. In time, she found more—on envelopes, in newspaper margins, on grocery bags. Brother Austin's intimate friend Mabel Loomis Todd set about copying them from Emily's enigmatic scrawl. After some years, Lavinia and Todd were able to convince the initially reluctant T. W. Higginson to edit and publish the first volume of Emily Dickinson's *Poems* in 1890. Both Todd and Higginson smoothed out her poetry, "correcting" grammar, meter, and rhyme. Eleven printings followed. In November 1891, volume two of *Poems* appeared, lasting five printings. By 1896, when volume three appeared, Emily Dickinson's poetry was receiving worldwide attention. In her life, she had published fewer than a dozen poems, all anonymously. The once-imagined Belle of Amherst had become, only posthumously, the Poet of Amherst.

In 1955, almost a lifetime (seventy years) after Emily Dickinson's death, Thomas Johnson published all 1,775 poems, uncorrected, as Emily had originally written them, allowing readers to experience for the first time the potent freshness of her voice. Johnson concluded, from studying poems, letters, and handwriting changes, that she had written most of her poems during a seven-year period between 1858 and 1865, when she was twenty-eight to thirty-five years old, what we recognize as her intellectual-soul stage of development.

Emily Dickinson: The Poetry

We grow accustomed to the Dark— 164 (419)
When Light is put away—
As when the Neighbor holds the Lamp
To witness her Goodbye—

A Moment—We uncertain step
For newness of the night—
Then—fit our Vision to the Dark—
And meet the Road—erect—

And so of larger—Darknesses—
Those Evenings of the Brain—
When not a Moon disclose a sign—
Or star—come out—within—

The Bravest—grope a little—
And sometimes hit a Tree
Directly in the Forehead—
But as they learn to see—

Either the Darkness alters—
Or something in the sight
Adjusts itself to Midnight—
And Life steps almost straight.

The poem's five stanzas begin in the medieval ballad form which became standard for many church hymns: a four-line stanza, with alternating lines of four and three feet in length, in a rhyme pattern of a-b-c-b. However, right away in the first stanza, line four's expected rhyme with line two's *away* is a slant rhyme, an open vowel, *goodbye,* but not just the same, as if reflecting a parting, a changing of ways, as we step away into the dark from the neighbor's lamp light.

The second stanza's lingering "m" sounds of "***mom***ent" are followed by seven "n" sounds, which, in their drawing-back gesture, reinforce the uncertainty: "Mome***n***t...u***n***certai***n***...***n***ew***n***ess...***n***ight—the***n***." However, the assonance of "f***i***t...v***i***sion," with its narrow, short "i" sound suggests that our limited vision is being almost fixed, aligned onto the largeness evoked by the more expansive vowel, "ah," in *dark*. The opening *dark* is reinforced in stanza three through "l***ar***ger—D***ar***knesses—." The rolling "r" extends the effect of the open "ah" even further. Even the negation of *star* reinforces the extent of these darknesses. The hyphen on each side of *Darknesses* suggests the silence beyond the invisibility of darkness.

In the fourth, penultimate stanza the recurrent "i" of "l***i***ttle...h***i***t...***i***n..." echoes the limited, human experience suggested in the process of stanza two's "f***i***t(ting) our V***i***sion." Yet, although the first three stanzas have each rung with slant rhyme, "away...goodbye; night...erect; Brain...within," reinforcing the disjunction, dislocation, of stepping into the dark, this stanza offers suddenly an exact rhyme: "Tree...see," evoking a coalescence made possible by learning to see in the dark.

The sounds in the final stanza embody the two poles of the riddle of how we grow accustomed to the dark. Either "Darkness alters," with its expansive "ah," or our contracted vision, embodied in the "i" sounds of "someth***i***ng ***i***n...***i***tself...M***i***dnight," adjusts. The answer is, of course, a bit of a dance, a symbiosis of the two. What is the dominant sound of the final stanza? The opening sound of the stanza is the diphthong "ei," or *I*, in *Either*. Whereas the first three stanzas rang in slant rhyme, and the fourth sounded in an exact rhyme, evoking a coalescing, the fifth moves the process even further by rhyming the middle two lines, back-to-back, in a kind of fusion: "sight...Midnight—". The same diphthong—hardly heard in the poem since the *Light* was put away in line two—definitely dominates the middle of the final stanza. The most important word in the final line of the poem, *Life,* sounds it again. Of what is this diphthong composed? Of the expansive "ah," and of the contracted "i." Officially the second sound in the diphthong is generally the longer cousin of "i," "ee," as in *five* ("fah-eeve"). However, in this context our association is legitimate. The diphthong "i" in *life* embodies both the expansive "ah" and the contracted "i"; the tension between these two sounds has permeated the poem as a whole.

It's as though the new sight becomes possible through a light that is neither lamp (artificial) nor Moon or star (natural), but arises out of our activity, interacting with nature. And, just as our ear has been taught by the poem that the adjusting struggle's slant rhymes have fused into straight rhyme in stanza four, and even a middle rhyme in stanza five, we quite expect that final line to rhyme, too, with *sight* and *Midnight*. But no, *Life* is only "almost straight," reminding us through slant rhyme, again, that the fit will always be only almost, however we accustom ourselves.

How has the spirit of the English language worked through Emily Dickinson? During the years when the United States suffered its Civil War, Emily wrote most prolifically. Whereas newspaperman Walt Whitman had lived in the thick of the worlds of Brooklyn and Manhattan, then traveled across the wild expanses of the young country, Emily traveled much, mostly in Amherst. Although Walt wrote expansively in ever-altering form, Emily concentrated in the little room of the short-lined, short-stanzaed, short poem, often echoing the hymn in structure. While Walt's poems at their best generate life, Emily's at their best distil light, illuminating as though through faces of a diamond, glinting with slant glance, like slant rhyme. Walt's poetry rides the swelling tides of the life-humor of the land and its many peoples; Emily's cuts its edge on wit, some of the keenest, most potentized wordwork in the language. Walt is macrocosmic; Emily is microcosmic. Walt is perhaps more feminine, generating consciousness through embrace; Emily is perhaps more masculine, cutting consciousness, as though pruning, weeding, through discernment.

In Elizabethan England in the 1600s, Shakespeare's vocabulary had expanded with his vision, while the language of the King James Bible had contracted, saying the most in the fewest words. In the 1840s, Emerson had traveled the newly united states, speaking to all kinds of people, letting the ear of the people help him find his voice; Thoreau had traveled much in Concord, revising his journals as the perfectionist craftsperson, revising and revising into *Walden*. In Victorian England in the 1850s and 1860s, Tennyson had filled the sky of the era; unknown Gerard Manley Hopkins wrote some of the most concentratedly modern verse of which the language has been capable.

Akin to Donne in concentrated wit, to Blake in some ways in terms of originality, Emily Dickinson anticipates James Joyce's *Finnegan's Wake* in opening up not the word itself, but certainly the phrasing, the line, with pauses, dashes, differing perspectives. She has the tough mind of steel, of diamond, the accuracy of an arrow. Emily is less singer than sayer. Whereas Walt loved opera; Emily loved her lexicon. Whitman lists, naming, re-sounding, like Adam, or a child. Emily defines anew, restates, in sentences, completing thoughts, flashing intuitions. Samuel Johnson, in the 1700s, had gathered the first dictionary of the English language, establishing spellings and meanings of the language then at work in speech and literature. Emily Dickinson, like an adolescent whose very thinking is fashioning the organs enabling new thinking, was creating her own dictionary of soul-spirit experience. Whereas Walt's consciousness rolls through his lines like ocean waves, Emily's burns like fire. In terms of lyric intensity, Emily Dickinson is Sappho's long-awaited first daughter.

Karl Shapiro said that all American poetry resides within the polarity of Whitman and Poe—Whitman's life-engendering consciousness and Poe's death-reflecting consciousness. It is just as valid to say that all American poetry is the offspring of the polarity of Whitman and Dickinson, the flower-and-fruit-father and the seed-mother. Both poets launch modern consciousness, and hence the English language, into the future.

Before considering how the evolution of the English language might affect the development of adolescents—in whom, after all, the future of the English language resides—let us notice a few dynamics in contemporary American speech.

Chapter 26

Contemporary American Speech

While *The Spirit of the English Language* attempts to understand the activities of the spirit of the language in poetry, it does not include modern and contemporary poetry within its scope. Nevertheless, it is worth glancing at some of the ways contemporary youth are using the English language. We will relinquish our attention to sound patterns and shift to speech patterns, still reflecting and affecting the spirit of the language.

There are several habits of speech among contemporary American youth that may seem innocuous, but that deserve understanding among parents, teachers, and anyone concerned with language and consciousness. When we wonder about new ways in the third millennium, pondering the unpredictable changes ahead of us in the coming several decades, we find that one of the best tools for meeting what may come is to look at the way children speak throughout their waking lives. Teachers and parents need to work together on children's language.

These concerns arise not from a statement of what is right or wrong. This writer is no grammarian speaking out in contrast to anti-grammarians. This is not a cry of the Alamo, holding out against the changing language of the masses. Language always changes; language changed more in Elizabethan England than at almost any other time. Poets need to be changing and revitalizing language; otherwise our language dies, and hence our consciousness weakens. Often, there has been a healthy interchange between the language of the streets or fields and the language among the educated groves of academia, an interchange between the established language patterns of the past and the percolating slang of the present. Such tension is needed if the language is to stay alive. The uniformity of our pervasive mass media is a major new force that is deadening that vital interchange.

As parents, as teachers, and simply as individuals, we need to choose what is timeless and essential in our language, so that our children and students can navigate clearly through the ever-changing, turbulent waters of the present and near future. We are not taking a stand on one side or the other in the perennial polarities between traditional and progressive, classic and Romantic, lawful and artful, established and pioneering, past and future. We are concerned primarily with the healthy development of children as individuals in healthy relationships to others; therefore we hope that our education works both traditionally and progressively, both "classically "and "Romantically," lawfully and artfully, in developing schools that, as they become established, continue to pioneer while drawing on the past to meet the future.

Six changes have been creeping into our American English at various times during the last fifty years, changes that may be indications of degenerating consciousness rather than changes that vitalize new consciousness. They are, in shorthand, unconscious uses of *like, good/well, who/that, each one/their, me/I, whatever.* If we understand, especially as teachers and parents, the nature of these increasingly unconscious confusions, we can work together to aid the health of our children's emerging and enduring consciousness in most essential ways.

Like

In a recent session of the full faculty meeting of the Green Meadow Waldorf School, focusing on the Humanities Curriculum, it emerged that the single most urgent concern about our children's speech is the pervasive abuse of the word *like.* It is a fine word, usually a preposition with a noun or pronoun as its object: "like a rock"; "like a bird"; "like her." The advertising firm in the 1950s for Winston-Salem cigarettes is probably responsible for jarring *like* loose from its clear role as a preposition and using it as a conjunction, followed by a clause, with a noun and a verb: "Winston tastes good, like a —— cigarette should." Ever since Homer, that role of conjunction, for a clause, had been played primarily by *as*, the good cousin of *like*.

In fact, one could say that Homer gave the clearest and finest mission to the word *like* and its companion *as*. The essential dynamic of the simile, one of the most important activities of the evolving Western mind, is to recognize and to state that two normally dissimilar objects are in fact similar: *A* is like *B;* a woman is like a tree. "Thetis..., rising like a dawn mist from the sea into a cloud..., soared aloft in heaven to high Olympos" (*Iliad*, 1, ll.496–499). The relationship is not one of mathematical equality—A = B—but rather one of comparison. One exercises imagination rationally. The fact of the similarity is stated explicitly through language. The possible similarities usually remain implicit and active in the imagination of the reader. When the similarity is recognized not simply between two objects, but between two activities, then *like* is replaced with *as*, which links two clauses. Homer's extended similes can become quite developed, taking on a life of their own.

> From the camp
> The troops were turning out now, thick as bees
> That issue from some crevice in a rock face,
> Endlessly pouring forth, to make a cluster
> And swarm on blooms of summer here and there,
> glinting and droning, busy in bright air.
> Like bees innumerable from ships and huts,
> Down the deep foreshore streamed those regiments
> Toward the assembly ground-and Rumor blazed
> Among them like a crier sent from Zeus.
>
> (Homer's *Iliad*, 2, ll. 81–90, tr. Fitzgerald)

In either case, the normal simile with *like,* or the extended simile with *as,* it is absolutely crucial that both the speaker/writer and the listener/reader are clear which image is the actual subject (called by literary scholars the "tenor") and which image is the "vehicle," to help us understand better the original, actual subject. In the extended simile, the actual subject is almost always a particular activity in a particular place, while the "vehicle" is almost always an activity that takes place almost anywhere, probably forever, any place, any time. There will always be, we hope, bees swarming on blooms of summer. The Homeric extended simile provides an eternal dimension within the activities of mortals on Earth. One can say that the Greeks, being guided into life on Earth by these great stories, were, through similes, not only shown the connections between things on Earth, but were also reminded of the timeless realm from which they had come.

Now that we have a historic and linguistic context for the role of *like* in our language and literature, we can turn our attention to the role of *like* in the life of the developing child. Our concern for children during the years of active Waldorf education is essentially that they incarnate into life in the healthiest way possible. We nourish young children artfully through imagination, always in the service of guiding them into the reality of the world in which we live, and at the same time the reality of the world that these children will help create.

As the child grows gradually, unfolding young thinking capacities, especially in fifth and sixth grades, paralleling humanity's developments in Greece and Rome, it becomes crucial that the child is grounded healthily in reality. We cannot become so lost in the swarming bees that we forget that the soldiers are actually running to the ships. The simile is meant to take us further inside the original image, not away from it. In literary language the "vehicle" is meant to illuminate the "tenor," not to eclipse it. We could also say, as parents and educators, that the simile should help us more fully incarnate, rather than excarnate.

Now, what happened with *like* about fifty years ago? Here is one amateur, pop linguist's version of the recent life and times of *like*. In the late 1960s, American society was cast into a tense duality. The hardening asphalt of the cool fifties was rent asunder by mere flowers, the flower children of the dawning of the new "Age of Aquarius." In the opposition between "repressed, oppressive" establishment and "uninhibited, liberated" hippies, the gesture of the young people was to expand their consciousness, out from and beyond the bedrock of day-to-day reality. The ignorant and indiscriminate use of drugs often gave the illusion of further expanding consciousness, to the extent that for some the connection to actual, daily reality evaporated. Or, to use a simile from those times, it was as though an astronaut, floating in space, severed that delicate connecting cord to the spaceship, which really connects one to life on Earth.

In our literary terms, the conscious connection between the actual image and the figurative image, between the tenor and the vehicle, between the actuality and the illuminating perspective, was lost. In terms of "*A* is like *B*," *B* lost *A*. "Like, I like went to the like store, and, you know, like I met like Freddie." The speaker is living, at best, completely in the world of the illuminating perspective. Yet there is no different reality to illuminate. There is no darkness to shed light on. The light has no bearing; the light is lost. In the language of our seniors studying *Faust,* there is no good without evil.

William Blake said, "Without Contraries, there is no Progression." This arbitrary proliferation of *like,* like a virus or cancer, robs both the speaker and the listener of the vitality, the dynamic of contraries, of clear polarity. The virus of misused *like* gives the speaker the illusion of living completely in the "illuminating perspective," yet the irony is that, in fact, it is only a weakened shadow of day-to-day reality, not at all that larger, timeless dimension of the vehicle in Homer's extended simile.

Unfortunately, the drug culture of the sixties spawned this senseless proliferation of *like,* permeating the verbal atmosphere in which the children now grow up. The insidious danger is that, like chemical, atmospheric pollution, the abusive misuse of *like* interferes seriously with the healthy incarnation process of the child. Growing children need to find a vital, conscious true connection to the Earth on which we live. Rather than incarnating growing children, this misuse of *like* excarnates and pulls them out from living actuality.

What can we parents and teachers do? First, be clear ourselves so that we do not thoughtlessly perpetrate such confusion. Second, gently correct the children any time we hear the misuse.

Children learn to speak from us as parents and teachers. By imitating, they form their habits early. We need to help those habits become clear, strong, true, and incarnating. Young ones don't need explanations; they just need to hear the correct way after any of their mistakes, and then they need to imitate correctly. Of course, our youth will speak their own peer lingo, which often includes this "likedy-like." When we're not present, naturally we cannot affect that. They will enjoy their slang jargon. That's fine; some of it is vital, new language. But, if we are clear at home and at school, they will know the difference. The whole reason for teaching foreign languages from first grade on is to develop mobility and flexibility of soul. If children grow up with the habit of speaking clearly, making true connections both at home and at school, then they will be able to think more clearly in high school and act more consciously in adult life. They will be able to make connections consciously, allowing the eternal to permeate the particulars of their lives. The right use of this splendid word *like* can make a crucial difference.

I can well imagine that at some future stage we may no longer need the word *like* to make connections. We will become so able to experience the thing itself that we will not need to let something else illuminate it for us. So far, however, as a stage in the process of illuminating our world, *like* continues to serve a fine function as we exercise our imaginations rationally. Parents and teachers, let us work together to help our children speak clearly, so that, through their speech, they know clearly what is what—what is like what and what like ain't.

Good / Well

In the last fifteen years, sports announcers and athletes have been largely responsible for turning *good* into an adverb. "Well, how'd the team play today?" "Good, good." "How do you think you'll do against Holy Cross tomorrow?" "I think we'll do good; we're ready." The confusion is becoming increasingly common outside the sports world; of course our young people imitate it. Is this one of those evolutionary shifts of language that we might as well surrender to and go with the flow? Perhaps. First though, let's consider the implications. How important is it to distinguish between an adjective and an adverb? Are they on the way to merging and becoming "adjerbs?" If so, should we help the merger or sustain the distinction? What difference does it make anyway?

An adjective, by definition, modifies a noun or pronoun. A noun is a person, place, thing, or idea. What do thing, place, person, and ideas have in common? Thing, place, person all exist in space. Idea exists, one might say, in inner space. All four have, in themselves, a stationary quality, a quality of being at rest. An adverb modifies a verb, another adverb, or an adjective. Whereas the adjective is usually connected directly to the noun, the adverb allows our consciousness to expand, flexibly, like a dog that wanders without getting lost. "The red team played, all things considered, and especially in spite of its injuries, quite well." The adverb *well* modifies the verb *played*. The adverb's connection to the verb is flexible, elastic; the adverb can be placed almost anywhere in the sentence.

The distinction between adjective and adverb is essentially linked to the distinction between noun and verb. How important is that distinction? Well, come to think of it, the essential unit with which we communicate our thoughts, the sentence, depends absolutely on the distinction between noun and verb. The quintessential sentence, "I am," consists of a pronoun and the verb meaning "to be." In Roman times a "sentence" expressed a feeling: *sentire*. In our times, a sentence expresses a thought. Absolutely essential, for a thought to have any dynamic, is the presence of a subject and a predicate, a noun and a verb. Without the verb, the noun remains at rest, inert. Without the subject (the noun), the verb remains undirected, unfocussed. Without either, thought has no dynamic, no life.

If we give up the distinction between adjective and adverb, we take a large step toward blurring and losing the distinction between noun and verb, the fundamental polarity that informs our ability to form and express dynamic thoughts. *Good* is usually an adjective. In "to do good," *good* is a noun, not an adverb. A good Samaritan does good through many selfless deeds. Yes, you will find in your dictionary a third listing for "good" as an adverb. And yes, *well,* an adverb, can of course work as an adjective, usually in terms of health of state of soul. "Are you well today?" So there is flexibility possible. But generally, helping our children to distinguish appropriately between *good* as an adjective and *well* as an adverb will help them distinguish more consciously between relationship to noun and relationship to verb, which will quicken both the accuracy and the dynamic of their thinking.

It is not surprising that the sports world would want to turn adjectives into adverbs. But, from an educational perspective, it is often precisely our young athletes who need the noun's distinction of place as a basis for a pure idea, to give them clear orientation in a world of continuous action. Our young people need to grow out of being continuous verbs, into becoming clear subjects. A clear distinction between adjective and adverb will help that process. For the adult, how we speak reflects how we think. For the child, how we speak affects how we become able to think.

Who / That

"Any person that speaks this way to another is highly inconsiderate." "Any girl that stays quiet in class through either fear or protection of the boys is being unfair to herself."

Simply, a person is "who." A place, thing, or idea, is "that" or "which." This is simple. Yet the tendency to dehumanize is powerful and pervasive, whether on Madison Avenue, in the computer world, in business, in the armed forces, in prisons, in public schools, even, lo and behold, possibly through careless language in our schools. The problem is not with *that* (or *which*) as adjectives. There is nothing wrong with "Which boy finished his work?" or "I see that child in the green shirt." The proper use of the appropriate relative pronoun is the simplest of ways to differentiate actively between what is human and what is not human. The person who... or whom... The thing that... or which... Each time children hear themselves referred to as "who" rather than "that" or "which," they subconsciously experience their humanity confirmed. Every individual lives with the question: Who am I? The corollary statement should at least be: I am who.

EACH ONE / THEIR

In the second half of the twentieth century, an emerging new consciousness has been struggling with the language, to find more accuracy in a particular dimension. Yet the frequent solution, the easy solution, reinforces a dangerous, different kind of unconsciousness. Simply put, the struggle for gender clarification has too often settled into a confusion of number.

For example, the traditional statement has been, "Everyone should put his coat on the hook." Or "Each student should finish his lunch before going outside." *Everyone*—every one—is singular, as are *everybody, anyone,* and *anybody.* The simple solution for the possessive pronoun, easier in days of single-sex schools, was to use the masculine possessive pronoun: "his coat" or "his lunch," unless only girls were involved. Culturally, "his" included both male and female. As people became more awake and sensitive to the gender implications of our language, a more accurate, careful statement became, "Everyone should put away his or her coat." While it is the most accurate form, this solution comes to feel a little strained and cumbersome, especially when repeated frequently. Unfortunately, and I'm afraid owing as much to lack of consciousness about number as to raised consciousness about gender, a too frequent statement is, "Everyone should hang up their coats." Initially, it sounds like a simpler, more inclusive solution.

But every young child is, at some stage, acutely sensitive to every clue to the actual laws of life and of the universe. *One* is a distinctive, powerful, unique experience, the seed of the gradually emerging individuality. *Each* (person) reinforces the singularity. To say "Everyone must put away their coats" means literally that each individual should be putting away the other students' coats: the plurally possessed coats. That is confusing, unless the teacher or parent actually means that. Each student should finish his or her lunch, not all the students' lunches, before going outside.

This confusion between singular and plural is not a light matter, because individuality is seriously threatened from two directions in our time. From outside, with pressure from media, statistics, large institutions, and the many of implications of natural science during the past several centuries, we can grow up feeling that each one of us is an inconsequential member of the masses, without an individual story. From inside, on the other hand, in this era of fast time and decreasing family cohesion, the soul is subject to forces that can pull it apart. Bipolar disorder, schizophrenia, and to the extreme, multiple personalities, are potent symptoms of the contemporary challenge of growing up with a healthy, integrated soul.

It has a profound effect on a young, impressionable, forming child when a parent or teacher, meaning "one" says "many," meaning singular says plural. Ralph Waldo Emerson wrote in his journal in 1837, "A believer in Unity, a seer of Unity, I yet behold two.... Cannot I behold the Universe without a contradiction?" (Whicher 62). Emerson learned to embrace contradictions. We want our students to be able to embrace contradictions. However, we want our students to be able to hear, to see, to think "one" when "one" is meant. The spoken confusion between singular and plural splits the child's growing consciousness of, and confidence in, the integrity of one, and hence in the clarity and actuality of both individuality and of unity. The corollary, of course, is that accuracy in relation to singular and plural will strengthen the child's growing consciousness of, and confidence in, the integrity of one, and hence in the clarity and actuality of his or her growing individuality, which is the center of one's actual capacity to experience unity.

What is the best solution at this time in the evolution of our language and consciousness? As parents and teachers, we owe it to our children to distinguish clearly between singular and plural. Then we have two choices. The truest choice, "Each student must finish his or her lunch" can feel at times like a strain, aesthetically clumsy, though it's better than the inaccurate "their." For the time being, the best solution seems to be to be accurate in terms of number, and to be flexibly inclusive in terms of gender. Elevate *her* to the generic status that *his* has always occupied, alternating the use of *his* with the use of *her,* allowing the students to develop the sense that either can be used flexibly in those inclusive group contexts to refer to each individual in the coeducational group. Not perfect, but if one feels it necessary, this solution does offer an aesthetic compromise, with clarifying consciousness.

I / Me

What may be the most crucial grammatical confusion in our children's speaking these days has emerged relatively recently, and I do not yet understand why. I do not remember it in the 1950s or in the 1960s. It is interesting that its spawning seems to coincide with what sociologists have called "the 'me' generation" of the 70s. It is astonishing how many of our high school students say, "Me 'n' Sarah played basketball yesterday." "Me, Jack, 'n' Josh drove through the snow yesterday." We remember five- and six-year-olds speaking this way—but high school sophomores, juniors, seniors well on the way toward becoming young men and young women?

First, let's look at the implications developmentally, then grammatically. After birth, a baby is like the still, though squirming, center of the turning Earth. A young baby doesn't go anywhere, yet its consciousness is, in a way, everywhere, all around, in every sight, smell, and sound. Gradually, in stage two, the more a child imitates and is formed by surrounding sounds, the more the child grows into speech. A child grows into naming things of the world, including his or her own name; "Sarah" or "Josh" is spoken like everyone else's name: as though from an outside perspective.

In stage three, the child starts to experience the first level of differentiation between oneself and the rest of the world. The child begins to say "me" instead of her or his name. The child becomes the receptive center of the universe: me, the object of everyone's attention. Me, the object. Me. They hold me. They feed me. They sing to me. And, less consciously, but most important, they love me.

Stage four appears first during stage three, usually sometime in a child's third year. Then the child first utters the most mysterious name "I," the name of each one of us, the name we all share, yet the name that no one else can call any of us. "I" is the object of no one else's attention or activity. The moment a child first says "I," the long journey has begun, from sucking center of the world to source/center of the world; from passive receiver of life to active giver of life; from object to subject.

This process in "stage four" continues until around the age of twenty-one; the evolution from a predominance of "me" toward an increasing predominance of "I" is subtly reinforced at several turning points in childhood. As many Waldorf school parents know, around the ages of nine and ten, a child inwardly experiences a deepening of the difference between the outer world of nature and the inner world of self. A child often experiences certain degrees of separation from one's family, a process by which the child's "I" becomes more conscious.

Sometime between the ages of twelve and fourteen, as puberty inaugurates new activity in the metabolic system and reproductive organs, the adolescent's soul opens inwardly in manifold dimensions. This new activity enriches the experience of the individual's inner world in relation to and often in contrast to the outer world, yet now with increasingly conscious thinking activity. By ages sixteen and seventeen, this process usually includes an experience of extreme inward isolation, like that of an Odysseus, a Parzival, a Hamlet, or a Jane Eyre. Yet, by twelfth grade, that very experience of inner isolation should make possible the individual's ability to enter the thinking experience of any other "I," as well as becoming an active, leading, primarily responsible source of life in the community, an "I," a subject actively influencing the world.

Pedagogically, in terms of the immediate tasks of primary and secondary education, this process culminates in twelfth grade. Whereas your four-year-old's language may still include a predominance of "me," your eighteen-year-old's language should certainly include a predominance of "I," with "I" always the subject, "me" always an object. Actually, that process of shift from "me" toward "I" continues through the late teens, as sometime around the traditional age of twenty-one, the individual has the experience that inwardly the long process of unfolding the "I" has come to a new stage of fulfillment as an adult "I" in the world. Sometime around this age of twenty-one, a new, inward experience becomes simply, "Here I am," with a new clarity and calm, however chaotically the world may be turning around the individual. The process of the development of the "I" continues, of course, in other ways, throughout adult life.

Before returning to the grammatical mystery of the word *I*, let us notice one more aspect of the developmental mystery of the "I." Yes, egotism is an unhealthy excess of self-absorption, usually with "me." Yes, in the high school we do make sure that students can write essays expressing objective, well-supported perspective, without "I..., I..., I...and me,...me,...me" in every other sentence. Yes, it is true that the highest capacity of the "I" is to serve another or to serve something higher than oneself. And yes, the best way to practice that capacity is through the good old, courteous habit of mentioning others before oneself. "Tom, Josh, Sarah, and I are going to a concert."

Be aware, however (especially adults in Eastern spiritual streams), that what one practices as an adult can have very different effects from what one experiences as a child. For children to be engaged in meditative practice oriented toward giving up, or dispelling, the "ego" can have lifelong deleterious effects on young people's ability later to find their individual ways as adults. It is one thing for a conscious, mature "I" to choose to "give up" or go beyond one's own "I." It is quite another for an only partially conscious child to be influenced to give up something that is hardly one's own yet. How can a child give up what has not yet been gained? Over the years, we have seen some children prematurely practicing concentrated meditations, with a consequence of extreme difficulty concentrating in adolescence and adulthood. Too often, well-intended but developmentally unaware efforts of parents in that direction can leave a child, in the wake of "I-lessness," actually collapsing in on "Me 'n' Sarah went to the store," an infantile, self-absorbed pendulum swing.

Now, let us return to the grammatical mystery—the first-person trinity of pronouns, *me, myself,* and *I*. Of course, the Scottish drunkard has long lost his "I" and makes his toast, "'Ere's ta me, maseln, 'n na' forgettin' ma wife's 'usban'!" But first, myself. Myself is reflexive. The mystery of myself is that it absolutely cannot exist without "I." Tom, Josh, Sarah, and myself cannot go to an important conference, be on an important committee, join a power breakfast. Oh, no. Myself can do absolutely nothing. That's the law of the living language. Only *I* can do, can be. You can't and they can't love myself or bring myself. Oh, no. Myself is almost like the shadow of "I" in a positive, Peter Pan sense, not a negative sense. Just as *I* is the name only I as an individual can call myself, only I can refer to myself, can transform myself. To say that Josh, Sarah, and myself are on the committee reflects subtle, unconscious self-absorption, a grammatical, reflexive equivalent of muscle flexing. Josh, Sarah, and (simply) I are on the committee; that's all. Myself, reflexive, is exclusively either the appositive (I, myself, will...) or the object of the subject I (I trust myself). No "myself" in a sentence without "I." Mystery number one. Mysteries of course merely conceal higher laws, which we already know subconsciously.

Mystery Number Two. "Me." *Me,* we all know, exists only as an object. The mystery of *me* is twofold. First, unlike *myself, me* does not, cannot, exist as an object of *I*. I cannot love me, take me, have me. Second, *me* exists, in fact, only as an object of the pronouns *you, he, she, it,* and *they,* or of nouns such as *policeman, teacher, friend,* etc. Essentially, whereas *myself* is the object of *I, me* is the object of the other. "Me" is incapable and not allowed to do anything out of its own will. "Me" has no will of its own. "Me" is the servant, the slave, the child, the passive object, determined usually by the subject of the other, or by a preposition. "He knows me." "She moves me." "They make me do this." "It frightens me." "You gave it to me."

Anytime we, parents and teachers, allow a child to say, "Me an' Sarah are going to the store," we reinforce that child's unconscious experience that, instead of that emerging individuality choosing out of growing, conscious free will to go with Sarah to the store, the child is instead impelled, as object not subject, by forces other than his or her own will, perhaps through peer pressure or Madison Avenue, to go to that store with Sarah. Who will write the script of that child's life? He, himself? She, herself? Or all the forces that want to control people who are weak enough individuals to allow themselves to be objects in life, rather than choosing freely to be subjects. "Sarah and I are going to the store." Put the other first, yet choose as an individual, as an actual subject, to go. Let *me* work as an object. There are many situations when that is appropriate. But don't let your child or student be an object when a subject is appropriate. Not "me am" but "I am."

And now the third mystery of the first-person trinity, or triad. Like shading in around light in a drawing, our considerations of myself and of me have already implied much about the mystery of "I." Only they define me. Only I define myself. But, no one defines "I." Only I...am.

I—perhaps the most vital, essential, pure single-sound word in our language. *I*—a diphthong of three vowel sounds, actually "ah-a-ee." Undetermined by any consonant sounds, compared to most names and indeed most words, *I* is unaffected by those sounds generally associated with the physical world, the outer world. The "ah" is open and sounds back deeper in the throat. The long "a" sounds more forward in the mouth. The "a" sound can evoke a horizontality; the eurythmy gesture usually includes some kind of a crossing of arms, a defining meeting. "Ee" sounds even more forward in the mouth, extending linearly forward and vertically, as is reflected in the eurythmy gestures of one arm reaching up and the other raying down.

I is in some ways the equivalent, in the world of nouns and pronouns, of the infinitive in the verb world. "She had run. She ran. She runs. She will run." Each such form of the verb "to run" is expressed in a particular, finite time: past perfect, past, present, future. The mystery of the infinitive *to run* is that, rather than being actualized into any particular time (or tense), the infinitive form of the verb *to run* remains in the state of complete potential with infinite possibility. The manifold mystery of *I* is that not only is it free of any consonant sounds, but it also remains undetermined by any force outside itself. Unlike any noun, *I* can never be an object. *I* is the infinite subject.

I, as the name no one else can utter, is also the subject no one else can initiate or command. *I*, in English, stands free, not embedded in the verb, as in Latin, Spanish, Italian: *te amo* (I love you), with the first person embedded in the verb ending. *I*, as a word, stands independent, free to choose its own verb. *I*, the most unencumbered of subjects, is literally the "infinitive" of subjects, the most universal of subjects, because it is the potential, the capacity, of each individual to say "I." Literally, in these times when English is becoming the lingua franca of most of the globe, the experience of saying "I" is on the way to becoming universal.

On another level, the purest thought deed connected with the purest subject is the simplest statement: "I am." This statement, the essence, even the name, of the Judeo-Christian divinity, reveals the immortal, spiritual nature of "I." The riddle of the "I am" is that it reveals what is most individual about the subject speaking it. No one else can utter it for that subject. Yet at the same time, *I* is the individual mystery for every individual. Hence each individual "I am" participates in the universal "I AM" of all humanity. The "I AM" of all humanity is infinite in its spiritual nature. Through one's own "I," one recognizes other "I" beings. Every time an "I" thinks, speaks, acts, the "I" of others awakens, stirs. Every time an "I" is a "me" or "myself" instead, the other "I" beings are pacified. An "I," active, has an activating effect on each individual it affects. So, the first-person trinity of pronouns (*me, myself*, and *I*) need to be allowed to have their proper relationship. Then they can influence me. I can transform myself. And I can be freely active, for everyone's sake.

Whatever

The sixth and final grammatical confusion is the youngest (or most recent), the simplest, and perhaps the most insidious. Where has it come from, this trail word, this tail word, of the 1990s? I wonder.

Whatever has a perfectly respectable history as a pronoun and as an adjective. Also as pronoun: "Do whatever you think is best. Whatever happens, keep the faith." As adjective: "Whatever merits the work has..." "Whatever the reason, she refuses to go." These are examples from *Webster's Dictionary*. As a pronoun, *whatever* is either the subject or the object of a verb, a dynamic part of a thought. As an adjective, *whatever* clearly qualifies, modifies, some particular noun.

"She can come if she likes. Whatever." "I think that's bad, whatever." "I might do it, whatever." How is this word working in the sentences? It does not seem to be working as any recognizable part of speech. Maybe it comes closest to an interjection, like "hooray" or "uh-oh." How is it affecting or reflecting the rest of the sentence? It does not affirm or reinforce. It does not ask, opening up. It does not negate, taking a stance in opposition. This word, used in a manner almost alien to the eight parts of speech, seems to undo, diffuse, and almost invalidate the preceding thought.

How might one punctuate the equivalent of this floating *whatever?* Not with the period of a statement, nor with a question mark of open exploration and consideration. And not with an exclamation point of excitement or command. The punctuation mark for the tailing "whatever" would have to be something like a squiggle—a drooping squiggle. Essentially, *whatever,* used this way, is the cop-out word. *Whatever* articulates the epitome of moral relativism, indifference, and impotence. *Whatever* expresses the attitude of twenty bystanders who see and hear a woman being slowly murdered without running to stop it or even lifting a finger to call the police. *Whatever* expresses the attitude that words lack meaning, and hence what one has just said doesn't matter. If what one does or says doesn't matter, what one feels or thinks also does not matter. And if that's the case, why live? This use of *whatever* is insidious. Whatever it is, it matters one way or the other. The point is to name it and find one's relationship to it. Then every thought, every word, every feeling, every action matters. Then we and the world we inhabit become fully alive.

Whereas the misuse of *like* is like a virus disintegrating our thinking, this misuse of *whatever* is like a virus disassociating, alienating, our attitudes and our actions. It will be a service to our students to help them out of the habit of using *whatever* as the cop-out word, restoring *whatever* to its clear, dynamic use as either pronoun or adjective. By simply asking them to follow *whatever* with words that complete a thought, we will help them use *whatever* either as a pronoun ("Whatever is the outcome...") or as an adjective ("Whatever the weather, we will go to Mystic Seaport."). Then our children will be exercising clarity of thinking and the will to complete a thought, while fostering elasticity of soul, consciously, which is profoundly different from "anything goes."

As we conclude these diagnoses of six contemporary misuses of our language, let us not forget that, primarily, we want our children (and ourselves) to be able to play in the language, to play with the language, to make up new language, to learn the laws of the language, to work as freely and flexibly as possible within those laws, to love the art of language, to go beyond the laws when artistically appropriate, to use the language so that it helps us all to think clearly, feel fully, and act truly. Yet, we want to recognize when certain developments pose real dangers. When we recognize such dangers, how we speak and how we help children to speak can make a crucial difference.*

---

* This chapter originally appeared, in slightly altered form, in *Renewal*.

Chapter 27

Twelfth Grade (Ages 17–18)

By twelfth grade, the senior has emerged into a contemporary world with such a bewildering range of forms of music, painting, architecture, poetry, movement, and so on that the world can appear quite formless artistically and literarily. Nevertheless, the senior has recently recapitulated the formal stages of development of English poetry: Old Anglo-Saxon, four-beat alliterative verse; Chaucer's Middle English in iambic pentameter with rhyming couplets; Shakespeare's blank verse; and the Romantic poets' organically evolving blank verse. Hence seniors have earned a newly constituted readiness to take a fresh step in consciousness, one of the most courageous, lonely adventures in the history of human culture.

As difficult as it was for the settlers of the New World to emancipate themselves beyond geographic, religious, legal, political, and economic stages to a true artistic independence, it is just as difficult for our teenagers to honestly earn an inner independence artistically. From painting in red, yellow, and blue in first grade through copying essays from teachers through fourth grade; from underemphasizing "creative" writing in fifth to eighth grades, to schooling the ninth graders' observation of the physical world and helping tenth and eleventh graders write in various forms appropriate to the corresponding stages of consciousness of the historical period they were studying, our whole education has tried to avoid prematurely demanding of Waldorf students or exposing them to the exercise of individuality before other members of the child's being (the physical, etheric and astral bodies) have matured healthily in relation to one another.

Twelfth graders embark on perhaps the most mysterious and challenging year of their whole Waldorf education. From one perspective, the senior arrives at the culminating year of the twelve, or even fourteen-year sequence in a great crescendo. Many experiences over the years—in preschool and kindergarten and each of the grades—ring both familiarly and anew as the seniors start, like Janus, to reflect back more consciously than ever before on what has come before. Seniors feel a great swelling momentum, like a wave, that they ride with a new poise not previously known.

From another perspective, the senior, also like Janus, looks ahead, farther and further than ever before. In terms of space, the senior looks out at the many possibilities for yet higher education and for further life experience. In the midst of those immense terrains of the world, the senior is looking for signs, listening for possible callings: What might my work in the world be? Even more important, subtle, and elusive, however—and here is the real heart of the mystery of twelfth grade—the senior is looking out for, listening in for, the growing experience of the emerging "I," the more clearly sounding individuality.

As full as the seniors feel, they are only halfway through the third seven-year stage of development: that of their soul (astral) body. Much remains to develop during the next several years. Yet in our Waldorf curriculum, we try to work pedagogically in ways that will artistically quicken and enhance the "I" faculties and capabilities, even though that experience will not really come into its own until the next time they are seniors, in college or university, usually around the age of twenty-one.

How can we educators work to serve a healthy awakening, a gentle exercising of this immanent "I" capacity? First, the students have been strengthening their life patterns and soul forces by practicing the previous forms of poetry, which acknowledges the soul body's continuing development, in contrast to thrusting ninth and tenth graders into the modern world of formlessness to navigate however they can, with whatever toll that might take on their undeveloped selves, sucking the forces from the development of the soul substance into premature "I" activity.

Nevertheless, based on that momentum and having trained them well to navigate the seas of imagination and consciousness according to certain rhythms and laws, we can ask the help of one of the pioneers of Western consciousness to guide them into the next step. In the context of the twelfth grade English main lesson, "The Birth of American Literature," the students hear Ralph Waldo Emerson in 1837 ask for a truly American scholar, and, in 1842, ask for a truly American poet, not just someone imitating Old World patterns.

Outwardly, Walt Whitman spent his teens, twenties, and early thirties writing unremarkable journalistic prose. Inwardly, however, Emerson's words were taking root. In a moment of undeliberate passion (see chapter 24), Walt Whitman wrote what was essentially America's first "free verse." In the ensuing years—in fact, through the rest of his life—he continued, yielding nine growing editions of *Leaves of Grass*. What does it mean for Walt Whitman to arrive at the end of a line of poetry without any formal guide dictating, suggesting, and ordering him in terms of what the form of the next line should be? Of course, with the rare exception of Ralph Waldo Emerson, most of the people reading his poetry in 1855 could not follow him from line to unpredictable line, precisely because they did not know how they were supposed to proceed, and hence they could not follow with open, fully engaged consciousness. Inwardly, they were not free enough to follow into such unordered waters of consciousness. They experienced only anarchy. Emerson, on the other hand, was flexibly awake enough to recognize the appropriate vitality of each line, adapting itself formally to whatever the particular nuance of that line's experience required, and treating each line with equal democratic importance, giving it its form according to its individual character, so that, in Galway Kinnell's image, each line emerges dripping wet with the experience. What does it mean for humanity to arrive at a moment when no outward form dictates the next step?

Twelfth graders can recognize and experience that Whitman's verse is not mere anarchy and not just "free" verse in the sense that anything that the poet writes is fair and equally vital. Students can experience when one of Whitman's lines is weak or does not fit artistically. The students can experience that the perhaps frightening "freedom" from the dictates of outer form may be accompanied by the frightening, but eternally exciting responsibility to listen openly, without preconception or prejudice, not only to the experience itself which is the subject of the poem, but to each moment of the recreation of that experience. That selfless openness to the changing, unpredictable essence of the other, whatever its character may be, is the essence of the mystery of the capacity of the "I." "Free" verse, the form for a revolution of consciousness, generated in North America, turns out to be the form of poetry most inwardly demanding, most strict, most challenging to, and hence most generating of, the inwardly free consciousness of "I" activity.

Had I the Choice

Had I the choice to tally greatest bards,
To limn their portraits, stately, beautiful, and emulate at will,
Homer with all his wars and warriors—Hector, Achilles, Ajax
Or Shakespeare's woe-entangled Hamlet, Lear, Othello—
    Tennyson's fair ladies,
Metre or wit, the best, or choice conceit to wield in perfect rhyme,
    delight of singers;
These, these, O sea, all these I'd gladly barter,
Would you the undulation of one wave, its trick to me transfer,
Or breathe one breath of yours upon my verse,
And leave its odor there.

Walt Whitman, *Leaves of Grass*

Song of Myself

. . . Water is all color, it is life.
Its endless forms and patterns have affected all of the
    creation,
More perhaps than any other single thing.
I have grown through the waters.

It is the vessel of my memories, it is the substance of my
body and mind.
My soul would be like water.

The air is laden with water, it is tired of it.
At night, when no one is looking, the air throws water
carelessly all over the ground.
But the sun, judge of all creation,
sentences the air to carry it through every day.
So every morning, it must painfully gather up every drop
once more.

To be warm and cozy, with smoke curling silently into the
air,
talking of love and lust, solitude and friendship,
paper plates and candles...
Or utterly alone, content as a stone.
The soothing sound of rain
like nothing else
sings me into complete contentment.
And if it fails, I know I must
seek it out, and learn from it,
and plead endlessly with it; for anything cannot we be
one?
I embrace it to the fullest, strip all restraints from my
body,
And twirl, soaked through the skin,
until my plea is acknowledged.

Snow is the happiness of rain,
we understand her far less than her brother,
she is too removed from our interests.
But for me she possesses a greater slice of heaven
than I find elsewhere,
I love her just as well as the coolest stream bed
imbued with all of the ripples,
nipples, waves and falls of the world.

Ocean, fullest of all habitats, overwhelms me with its life,
No, fresh water is more my cup of tea.

NICHOLAS ALEXANDRA, GMWS, 1997

Just as ninth graders live naturally in the contemporary "language of the times," twelfth graders reenter the present through the curriculum, but now having been consciously re-oriented in the context of humanity's evolution, from ancient cultures through Greek, Roman, Medieval, Renaissance eras into the immediacy of the modern world. Hence, in addition to the main lesson on the birth of American literature, it is fortunate for seniors to have the opportunity to explore contemporary consciousness through electives such as Modern Poetry, African American Literature, Native American Literature, or Latin American literature. Modern Poetry might include such poets as Yeats, Pound, Eliot, Frost, Stevens, and Williams, then Bishop, Cummings, Jeffers, Roethke, Plath, and Wilbur, then Ginsberg, Snyder, Heaney, Kinnell, Oliver, and so on. African American Literature might include fables, blues, *Song of Solomon* by Toni Morrison, and poetry by Langston Hughes, Gwendolyn Brooks, Lucille Clifton, Rita Dove, and Maya Angelou. Native American Literature may include books such as *Black Elk Speaks* by John Neihardt, *Love Medicine* or *The Beet Queen* by Louise Erdrich, *Ceremony* by Leslie Marmon Silko, *The Book of the Hopi* by Frank Waters, *House of Dawn* by N. Scott Momaday, *Fool's Crow* by James Welch, and poetry by Joy Harjo and Sherman Alexie. Latin American Literature may include *One Hundred Years of Solitude* by Gabriel Marcia Marquez, *The Storyteller* by Mario Vargas Llosa, *The Years With Laura Diaz* by Carlos Fuentes, and poetry by Pablo Neruda, Gabriela Mistral, and Octavio Paz.

Twelfth graders should emerge into the world feeling that their emerging individualities have been enlivened, strengthened, elaborated, articulated, and quickened through having experienced the evolving activity of the spirit of the English language. Since the spirit of our times has an especially strong partnership with the spirit of the English language, as English becomes the global language, seniors can experience all the more strongly that, through the Word, they can know the world, hence engendering the becoming self.

Chapter 28

Speech and Drama in High School

One cannot discuss a study of the effect of the English language on stages of adolescent development without stating the obvious: Especially crucial to developing teenagers is how the mother tongue, English, lives in daily use. Each student entering each classroom should experience, usually unconsciously, that the very air in the room, the very atmosphere, has been permeated by, even formed by, carefully spoken sounds. Students should experience that the sentences have been formed meaningfully, that the phrases have been crafted carefully, that the words have been chosen thoughtfully, that the sounds have been uttered artfully.

How distinctly one articulates consonant sounds affects the vitality with which one incarnates in relation to the things and elements of the outer, physical world. How clearly and fully one voices vowel sounds affects the artfulness with which one's inner, soul life can be articulated consciously. The artful combining of these two, consonants and vowels, to form each word, is an "I" activity, strengthening, exercising one's I AM, and in the process actually weaving life body and astral body together healthily through wakeful, artful speech.

Ideally, all teachers would be doing some speech exercises and some recitation at the beginning of every main lesson, every day, whatever the subject, throughout the four years. Most "run-through" English classes can include some recitation.

A potential Speech and Drama Curriculum, based on the stated constant activity and attention of all teachers and students, might include the following:

Ninth Grade

Reading/enacting scenes in class in The Story of Drama
One-minute impromptu speeches
One-minute prepared speeches
Two-minute prepared speeches
Individual recitations
Group recitations
Oral book reports
Class meeting discussion protocol
Individual offerings in High School Poetry Evening
Class offerings in all-school assemblies

Tenth Grade

Tenth-grade play
Individual recitations
Group recitations
Oral book reports
Debating Club?
Drama Club?
Class meeting discussion protocol
Individual offerings in High School Poetry Evening
Class offerings in all-school assemblies

Eleventh Grade

Presentation of monologues, dialogues in Chaucerian Middle English
Writing and enacting dramatic monologues
Oral Reports on Foreign Exchange experience
Individual recitations
Group recitations
Oral book reports
Debating Club?
Drama Club?
Class meeting discussion protocol
Individual offerings in High School Poetry Evening
Class offerings in all-school assemblies
Final assembly skit on Senior Class

TWELFTH GRADE

Individual recitations
Group recitations
Debating Club?
Drama Club?
Class meeting discussion protocol
Class offerings in all-school assemblies
Individual offerings in High School Poetry Evening
Five-minute Senior Speech to whole High School
Discussion group guides in High School Week
Twenty-to-thirty minute presentation to whole high school community of Independent Senior Project
Twelfth-Grade Play
Two student speakers at graduation

Chapter 29

Conclusion

Human development is mysterious and complex. Through attention over the years, we scholars and educators can become increasingly aware of nuances, whether subtle or clear, and qualitative differentiations in evolving stages of the English language in poetry. Such differences become ever clearer signals of altering consciousness in those people living in, "speaking," that particular form of the English language. Poetry, as the most artful form of language, may be the vessel for the fullest striving of consciousness of a given people at a given time. We poets can become ever more aware of what experiences, of what consciousness, our sound-uses are generating.

One of Rudolf Steiner's many gifts to those of us working in Waldorf education is a quite fully developed picture of natural stages of development in an individual life. Simplistically, the generalized picture includes the following large brush strokes (see table). We are aware that the growing individual's development is

Stages of Human Development

ages 1–7:	primary development of	physical body
7–14:	primary development of	life (ether) body
14–21:	primary development of	soul (astral) body
c.21	emergence of	"I" (I AM)
21–28:	development of	sentient soul
28–35:	development of	intellectual (rational, or mind) soul
35–42:	development of	consciousness (spiritual) soul
etc…		

naturally a microcosmic recapitulation of stages of development that all of humanity has experienced over large periods of time.

Part of the art of Waldorf Education is to work as harmoniously as possible with those natural developmental stages. Part of the art of Waldorf Education is to work more than naturally with those stages, to work artfully. God creates nature. Human beings recreate and transform nature through art.

English teachers can help students emerge, in their twenties, into the world, as healthily composed individuals, with a rich "remembrance" of much of English literature and all it reveals of the mysteries of human experience. Such students will be naturally ready to embark upon their next stage of development, that of the sentient soul, in their twenties. However, the degree to which we can guide students through vitally conscious experience of the altering stages of the English language itself, as embodied in poetry, strongly affects the degree to which our students will be able to 1) develop the soul substance of the astral body itself in lawful accord with the evolving stages of humanity; 2) by being "conscious" of these language changes, quicken the maturing activity of the I AM ("I") itself; 3) by creating soul substance through language reflecting Humanity's major stages of development, form already a living, conscious basis in the astral body for each of the ensuing soul members: sentient soul, intellectual soul, and consciousness soul. This means the emerging individual will meet those stages of his or her development not only naturally, but also with a conscious, vital "head start" through the "seedlike" soul substance that the language engendered in adolescence.

Then all of us, scholars, poets, educators, and students alike, will be better able, through our language, not just to reflect what is around us, but also to generate new, vitalizing consciousness. We will work in partnership with the spirit of the English language.

Through literature, we remember;
through us, language engenders.

WORKS CITED

Abrams, M. H., et al., eds. *The Norton Anthology of English Literature*. New York: Norton, 1968.

Ackroyd, Peter. *Blake, A Biography*. New York: Alfred A. Knopf, 1996.

Armstrong, Margaret. *Trelawney. New York:* Macmillan, 1940.

Baigent and Leigh. *Temple and Lodge*. New York: Arcade, 1989.

Bate, W. Jackson. *John Keats*. Cambridge, MA.: Cambridge University Press, 1963.

Baugh, Albert A. *A History of the English Language*. New York: Appleton-Century Crofts, 1957.

Bembridge, Paul. "The Rosicrucian Resurgence at the Court of Cromwell," White, Ralph, ed. *The Rosicrucian Enlightenment Revisited*. Great Barrington, MA: Lindisfarne Books, 1999.

Bergonzi, Bernard. *Gerard Manley Hopkins*. New York: Macmillan, 1977.

Bo, Bentja Katya (Norwegian). "Old Norse Language and Literature." Threefold Educational Foundation, Spring Valley, New York. May 11, 1995.

Briggs, Harold, ed. *Complete Poetry and Selected Prose of John Keats*. New York: Modern Library, 1951.

Brooks, Van Wyck. *New England:Indian Summer*. New York: Dutton, 1940.

———. *The Times of Melville and Whitman*. New York: Dutton, 1947.

Chase, Richard, *Walt Whitman Reconsidered*. New York: William Sloane Associates, 1955.

Castle, Terry. "Mad, Bad, and Dangerous to Know." *New York Times on the Web* April 13, 1997; review of Phyllis Grosskurth, *Byron: The Flawed Angel*, Boston: Houghton Mifflin, 1997.

Coleridge, Henry Nelson. *Biographical Supplement to the Biographia literaria*. (letter to Poole, October, 1797). London, c.1834.

Coleridge, Samuel Taylor. Aids to Reflection, Aphorism IV, Selected Poetry and Prose of Coleridge, ed. Donald A. Stauffer. New York: Modern Library, 1951.

———. *Specimens of the Table Talk of Samuel Taylor Coleridge*. London, John Murray, 1837.

Eliot, T. S. *Andrew Marvel, Selected Essays, 1917–1932*. New York: Harcourt Brace, 1932.

———. "Whitman and Tennyson" in *Walt Whitman: A Critical Anthology* (Francis Murphy, ed.). Baltimore: Penguin, 1969.

Emerson, Ralph Waldo, "Shakespear, or, The Poet," in *Representative Men: Seven Lectures*, Modern Library, 2004.

Erdman, David V. *The Illuminated Blake*. New York: Dover, 1974.

Faulkner-Jones, D. E. *The English Spirit*. London: Rudolf Steiner Press, 1935.

Ford, George, et al., eds. *The Norton Anthology of English Literature*. New York: Norton, 1968.

Frazier, Charles. *Cold Mountain*. New York: Atlantic Monthly Press, 1997.

Gardner, John. *The Life and Times of Chaucer*. New York: Knopf, 1977.

Gardner, W. H. *Gerard Manley Hopkins: Poems, and Prose*. London: Penguin, 1963.

Grosskurth, Phyllis. *Byron: The Flawed Angel*. Boston: Houghton Mifflin, 1997.

Gura, Philip. *The Wisdom of Words*. Middletown, CN.: Wesleyan University Press, 1981.

Harding, Walter. *The Days of Henry Thoreau*. New York: Dover Publications, 1962.

Hazlitt, William. *The Spirit of the Age: Contemporary Portraits*. Charleston, SC: BiblioBazaar, 2006.

Hollander, John & Frank Kermode, eds. *Oxford Anthology of English Literature*. New York: Oxford University Press, 1973.

Holmes, Richard. *Coleridge: Early Visions*. New York: Viking Press, 1990.

Johnson, Samuel. "The Life of Cowley," *Lives of the English Poets*. London: Oxford University Press, 1952; see vol. 1, pp. 12–16, for Johnson's account of the metaphysical poets.

Kermode and Hollander, eds. *Oxford Anthology of English Literature*. New York: Oxford University Press, 1973.

Kinnell, Galway. "William Blake," lecture. Metropolitan Museum of Art, New York. June 15, 2001.

Knottenbelt, Johanna. *The Art of Poetry in the Light of Anthroposophy*, Wiersma-Ter Braak, 1973.

Martin, Robert Bernard. *Tennyson: The Unquiet Heart: A Biography*. New York: Oxford University Press, 1980.

Martz, Louis. *Seventeenth Century Verse*. Garden City, NY: Anchor Books, 1963.

Maurois, André. *Ariel: The Life of Shelley*. New York: Penguin, 1985.

McCrum, Robert, William Cran, & Robert Macneil. *The Story of English*. New York: Viking Press, 1986.

Melville, Herman. *Moby-Dick*. Berkeley: University of California Press, 1979.

Meres, Francis, *Palladis Tamia: Wits Treasury: Being the Second Part of Wits Common-wealth*. London, 1598.

Nichol, John. *Byron*. London, 1880 (New York: HMS Press, 1968).

Nicolson, Adam. *God's Secretaries: The Making of the King James Bible*. New York: HarperCollins, 2003.

Perkins, David. *English Romantic Writers*. New York: Harcourt Brace Jovanovich, 1967.

Richards, I. A., ed. *The Portable Coleridge*. New York: Viking Press, 1950.

Richardson, Joanna. *The Pre-Eminent Victorian: A Study of Tennyson*. Jonathon Cape: London, 1962.

Schmidt, Michael. *Lives of the Poets*. New York: Vintage Books, 1998.

Sewall, Richard B. *The Life of Emily Dickinson*. Cambridge, MA: Harvard University Press, 1974.

Sisman, Adam. *The Friendship: Wordsworth & Coleridge*. New York: Viking, 2006.

Steiner, George. "The Good Books." *The New Yorker* January 11, 1988.

Steiner, Rudolf. *Speech and Drama*. "Speech-formation and the Dramatic Arts" (Dornach, September 5–23, 1924). London: Rudolf Steiner Press, 1959.

Taplin, Gardner. *The Life of Elizabeth Barrett Browning*. New Haven: Yale University Press, 1957.

Trelawney, Edward John. *Records of Shelley, Byron, and the Author*. London, 1878.

Whicher, Stephen E., ed. *Selections from Ralph Waldo Emerson*. Boston: Houghton Mifflin, 1957.

Woodberry, George, ed. *The Complete Poetical Works of Percy Bysshe Shelley*. Boston: Houghton Mifflin, 1901.

Wyatt, Isabel. *Chaucer and the Modern Consciousness*. Unpublished Manuscript. England, c.1970.